Employment Deconcentration in European Metropolitan Areas

The GeoJournal Library

Volume 91

Managing Editor: Max Barlow, Toronto, Canada

Founding Series Editor:
Wolf Tietze, Helmstedt, Germany

The titles published in this series are listed at the end of this volume.

Employment Deconcentration in European Metropolitan Areas

Market Forces versus Planning Regulations

Edited by

ERAN RAZIN
The Hebrew University of Jerusalem, Israel

MARTIN DIJST
University of Utrecht, The Netherlands

and

CARMEN VÁZQUEZ
University of Castilla-La Mancha, Spain

 Springer

A C.I.P. Catalogue record for this book is available from the Library of Congress.

ISBN 978-1-4020-5761-8 (HB)
ISBN 978-1-4020-5762-5 (e-book)

Published by Springer,
P.O. Box 17, 3300 AA Dordrecht, The Netherlands.

www.springer.com

Printed on acid-free paper

In memory of Frans Dieleman and
Arie Shachar

Table of Contents

Contributing Authors

Annet Bogaerts

Junior researcher at the Urban Geography Department, Faculty of Geosciences Utrecht University, 2003-2005, and member of the EU-funded SELMA. At present she is employed at 'RIGO Research Institute for the Built Environment', a consulting company specialising in urban policy, policy evaluation, urban regeneration and quality of life.

Simone Di Zio

Has a degree in Economics and PhD in Statistics and is a researcher at the d'Annunzio University, Chieti-Pescara, Italy. His research interests focus on Fractal Geometry, Spatial Statistics, GIS, Decision Support Systems and Multi-Criteria Analysis. He has been member of the research teams of the EU funded projects ESPON and SELMA.

Frans Dieleman (1942–2005)

Professor in Urban and Rural Geography at the Faculty of Geosciences, Utrecht University. He published extensively on themes of residential mobility, housing choice, social housing, the development of urban form in Northwest Europe and the relationship between urban form and travel behaviour, methodologies, spatial planning and related geographic topics. He served in various administrative positions such as Dean of the Faculty of Geosciences and director of the Netherlands Graduate School for Housing and Urban Research (NETHUR). In 2004 he was appointed as professor of Methodology and Technology of System Innovation in Spatial Development at Delft University. Recently, he also worked as advisor for the Organisation of Applied Natural Sciences Research (TNO) and the Netherlands Institute of Spatial Research (RPB). Over the years 2002-2004 he served as project coordinator for the SELMA consortium.

Martin Dijst

Professor of Urban Development and Mobility at the Urban and Regional research centre Utrecht (URU), Faculty of Geosciences, Utrecht University. He specializes in transportation research and urban development. He has published widely in international journals, such as Transportation, Transportation Research A, Urban Geography, Urban Studies, Environment and Planning A and B, Journal of Transport Geography, Geojournal, and TESG. Additionally, he has served as external advisor in several national and international research programs. From 2005 he acted as the SELMA project coordinator.

Yaakov Garb

Yaakov Garb is a Visiting Assistant Professor at Brown University and a Lecturer at the Blaustein Institutes at Ben-Gurion University (Sede Boqer). A former Director of the Central European programs of the Institute for Transport and Development Policy (New York), he conducts interdisciplinary environmental, urban, and social analysis, most recently writing on the politics of mobility in Israel and Palestine.

Stan Geertman
Associate Professor in Geographical Information Science at Utrecht University and Visiting Professor at the International Institute for Geo-Information Sciences and Remote Sensing (ITC). His research focuses on Planning and Decision Support Systems (PSS/DSS). He has published widely in international journals and has been a member of national and international conference organizations. At present he is Programme Director of the interuniversity Master of Science programme 'Geographical Information Management and Applications' (GIMA).

Peter Hartoft-Nielsen
Civil engineer and PhD. He has been employed for the last two decades at the National Spatial Planning Department specializing in the urban environment and planning in Greater Copenhagen. During periods on leave: research on urban development, location and travel behaviour at the Danish Centre for Forest, Landscape and Planning. Since 2004 he has worked on a new Planning Act and on special provisions on spatial planning in Greater Copenhagen. At present he serves as project manager on the National Planning Directive for the Greater Copenhagen (The 2006 Finger Plan).

Ángel Jodra
Research member of the Laboratory on Urban and Social Geography, the Department of Geography at the Autonomous University of Madrid. Over the last eight years he has worked on various European projects such as *TELECITYVISION: Information Society and Urban Development in European Comparison, URBANEYE. On the Threshold to Urban Panopticon?* and *SELMA Spatial Deconcentration of Economic Land Use and Quality of life in European Metropolitan Areas*; as well as in different Spanish projects.

Armando Montanari
Professor of Urban Economics, Business School, d'Annunzio University, Chieti-Pescara, Italy. He is involved in multinational comparative analysis on the issues of urban and regional restructuring in Europe, and on human mobility (1979-2006). He has published about 150 books and articles on these topics, about half of them in English, French, Spanish and Japanese.

Martin Ouředníček
Assistant Professor in the Department of Social Geography and Regional Development of the Faculty of Science, Charles University in Prague, the Czech Republic. His research covers urban and settlement geography, specializing in socio-spatial structures, migration, urbanisation and suburbanisation processes.

Antonio J. Palacios
Obtained a PhD in January 2005 at the Autonomous University of Madrid. His thesis, focused on multi-deprived neighbourhoods in Spain. He has recently been involved in various European research projects such as *TELECITYVISION: Information Society and Urban Development in European Comparison* and *SELMA Spatial Deconcentration of Economic Land Use and Quality of life in European Metropolitan Areas.*

Eran Razin
Associate Professor in the Department of Geography and Institute of Urban and Regional Studies, the Hebrew University of Jerusalem. He specializes in local government and urban development and has also studied aspects of immigrant enterprise and the urban milieu. His research has been published in journals such as: *Urban Studies, Environment and Planning C, Urban Affairs Review, Political Geography, Geografiska Annaler, TESG, Journal of Urban Affairs, Urban Geography* and *International Migration Review.*

Arie Shachar (1935–2006)
Professor in the Department of Geography and the Institute of Urban and Regional Studies, The Hebrew University of Jerusalem. His main areas of interest were economic globalization and urban development and national and metropolitan planning. He directed the preparation of the Israeli National Outline Plan (Tama 35). His recent publications included two edited volumes, one entitled "Tel-Aviv and Frankfurt – Emerging Nodes in the Global Economy" and the other evaluating the impact of the Intel Corporation on a small town in Israel (Kiryat-Gat). He received the Israel Prize in 1999 for his contributions to urban geography and urban planning.

Ian Smith
Senior research fellow at the Cities Research Centre, Faculty of the Built Environment, University of the West of England – Bristol. His research centres on policy analysis and policy evaluation of spatial and urban policy within both metropolitan and rural areas.

Barbara Staniscia
Has a Master degree in Local Development and a PhD in Economic Geography. She is a researcher at the d'Annunzio University, Chieti-Pescara, Italy. She has been a member of EU-funded research projects, such as MIRE, ESPON, SELMA, and has conducted research on urban dynamics, human mobility, local development and spatial effects of EU policies.

Luděk Sýkora
Associate Professor at the Department of Social Geography and Regional Development, Faculty of Science, Charles University in Prague. His research focuses on

urban restructuring, impacts of globalisation on urban transformations, real estate development, housing and housing policy and urban planning in post-communist cities.

Manuel Valenzuela

Principal researcher of the Laboratory on Urban and Social Geography and Professor of Human Geography at the Autonomous University of Madrid since 1981. His research interests focus on two main areas: urban geography and geography of tourism and leisure. He is a member of the advisory boards of both Spanish and European scientific geography journals and is a member of the committee for the International Geography Award "Vautrin Lud". He has written or coordinated twelve books, forty book chapters, fifty journal papers and a similar number of contributions to proceedings.

Carmen Vázquez

Associate Professor of Geography at the Faculty of Humanities, University of Castilla-La Mancha, 1999 up to date. She started her academic career working on urban social geography topics dealing with urban social segregation. Over time, her research interests broadened to include transport infrastructure and information and communication technologies (ICTs) in cities as well as processes of deconcentration and urban sprawl. She has published two books, 17 book chapters and 20 articles in both Spanish and European journals.

Preface

European metropolitan areas have experienced a marked reorganization associated with the processes of globalization and the European integration of economic activities on various spatial scales. Much of this change is particularly evident at the edge of central cities, further away at suburban locations and on the fringes of expanding metropolitan areas. These spatial processes of urban expansion, sprawling development, and employment deconcentration present constant challenges to urban quality of life, raising concerns about excessive consumption of land and energy, traffic congestion, and so forth. These concerns prompt the formulation of public policies at various levels of government: European Union agencies, national, and sub national public authorities.

The challenges posed by the spatial reorganization of economic activities within European metropolitan areas and their implications for the quality of life inspired the research project sponsored by the European Commission 5th Framework, entitled: Spatial Deconcentration of Economic Land Use and Quality of Life in European Metropolitan Areas (SELMA). The primary goal of SELMA was to design urban planning and management strategies to ensure the maintenance of the quality of life in European metropolitan areas. To this end, three broad activities were defined. The first focused on the identification and analysis of the driving forces and dynamics behind the process of economic land-use deconcentration in metropolitan areas. An analysis of the impacts of these processes on urban quality of life formed the heart of the second activity. Finally, the effectiveness of the public policy response to the challenges of economic land-use deconcentration in various governance systems was assessed. These activities were carried out in 14 metropolitan areas in seven countries: Denmark, the United Kingdom, the Netherlands, the Czech Republic, Spain, Italy, and Israel.

This book presents the results of part of the SELMA endeavour, focusing mainly on the development trends over a 10-year period relating to the form and magnitude of employment dispersal and the role of public policies in creating the present processes. The main objective was to provide the infrastructural knowledge base relating to European urban trends and to provide rich comparative case-study evidence. In the scientific literature, the broad phenomenon of urban sprawl has been discussed widely. However, most studies have featured patterns, processes, and policy debates in the United States and concentrated mainly on residential spatial reconfigurations. The few studies of the deconcentration of economic land uses are limited in scope and in most cases lack a cross-national comparative perspective. Such a perspective can contribute substantially to the explanation of the patterns and processes of deconcentration, in particular to the assessment of the impact of different governance systems and public policies on deconcentration. In this book we discuss the scale and form of economic deconcentration and quality-of-life implications within selected metropolitan areas, referring to attributes of governance systems, thus aiming to provide useful insights for possible changes in metropolitan governance and policies.

This book is dedicated to the memory of Professor Frans Dieleman and Professor Arie Shachar – two leading urban geographers, kind and wise human beings, who initiated the SELMA project.

Frans Dieleman of Utrecht University led the SELMA project until, sadly, he suddenly passed away on 11 April 2005. His death was a great loss for the SELMA consortium. He was well-respected scientist in the international geographic and planning community and an expert on housing, transportation, urban development, methodologies, spatial planning, and related topics. His management qualities were renowned both within academia and beyond. It was an honour for the SELMA consortium to have such an experienced and highly esteemed scholar as coordinator. His was a truly influential voice in the many debates and the development of the project. Frans Dieleman will be remembered as a gifted scientist and a much-loved coordinator of SELMA.

Arie Shachar of the Hebrew University of Jerusalem pioneered urban geography in Israel and became a renown geographer and urban planner worldwide, directing international research programs. In Israel he played a leading role in formulating the Tel Aviv metropolitan plan and the National Outline Plan. Abroad he was engaged in many international planning consultancy efforts, even serving in 1978 as an advisor to the White House conference on balanced national growth and economic development. He was a leader and a "scientific" entrepreneur, initiating and directing countless ventures in basic and applied research. He also played a major role in initiating the SELMA project, and served as its scientific coordinator. While still engaged in an impressive array of new such ventures, he passed away in September 2006.

We acknowledge the various organizations that have contributed to this program. The SELMA project is funded by the European Community under the *Energy, Environment and Sustainable Development* FP5 Programme (1998-2002), Key Action 4 *City of Tomorrow and Culture Heritage* (contract no. EVK4-CT-2002-00102). This project could not have been carried out successfully without the unrestrained energy of all the partners: Utrecht University, Faculty of Geosciences, Urban and Regional research Centre (The Netherlands), Hebrew University of Jerusalem, Department of Geography Faculty of Social Sciences (Israel), Universidad Autonoma de Madrid, Department of Geography, Research Laboratory for Urban and Social Geography (Spain), University G. d'Annunzio – Chieti – Pescara, Dipartimento di Economia e Storia del Territorio (Italy), University of the West of England – Bristol, Faculty of the Built Environment, Cities Research Centre (United Kingdom), Charles University Prague, Faculty of Science, Department of Social Geography and Regional Development (Czech Republic), Skov & Landskap, Danish Centre for Forest, Landscape and Planning, Department of Urban and Regional Planning (Denmark), By-og-Byg, Danish Building and Urban Research, Housing and Urban Research Division (Denmark), and the RIVM-Netherlands Environmental Assessment Agency (The Netherlands).

Although they have not contributed to this book directly, the end-users involved in the program have given valuable and constructive comments on the work activities and reports of the SELMA project. The following end-users' organizations were involved: City of Utrecht; Department of Strategic Planning (The Netherlands), The Netherlands Ministry of Housing, Spatial Planning and the Environment (The Netherlands), Ministry of Interior of Israel, Planning Administration (Israel), Comune di Roma Dipartimento XIV per lo sviluppo locale, per la formazione e per il lavoro (Italy), Distretto dell'Audiovisivo e dell 'ICT (Italy), Eastleigh Borough Council (United Kingdom), Southampton City Council (United Kingdom), Czech-Invest, Industrial Properties and Regions Department (Czech Republic), City of Brno, Office of City Development (Czech Republic), and the Danish Ministry of Environment and Energy, Spatial Planning Department (Denmark).

In completing this book we consider ourselves very fortunate to have had the help of Anne Hawkins for the English-language editing, and Tamar Sofer, the Cartographic Laboratory of the Department of Geography, the Hebrew University of Jerusalem, for the cartographic contributions.

1 Introduction: Deconcentration of economic activities within metropolitan regions: A qualitative framework for cross-national comparison

Eran Razin

Department of Geography, The Hebrew University, Jerusalem 91905, Israel

Abstract: The chapter outlines a comparative framework for the study of employment deconcentration within metropolitan areas, aiming to explain processes and forms of deconcentration and the impact of different governance systems. It introduces processes of deconcentration, followed by a discussion of the two extremes of the spectrum among developed economies: the United States and Western Europe. Governance systems, assumed to be major explanatory factors of deconcentration, are defined by various combinations of welfare state regimes and central government-local government relationships. A classification of market determinants is followed by a classification of types of employment deconcentration, linking these types with governance systems. Also mentioned is the broader context that includes residential sprawl, quality-of-life outcomes and particular policy packages. The chapter concludes with some preliminary remarks on the national case studies discussed in subsequent chapters

Key words: Employment deconcentration, sprawl, governance, welfare state regimes

1.1 Introduction

The deconcentration of economic activities has become a familiar sight at the edges of large European metropolitan areas. Such deconcentration has ceased to be dominated by manufacturing plants, warehouses, and other facilities that can now hardly locate in inner urban locations. Hypermarkets, superstores, and do-it-yourself stores now proliferate at urban fringe locations in numerous metropolitan areas; such locations frequently serve as nuclei for the evolution of major suburban retail, service, and entertainment concentrations. Modern suburban office complexes have also become prominent in the economy of certain European metropolitan areas.

In American metropolitan areas, employment deconcentration came earlier and on a much larger scale; it has now also become a policy concern in Europe. In many ways, the urban landscape formed by employment deconcentration in Europe resembles the North American prototype, as reflected by big-box retail structures and their surrounding parking lots, single-use modern office complexes, entertainment centres, warehouses and distribution concentrations, all located in accessible suburban locations along main roads and near motorway intersections. This scenario raises the question of whether market forces and

1

E. Razin et al. (eds.), Employment Deconcentration in European Metropolitan Areas, 1–27.
© 2007 *Springer.*

technological improvements work towards the formation of North-American-type patterns of deconcentration of economic land uses in Europe, or whether European metropolitan areas remain fundamentally different.

Numerous studies have assessed the broader phenomenon of urban sprawl, but the bulk of research, which has become particularly voluminous since the 1990s, has focused on processes and policy debates in the United States (recent examples include Gillham, 2002; Wiewel & Persky, 2002; Burchell *et al.*, 2005; and Wagner *et al.*, 2005). Moreover, most studies have dealt in general with urban form or specifically with residential sprawl. The deconcentration of economic land uses has not received the same systematic coverage, although a few recent studies have focused on employment deconcentration. Persky & Wiewel (2000) have provided a cost-benefit analysis of employment deconcentration in the American context, and Lang (2003) focused on the deconcentration of office space in American metropolitan areas.

Interest in sprawl has also grown in Europe, with transportation and environmental aspects frequent subjects for debate (for example, Breheny, 1995; Dieleman *et al.*, 1999). American-European comparisons have been inspired by the desire of anti-sprawl advocates in the United States to learn lessons from European policies and experiences of compact development (Nivola, 1999; Beatley, 2000). Studies of the location of economic activities in European countries have emphasized trends of deconcentration and discussed the effectiveness of public policies attempting to influence the location of retail and other business establishments (Guy, 1998; Schiller, 2001). However, these studies have usually been limited in their scope and, in most cases, have lacked a cross-national comparative perspective.

A comparative perspective on the deconcentration of economic activities is capable of contributing substantially to the explanation of processes and forms of deconcentration, particularly to the assessment of the impact of different governance systems on deconcentration. Such assessment offers insights for formulating and evaluating public policies that concern sprawl, not only by surveying the range of policies employed in different countries, but also by demonstrating that specific policy packages should be fitted to particular governance systems. Insight can also be provided into the implications of reforming metropolitan governance on deconcentration.

Our book has the following objectives:

1. To identify the forms and processes of employment deconcentration in selected metropolitan areas within Europe (and in Israel), commenting on whether the processes in Europe are fundamentally different from those that took place in North America, and whether processes in European metropolitan areas indicate a unique European model or a variety of models of deconcentration.
2. To assess the determinants of employment deconcentration in different European countries and in different metropolitan areas within these countries.
3. To position the forms and processes of employment deconcentration in European metropolitan areas within a broader cross-national comparative framework

defined by combinations of governance attributes and market characteristics that produce particular forms of deconcentration.

4. To assess possible governance and policy implications of the deconcentration process in the light of specific metropolitan circumstances and local values.

We suggest that a European type of employment deconcentration could be defined in a broad sense, diverging fundamentally from the United States type in both market and governance attributes. Similarly, European employment deconcentration diverges from the Canadian variant of the US type, primarily in market attributes. The European type presents a context of low population growth, highly developed economies, and the long urban history reflected in an urban fabric that constrains options for the location of economic activities. The European type is also characterized by a fairly broad consensus over welfare state values that implies acceptance of public policy controls over the location of economic activities.

Nevertheless, we also suggest that a broad variety of types of deconcentration can be observed in European metropolitan areas – diversity that results from variations in governance and market attributes and is sometimes obscured by the more striking differences between European and North American metropolitan areas. We identify four main deconcentration types in European metropolitan areas: (1) a highly-regulated continental-northern European type; (2) a slightly less regulated British type; (3) a southern European type, where lower levels of regulation-enforcement could be expected; and (4) a post-communist central European type, characterized by lower standards of living and by either low levels of regulation-enforcement or antagonism towards central planning. Intra-national variations in processes and forms of deconcentration are also marked; variations in size, economic base, geographical specificities, and metropolitan governance attributes can be expected.

This introductory chapter puts forward a comparative framework for the national case studies that follow, providing insights on the desirability and feasibility of various policy measures that concern employment deconcentration in different market and governance contexts. The chapter starts with a general introduction to the processes of employment deconcentration, followed by a discussion of the two extremes of the spectrum among developed economies – the United States and Western Europe. We then suggest a classification of governance systems defined by various combinations of welfare state regimes and central government-local government relationships. We also define the market determinants of deconcentration. There follows a classification of the dependent variable – types of employment deconcentration – linking types with governance systems. We emphasize the broader context that includes residential sprawl influenced by similar determinants, but having its own independent influence *on* employment deconcentration as well as being influenced *by* employment deconcentration. Quality-of-life outcomes are also mentioned, because these outcomes influence policies and aspects of governance that in turn lead to the modification of forms of employment deconcentration. We then link deconcentration types, associated with quality-of-life, market, and governance attributes, with particular policy packages. Finally, the chapter provides some preliminary remarks on the national case studies discussed in subsequent chapters; these are compared more thoroughly in the concluding chapter of this book.

1.2
The magnitude and form of employment deconcentration

In recent decades, urban sprawl, characterized by leapfrog and strip development, low densities, automobile dependence, and the spatial separation of land uses, has become a major issue in the policy and planning agenda in many metropolitan areas throughout the Western world (Beatley, 2000; Bourne, 1992). Sprawl is to a large extent a market-driven phenomenon, a response to the widespread preference for low-density housing and an embrace of the freedom and convenience that car ownership brings. Thus, the positive quality-of-life implications of sprawl for large segments of the population cannot be ignored. However, sprawl also has negative impacts on aspects of sustainable development and social justice; these impacts have been a source of extensive debate (Ewing, 1997; Gordon and Richardson, 1997; Gillham, 2002). An evaluation of the pros and cons of sprawl does not mark the end of the debate; it also raises such questions as how to measure it (Galster et al., 2001), how to assess its root causes (Razin and Rosentraub, 2000), and how public policies might influence the magnitude and pattern of urban deconcentration.

The study of sprawl has to distinguish between residential and non-residential variants, the latter involving various commercial, entertainment, industrial, office, warehousing, and public facilities. Although both processes are interrelated, they differ substantially in their dynamics and economic, social, and environmental effects. Residential sprawl has received more attention in the past, as employment deconcentration is largely perceived as an outcome of the decentralization of population from metropolitan cores. However, evidence in recent years has shown that the deconcentration of employment – particularly of retail centres and offices – is a policy challenge in itself, since its impact on travel, accessibility, and future urban form is significant (Bourne, 2001; Lang, 2003). Moreover, the deconcentration of employment has also been perceived as a cause rather than the result of residential sprawl: households could be moving closer to new employment opportunities in the periphery rather than retail establishments locating close to a newly suburbanized population.

In Europe, population sprawl has not been considered a policy issue of prime significance, partly because limited population growth has meant that residential sprawl has been moderate and has not affected travel behaviour in a fundamental way (Dieleman et al., 1999). However, the deconcentration of business uses has become an important policy issue, increasingly viewed as a major factor in the modification of travel patterns and consequent increase in energy consumption, and in the accessibility of particular population groups to jobs, services and amenities.

An evaluation of employment deconcentration needs to refer first to the *magnitude* of the deconcentration of retail (including restaurants and entertainment), office and industrial space, measured by number of jobs, land area or floor space located in various parts of the metropolitan area. Deconcentration measures could refer to trends of change in the central city of the metropolitan area versus its inner and outer suburbs. Measures could also compare the historic CBD with new employment concentrations, or continuously built-up urban areas with development in urban-rural fringe areas. Results depend on the spatial unit of analysis employed; thus, in order to avoid the ecological fallacy – the invalid transfer of conclusions from spatially aggregated analysis to smaller areas or to the individual level – reference is also made to smaller units of analysis. Trans-national comparative studies, however, may have to sacrifice the accuracy of the insights on specific forms of deconcentration, limited as they are to the data and information available for the metropolitan areas compared.

A second main aspect for evaluation concerns *forms* of deconcentration, distinguishing low-density scattered patterns from polynucleated growth (a polycentric spatial structure that includes suburban nodes and even edge cities that can overshadow the historic CBD). The evaluation of patterns also refers to specific spatial configurations of deconcentration, for instance commercial strips and leapfrog development, as well as to the distance of deconcentrated functions from the city centre or from the central city.

The magnitude and form of employment deconcentration should be evaluated separately for different economic activities. One could hardly expect manufacturing and warehousing to remain in dense urban environments, expect for small enterprises of special types. The major issue concerning the decentralization of manufacturing and warehousing is therefore whether decentralization leads to a scattered or a polycentric pattern. The magnitude and form of retail deconcentration, only partly an inevitable consequence of metropolitan expansion, depends on particular public policies and market circumstances (Guy, 1998). Offices are the function that could be expected to remain most concentrated in historic CBDs and in the central cities of metropolitan areas, or at least to concentrate in edge cities should they leave the downtown area (Garreau, 1991). Whereas high-technology manufacturing can be expected to prefer suburban and exurban locations, even when involving high transaction costs, start-ups and R&D activities, communication, software and technical services can be expected to locate in both inner city and suburban locations – the inner city tending to attract smaller businesses and start-ups (Simone Gross, 2005).

Although policies of historic preservation may limit opportunities for office development in historic CBDs, pushing office construction to the periphery, the CBD usually remains the preferred location for front-office activities. This is the place with the densest pattern of face-to-face contacts between members of the high-order service industries, except for edge cities in some North American metropolitan areas. In North America, however, office construction has also undergone a process of suburbanization that has also led to a pattern of scattered rather than polycentric development (Lang, 2003). Finally, different commercial uses, including various forms of retail, offices, hotel, and public uses such as convention centres, municipal offices and libraries, can be found to converge over time in specific locations in the periphery, for instance in the vicinity of regional shopping malls. These concentrations do not necessarily constitute edge cities or new downtowns, although they may provide the basis for their emergence (Moretti & Fischler, 2001).

The magnitude and form of sprawl are influenced by private and public decision-making as well as by civil society actors. The role of public action in promoting or controlling urban sprawl has been a source of considerable debate (Duany et al., 2000), for example over the balance between investment in highway construction and investment in public-transit systems – a balance that can considerably influence patterns of land use and urban form. Fuel pricing (by means of taxes), energy policies, housing policies, systems of taxation and agricultural subsidies, not to mention local zoning, are further relevant public policies that influence patterns of sprawl (Nivola, 1999).

1.3
The extreme archetypes: the United States and Western Europe

The two extreme archetypes in the spectrum of processes of employment deconcentration in developed economies are described in this section as a first step in the formulation of a broader cross-national framework for comparing the phenomenon. Metropolitan areas of the United States, at one end of the spectrum, are considered to be prototypes of sprawling patterns of deconcentration in a weak regulatory environment. West European metropolitan areas, at the other end, represent compact patterns of development and strict measures to control sprawl. Despite some convergence of trends in North America and Europe (Kay, 2002), substantial differences between the two continents remain with respect to the processes of urban development (Nivola, 1999).

1.3.1
The United States type

The United States represents the case of archetypical sprawl, both of residential and economic activities (Gillham, 2002): commercial strips; leapfrog development; suburban automobile-dependent concentrations of retail and entertainment; suburban office complexes; edge cities that in some cases surpass the CBD in floor space and economic dominance; and perhaps edgeless cities, where offices disperse even from the large suburban concentrations – all these evolved in the United States earlier and to a greater extent than anywhere else.

Prime market forces responsible for the extreme position of the United States are usually assumed to include a high standard of living, high motorization rates, high population growth compared with most developed countries, the abundance of land, and the racial tensions and crime that frequently plague metropolitan cores. Transportation technologies, particularly those associated with the automobile, were adopted earlier and on a greater scale in North America than in Europe, thus accelerating the processes of dispersion. Early adoption of new telecommunication technologies, from the telephone to the computer and most aspects of digital capacity, and even innovations such as air conditioning, have also contributed to more sprawling patterns of development in North America than in Europe.

In terms of public policy, the United States is characterized by a marked influence of *laissez-faire* ideologies and a strong emphasis on property rights. Attempts to control the ambitions of developers and property owners meet little sympathy in the courts (Stanilov, 2004). The United States is also considered as a prototype of decentralization (Razin, 2000). Local governments are largely autonomous in land–use planning, and regional growth-management or smart-growth frameworks are rather weak. Municipal fragmentation also contributes to employment deconcentration – the weakness of central cities lead businesses to deconcentrate from them. Local government expenditures are heavily dependent on self-generated revenues; consequently, inter-municipal competition over rate-able land uses that are beneficial for their fiscal viability (primarily businesses) leads to the further scatteration of businesses within suburban space, offsetting the tendency of some businesses to cluster in selected nodes as a result of agglomeration economies. Strong ties between the business community and local leaders and low energy costs can also be regarded as governance and policy variables that encourage sprawl.

Some public decisions made in the 1950s that had a particular effect on accelerating the deconcentration of economic activities in the United States were the large federal investment in interstate highways and other elements of road infrastructure, and legislation in1954 for the accelerated depreciation of income-producing property. This anti-recession move made by a Republican government remained in effect until the 1980s (Hayden, 2003). This step explicitly encouraged mass investment in new suburban shopping malls and other commercial real estate. Successive rounds of investment and the cost of maintaining and upgrading existing facilities rendered them economically unviable. They were eventually sold and abandoned while new income-producing properties were developed further away from the urban core. It is commonly assumed that market forces encouraging deconcentration in the United States have been accompanied by federal tax concessions and subsidies, local government subsidies that helped deconcentrate economic activities and build edge cities and "edge nodes" at metropolitan fringe locations (Hayden, 2003). These concessions and subsidies have not been offset by the public funding provided to the regeneration of downtowns, to urban renewal and to mass-transit projects. In fact, widespread policies of downtown regeneration in the United States are not aimed specifically at curbing employment deconcentration, and have minimal impact on patterns of development in suburban space and beyond.

1.3.2
The European type

At the other end of the spectrum are the West European countries, where strict measures aimed to control urban development and curb deconcentration of economic activities are enforced with varying degrees of effectiveness. The Netherlands, Germany, and the Scandinavian countries are considered to be prime examples of this highly-regulated type, characterized by relatively compact urban development, thriving city centres, limited retail deconcentration, and office deconcentration that largely depends on whether the construction of modern office buildings in historic city centres is restricted by preservation considerations.

Nevertheless, even in countries at this end of the spectrum, policies that control the deconcentration of economic activities face new challenges. From the governance side, processes of political decentralization, such as those operating in the Netherlands, can be associated with the transfer of land-use planning powers to lower-level governments, rendering control mechanisms countering sprawl less effective.

Changes in the markets, however, seem to pose the major dilemmas. First, it is difficult to ignore the growing popularity of big-box retail, such as large Ikea and Toys-'R'-Us stores, do-it-yourself stores that sell a broad range of merchandise, and superstores, all providing convenience and economies of scale. These establishments require large tracts of land and depend on low land costs – requirements that preclude location in CBDs and pull them towards the urban fringe. Factory outlet centres – another retail innovation imported from North America – also contribute to the deconcentration of retail in certain European metropolitan areas.

Second, innovation in communication technologies – the emergence of "cyber-cities" – make it more difficult for dense urban concentrations to anchor high-technology, office and high-end service jobs (Simone Gross, 2005), reducing the agglomeration economies for these high-transaction-cost activities. Inter-local competition could thus move from striving for advantages in production to advantages in consumption. The continued concentration of high-end jobs in urban centres increasingly depends on the amenities offered by dense urban environments (Glaeser et al., 2001). Core areas of world cities and a few downtowns of smaller urban areas do well in the competition over amenities, but many other cities could find it difficult to compete with suburban and exurban locations. In the case of retail location, city centres in large British cities frequently manage to thrive despite retail deconcentration; it is the High Streets of smaller cities and towns that seem to suffer most from deconcentration.

Third, expanding flexible production and distribution systems require large low-density sites with good access to the inter-urban road network (Dieleman & Wegener, 2004).

Finally, the distinction between economic activities is becoming increasingly blurred. As stated above, the deconcentration of manufacturing and warehousing is considered to be inevitable, even desirable, owing to both the inability to meet their needs for land in inner city locations and the possible environmental nuisance associated with some of these facilities. Industrial parks in metropolitan fringe locations could attract high-tech industries, usually considered to be lucrative tenants. However, it is hard to distinguish between high-tech activities and ordinary offices, so that in practice it may become impossible to stem the exodus of office activities, both front offices and back offices, from inner city locations to automobile-dependent sites at the metropolitan fringe. Retail could also penetrate industrial areas through the establishment of do-it-yourself stores (Schiller, 2001) and warehouses, which could provide another fissure in the anti-sprawl policy, since they are readily convertible into big-box retail operations.

The deconcentration of non-manufacturing activities therefore becomes diffi-cult to control although market forces also work to limit sprawl in Western Europe. These forces include minimal population growth, high land prices, phys-ical obstacles to sprawl such as the high cost of development on Dutch polders, and the unique amenities offered by historic city cores in some European cities (see chapter 6 in our book). Greater acceptance of planning and policies imposed from above is a policy variable that still distinguishes Europe from the United States. Thus, although suburban concentrations of retail space have also pene-trated Western Europe, their magnitude has remained a small fraction of those in American metropolitan areas (Stanilov, 2004).

1.3.3
Variations within the extremes

It should be noted that considerable variations exist within the United States and West European extremes. The spatial deconcentration of retail sales in American metropolitan areas is influenced by the level of dependence of local government finance on taxes collected from businesses (sales tax and property tax) and by the existence of planning policies that include restrictive urban growth boundaries (Wassmer, 2002). There are sporadic attempts at growth management and smart growth in American metropolitan areas: Portland, Oregon is the most publicized example (Abbott, 1997; Dieleman & Wegener, 2004).

Variations within Europe are greater. Great Britain, for example, implements interventionist regulations that concern retail location, but these have been bypassed through the establishment of large supermarkets/superstores that almost become mini-shopping malls, the establishment of do-it-yourself stores on industrial estates that grow to become major retail outlets, the establishment of major shopping malls in enterprise zones exempt from planning regulations (Schiller, 2001), and the conversion of industrial structures and warehouses into big-box retail establishments. Less effective enforcement of regulations could be expected in Southern European metropolitan areas – namely, in Spain and Italy – but these are still characterized by relatively strong monocentrism.

Major metropolitan areas in post-communist Europe, particularly in the Czech Republic, Hungary, and Poland, present an interesting variation: they are characterized by lower standards of living and either low levels of enforcement of regulations or antagonism towards communist-style central planning. Whereas suburban development in the communist era was largely confined to high-rise apartment blocks and large industrial estates, post-communist metropolitan development has been characterized by the considerable deconcentration of economic activities, particularly retail – shopping centres, entertainment and big-box retail establishments near major suburban intersections – and warehousing (Sykora *et al.*, 2000). Diverging from the trends in most developed countries, the suburbanization of retail even preceded the low-density residential deconcentration of the middle class; deconcentration was financed by foreign corporations and was less dependent on the purchasing power and capital accumulation of the local population. The spatial pattern of investment in economic activities in places such as Prague seems to have followed a North-American economic-geography textbook, with far weaker regulations than in Western Europe. Some post-communist metropolitan areas seem to combine typical European urban patterns with American locational trends led by market processes.

1.4
A cross-national framework for comparing employment deconcentration

1.4.1
Governance systems

The above description of the two extremes and variations between them can serve as a basis for the formulation of a broader comparative framework for employment deconcentration. We assume that governance systems are major explanatory factors of employment deconcentration. Two major dimensions of governance we expected to influence sprawl in general, and employment deconcentration in particular, are the welfare state regime and central government-local government relationships (Figure 1.1).

Welfare state regimes are largely defined by the levels of public intervention in market processes and the regulation of the economy in the name of the public good; welfare state regimes are usually sensitive to aspects of social justice and sustainable development rather than primarily to efficiency and economic growth. The United States and West European countries represent the two ends of the spectrum (Esping-Andersen, 1990). The liberal welfare state – the United

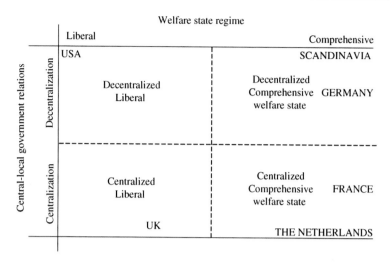

Fig. 1.1 Governance systems

States – is characterized by a less regulated economy, in which relatively limited welfare state mechanisms are targeted at clientele of low income. The comprehensive welfare state refers to continental West European countries, such as France, Germany, and Scandinavian countries. Esping-Andersen (1990) also distinguishes between the corporatist welfare state (Germany, for example), in which the state is ready to replace the market as a provider of services, and the social-democratic (Scandinavian) welfare state that places a greater emphasis on equality. This latter distinction seems, however, to have lost its significance (Kloosterman, 2000). A more significant variation among continental European welfare states, one which potentially has implications for the location of economic activities and policies towards sprawl, refers to the nature and extent of adjustments in response to pressures on the welfare state. These pressures are caused by escalating costs associated with demographic changes, technological advances in health care, and increasing exploitation of welfare benefits, strained public budgets, globalization that leads to intensified competition and precludes the ability to shield the high costs of financing generous welfare benefits from lower-cost international competitors, and greater socio-ethnic diversity that could reduce the social solidarity embedded in the welfare state.

The liberal welfare state is dominated by *laissez-faire* approaches embedded in neo-liberal or neo-conservative ideologies, whereas in comprehensive welfare states there is as yet no significant support for ideologies labelled as such; initiatives to adjust the welfare state in the light of growing pressures defy political labels. Centrally-imposed land-use policies that aim to control sprawl and intervene in the location of economic activities are expected to be more politically acceptable in comprehensive welfare states. Higher taxes on fuel, greater publicly-subsidized investment in public transportation, and high subsidies to agriculture can also be expected in the more comprehensive welfare states. Anglo-Saxon countries, such as Britain and Canada, lie between the United States and continental European archetypes; Britain in particular represents a case of retreat from the comprehensive model, although retaining a far more interventionist approach than the United States.

A relevant sub-dimension of the welfare state regime refers to the level of enforcement of welfare state regulations (Freeman & Ogelman, 2000). Most of West Europe (except for some Mediterranean regions) and North America are regarded as a high-enforcement environment, but low levels of enforcement are attributed at times to southern European countries and, more recently, to post-Communist Europe. These low levels could reduce the effectiveness of policy measures that aim to control patterns of urban development.

The second major relevant dimension of governance – central government-local government relationships – distinguishes between systems in which substantial powers, political autonomy, and financial capacity are devolved to local governments, and systems in which upper-level government agencies either possess substantial powers to direct local affairs or closely monitor and control functions performed by local authorities. In these latter systems, local authorities usually only possess limited political autonomy and are either constrained by meagre financial resources or depend substantially on grants from higher-level governments.

Land-use planning and local-government finance are the two aspects of central-local government relationships most relevant to employment deconcentration. Far-reaching decentralization of land-use planning combined with a high dependency of local authorities on taxes and levies paid by businesses are the conditions most expected to encourage the deconcentration of economic activities.

The level of local government fragmentation (consolidation versus fragmentation) is a sub-dimension of central government-local government relationships. When land-use planning is decentralized and local governments depend on taxes and levies paid by businesses, high levels of municipal fragmentation could lead to a particularly scattered pattern of deconcentration. When higher-level governments retain control over land-use planning, or at least have powers to determine policies at the regional and national levels and intervene when local decisions deviate markedly from these policies, and when local government finance does not depend on revenues from businesses, municipal fragmentation is less relevant for patterns of economic deconcentration. However, even in this last case, the interests of landowners still tend to influence land-use planning decisions more in small local authorities than in large cities or regional municipalities.

The above two dimensions – the welfare state regime and the central-local government relationships – define four extreme governance systems (Figure 1.1). The United States is considered as the archetypical decentralized liberal system in which markets predominate, taxes – including those on fuel – are relatively low, and there are few checks on employment deconcentration. At the other end, the Netherlands represents a centralized comprehensive welfare state where public controls on deconcentration could be most effective. The Dutch case represents perhaps the epitome of the centralized welfare-state model. A long tradition of central planning and centrally-imposed reforms has been augmented by a near-total dependence of local governments on central grants (Razin, 2000). To a lesser extent, France also represents an example of such a system that is characterized by extremely high levels of municipal fragmentation (Hoffmann-Martinot, 2005).

The other two corners of Figure 1.1 – decentralized comprehensive welfare states and centralized liberal systems – combine components that seem contradictory, because comprehensive welfare states are expected to require political centralization, whereas liberalism is usually expected to be associated with decentralization. The decentralized comprehensive welfare state is best represented by Scandinavian countries and, to a lesser extent, by Germany (Wollmann, 2000, 2004). The combination of a centralized liberal system is less common. Britain since Thatcher has moved considerably in that direction (Stoker, 2004), although its welfare state is still more comprehensive than that of the United States.

Southern European countries, post-communist countries, and Israel do not fit any of the four corners of Figure 1.1. Placing these countries in the figure requires in-depth examination of their governance attributes. In terms of welfare state regimes, according to prevailing perceptions, the above countries are characterized, to varying degrees, by lower levels of regulation enforcement than other West European or North American countries. This attitude implies lax attitudes towards construction without permits and corruption in the planning and development process. Less comprehensive welfare-state mechanisms in these countries could reflect market attributes, namely lower incomes, but in post-Communist Europe and in Israel this attitude could also be associated with antagonism to Communism or socialist values – values that open doors to the somewhat greater influence of neo-liberal ideologies than in Western Europe. Needless to say, even if progressing towards the US decentralized liberal system, deconcentration outcomes would remain profoundly different from those in US metropolitan areas owing to the differences in market attributes. Levels of political decentralization also vary substantially between the above countries, although none can be regarded as decentralized as the United States or Scandinavian countries.

1.4.2
Market determinants of employment deconcentration

Market attributes influencing the deconcentration of economic activities have been discussed extensively in the sprawl literature. In Figure 1.2, these attributes are grouped into six interrelated categories.

The first category refers to land values and the geographical constraints that influence land values and development costs. These constraints include the scarcity of developable land, topographic and climatic constraints on the availability of land and on densities, and other physical constraints such as the high development costs on Dutch polders. High land values are expected to encourage more intensive

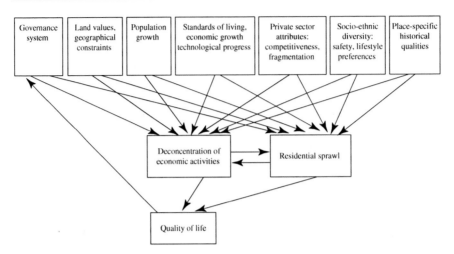

Fig. 1.2 A framework for evaluating deconcentration of economic activities in metropolitan areas

compact development, although very low land values could be associated with very limited employment deconcentration as a result of a lack of demographic and economic growth. Indeed, land values are influenced by other explanatory factors included in Figure 1.2, primarily demographic and economic growth. Infrastructure and accessibility can also form geographical constraints, but economic growth and technological progress, defined as separate explanatory factors, can usually overcome such constraints.

Population growth is a prime factor influencing development pressures, including those for the development of economic land use in metropolitan fringe areas. Rapid population growth encourages deconcentration, but the development and deconcentration of economic activities also takes place when population is stagnant or even declining, as is the case in many European metropolitan areas and in some American ones — Cleveland, for example. In this case, deconcentration is either fuelled by economic growth and technological development or reflects competition in which investment in new commercial and office space comes at the expense of older facilities. Population growth can be regarded as an exogenous factor at the national level, but governance and market-related explanatory factors at the metropolitan level do influence population growth.

Standards of living, economic growth, and technological change represent a third category of market attributes that reflect economic and technological progress. Economic growth and high standards of living lead to an increase in land consumption per capita for both residential and non-residential uses. High rates of motorization, encouraging deconcentration, are primarily an outcome of high levels of economic well-being. Technological change has led to the realization of new levels of economies of scale associated with the concentration of retail and distribution activities in larger space-consuming structures that tend to locate in urban and metropolitan fringe areas (Schiller, 2001). However, such progress does not necessarily lead to a scattered pattern of deconcentration. The use of cars and the realization of economies of scale can lead to the emergence of poly-centric forms in which economic activities form even larger-scale operations in car-accessible suburban locations where sufficient developable land is available. A parallel process of scatteration can occur in specific economic activities: the potential impact of communication technologies on encouraging scattered forms of footloose businesses (Simone Gross, 2005) and on the overall demand for office and retail space is still unclear.

A fourth category of market attributes refers to the competitiveness and fragmentation of the real-estate market. A market dominated by a few large developers could produce a more polycentric pattern dominated by large-scale projects of business parks, office complexes, and shopping centres. A market characterized by the proliferation of small and medium-sized developers would produce a more scattered pattern, particularly when land ownership is also fragmented.

Socio-ethnic diversity is usually considered as an explanatory factor where ethnic tensions accelerate suburbanization. Most commonly, such tension is attributed to the friction between the white and African-American populations in American metropolitan areas, where the fear of crime and poor school quality were among the reasons for white-flight into suburban locations. It has been argued that sprawl-reducing metropolitan governance arrangements, such as the directly-elected regional authority in Portland, Oregon, and the tax-base-sharing mechanism in the Minneapolis-St Paul metropolitan area have become politically feasible owing to the relative lack of ethnic tensions in these metropolitan areas, where deprived African-American and Hispanic communities are small. Safety problems associated with high levels of crime in CBDs surrounded by poor ethnic neighbourhoods used to be quoted as major motives for the exodus of businesses from the downtowns of American metropolitan areas. Black riots in the 1960s hastened that process.

Several decades of public efforts to revitalize American downtowns (Ford, 2003) have produced some results, but have hardly influenced deconcentration processes. The economy of many revitalized downtowns have remained volatile and attracting substantial retail back into city centres has been difficult, not so much because of ethnic tensions or crime, but because of insufficient purchasing power in the vicinity of the CBDs. Downtowns have suffered from inferior accessibility to the suburban middle class; most high-threshold retail activities have sufficient markets to operate in suburban locations.

Socio-ethnic diversity also influences values and tastes. However, it is unclear whether this cultural-lifestyle factor has an independent effect on preferences that concern residential densities and shopping behaviour, or whether different preferences largely reflect variations in incomes and other market and policy constraints.

Finally, place-specific historic qualities can influence the deconcentration of economic activities in diverse ways. On the one hand, the strict preservation of historic city centres could force large-scale office activities, such as the head-quarters of large corporations, to move out to suburban locations, because of the inability to develop modern facilities in the preserved centre. On the other hand, thriving historic centres that offer unique qualities in the metropolitan area could attract high-end retail and office activities and slow down deconcentration.

1.4.3
Forms and processes of employment deconcentration

The above governance and market determinants produce a variety of types of employment deconcentration that cannot be measured on a single scale. Quantitative attempts to measure sprawl, based, for example, on the eight measures suggested by Galster and colleagues (2001), are limited in their ability to depict major attributes of employment deconcentration, and face limitations in data availability and quality. A more qualitative taxonomy suggested in the framework of the SELMA project (Montanari *et al.*, 2004) is based on four main attributes of deconcentration: magnitude (small-scale or large-scale); physical form (concentrated or scattered); sectoral composition (industry-led, services-led or commerce-led); and government-policy context (planning-led or market-led).

Table 1.1 suggests a framework for comparison that distinguishes only two main scales: (1) spatial form and (2) process and policy. The spatial form scale includes four levels of deconcentration. The lowest is defined as *limited polycentric*, usually led by industry and warehousing. At higher levels, deconcentration is led by retail and offices, displaying both *scattered forms* and the evolution of *edge nodes* or even an *edge city* that competes with or even eclipses the historic CBD. The most deconcentrated forms are scattered, led by offices. These four levels do not encompass all possible combinations of magnitude, physical form, and sectoral composition, but only rarely would metropolitan areas diverge radically from one of the defined levels.

The process-and-policy scale includes three levels (Table 1.1). At one end are comprehensive and effective compact-development policies and at the other end are policies that are either ineffective or take a *laissez-faire* approach. Between these poles are anti-sprawl policies that are considerably influential, although policy deviations are more common than in the more effective policies of compact development.

Whereas the various dimensions of forms of employment deconcentration can be collapsed together into one scale with a minimal loss of information, the process and policy scale has to be retained as a separate scale, because similar policies and processes can lead to very different forms owing to differences in market attributes. For example, even if governance systems in post-communist metropolitan areas evolve to resemble the United States' decentralized liberal typology, and even

Table 1.1 Forms and processes of employment deconcentration and their relationship with governance types: a framework for comparison

		Process and policy		
		Comprehensive and effective compact development policies	Comprehensive compact development policies, occasional deviations	Ineffective enforcement of policies or laissez faire approaches
Form	Limited, polycentric, usually led by industry & warehousing	**A** **B**		
	Polycentric, limited scattered development, led by retail	**A** (market characteristics promote deconc.) **B** (market characteristics promote deconc.)	**A** (limited enforcement) **B** (limited enforcement) **C**	**A** (ineffective enforcement) **B** (ineffective enforcement) **D** (low incomes)
	Substantial polycentric and scattered, edge city phenomena	**B**	**B** **C**	**D**
	Substantial, scattered, led by offices			**D**

Notes: The positioning of each extreme type of governance system in the Table is only suggested.
A – Centralized comprehensive welfare state.
B – Decentralized comprehensive welfare state.
C – Centralized liberal.
D – Decentralized liberal.

if subsequent policies and processes resemble those of American metropolitan areas, the spatial outcomes would be very different, because of differences in the standard of living, in the historic qualities of cities, and in other market variables.

1.4.4
Linking governance types to deconcentration types

Different governance systems lead to different types of employment deconcentration; Table 1.1 suggests likely types of deconcentration for each of the four extreme governance systems specified in Figure 1.1. The decentralized liberal governance system, characterizing American metropolitan areas, is likely to produce one of the two most scattered forms. Strong local political autonomy, the dominance of elected local residents in land use and zoning decisions, the financial autonomy of local communities, and inter-local competition over the tax base are argued to be important factors that encourage sprawl in the United States (Jacobs, 2003). Outcomes would be influenced, however, on market characteristics and on variations in land-use policies. Lower standards of living and geographic-historic constraints could lead to more compact outcomes characterized by only limited scattered development. Pure *laisse-faire* in land-use development is unfeasible in modern metropolitan areas; even metropolitan areas such as Houston are not pure *laissez–faire*. Thus, policy variations also influence deconcentration within decentralized liberal systems. Lower dependence of local government finance on taxes paid by businesses also eliminates an engine of economic deconcentration.

The centralized comprehensive welfare state produces concentrated development forms. For example, spatial planning and tax regulations in Japan promote much more inter-local cooperation and service equity than in the United States, leading to compact forms of development (Jacobs, 2003). Similarly, centralized national spatial plans make a major contribution to Dutch compact development. Outcomes are nevertheless influenced by market characteristics. Despite very high levels of economic and technological development in both Japan and the Netherlands, the extreme scarcity of land is a powerful market characteristic that encourages compact development in both. However, although office activities under this governance type could be expected to remain concentrated in city centres, the unique nature of historic city centres in the Netherlands compels large-scale office activities to decentralize into compact-office concentrations at city edges or along major motorways.

The ineffective implementation of policies could also lead to increased deconcentration in a centralized comprehensive welfare state. The challenge posed by changing technologies – big-box retail establishments and the blurred distinction between economic activities – and by high standards of living, also presses towards the second category of forms of deconcentration (Table 1.1).

The impact on employment deconcentration of the two latter extreme types of governance – the decentralized comprehensive welfare state and the centralized liberal state – is more difficult to anticipate. In a decentralized comprehensive welfare state, a broad societal consensus over sustainable development is more likely than in a decentralized liberal system and equalization mechanisms associated with the comprehensive welfare state could reduce the incentive to compete over taxpaying economic land uses. As in the centralized comprehensive welfare state, market pressures and weaker enforcement could increase deconcentration. A partly planned polycentric deconcentration is also a possibility. Whereas Scandinavian and German metropolitan areas are likely to represent the stricter compact development policies in decentralized comprehensive welfare states, Toronto in the Canadian Province of Ontario is an example of a polycentric pattern in such a governance regime (Shearmur and Coffey, 2002); the local authorities in Canada are rather weak, but the political system is more decentralized than in the European comprehensive welfare states.

A centralized liberal state could be characterized by intermediate levels of policies and forms of deconcentration. Centralized mechanisms in such a state have a substantial ability to constrain deconcentration. In Britain, centralized compact development policies are in place, including policies to curb out-of-town retail development that harms city-centre high-street retail. However, deviations are more likely than in a comprehensive welfare state (Schiller, 2001) associated with a liberal *laissez-faire* ideological environment, including mechanisms such as planning gains and planning obligations that provide incentives for public authorities to approve projects that are not always in line with long-standing policies (Ratcliffe *et al.*, 2004). Nevertheless, the divergence of spatial outcomes of the decentralized liberal system – the United States – from outcomes of the other three governance systems defined in Figure 1.1 can be expected to be far greater than the divergence in spatial outcomes when these other three systems are compared with each other.

Table 1.2 displays the expected association between governance and decon-centration, based on the generalizations presented in Table 1.1. Both Tables can serve as a framework in which to compare metropolitan areas in different countries. Table 1.2 includes a more simplified classification of deconcentration patterns, based solely on magnitude and form, displaying the association between these patterns and types of governance. Variations in magnitude and form of deconcentration among metropolitan areas of the same governance category are explained by variations in market determinants, in policies and their effective implementation, and by variations in governance attributes within each of the four governance categories. Nevertheless, the Table does indicate some combina-tions of deconcentration and governance that could hardly be expected under any circumstances.

Table 1.2 The expected association between governance and employment deconcentration

Magnitude and form of deconcentration	Governance system			
	Centralized comprehensive welfare state	Decentralized comprehensive welfare state	Centralized liberal	Decentralized liberal
Small-scale concentrated	V	V		
Small-scale scattered	V	V	V	V
Large-scale concentrated (polycentric)		V	V	V
Large-scale scattered				V

1.4.5
The role of residential sprawl, quality of life impacts
and counter-influences

Assessing the impact of governance and markets on the deconcentration of economic activities has also to refer to residential sprawl and to quality-of-life outcomes of deconcentration and sprawl that have a counter-influence on governance and policy (Figure 1.2). Similar determinants influence both residential sprawl and the deconcentration of economic activities, but residential sprawl by itself is a factor that encourages the deconcentration of economic activities. Retail and service establishments seek proximity to markets and businesses seek proximity to large pools of suitable labour. Employment deconcentration then further encourages the suburbanization and exurbanization of population. In fact, the deconcentration of economic activities that is not initially a product of residential suburbanization can trigger a process of residential suburbanization and sprawl. This process has perhaps not occurred in countries such as the highly-regulated Netherlands, where employment deconcentration has been slow to follow residential deconcentration, despite a growing spatial mismatch between workers and places of work (Schwanen *et al.*, 2004). However, in less regulated circumstances, employment deconcentration that erodes the job-accessibility advantage of central locations can prompt households to deconcentrate, even if the end result is not necessarily shorter commutes.

Sprawl in general and employment deconcentration in particular influences the quality of life considerably. Defined broadly, quality-of-life outcomes can be grouped into three categories: economic, social, and environmental. Economic outcomes include the costs of infrastructure and waste resulting from the under-utilization of existing infrastructure, the costs of real estate development, the costs of congestion, and economies of scale in various economic activities. Social outcomes refer to fiscal and service-level disparities, access to jobs (particularly for low-income populations), access to amenities, the availability of affordable housing (Downs, 2004), safety, civic engagement, and catering for people's subjective lifestyle preferences. Environmental outcomes refer to the waste of farmland, damage to environmentally fragile land, nuisances and hazards associated with the proximity of certain economic activities to residential areas, pollution, the emission of greenhouse gases, and the impact on health (including obesity).

With some exceptions, most notably Gordon and Richardson (1997) and Bruegmann (2005), authors accept the overriding costs of sprawl, even in the United States (Persky & Wiewel, 2000; Burchell *et al.*, 2005), although not necessarily its translation into policy action. The acknowledged benefits of sprawl usually refer to residential sprawl, primarily lower housing costs, larger lot sizes, and consumer preferences for lower-density living. Employment deconcentration offers some advantages to customers and employees, and enables the realization of economies of scale and cost savings for businesses. However, on the whole employment sprawl tends to be viewed even more negatively than residential sprawl. Among proposed anti-sprawl prescriptions, new urbanism explicitly links residential and employment deconcentration and advocates mixing housing with commercial space in a compact, walkable urban environment (Langdon, 1994; Daniels, 1999).

Linking particular patterns of employment deconcentration with possible outcomes is an endeavour beyond the scope of this book. It should nonetheless be recognized that, although governance and policy shifts take place in the context of macro-societal processes – in recent decades namely globalization, the liberalization of markets, pressures on the welfare state and decentralization (Salet *et al.*, 2003) – the quality-of-life outcomes of sprawl and deconcentration have a counter-influence on governance and policy. The influence of quality-of-life outcomes is both direct and indirect. Direct influences include conscious changes made in response to these outcomes, such as in local government organization, metropolitan governance structures, land-use planning, and transportation policy. Indirect influences include possible greater political conservatism associated with suburbanization (Walks, 2004). The interaction between governance, employment deconcentration, and quality of life, influenced by external market determinants should be taken into account in evaluations of employment deconcentration within metropolitan regions and their policy implications.

1.4.6
Policy packages, governance and deconcentration

Policy options that aim to constrain sprawl and employment deconcentration are all, to some extent, uphill efforts needed to counteract powerful market pressures. Such policies can be classified into four main types (Persky & Wiewel, 2000; Gillham, 2002):

1. Policies that directly constrain sprawl and deconcentration through land-use controls/regulatory growth controls: zoning controls, transit oriented development, urban growth boundaries, land acquisition, transfer of development rights.
2. Policies that constrain sprawl and deconcentration through financial penalties and incentives: impact fees, tax incentives.
3. Policies that deal with unequal outcomes associated with deconcentration, thus reducing some of the motivation to promote deconcentration: revenue/tax base sharing, equalization grants and other local government reforms: "regionalism", affordable housing strategies.
4. Policies that deal with the regeneration of older urban centres: enhancing the efficiency of places that are currently not efficient from a market perspective. Downtown redevelopment programs, brownfield and greyfield redevelopment.

Governance influences policy discourses and policy prescriptions. Even policy labels such as growth management, smart growth, new urbanism, compact city, and multifunctional land use differ from place to place (Dieleman & Wegener, 2004).

Policy choice thus has to acknowledge governance constraints and proposed policy packages have to fit particular governance attributes (and market conditions). Such a fit refers not only to the level of interventionism: that is, to the balance between planning restriction and *laissez-faire* approaches, and to the effective enforcement of policies. Rather, the closeness of fit refers to the particular nature of policies that are ideologically acceptable and feasible given political and market circumstances.

Of the four policy types defined above, the first and the third – direct land-use planning constraints and equalization mechanisms – can be expected to predominate in the policy packages in comprehensive welfare states, whether centralized or decentralized. Policy initiatives of these types can occasionally be found in a decentralized liberal governance system, but there they can be expected to remain rather marginal. Policies of the second and the fourth types – financial tools and the regeneration of centrally-located declining concentrations of economic activities – could be attempted more frequently in decentralized liberal systems, having less friction with market-oriented ideologies. Such policies are less essential in comprehensive welfare states, although brownfield redevelopment could be practised widely in metropolitan areas where brownfields have a marked presence.

Appropriate policy packages should take into account market determinants that vary considerably from place to place. These determinants also influence the range of effective policy packages that can be employed in a particular metropolitan area. In fact, an attempt can be made to link particular policy packages to the various combinations of types of deconcentration and types of governance specified in Tables 1.1 and 1.2.

Desired quality–of-life outcomes could require changes in governance rather than solely policy adjustments. Whereas modifications in the welfare state regime is a macro-societal process that can hardly be expected to be triggered by debates over sprawl and deconcentration, modifications in the central government-local government relationships dimension are more likely to be suggested as a response to urban expansion processes. Such modifications refer to formal local government reforms as well as to steps meant to change the 'rules of the game' of local governance. In some cases, these modifications can be considered merely as policy adjustments of the third type, but substantial changes can be regarded as modifications in governance that have an impact on the range of feasible policies.

1.5
The case studies – some preliminary remarks

Following this introductory chapter, the book consists of eight chapters each of which features a specific national case study. Three chapters represent northern Europe (the Netherlands, Denmark, England), three represent the southern European-Mediterranean region (Spain, Italy, Israel) and two deal with post-communist central Europe (the Czech Republic and a general chapter on retail deconcentration). Most chapters present information on two metropolitan areas, usually a large one (North Randstad, Copenhagen, Bristol, Madrid, Rome, Tel

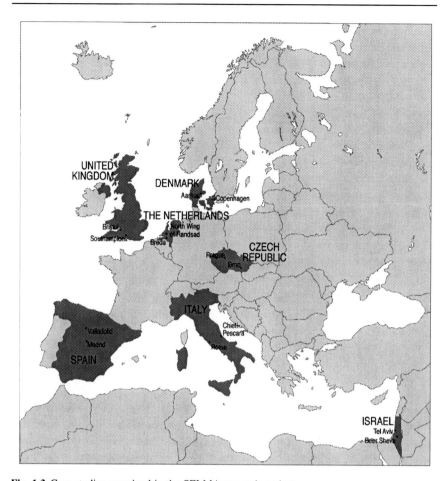

Fig. 1.3 Case studies examined in the SELMA research project

Aviv, Prague) and a smaller one (Figure 1.3). The chapters describe patterns of employment deconcentration, their governance and policy context in each of the metropolitan areas (usually providing more details on the larger metropolitan area and examining to what extent the smaller metropolitan area displays similar or different patterns and processes). A comparative chapter follows the eight case-study chapters.

The chapters reveal considerable variations in the magnitude, form, and process of employment deconcentration within metropolitan areas in Europe. However, evidence from the case studies does not confirm the anticipated distinction between Northern and Mediterranean Europe. Indeed, the northern Europe case studies represent the high-regulation model well, each within a somewhat different governance context: the Netherlands as a centralized comprehensive welfare state, Denmark a decentralized comprehensive welfare state (although displaying marked centralization in land use planning controls on sprawl), and Britain a centralized liberal welfare state. The regulation of employment deconcentration in the metropolitan areas of each of these three countries encounters mounting pressures associated with economic and political change at the supra-national level. In Britain, some attempts are being made to reconstruct the barriers to deconcentration lowered by the liberal transformation of its welfare state, particularly for retail. In the Netherlands, the rapid deconcentration of employment away from the central cities – probably a consequence of the rapid economic growth and the unique urban structure of the Randstad – has retained a compact polycentric form. Recent trends of the decentralization of powers and deregulation in the Netherlands impose a certain level of uncertainty on the continued effectiveness of compact city policies, although public support for policies to retain the viability of historic city centres remain strong and a wide-scale process of retail deconcentration seems highly unlikely. Denmark seems to provide the most stable governance and policy environment to control deconcentration of economic activities; occasional deviations from policy are largely exceptions that demonstrate the general high effectiveness of the high-regulation policies that are already embedded in a decentralized political system.

Metropolitan areas located in Mediterranean Europe could have been expected to display a less planned pattern of deconcentration, resulting from loose management practices and low levels of enforcement of legislation and regulations. However, less explicit policies towards deconcentration and lower levels of enforcement has not appeared to produce extensive deconcentration. In fact, metropolitan areas in both countries have so far seemed to retain a strong monocentric employment distribution, perhaps reflecting a market phenomenon associated with the superior qualities offered by historic city core locations, at least in the largest metropolitan areas. Public efforts are thus geared towards alleviating pressure on the urban core through polycentric deconcentration.

The Czech Republic and Israel seem to diverge most from prevailing European trends; they are both influenced by the employment deconcentration processes that characterize the decentralized, liberal, United States type of governance. This uniqueness could reflect the major political shift away from communist or strong socialist-ideological orientation in both countries. These experiences could be relevant to other centralized or formerly centralized emerging economies, such as China. Future deconcentration of economic activities under these circumstances could face contradictory pressures. On the one hand, strong market pressures could lead through metropolitan governance in these countries to follow decentralized liberal patterns – variations from American metropolitan areas mainly reflecting market attributes. On the other hand, the fundamentally more centralized political culture, the influence of the values of other members of the European Union (particularly in post-communist countries that have joined the EU), and the scarcity of land (particularly in Israel), could enhance a counter-trend of reconstructing regulation to constrain deconcentration.

The following chapters present details and evaluations of the selected case studies, enabling the assessment of the proposed comparative framework, its policy, governance, and quality-of-life implications in the concluding chapter.

References

Abbott C (1997) The Portland region: where city and suburbs talk to each other – and often agree. Housing Policy Debate 8:11–51

Beatley T (ed) (2000) Green urbanism, learning from European cities. Island Press, Washington, DC

Bourne LS (1992) Self-fulfilling prophecies? Decentralization, inner city decline, and the quality of urban life. J Am Plann Assoc 58:509–513

Bourne LS (2001) The urban sprawl debate: myths, realities and hidden agendas. Plan Canada 41(4):26–28

Breheny M (1995) Counter-urbanization and sustainable urban forms. In: Brotchie J, Batty M, Blakely E, Hall P, Newton P (eds) Cities in competition: Productive and sustainable cities for the 21st century. Longman, Melbourne, Australia, pp 402–429

Bruegmann R (2005) Sprawl, a compact history. The University of Chicago Press, Chicago

Burchell RW, Downs A, McCann B, Mukherji S (2005) Sprawl costs, economic impacts of unchecked development. Island Press, Washington, DC

Daniels T (1999) When city and country collide, managing growth in the metropolitan fringe. Island Press, Washington, DC

Dieleman FM, Dijst MJ, Spit T (1999) Planning the compact city: the Randstad Holland experience. Eur Plann Stud 7:605–621

Dieleman F, Wegener M (2004) Compact city and urban sprawl. Built Environ 30:308–323

Downs A (ed) (2004) Growth management and affordable housing, do they conflict? Brookings Institution Press, Washington, DC

Duany A, Plater-Zyberk E, Speck J (2000) Suburban nation: the rise of Sprawl and the decline of the American dream. North Point Press, New York

Esping-Andersen G (1990) The three worlds of welfare capitalism. Princeton University Press, Princeton, NJ

Ewing R (1997) Is Los Angeles-style sprawl desirable? J Am Plann Assoc 63:107–126

Ford LR (2003) America's new downtowns, revitalization or reinvention? The Johns Hopkins University Press, Baltimore

Freeman GP, Ogelman N (2000) State regulatory regimes and immigrants' informal economic activity. In: Rath J (ed) Immigrant businesses, the economic, political and social environment. Macmillan, Houndmills, 107–123

Galster G, Hanson R, Ratcliffe MR, Wolman H, Coleman S, Freihage J (2001) Wrestling sprawl to the ground: defining and measuring an elusive concept. Housing Policy Debate 12:681–717

Garreau J (1991) Edge city: life on the new frontier. Anchor Books, Doubleday, New York

Gillham O (2002) The limitless city, a primer on the urban sprawl debate. Island Press, Washington, DC

Glaeser EL, Kolko J, Saiz A (2001) Consumer city. J Econ Geogr 1:27–50

Gordon P, Richardson HW (1997) Are compact cities a desirable planning goal? J Am Plann Assoc 63:95–106

Guy CM (1998) Controlling new retail spaces: the impress of planning policies in Western Europe. Urban Studies 35:953–979

Hayden D (2003) Building suburbia, green fields and urban growth, 1820—2000. Vintage Books, New York

Hoffmann-Martinot V (2005) Towards an Americanization of French metropolitan areas? In: Hoffmann-Martinot V, Sellers J (eds) Metropolitanization and political change. VS verlag fur Sozialwissenschaften, Wiesbaden, pp 231–264

Jacobs AJ (2003) Embedded autonomy and uneven metropolitan development: a comparison of the Detroit and Nagoya auto regions, 1969–2000. Urban Studies 40:335–360

Kay JH (2002) In Holland, the pressures of American-style urban sprawl. The Christian Science Monitor, October 3 (http://www.scmonitor.com/2002/1003/p13s01-stgn.html)

Kloosterman R (2000) Immigrant entrepreneurship and the institutional context: a theoretical exploration. In: Rath J (ed) Immigrant businesses, the economic, political and social environment. Macmillan, Houndmills, pp 90–106

Lang RE (2003) Edgeless cities, exploring the elusive metropolis. Brookings Institution Press, Washington, DC

Langdon P (1994) A better place to live, reshaping the American suburb. Harper Perennial, New York

Montanari A, Staniscia B, di Zio S (2004) Spatial Deconcentration of Economic Land Use and Quality of Life in European Metropolitan Areas, Taxonomy of Economic Land Use Deconcentration. Project funded by the European Community under the Energy, Environment and Sustainable Development Programme, Key Action 4, City of Tomorrow and Cultural Change.

Moretti GP, Fischler R (2001) Shopping center development and the densification of new suburban cores. Journal of Shopping Cent Res 8(2):83–116

Nivola PS (1999) Laws of the landscape, how policies shape cities in Europe and America. Brookings Institution Press, Washington, DC

Persky J, Wiewel W (2000) When corporations leave town, the costs and benefits of metropolitan job sprawl. Wayne State University Press, Detroit

Ratcliffe J, Stubbs M, Shepherd M (2004) Urban planning and real estate development, 2nd edn. Spon, London

Razin E (2000) The impact of local government organization on development and disparities – a comparative perspective. Environ Plann C: Gov Policy 18:17–31

Razin E, Rosentraub M (2000) Are fragmentation and sprawl interlinked? North American evidence. Urban Aff Rev 35:864–879

Salet W, Thornley A, Kreukels A (2003) Institutional and spatial coordination in European metropolitan regions. In: Salet W, Thornley A, Kreukels A (eds) Metropolitan governance and spatial planning, comparative case studies of European city-regions. Spon, London, pp 3–19

Schiller R (2001) The dynamics of property location, value and the factors which drive the location of shops, offices and other land uses. Spon Press, London

Shearmur R, Coffey WJ (2002) A tale of four cities: intrametropolitan employment distribution in Toronto, Montreal, Vancouver, and Ottawa-Hull, 1981–1996. Environ Plann A 34:575–598

Schwanen T, Dijst M, Dieleman FM (2004) Policies for urban form and their impact on travel: the Netherlands experience. Urban Studies 41:579–603

Simone Gross J (2005) CyberCities. In: Wagner FW, Joder TE, Mumphrey AJ Jr, Akundi KM, Artibise AFJ (eds) Revitalizing the city, strategies to contain sprawl and revive the core, M.E. Sharpe, Armonk, NY, 274–309

was put in force in the late 1970s and early 1980s; it was successful in concentrating suburban residential growth into the selected designated growth centres of Nieuwegein, Almere, Houten, and Huizen in the Northwing of the Randstad, while stemming urban sprawl in the Green Heart (Faludi & Van der Valk, 1990; Dieleman et al., 1999).

This policy of 'concentrated deconcentration' was brought to an end during the 1980s, because it had a negative impact on population size and employment in central city areas (MVROM, 1988; Dieleman et al., 1999; Hajer & Zonneveld, 2000). A new policy of 'compact urban growth' was implemented. As formulated in the Fourth Physical Planning Memorandum Extra (VINEX) (MVROM, 1991), this new policy guided urban growth into (re-)development locations within existing cities (brownfield sites) and towards new greenfield sites directly adjacent to the built-up areas of the larger cities. Leidsche Rijn – the greenfield development immediately to the west of Utrecht – is the largest of these VINEX locations; some 35,000 dwellings and 10,000 jobs have been created there (Van der Burg & Dieleman, 2004).

In addition to this VINEX-policy, the Fourth Physical Planning Memorandum (MVROM, 1988) also introduced a policy for the location of firms: the A-B-C location policy, which could support the concentration of urbanization and the preservation of green areas. This policy was formulated to discourage the use of the private car and promote public transport, cycling and walking in economic commuting. A locations were close to main railway stations; B locations were situated in development nodes outside the larger CBDs and the centres of smaller urban settlements, were reasonably well connected to public transport, and readily accessible by car; C locations had good motorway access – typical examples were business zones in the urban fringe or alongside motorways. The intention of this policy was to guide new employment and public services – especially those attracting many visitors or requiring high levels of employment– towards A and B locations. This policy turned out to be difficult to implement and many economic developments took root at 'wrong' locations, in particular at C locations (Schwanen et al., 2004). One important reason appeared to be that local government authorities often gave higher priority to attracting new employment (read: new jobs and income) than to strict adherence to locational rules. It will be apparent that the 'hierarchical and very centralized' Dutch planning system described in the introduction leaves considerable room for local spatial policy initiative and power. Another reason for the unwanted development in C locations was the underestimation of the growth in employment in the office sector during the 1990s that could not be fully accommodated in A and B locations. As a result, the largest employment growth in the 1990s occurred at C locations. Consequently, the A-B-C location policy has been extensively modified (MVROM, 2001).

Finally, since 1973, Dutch retail policy has been highly effective in barring the establishment of out-of-town shopping malls. These were perceived to be a threat to the vitality of town centres and likely to generate extensive private car use. Many shops are still located within the built-up areas of cities and towns and within walking or cycling distance for local residents (Evers, 2002). Recently, the national retail planning policy was abolished, since it was blamed for curtailing retail productivity and competitiveness and creating barriers to new firms entering the retail market (Evers, 2002). However, at the local level regulations are still in force preventing the development of out-of-town hypermarkets and shopping malls, although the first signs of the liberalization of this retail locational policy can be found (outlet markets, furniture boulevards, and so forth).

2.2.2
Spatial coherence

While the principles of 'concentrated deconcentration' and 'compact urban growth' relate to the physical aspects of urban activities, the principle of 'spatial coherence' is based on the functional aspects of these activities. Since the publication of the Fourth Physical Planning Memorandum (MVROM, 1988), the Dutch government has encouraged the concentration of related strong economic functions in specific areas readily accessible by main infrastructure (mainports such as Rotterdam harbour and Amsterdam Schiphol Airport, for example). A related functional policy objective that also features in this Memorandum is that of concentrating people's daily activities within the borders of compact daily urban systems (WRR, 1998). This policy promotes the intermingled localization of home, work, and services so as to avoid unnecessary travel movements.

2.2.3
Spatial differentiation

The third principle is that of 'spatial differentiation': the preservation and enforcement of diversity within the urban or rural landscape. To prevent areas becoming monotonous, attractive features of Dutch scenery, such as historic sites, would be preserved with robust measures. Rural areas to be preserved include parts of the 'Green Heart' in the centre of the Randstad and the Ecological Main Structure, and natural buffer zones separating cities/villages to prevent the development of continuous built-up areas.

The national government set up an extensive urban renewal program in the same period as the 'compact urban growth' policy. Subsidies were given to upgrade existing housing stock. Unfortunately, the urban renewal policy showed little concern for retaining or attracting employment in the city core areas. This neglect has certainly been one of the main causes of the economic deconcentration processes in the larger Dutch cities. The majority of jobs in many cities can now be found in new employment concentrations outside the original city centres (Schwanen *et al.*, 2004).

2.2.4
Hierarchic urbanization

The principle of 'hierarchic urbanization' promotes the development/preservation of rank-size within urbanization and a policy to prevent the levelling off of the existing Dutch urban structure. 'Urban nodes' and 'Randstad International' are examples of policy concepts aimed at the development of an urban hierarchy (MVROM, 1988). The first refers to the selection of certain urban nodes in which selective urban policies and governmental finances are concentrated, primarily for reasons of efficiency. The 'Randstad International' policy is intended to concentrate important economic developments in the economic heartland of the Netherlands and make the Randstad an attractive location for international companies (WRR, 1998).

2.2.5
Spatial justice

The fair distribution of economic activities has always been an important objective of Dutch planning policy. Nowadays, the aim is a fair distribution across the country of growth potential rather than an equal distribution of economic activities. This objective is reflected in the planning concept 'regions on their own strengths', which means that each region should achieve economic growth through its own strengths and make optimal use of its own economic potential (WRR, 1998).

These principles of Dutch spatial planning have successfully guided spatial developments in the last few decades. The question that arises is how these principles influenced economic concentration/deconcentration processes in the 1990s in the Netherlands and how this worked out for the two selected regions: the Northwing of the Randstad and the Breda region. That is the main issue addressed in this chapter. In the next section we first discuss some research-analytical issues.

2.3
Data and methodological issues

To analyse the deconcentration of the economic sectors we have made use of LISA data (*Landelijk Informatiesysteem Arbeidsplaatsen* [National Information System for the Working Population]) for the years 1991, 1996, and 2000[1]. Information on the number of employees per economic sector in the study areas is stored in the LISA files. It should be noted, however, that changes in the course of time in the classification and comparative methods necessitated certain adjustments to this dataset before temporal comparisons could be made appropriately.

The employment data have been classified in three economic sectors:

- Retailing/consumer services: wholesale and retail trade, hotels, health institutes, education, household goods, and so forth.

- Producer services: companies working in finance, business administration, and transport;
- Manufacturing/construction: electricity, gas, and water utilities, construction and manufacturing companies.

We have used two different approaches in our analysis of the spatial deconcentration of economic land use. In this way we were better placed to identify the differentiations in spatial patterns and the underlying spatial processes and investigate them in more depth.

In the first approach, we subdivided the urbanized regions into concentric urban and suburban zones starting from the centre of the central city (monocentric region) or cities (polycentric regions). This subdivision resulted in four functional zones (Figure 2.2):

- CBD or centre of the central city;
- The rest of the central city;
- Inner suburban ring;
- Outer suburban ring.

These functional zones are based on neighbourhood boundaries, municipal boundaries, and the 'daily urban systems[2]' of the cities (see Van der Laan, 1998). The neighbourhood boundaries are used to define the 'centre' of a central city. In the Northwing of the Randstad a 'centre' can only be distinguished in Amsterdam and Utrecht. The municipal boundaries of the main cities are used to define the

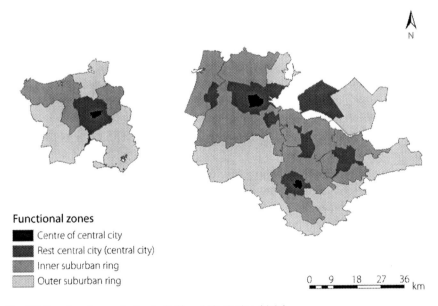

Functional zones

- Centre of central city
- Rest central city (central city)
- Inner suburban ring
- Outer suburban ring

0   9   18   27   36 km

Fig. 2.2 Functional zones in Breda (left) and Northwing (right)
Source: Statistics Netherlands, 2000

'rest of the central city'. The borders of the daily urban system are used for the definition of the 'inner suburban ring'. In fact, this 'inner suburban ring' is the daily urban system minus the central cities (the centre of the central city and the rest of the central city). The 'outer suburban ring' is based on the relationships of the main cities with the municipalities outside the daily urban system.

The second approach to the analysis of the deconcentration of economic functions follows the work of Galster and colleagues (2001). For residential deconcentration, they developed a conceptual definition of sprawl based on eight dimensions: centrality, density, concentration, continuity, nuclearity, mixed use, clustering, and proximity. They operationalized and tested these dimensions successfully for 13 urbanized areas in USA. For the purpose of our analysis, we selected three of these dimensions:

- Density: The average number of employees per square metre of developable land in an urban area;
- Centrality: The degree to which development in an urban area is situated close to the CBD;
- Mixed use: The degree to which two or more different land uses are intermingled in the same small area and how far this pattern is typical throughout the urban area.

The starting point for this second analysis is a raster of 250m by 250m superimposed on the study area. Within the raster a distinction is drawn between developable areas such as agricultural land, and other areas such as water, nature, and forests. The calculation of the indices of sprawl is based on the surface area of developable land within the grids. A summary of our calculation and visualization methods for the sprawl indices is given in Bogaerts et al. (2003a).

2.4
Dynamics in employment distribution over functional zones

The 1990s are known as a decade of exceptionally strong economic growth in the Netherlands. At 26 percent, the employment growth was well above that of the USA or of European countries as a whole; this growth is attributed to the comparatively advantageous development of labour costs in the 1990s (Atzema & Van Dijk, 2004). When employment growth in the Northwing of the Randstad is compared with the Netherlands as a whole, it becomes clear that the regional growth was stronger than in the rest of the country. Between 1991 and 2000, the number of jobs increased by 36 percent. With a growth of 104 percent, the producer services account for a large share of the new employment. In the Breda region, at 30 percent the employment growth is slightly higher than the Dutch average, but less than that of the Northwing. This difference can be envisioned as a clear identification of the different economic positions of the two regions within the Dutch economic situation. In the Breda region, the enormous growth in producer services also stands out (64 percent). In both regions the retailing/consumer sector also increased substantially, although less than the producer services (32 percent in the Northwing and 37 percent in the Breda region). Manufacturing/construction hardly increased in either the Northwing (0.7 percent) or in the Breda region (7 percent).

Against this background of general trends in employment growth, in this section we present our analysis of the different functional zones of the Northwing and Breda region in the development of employment for the period 1991–2000. We centre our discussion on (1) the growth of employment in each zone and (2) the changes in the share in employment of each functional zone. In addition to total employment, we have analysed the dynamics for the three identified sectors: retailing/consumer, producer services, and manufacturing/construction.

Figure 2.3 shows that, in the period 1991 to 2000, employment increased substantially in both regions, particularly in the zones outside the centres of the central cities. So the rest of the central cities, especially the suburban zones, enjoyed a substantial growth rate. This increase in employment was largely caused by the expansion of the producer services in the Northwing of the Randstad and the Breda region. However, the growth rates of these regions differ substantially: while in the Northwing the inner and to a lesser extent the outer suburban ring show the biggest growth rates, within the Breda region the highest growth rate in producer services employment can be found in the rest of the central city and to a lesser extent in the suburban zones. The difference in the scale of developments between the regions is clear to see. Moreover, the outcome of the policy of compact urban growth is clearly illustrated in this development. With regard to retailing/consumer services, development growth was more or less equal in all other functional zones outside the city centres, both within the Northwing and the Breda region. The manufacturing/construction sector shows a slight overall increase in employment in both regions, with the exception of the centres of the central cities in the Northwing of the Randstad, where employment in this sector has decreased substantially.

In general terms, this uneven employment development between the centres of the central cities on the one hand and the rest of the central cities and suburban zones on the other can probably be attributed to the intense competition for space in these areas, the consequent high rents, and restricted expansion potential. Obviously, firms with a high demand for extensive floor space such as transport or car rental firms or business administration have moved to out-of-town-centre locations. In addition to this competition for space, the urban renewal policy referred to above showed little interest in attracting or even retaining employment in the centres of the central cities. In fact, this policy was focused on residential and social upgrading rather than economic upgrading. This preference may well have contributed to the uneven employment development spread.

These trends are reflected in the development in employment share of each functional zone as illustrated in Table 2.1. In general terms, it can be seen that, although in an absolute sense employment levels within the centres of the central cities increased rather than decreased, in a relative sense the share decreased in

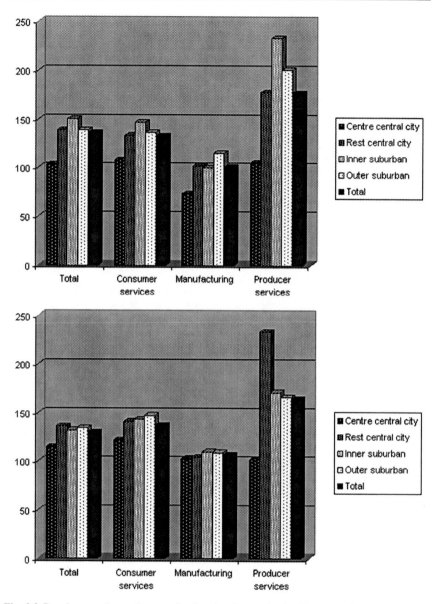

Fig. 2.3 Development in employment for functional zones in the Northwing (above) and Breda regions (below) 1991-2000 (1991=100)
Source: LISA 1991-2000

Table 2.1 Total employment and development in share of employment of each functional zone: Northwing (above) and Breda region (below) 1991–2000 (percent)

		Total employment		Retailing/ consumer		Manufacturing/ construction		Producer services	
		Absolute	Share	Absolute	Share	Absolute	Share	Absolute	Share
Centre of	1991	239988	19.4	133682	20.7	19431	7.6	85485	26.7
central city	2000	248276	14.8	143786	16.8	14255	5.6	89983	15.9
Rest	1991	422342	34.2	228020	35.4	77552	30.4	114467	35.8
central city	2000	586690	34.9	302940	35.5	79237	30.9	203392	36.0
Inner	1991	430785	34.8	206268	32.0	120174	47.1	95176	29.8
suburban ring	2000	647347	38.5	301966	35.4	119752	46.7	221861	39.3
Outer	1991	143426	11.6	76812	11.9	37718	14.8	24448	7.6
suburban ring	2000	198785	11.8	104650	12.3	43356	16.9	48949	8.7
Total	1991	1236541	100	644782	100	254875	100	319576	100
urbanised area	2000	1681098	100	853342	100	256600	100	564185	100

		Total employment		Retailing/ consumer		Manufacturing/ construction		Producer services	
		Absolute	Share	Absolute	Share	Absolute	Share	Absolute	Share
Centre of	1991	32261	22.4	21124	29.7	3654	8.1	7426	30.7
central city	2000	37050	19.8	25689	26.4	3756	7.8	7588	19.1
Rest	1991	39295	27.2	18647	26.3	12719	28.2	5901	24.4
central city	2000	53538	28.6	26331	27.1	13242	27.4	13750	34.6
Inner	1991	41724	28.9	17212	24.2	17410	38.6	6585	27.2
suburban ring	2000	55175	29.5	24587	25.3	19101	39.5	11232	28.3
Outer	1991	30916	21.4	14034	19.8	11319	25.1	4278	17.7
suburban ring	2000	41385	22.1	20613	21.2	12282	25.4	7112	17.9
Total	1991	144196	100	71017	100	45102	100	24190	100
urbanised area	2000	187148	100	97220	100	48381	100	39682	100

Source: LISA 1991–2000

favour of all the out-of-centre functional zones in both the Northwing and the Breda region. In the Northwing in particular, the inner suburban zone attracted a substantial share of this suburbanization process. However, despite this overall suburbanization trend, about 50 percent of all employment has remained within the boundaries of the central cities. For instance, for the producer services sector, 52 percent and 54 percent respectively is still situated in the cities of the Northwing and Breda region. From this observation it can be concluded that, within this sector, a clear differentiation has taken place; some parts still consider the central city to be a valuable location, even economically speaking, despite the competition for space and high rents, while others have found suitable locations in the suburban zones. This upcoming of new suburban office space can be encountered along out-of-town main highways and around suburban railway/metro stations; some quite extensive office areas were constructed during the 1990s (Amsterdam South East, for example).

On the basis of these analyses, one can conclude that, during the 1990s, employment growth took place primarily within the rest of the central cities and the suburban zones, although the centres of the central cities preserved their employment levels in an absolute sense. This statement holds for both the Northwing and Breda region and for all the sectors listed, with the exception of manufacturing in the centre of the central cities in the Northwing of the Randstad; employment growth decreased there substantially in both absolute and relative terms. Moreover, the substantial overall growth rates of the producer services sector surpassed all other employment developments, although consumer sector employment also increased markedly. In conclusion, although no massive deconcentration took place in the 1990s in the sense of a substantial moving out of employment from city centres to suburban locations, the suburban growth rates far exceeded those of the cities. Taken together, the Dutch planning principles of 'concentration', 'spatial coherence', and 'spatial differentiation' seem to have limited the extent and the territory over which economic functions have deconcentrated.

2.5
Dimensions of employment deconcentration

In the previous section, the deconcentration processes for designated urban and suburban zones of the Northwing and the Breda region were analysed. This section describes a more detailed analysis obtained by making use of the level of employment sprawl indices (see Galster *et al.*, 2001; Bogaerts *et al.*, 2003b). The emphasis is on three sprawl indices: density, centrality, and mixed use. A raster of 250m by 250m is superimposed on the study area and a distinction is drawn between developable areas (agricultural land) and non-developable areas (water, nature, and forests). The calculations of the sprawl indices are based on the developable areas.

2.5.1
Density

Density is probably one of the most frequently used measures to capture urban development patterns. Density can be defined as the average number of employees (or the surface area of economic land use) per hectare of developable land in the urban area. The level of density is calculated by counting the number of employees per 250 by 250 metre raster and dividing this number by the developable surface within this raster.

Figure 2.4 shows the development in total employment density for the Northwing. In general, the centres of the cities have by far the highest employment densities; the density decreases with distance from the centre. Looking at the development in employment density, there appears overall to have been a substantial increase in employment density, which has taken place primarily as an extension and intensification of existing employment concentrations. For the few developments taking place at new locations, the infrastructure appears to have been

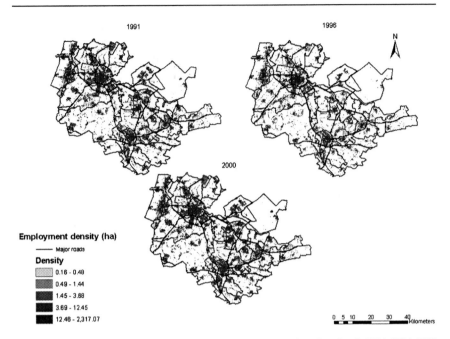

Fig. 2.4 Level of total employment density in the Northwing of the Randstad, 1991-1996-2000
Source: LISA 1991-1996-2000

a conductor for these, so that new employment developments take place along highway networks.

This picture for the Northwing corresponds largely with that of the much smaller Breda region. There, the highest employment densities can be found in the central cities of Breda and the surrounding municipalities of Etten-Leur and Oosterhout. Again, employment density decreases as distance from the city centres increases. As in the Northwing, the development of employment densities between 1991 and 2000 primarily took place in the form of extensions and intensifications of existing employment centres. New employment developed on just a few areas in an East-West band within the Breda region; there again, the infrastructure was an important stimulator. Local and regional spatial policies also contributed to these new East-West developments through the active stimulation of links to Roosendaal in the West and Tilburg in the East.

Differentiating these general trends in employment density for the sectors identi-fied makes some differences clear. Retailing/consumer services are highly concen-trated in the city centres and their increase in employment density can mainly be found at or adjacent to existing locations. This preservation and extension of existing spatial pattern is expected to be a consequence of the strict national retail policy, mentioned above as part of the urban concentration policy of the 1990s, which prohibited the development of huge out-of-town shopping centres and hypermarkets far away from the cities. The exceptions to this rule can be seen in the outskirts of the central cities and consist primarily of Do-It-Yourself stores and retailers in furniture and domestic decoration. The growth of this kind of suburban-located retailing/consumer services employment concentrations is, however, quite substantial. As a result, despite the fact that no huge distant out-of-town shopping malls were constructed in the Dutch case study areas during the 1990s, some suburban growth took place in this sector on a more modest scale and distance.

Producer services and their development took place not only in the city centres, but also at the edge of central cities and in suburban locations. This statement applies to both the Northwing of the Randstad and the Breda region. Moreover, the layout of the suburban developments is concentrated: subcentres alongside infrastructure nodes or in smaller towns such as IJsselstein and Mijdrecht. These developments can be contrasted with economic spatial developments elsewhere, where they take the form of extensive widely-spread developments (in USA, for example). This clustering in the Netherlands can be attributed to the planning principles of 'concentration' and 'spatial coherence' referred to above.

Employment concentration and development in the manufacturing/construction sector spread around the area of the central cities and along main roads and motorways on the outskirts of central cities and within suburban locations. This is the case for both the Northwing and the Breda region.

On the basis of these density figures, one can state that the density of employment increased primarily as an extension and intensification of existing employment concentrations. Moreover, infrastructure can be considered a conductor for new developments, since many new developments are concentrated alongside highway networks. One cannot conclude from the employment density figures that a massive process of economic deconcentration took place within the Dutch context, at least not in a massive, dispersed fashion. No large-scale urban sprawl of employment operating at the expense of the cities can therefore be identified. On the contrary, one must conclude that the existing employment locations strengthened their position. Employment densities increased not only in city centres (retailing/consumer services), but also in suburban locations (producer service sector). In the figures concerning our next measure, 'centrality', the picture becomes clearer. Moreover, the density figures show that even suburban development took place primarily as an extension and intensification of existing employment concentrations, also in the form of concentrated/clustered development. This concentration can be attributed to a considerable extent to the Dutch policy of the concentration of urbanization and the preservation of 'green areas'.

2.5.2
Centrality

'Centrality' indicates the degree to which employment (or economic land use) is located close to the centres of cities and towns. A loss of centrality is often seen as a reference to increasing sprawl within, and in the proximity of, an urban area. The level of centrality is measured by calculating the average distance of employment from the city centre. Concentric circles one kilometre apart are drawn from the city centre outwards. The Northwing has a polynuclear structure with several centres, so the centrality is measured for each of these separately. To visualize centrality, the employment density is calculated and shown for each kilometre ring. Note that the centrality measure takes the mean density value of a ring and so does not permit the identification of concentrations in one or more directions within that ring.

Figure 2.5 shows the level of total employment centrality in the Northwing. The employment density is shown in that zone.

In Figure 2.5, two zones can be seen where the employment density is relatively high: the centre of the city, and the surrounding suburban municipalities. In the area between these two zones the employment density is relatively low. This picture applies in general terms to both the Northwing and the Breda region; Amsterdam and Utrecht show a more gradual overall decrease of employment density from the city centre. Moreover, the location of this intermediate zone is much closer to the city centre in the Breda region than it is in the Northwing, probably as a result of the difference in scale (the small size of the city of Breda in comparison with the Northwing). These buffer zones between towns reflect the 'spatial differentiation' principle of Dutch planning policy. The intermediate zones of relatively low density could be the result of this policy.

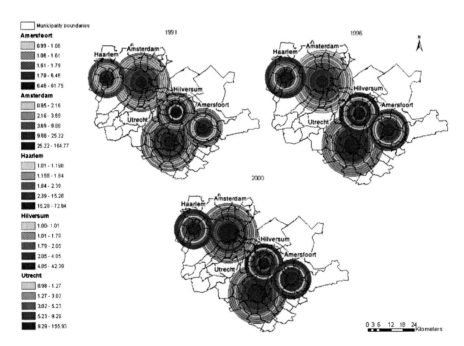

Fig. 2.5 Level of total employment centrality in the Northwing region, 1991-1996-2000
Source: LISA, 1991-1996-2000

The overall development of centrality between 1991 and 2000 shows a clear picture: in the surrounding municipalities, the growth of the level of employment density exceeded the growth in the town centres. As a consequence, centrality decreased between 1991 and 2000, although the city centres remain important areas of employment concentration, as previous density discussion makes clear Moreover, the centrality figures and maps show that in the 1990s, although the intermediate 'lower' density zones remained vibrant, they declined in magnitude. As a consequence, the density differences between the zones levelled out and overall the centrality decreased during the 1990s.

In contrast with the other two economic sectors, the overall level of centrality for manufacturing/construction is quite low. This is in line with the extensive space needs of most firms in this sector and the increasing competition for space and subsequent high costs in the town centres.

On the basis of these centrality figures, one can state in general terms that centrality has decreased for all the economic sectors within both case study areas. This is primarily the result of the substantial employment developments during the 1990s, particularly in the suburban zones. These developments can be attributed to the increasing competition for space in the town centres and probably also to the Dutch policies of 'spatial differentiation' and 'A-B-C location policy' (see section 2).

2.5.3
Mixed use

The 'mixed use' indicator measures the degree to which two or more different land uses coexist (Galster *et al.*, 2001, p. 995). The level of 'mixed use' in an area is determined by measuring the average employment density there and comparing it with the population density.

Figure 2.6 shows the level of mixed use in the Northwing of the Randstad. The areas with the highest level of mixed use of employment – defined here as a combination of employment and population, thus a mix of working and living – are found mainly in the town centres. The areas with a low level of mixed use (mono-functional areas) can be found in the city centres as well as in the outskirts and more suburban regions. The level of mixed use of employment decreases with distance from the centre of the city. Moreover, mixed use increases in the course of time, a development that is visible in both the Northwing and in the Breda region. The 'spatial coherence' principle of Dutch planning is clearly reflected in the resulting development patterns (see section 2). It is argued that one of the principles of Dutch planning is the formation and encouragement of compact daily urban systems, thereby avoiding unnecessary commuting.

The analysis of the level of mixed use of employment for the different economic sectors allows the following observations to be made. Similar pictures of mixed use are shown for both the Breda region and the Northwing of the Randstad. For retailing/consumer services, the level of mixed use is high in comparison with the

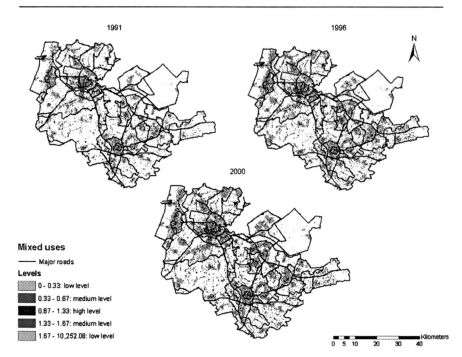

Fig. 2.6 Level of mixed uses in the Northwing of the Randstad, 1991-1996-2000
Source: LISA 1991-1996-2000 and KWB Statistics Netherlands, 1994-1997-2001

other sectors; moreover, the level increased between 1991 and 2000. At the same time, areas of mono-functional retailing/consumer employment are developing in the outskirts of the towns. Without doubt, this differential development – highly-mixed consumer services in the centres; low mix of consumer services in the outskirts – parallels the quite extreme diversification within this sector: from small specialized retail shops and hairdressers to supermarkets, large shops for furniture, hospitals, and public transport companies. The firms needing extensive space within this sector are more likely to be located at the outskirts of towns. Intermingling these kinds of economic function with residential functions was not an explicit spatial policy. In contrast, in the centres of Dutch towns the intermingling of living and working (in shops, for example) has long been the spatial policy, in particular for reasons of security and liveability (see below).

For producer services, the picture of mixed use is similar to that for retailing/consumer services: high levels of mixed use in the city centres; lower levels in the outskirts and suburban locations. However, areas of mono-functional employment of producer services can also be found in the city centres of the largest cities.

The level of mixed use in the manufacturing/construction sector appears to be significantly lower than the level in the other sectors, which is as expected from the characteristics of this sector: extensive need for space; nuisance from noise, and so forth. Moreover, and in agreement with these characteristics, the level of mixed use decreased between 1991 and 2000 and the development of mono-functional employment in manufacturing/construction is moving away from the town centres.

Reasons can be found for these differential developments in mixed use in the various Dutch spatial policies. First, in all the large Dutch municipalities, the local government authority has encouraged the return of the residential function in the city centres for reasons of liveability, security, and so forth. So, the traditional leisure shopping centres of Dutch cities became more mixed during the 1990s, partly because once again apartments were built above shops. This spatial policy has been made explicit and its positive effects are shown in the figures presented. Second, the Dutch policy of 'hierarchic urbanization' has also influenced the city centres. As indicated in sections 1 and 2, retail policy in particular has embraced and preserved the notion of the 'hierarchy of centres', in which the centres of the central cities continued to be the location for the most specialized shops and firms with the entire city as its consumer market, while the suburban locations became host to the facilities and services at the neighbourhood level. One of the consequences of this policy has been the preservation and even reinforcement of the city centre as a central and sustainable shopping area (consumer services). This policy has also contributed to mixed use in the city centres. Third, given the pressure on the Dutch land market and the related high prices per square metre, especially in the city centres, there is a tendency for spatial differential selection: services and firms needing a small area and with a high dependency on visitors passing by can be found in the centres of the towns; services and firms needing an extensive area and with less dependency on passing visitors seek cheaper and larger locations at the outskirts of the cities. The outcome of these large-scale developments with low mixed use at the outskirts of the towns is mono-functionality. This feature can also be seen as an exemplification of the Dutch policy of the 'concentration of urbanization' (see section 2). Fourth, during the 1990s almost all medium-sized and large cities in the Netherlands undertook the restructuring of the areas within the city centres in the vicinity of the central railway stations (brownfield locations). Luxury apartments to re-introduce high income groups into the city centres and mono-functional office areas of producer services can be found there (financial services, lawyers, government institutions, and so forth This restructuring could be the reason for the centrally-located mono-functional areas of producer services. In fact, the central localization of these producer services can be considered a minor success of the much criticized ABC-location policy, since these services are often visitor-intensive and situated near railway stations (see section 2).

2.6
Conclusions and discussion

In this chapter, we have analysed the concentration and deconcentration processes of three economic sectors in the 1990s for the case study areas of the Northwing of the Randstad and the Breda region, and assessed the impact of five planning principles of the Dutch planning system. In this concluding section we discuss these issues and the anticipated effectiveness of the Dutch planning system in the near future.

In general terms, it can be stated that employment growth usually takes place within suburban zones, although the centres of the central cities have preserved their employment magnitude in an absolute sense during this period. This process can be observed in the monocentric Breda region on a modest scale, and on a more extensive scale in the polycentric Northwing of the Randstad. Moreover, this growth pattern appears to apply to all three identified sectors, although the substantial growth rates of the producer services sector in the outer centres areas outweigh all other employment developments. As a consequence of these multi-focal developments, the centrality within the Breda region and the Northwing of the Randstad decreased between 1991 and 2000, although the cities of Amsterdam and Utrecht form the exception to this general rule since both centres preserved their centrality. At the same time it should be noted that, in terms of employment growth, there were no large-scale out-of-town developments located far from the central cities: the increase of employment density took place primarily as extensions and intensifications of existing employment concentrations. Moreover, it appears that, particularly for new economic developments, highways and to a lesser extent railway stations form the prime conductor for the new developments: new employment, especially in producer services, developed in clusters along the main infrastructure and on infrastructure nodes. Retailing/consumer services clearly followed developments in population densities, preserving their position primarily in the city centres and growing in shopping centres located within suburban communities. The more distant out-of-town shopping centres (shopping malls) so familiar in other countries hardly exist in the Netherlands, except for some dedicated categories such as Do-It-Yourself stores and large retailers in furniture and domestic decoration or outlet shops. These firms needing extensive floor space have found much cheaper locations at the outskirts of the central cities, where accessibility by car is the main criterion. Manufacturing/construction can usually be found spread around the central cities area and alongside the main roads and highways in the outskirts of central cities and in designated areas in more suburban locations. This generalization applies to both the Northwing and the Breda region.

So, in short, on the basis of the above, one has to conclude that no massive deconcentration took place in the Netherlands during the 1990s, despite the fact that most employment growth was in the out-of-centre areas. It seems that the 'concentration of urbanization', 'spatial coherence' and 'spatial differentiation' principles of Dutch spatial planning policy limited both the one-sided direction and the magnitude by which economic functions were deconcentrated.

The 'concentration' principle effectively limited the dispersed sprawl of economic functions over the total metropolitan area, since even suburban decon-centrated development took place in quite a concentrated manner along highways, at infrastructure nodes, and on designated sites. Question marks can, however, be set against claims for the effectiveness of this policy, in particular the A-B-C location policy. Its central purpose was to concentrate employment and visitor-intensive firms near public transport nodes. From the empirical analysis it appears that much of the new economic development took place close to main roads and highways. It can be seriously questioned whether all these firms can be characterized as employment- or visitor-extensive. However, the speed of the developments played an important part in the mismatch between policy and reality. Moreover, many firms were not overly disappointed when they found that they did have to establish themselves on C locations. In contrast with C locations, A and B locations were characterized by high land prices, poor accessibility by car, and no or very expensive parking lots.

The 'spatial coherence' principle provided a mixed picture in the 1990s. The city centres retained and even increased their high degree of mixture, a situation which can be attributed to the explicit policy of stimulating living in city centres, in particular above department stores (retailing/consumer services) and offices (producer services). This policy of mixing working and residential functions can be justified as a means of preserving/improving the liveability of city centres and from security considerations. Moreover, the policy contributes to a reduction in commuting movements. The level of mixed use decreases with distance from the city centre. The development of mono-functional employment areas has taken place in particular in the outskirts of the towns, although a few areas of mono-functionality can also be found in the centres of the bigger cities. The restricted appearance of mono-functional areas can be attributed to different spatial policies, for example: preventing nuisance arising from mutually conflicting functions (parking, noise, smell); concentrating similar functions together spatially for efficiency (infrastructure costs).

The effectiveness of the 'spatial differentiation' principle is reflected in particular on the outskirts of the towns. Economic developments have taken place there in a concentrated manner rather than spreading over whole metropolitan areas. Outer areas have been preserved from the negative consequences of dispersed economic development, including nuisance and superfluous traffic movements. Clear examples of these preservation and differentiation policies can still be found at the outskirts of the city of Breda and the surrounding municipalities of the medium-sized cities of Haarlem and Hilversum in the Northwing. Urbanization pressure on these areas is growing enormously, however, and the green buffer zones between the urbanized areas are being filled in. This process will doubtless lead eventually to one monotonous built-up area.

The principles of 'hierarchic urbanization' and 'spatial justice' are much harder to recognize in the empirical material investigated in this study. What has become clear, however, is that, although in relative terms growth in employment in the Northwing of the Randstad is comparable with that of the Breda region (36 percent and 30 percent respectively), in absolute terms they are of a different order of magnitude (see Table 2.2). The policy principle of 'hierarchic urbanization' will no doubt persist.

Table 2.2 Population growth and employment growth within the central cities of both study areas, 1991–2000 (percent)

	Population		Employment	
	Absolute, 2000	Development 1991–2000 (index)	Absolute, 2000	Development 1991–2000 (index)
Northwing				
Amsterdam*	874,053	112	483,137	130
Utrecht	233,667	101	180,535	120
Haarlem	148,484	99	64,311	101
Amersfoort	126,143	124	64,209	135
Hilversum	82,177	97	42,774	152
Breda region				
Breda	160,615	106	90,588	127

*Note that in this research Almere is part of the Amsterdam central city area.
Source: LISA 1991-2000, Statistics Netherlands- Statline.

This assessment of the effectiveness of the Dutch planning principles in guiding the spatial development of the various economic sectors brings us to a consideration of the future prospects of Dutch spatial planning policy. Spatial planning has recently changed substantially. One change is that, until recently, the national government had most directive power in spatial planning. This power structure will now change so that a substantial part of the national power will move to the regional level, and the provinces are expected to coordinate communication and decision making processes with the wide range of parties involved (municipalities, provinces, water institutions, important private and public stakeholders, and so forth). This decentralization will doubtless result in tailor-made solutions capable of dealing with the inevitable spatial conflicts that will arise between the participants involved.

Some fundamental changes in Dutch spatial planning policy concern the placing of people's activities within the boundaries of daily urban systems, the principle of 'spatial coherence', and the introduction of the new concept of a *Network Society* (MVROM, 2004). In the recently published Memorandum *Nota Ruimte* (National Spatial Strategy) the emphasis on the compact growth of isolated cities has made way for the new concept of the 'Network Society', in line with the principles of 'hierarchic urbanization' and 'spatial justice'. Towns and cities are no longer envisioned as separate entities, but interconnected and forming 'networks on different hierarchical scales' (Hajer & Zonneveld, 2000; Healey, 2004). The underlying idea is the interrelationship between separate towns (mutual dependency) and the consequent need for cooperation and mutual adjustment (specialization). The internal economic specialization of centres/towns in a network is expected to increase flows between centres/towns within the network and consequently the interaction between them. Moreover, the growth in importance of connections opens the potential for new developments at new locations, such as infill locations between interconnected urbanized areas (Hajer & Zonneveld, 2000).

Taking the two considerations together, we have to place serious doubts against the capability of the current policy, which up till now has been effective, of preventing large-scale deconcentration of economic development far beyond the boundaries of existing cities. Decentralized powers and changing spatial concepts will change the planning process and the content of spatial decision-making and finally the resulting outcomes. There will probably be large-scale spatial deconcentration of appropriate economic activities such as producer or manufacturing/construction services or large-scale retailing/consumer services in the form of malls. Some such 'outlets' have already appeared on the Dutch landscape. The familiar concepts of 'edgeless city' (Lang & LeFurgy, 2003) or even 'urban field' will then come into the picture.

Notes

[1] We were able to make use of LISA data within the Selma project thanks to our project partner RIVM.
[2] The 'daily urban system (*stadsgewest*)' can be described as a structure of one or more large cities and surrounding smaller cities/municipalities that are 'combined' in a functional relationship of mutual relationships (Zonneveld, 1991, p. 224).

References

Atzema O, van Dijk J (2004) The persistence of regional unemployment in the Netherlands. Utrecht University, Utrecht

Bogaerts A, Dieleman FM, Dijst M, Geertman S (2003a) Case study analysis: technical report. URU, Utrecht University, Utrecht

Bogaerts A, Dieleman FM, Dijst M, Geertman S (2003b) Case study analysis the Netherlands: work package 1 SELMA program. URU, Utrecht University /MNP, RIVM, Utrecht/Bilthoven

van der Burg A, Dieleman FM (2004) Dutch urbanization policies: from 'compact city' to 'urban network'. Tijdschrift voor economische en sociale geografie 95(1):108–116

Cervero R (1995) Planned communities, self-containment and commuting: a cross-national perspective. Urban Studies 32(7):1135–1161

Davoudi S (2003) Polycentricity in European spatial planning: from an analytical tool to a normative agenda. Eur Plann Stud 1(8):979–999

Dieleman FM, Faludi A (1998) Polynucleated metropolitan regions in Northwest Europe: theme of the spatial issue. Eur Plann Stud 6(4):365–377

Dieleman FM, Dijst M, Spit TJM (1999) Planning the compact city; the Randstad Holland Experience. Eur Plann Stud 7(5):605–621

European Commission (1997) The EU compendium of spatial planning systems and policies. Luxembourg: Office for Official Publications of the European Communities. (Regional Development Studies 28)

Evers D (2002) The rise (and fall?) of national retail planning. Tijdschrift voor economische en sociale geografie 93(1):107–113

Faludi A, van der Valk A (1990) Rule and order: Dutch planning doctrine in the Twentieth century. Kluwer, Dordrecht

Galster G, Hanson R, Ratcliffe MR, Wolman H, Coleman S, Freihage J (2001) Wrestling sprawl to the ground: defining and measuring an elusive concept. Housing Policy Debate 12(4):681–717

Hajer M, Zonneveld W (2000) Spatial planning in the network society – rethinking the principles of planning in the Netherlands. European Planning Studies 8(3):337–355

Healey P (2004) The treatment of space and place in the new strategic spatial planning in Europe. International Journal of Urban and Regional Research 28(1):45–67

van der Laan L (1998) Changing urban systems: an empirical analysis at two spatial levels. Regional Studies 32:235–247

Lang RE, LeFurgy J (2003) Edgeless cities: examining the noncentered metropolis. Housing Policy Debate 14(3):427–460

MVRO (1966) Second physical planning memorandum. Ministry of Housing and Physical Planning, The Hague

MVROM (1988) Fourth spatial planning memorandum. Ministry of Housing, Physical Planning and the Environment, The Hague

MVROM (1991) Fourth spatial planning memorandum extra. Ministry of Housing, Physical Planning and the Environment, The Hague

MVROM (2001) Fifth spatial planning memorandum 2000/2020. Ministry of Housing, Physical Planning and the Environment, The Hague

MVROM (2004) Spatial Memorandum: space for development. Cabinet Council The Hague

Razin E (2000) The impact of local government organization on development and disparities: a comparative perspective. Environ Plann C: Gov Policy 18:17–31

Schwanen T, Dijst M, Dieleman FM (2004) Policies for urban form and travel: The Netherlands experience. Urban Studies 41(3):579–603

Wetenschappelijke Raad voor het Regeringsbeleid (WRR) (1998) Ruimtelijke Ontwikkelingspolitiek. SDU uitgevers, The Hague (Rapporten aan de Regering nr. 53)

Zonneveld W (1991) Conceptvorming in ruimtelijke planning: encyclopedie van planconcepten. Planologisch Demografisch Instituut van de Universiteit van Amsterdam, Amsterdam

3 Deconcentration of workplaces in greater Copenhagen: Successes and failures of location strategies in regional planning

Peter Hartoft-Nielsen

Ministry of the Environment, Spatial Planning Department, Danish Forest and Nature Agency, Haraldsgade 53, DK-2100 Copenhagen, Denmark

Abstract: Urban development in Greater Copenhagen exemplifies the complexity of the interplay between overall regional planning and other factors influencing urban development, including the market. The Finger Plan of 1948 has succeeded in creating a well-functioning urban region and preventing urban sprawl. The location strategies of urban functions within the urban zone have led to both failures and successes. The secondary centres outside the central cities have not developed as planned; neither has the policy of promoting new office developments outside the central cities within walking distance from a railway station. On the other hand, the political decision to revitalize the City of Copenhagen has been a success and has positively influenced the implementation of the strategy of locating office firms within walking distance of a station. Potential barriers to the implementation of location strategies are identified and discussed together with the effects on travel behaviour, the environment, and living conditions

Key words: Greater Copenhagen, regional planning, location strategies, office location, travel behaviour

3.1
Introduction

Urban development in Greater Copenhagen demonstrates the complex interplay between overall regional planning and other factors influencing urban development, including the market. Urban development has been controlled through comprehensive regional planning for nearly sixty years. Since 1974, regional planning has had binding guidelines and has been carried out in accordance with an Act. The main principle – the Finger Plan – has been implemented, even though the urban fingers have been thicker than intended. The development in radial urban fingers along railway lines and with green wedges between the fingers is easy to recognize on a map. Compared with many other European Cities, the planning principles have succeeded in creating a well-functioning urban region and preventing urban sprawl.

The deconcentration of people and jobs took place during the 1960s, 1970s, and 1980s, as intended in the regional plans. The car congestion problems in the central parts of the urban region are quite limited. Travel by bicycle or public transport has an important role. But secondary centres outside the City of Copenhagen have not developed as planned. Consequently, congestion problems have grown, especially on the ring roads.

E. Razin et al. (eds.), Employment Deconcentration in European Metropolitan Areas, 53–87.
© 2007 *Springer.*

The 1989 Regional Plan for Greater Copenhagen ought to be as well-known as the 1948 Finger Plan. The 1989 Plan includes all aspects of spatial development and physical planning. Until the late 1980s, regional planning in Greater Copenhagen was mostly concerned with managing urban growth. The motto of the 1989 Regional Plan was "make a better town, not a bigger town". The 1989 Regional Plan reintroduced and reinterpreted the finger structure. The Plan introduced a new location strategy based on increasing the building density, refining the existing urban centres around the railway stations, and using other business sites and districts more extensively. New office developments were only to be located within walking distance from a railway station. Thus, the conversion and development of the existing urban areas featured more strongly in this regional plan than in earlier regional plans.

The implementation of the location policy has, however, been limited. Despite extensive regulatory authority, spatial planning has not been able to manage construction and development as intended. The strategy operates in a political and economic space where different interests conflict. In contrast, the political decisions taken to promote urban development in the central part of the region have been a success. Thus, urban development in Greater Copenhagen has resulted from market forces and specific political decisions and planning.

This chapter briefly presents Greater Copenhagen and its overall development. We describe the trends of recent decades in the location of workplaces and the composition of the population in the various urban rings. We then discuss why employment became deconcentrated and then reconcentrated in the 1990s. Regional planning and the associated strategies for locating workplaces are presented. The chapter concentrates on two location strategies: developing secondary centres in the periphery from the 1960s to the 1980s; the policy of promoting location in the vicinity of stations in the 1990s. We describe the potential barriers to implementation and the extent to which the overall location strategies have been instigated. The chapter concludes with a brief discussion of the consequences of the deconcentration and subsequent reconcentration of workplaces in Greater Copenhagen, stressing the effects on transport and the environment and on the residents of the Cities of Copenhagen and Frederiksberg and their suburbs.[1]

3.2
Greater Copenhagen

Copenhagen is Denmark's capital city. In 2002, the City of Copenhagen had 0.5 million inhabitants and Greater Copenhagen 1.8 million. Greater Copenhagen is the political, administrative, educational, and research centre of Denmark and accounts for about 41 percent of Denmark's economic output. One third of Denmark's population lives in Greater Copenhagen. Eight universities are located there, with about 70,000 enrolled students. Two thirds of both public and private research in Denmark takes place in Greater Copenhagen. Public services and financial & business services are the largest economic sectors. Key developing industries are biotechnology, medical equipment, pharmaceuticals, information technology, telecommunication services, and tourism. Copenhagen Airport – one of the largest in Europe – is located close to Copenhagen city centre, thereby ensuring excellent accessibility to the rest of the world (Figure 3.1).

Greater Copenhagen is the north-eastern part of the island of Sjælland (Figure 3.2). The accessibility of Greater Copenhagen has increased dramatically in recent years. New large-scale bridges and tunnels have opened up new hinterlands in the rest of Denmark and in southern Sweden (Figure 3.2). The Great Belt Fixed Link opened in 1998 and has enhanced accessibility to Copenhagen from western Denmark and continental Europe, reducing the travel time between Copenhagen and Denmark's other cities by more than an hour. Furthermore, in 2000 a fixed link for cars and trains opened between Copenhagen and Malmö in Sweden. Trains run between Copenhagen and Malmö every 20 minutes; the travel time is 37 minutes. Malmö has 265,000 residents; Skåne, the area surrounding Malmö, has about 1.1 million people.

3.2.1
The metropolitan area is expanding, but administratively divided

Greater Copenhagen is currently administered under the Act that delegates the responsibility for regional planning to the Greater Copenhagen Authority. The metropolitan area is gradually developing into an urban landscape comprising a network of urban areas. The commuting region is growing. The two neighbouring counties are becoming part of the commuting region, with 60,000 people travelling every day from these counties to Greater Copenhagen; this number grows every year. Furthermore, the metropolitan area is expanding across national borders. Although still infrequent, commuting from southern Sweden to Copenhagen has grown substantially since the fixed link opened. In due course, a unified Öresund region is expected to emerge, with a total population of 3.5 million.

Greater Copenhagen is divided administratively into five county units and 50 municipalities; the Cities of Copenhagen and Frederiksberg[2] are both municipalities and counties. The Greater Copenhagen Authority, which was established in 2001, is responsible for numerous regional tasks, including the regional planning of Greater Copenhagen as a whole. The Authority Council comprises politicians from the five counties. Comprehensive regional planning has, however, been in operation in Greater Copenhagen for nearly six decades.[3]

3.2.2
Trends in population and workplaces

The population of Greater Copenhagen grew steadily and substantially from 1900 to 1975 and then stagnated and even declined from 1975 to 1990. Growth has returned since 1990. Regional economic development shifted remarkably during

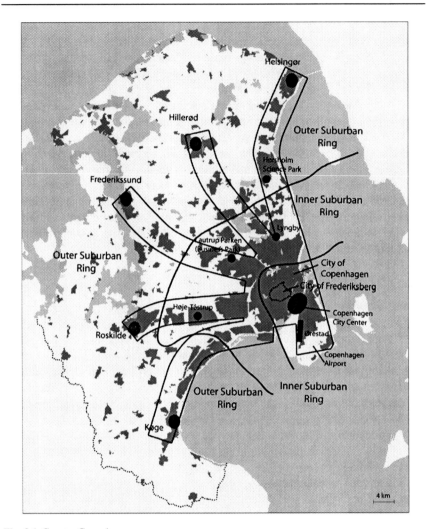

Fig. 3.1 Greater Copenhagen
The map shows the location of different towns and sites in Greater Copenhagen. The three urban rings and the finger structure are shown, as are the central cities – the cities of Copenhagen and Frederiksberg – and the five urban fingers now reaching the five provincial towns in a distance of 30 to 40 km from Copenhagen city centre: Helsingør (Elsinore, 46,000 people), Hillerød (28,000), Frederikssund (14,000), Roskilde (43,000) and Køge (33,000). The map also shows two subcentres: Høje-Taastrup and Lyngby, two business parks: Lautrupparken and Hørsholm Science Park and the new urban development: Ørestad

the 1990s (Table 3.1). From 1984 to 1993, the number of workplaces in the Greater Copenhagen commuting region declined, but grew in the rest of Denmark.

From 1994 to 2002, Greater Copenhagen acquired 107,000 new workplaces, an 11.8 percent increase versus 4.9 percent in the rest of Denmark. Thus, Greater

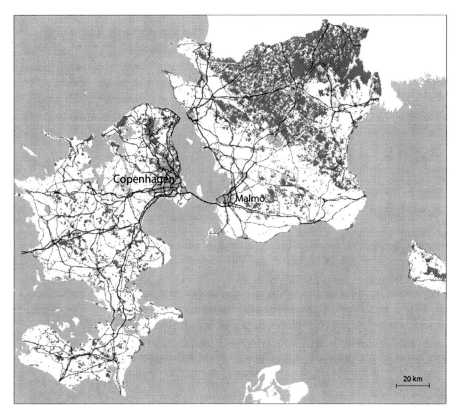

Fig. 3.2 The Oresund Region
The Greater Copenhagen Area is the north-eastern part of the island of Sjælland, Denmark. In 2000 a fixed link for cars and trains crossing the Sound (20 km) opened between Copenhagen and Malmö in the Southern part of Sweden

Table 3.1 Percentage growth in workplaces in commuting regions in Denmark, 1984–1993 and 1994–2001

Commuting region	1984–1993	1994–2001
Greater Copenhagen commuting region (including parts of Vestsjælland and Storstrøm Counties)	−1.3%	10.8%
Three cities (Aarhus, Odense and Aalborg) exceeding 100,000 population	5.9%	8.5%
Ten large towns (population 30,000–75,000)	7.0%	5.8%
Eight medium-sized towns (population 20,000–30,000)	4.7%	3.1%
Small towns	0.4%	1.4%
Denmark as a whole	2.7%	7.4%

Source: Spatial Planning Department, Ministry of the Environment, 2003.

Copenhagen's recent growth rate has been 2–3 times higher than that of the rest of Denmark. Trends in unemployment are similar. The unemployment rate in Greater Copenhagen declined from 12.3 percent in 1994 to 4.4 percent in 2001 and from 16.8 percent to 5.5 percent in the City of Copenhagen. "Business activity" is the largest of the 27 sectors (according to NACE/DB03) and has grown substantially. From 1993 to 2002, about 60,000 jobs were created in this sector: a 73 percent increase. Employment in most sub sectors within manufacturing is decreasing, as it is in public administration.

3.3
Spatial development in the urban rings of greater Copenhagen

Greater Copenhagen can be divided into three spatial units, each roughly representing one of the three urban rings: the central city, defined as the Cities of Copenhagen and Frederiksberg; the inner suburban ring, defined as Copenhagen County; and the outer suburban ring, defined as Frederiksborg and Roskilde Counties (Figure 3.1). Each of these units accommodates about one third of the population in Greater Copenhagen. The intraregional trends in population and workplaces in Greater Copenhagen have followed the classical pattern: urbanization, suburbanization, desuburbanization, and then (in the 1990s) reurbanization.

3.3.1
Population

The population of the Cities of Copenhagen and Frederiksberg peaked in 1950 at 887,000 and declined to 550,000 in 1991, when the population started to grow again. During the 1990s, the populations of the Cities of Copenhagen and Frederiksberg grew more rapidly than the population of Denmark as a whole and Greater Copenhagen (Table 3.2). In any event, the net inward migration to the City of Copenhagen seems to have stopped, probably because housing prices have risen substantially and there are few affordable dwellings available.

All the concentric belts experienced population growth from 1990 to 2002 (Table 3.3). The substantial growth in the innermost belt was remarkable. The weakest growth rates were in the old suburbs in the belts 5 to 25 km from the city centre.

The population growth in the innermost belt is the result of the growth in the inner districts of the City of Copenhagen. This growth represents a break in 40 years of urban development in the Greater Copenhagen Area. The social composition of the population in the inner districts of the central municipalities has changed in quite a dramatic way. In the 1970s, the inner areas had a substantial overrepresentation of elderly people and manual workers. The elderly residents from that period have now died, and the manual workers and the middle-aged

Table 3.2 Population in Greater Copenhagen and its geographical units in 1971, 1980, 1990 and 2002 and area and population density in 2002

	Number of munici- palities	Population (Thousands)								Area in 2002	Population density in 2002
		1971		1980		1990		2002			
		n	%	n	%	n	%	n	%	km²	perkm²
Central cities	2	728	41%	587	34%	552	32%	590	33%	97	6,076
Inner suburban ring	18	617	35%	627	36%	601	35%	617	34%	528	1,174
Outer suburban ring	30	415	24%	531	30%	558	33%	605	33%	2,239	270
Greater Copenhagen	50	1,759	100%	1746	100%	1711	100%	1815	100%	2,862	634

Source: Statistics Denmark.

Table 3.3 Total population in Greater Copenhagen in 1990 and 2002 according to concentric distance belts from the Copenhagen Town Hall

Distance to city centre (km)	Population					
	1990		2002		Growth, 1990–2002	
	n	%	n	%	n	%
0–5	466,237	27.3%	499,782	27.6%	33,545	7.2%
5–10	329,959	19.4%	340,822	18.9%	10,863	3.3%
10–15	224,450	13.2%	229,676	12.7%	5,226	2.3%
15–20	150,934	8.9%	159,876	8.8%	8,942	5.9%
20–25	86,755	5.1%	90,539	5.0%	3,784	4.4%
25–30	101,788	6.0%	109,172	6.0%	7,384	7.3%
30–35	117,934	6.9%	128,190	7.1%	10,256	8.7%
35–40	103,984	6.1%	113,732	6.3%	9,748	9.4%
40–45	57,821	3.4%	62,262	3.4%	4,441	7.7%
45–50	40,075	2.4%	44,362	2.5%	4,287	10.7%
> 50	24,786	1.5%	29,404	1.6%	4,618	18.6%
Total	1,704,723	100.0%	1,807,817	100.0%	103,094	6.0%

Source: Danish Centre for Forest, Landscape and Planning, calculated using a geographical information system from 100 m by 100 m grid data from Statistics Denmark.

moved out to the suburbs. The city centre population was replaced by independents and immigrants from prosperous countries, while from the late 20th century the surrounding inner areas have accommodated students, recent graduates, and immigrants from poorer countries.

During the last twenty years, the average age of the population in the City of Copenhagen has declined by 6 years, while at the same time the average age of Danes as a whole has increased by 3 years. Twenty years ago, one of the most remarkable differences between the population in the rest of the country and that of the City of Copenhagen was its huge overrepresentation of old people. Today, elderly people are underrepresented compared with the population of Denmark as a whole. The number of people aged 65 years and more decreased by 40 percent from 1980 to 2000 (from approximately 120,000 to 70,000), while at the same time the number of people aged 20 to 29 years increased by 40 percent (from approximately 90,000 to 130,000). Forty-two percent of the population in the City of Copenhagen is between 20 and 37 years of age, while the same age group only makes up 24 percent of the population in the rest of Denmark. The prognosis is that the population in the City of Copenhagen will stay young for the next 20 years, while becoming older in the rest of Denmark.

3.3.2
Workplaces

The more than 1 million workplaces in Greater Copenhagen are dispersed throughout most of the urban zones. Companies, public institutions, and other workplaces in Greater Copenhagen became considerably deconcentrated from the 1960s to the early 1990s. The proportion of workplaces located in the Cities of Copenhagen and Frederiksberg declined from 50 percent in 1970 to 39 percent in 1990 and then stabilized (Table 3.4). Since 1994, when a new period of economic growth started, the proportions of workplaces in the three spatial units (urban rings) have stabilized.

In 1945, about 40 percent of the total workplaces in Greater Copenhagen were located in the Copenhagen city centre (the historic centre). Today, the city centre still has the highest spatial concentration of workplaces, but only one tenth of all workplaces in Greater Copenhagen. Nevertheless, the city centre experienced economic growth during the 1990s. The traditional central district has been expanded to include parts of the waterfront in an area extending several kilometres north and south of the city centre. In addition, Ørestad, a large secondary centre, is being developed on a

Table 3.4 Distribution of total workplaces in Greater Copenhagen according to geographical units or urban rings, 1970, 1981, 1990 and 2002

	1970	1981	1990	2002
Cities of Copenhagen and Frederiksberg	50%	45%	39%	38%
Inner suburban ring: Copenhagen County	29%	32%	36%	37%
Outer suburban ring: Frederiksborg and Roskilde Counties	20%	23%	25%	25%
Total	100%	100%	100%	100%

Source: Danish Centre for Forest, Landscape and Planning, calculated using a geographical information system from 100 m by 100 m grid data from Statistics Denmark.

greenfield site within the boundaries of the City of Copenhagen, between the city centre and Copenhagen Airport. A new Metro links Ørestad directly with the railways and motorways connecting Denmark and Sweden and with the central districts of Copenhagen and Frederiksberg. Southern Ørestad will probably become Greater Copenhagen's first edge city, located only 5 km from the city centre.

More than half the workplaces in Greater Copenhagen are located within 10 km from the city centre and two thirds are within 15 km (Table 3.5). The City of Copenhagen is bounded by the sea to the east and to the south. Thus, each concentric distance belt in Tables 3.3 and 3.6 is only 150°C and not a full circle. The number of workplaces is growing in all the belts from 5 km to 35 km from the city centre. In general, the proportions of workplaces in the various distance belts were quite stable from 1990 to 2002.

3.3.3
Economic sectors

The urban economic sectors can be classified in three categories: retailing and consumer services; manufacturing and construction; and producer services (Table 3.6). Data for these categories is defined based on the 27 sectors (NACE/DB03). In 2002, retailing and consumer services accounted for 55 percent of the workplaces in Greater Copenhagen, producer services for 28 percent, and

Table 3.5 Numbers and percentages of workplaces in Greater Copenhagen according to concentric distance belts (five-kilometre belts from Copenhagen Town Hall), 1990 and 2002

Distance to city centre (km)	1990		2002		Growth, 1990–2002	
	n	%	n	%	n	%
0–5	338,996	37.1%	338,773	35.3%	−223	−0.1%
5–10	161,109	17.6%	168,460	17.6%	7,351	4.6%
10–15	132,165	14.5%	141,850	14.8%	9,685	7.3%
15–20	63,462	6.9%	71,611	7.5%	8,149	12.8%
20–25	38,586	4.2%	43,753	4.6%	5,167	13.4%
25–30	34,010	3.7%	41,032	4.3%	7,022	20.6%
30–35	63,721	7.0%	69,932	7.3%	6,211	9.7%
35–40	39,905	4.4%	39,724	4.1%	−181	−0.5%
40–45	21,000	2.3%	21,843	2.3%	843	4.0%
45–50	13,529	1.5%	13,451	1.4%	−78	−0.6%
> 50	6,672	0.7%	8,605	0.9%	1,933	29.0%
Total	913,155	100.0%	959,034	100.0%	45,879	5.0%

Not all workplaces have an exact address. The proportion of workplaces not included in this table for this reason comprised 4.5% in 1990 and 5.2% in 2002.
Source: Danish Centre for Forest, Landscape and Planning, calculated using a geographical information system from 100 m by 100 m grid data from Statistics Denmark.

Table 3.6 Total workplaces (excluding agriculture and other primary production) in Greater Copenhagen in 1993 and 2002 according to three spatial units and three urban economic categories: retailing and consumer services; manufacturing and construction; and producer services

1993	Total workplaces		Retailing and consumer services		Manufacturing and construction		Producer services	
Spatial unit	n	%	n	%	N	%	n	%
Central cities	343,526	38.3	199,509	39.1	43,683	25.3	100,334	46.5
Inner suburban ring	330,214	36.8	177,804	34.9	75,683	43.8	76,727	35.6
Outer suburban ring	224,287	25.0	132,418	26.0	53,345	30.9	38,524	17.9
Greater Copenhagen	898,027	100	509,731	100	172,711	100	215,585	100

2002	Total workplaces		Retailing and consumer services		Manufacturing and construction		Producer services	
Spatial unit	n	%	n	%	N	%	n	%
Central cities	378,322	37.9	215,729	38.9	36,508	21.9	126,085	45.5
Inner suburban ring	369,011	37.0	189,014	34.1	74,871	44.9	105,126	37.9
Outer suburban ring	250,716	25.1	149,467	27.0	55,386	33.2	45,863	16.6
Greater Copenhagen	998,049	100	554,210	100	166,765	100	277,074	100

Growth 1993-2002	Total workplaces		Retailing and consumer services		Manufacturing and construction		Producer services	
Spatial unit	n	%	n	%	N	%	n	%
Central cities	34,796	10.1	16,220	8.1	−7,175	−16.4	25,751	25.7
Inner suburban ring	38,797	11.7	11,210	6.3	−0,812	−1.1	28,399	37.0
Outer suburban ring	26,429	11.8	17,049	12.9	2,041	3.8	7,339	19.1
Greater Copenhagen	100,022	11.1	44,479	8.7	−5,946	−3.4	61,489	28.5

Source: Danish Centre for Forest, Landscape and Planning based on data from Statistics Denmark.

manufacturing and construction for 17 percent. The most substantial growth has been in producer services (Table 3.6).

The distribution of workplaces in retailing and consumer services according to spatial unit is similar to that of total workplaces, but disproportionately slightly more concentrated in the central cities. Producer services are disproportionately concentrated in the Cities of Copenhagen and Frederiksberg, while manufacturing and construction are disproportionately concentrated in the outer suburban ring.

Producer services have grown most rapidly in the inner suburban ring and in the Cities of Copenhagen and Frederiksberg, whereas retailing and consumer services have grown most rapidly in the outer suburban ring. Manufacturing and construction employment has declined slightly overall, with slight growth in the outer urban ring and substantial decline in the Cities of Copenhagen and Frederiksberg.

Based on the 825-sector level (NACE/DB03), the Greater Copenhagen Authority has constructed a dataset for various economic sectors indicating the degree to which the sector is bound to a specific area. For instance, kindergartens, primary schools, and municipal services serve the local area; secondary schools, the semi-local area; and hospitals, the regional area. The following categories are used: site-fixed, local, semi-local, regional, national, and global.[4]

In 2001, regional, national, and globally-oriented workplaces were slightly over-represented in the Cities of Copenhagen and Frederiksberg and in Copenhagen County. But these workplaces only accounted for 23 percent of the total growth in Greater Copenhagen from 1993 to 2001 versus 77 percent for locally and semi-locally-oriented workplaces. This lower figure for Copenhagen's share of the total growth could be one reason for the relatively uniform spatial distribution in workplace growth during the 1990s. Some municipalities in the inner suburban ring have the highest concentrations of regionally, nationally, and globally-oriented workplaces. These are located in various parts of the ring, mostly 10–15 km from the Copenhagen city centre.

3.4
Why did employment deconcentrate in the 1960s, 1970s and 1980s and reconcentrate in the 1990s?

No study in Denmark has systematically analysed the driving forces and regulatory potential related to urban development. Knowledge of the forces driving the deconcentration of workplaces is therefore limited. Nevertheless, some aspects can be featured.

Radical growth in dwelling space per capita and floor space per workplace was an important cause of the declining population and the stagnation in the number of workplaces in the Cities of Copenhagen and Frederiksberg and thus deconcentration. The space used per workplace has increased by 0.5 m^2 annually in the last few decades, despite the shift from industrial workplaces requiring substantial space to office and service workplaces requiring less. Increased affluence and technological development have driven this trend. Increased affluence also radically increased the housing floor space per capita from the beginning of the 1960s. The increases were so great, the Cities of Copenhagen and Frederiksberg could no longer contain all the workplaces and inhabitants.

Much of the growth in jobs since the 1960s has been associated with the development of the welfare society. Public-sector growth has been decentralized within municipal sectors providing services to the general public. Most of the growth in jobs has therefore occurred in citizen-oriented sectors in local areas, and the settlement pattern from 1960 until the early 1990s shifted strongly towards the suburbs.

Manufacturing jobs shifted extensively away from the Cities of Copenhagen and Frederiksberg in the 1960s and 1970s. The space used per workplace increased, and new production methods created a demand for new types of building. Many workplaces moved to the inner suburban ring or even more peripherally; others left Greater Copenhagen or closed.

Furthermore, many traditional city-centre-oriented companies and public institutions moved to the suburbs between the early 1970s and the early 1990s. The lack of space, obsolete buildings, and desire for improved accessibility by car seem to have been important reasons for locating outside dense urban areas. Greenfield construction was easier than converting buildings in inner cities. Companies were drawn to easily accessible, undeveloped, larger and less expensive building sites that were ready for development.

3.4.1
Reconcentration processes

Population and job growth stagnated in Greater Copenhagen in the 1970s and 1980s. The City of Copenhagen had substantial economic problems and came close to being placed under the economic administration of the state in the late 1980s. In March 1989, the Government of Denmark therefore initiated studies to determine how to re-establish growth in Greater Copenhagen. In March 1990, Denmark's Folketing (parliament) debated the future of Greater Copenhagen for the first time in decades. This debate was followed by the adoption of numerous large investment projects in Greater Copenhagen.

The Governments of Denmark and Sweden decided to link Copenhagen and Malmö in 1991; this link was completed on schedule in 2000. This investment was associated with several others to link the combined bridge and tunnel to the railways and motorways in Greater Copenhagen. Furthermore, a Metro was planned to serve parts of central Copenhagen and a new district, Ørestad, between the Copenhagen city centre and Copenhagen Airport (Figure 3.1). Ørestad is being developed on 310 ha jointly owned by the state and the City of Copenhagen. Legislation regulating Ørestad and the Metro was adopted in 1992, and a company was established to plan and carry out urban development and build the Metro. The idea was to sell land in Ørestad to finance the Metro. A total of 3.1 million m^2 of new buildings will be built there in the next few decades, mostly offices, but mixed with dwellings and cultural and educational institutions. A new, dense district with

60,000 workplaces and at least 20,000 inhabitants is planned. The first phase of the Metro was completed in the autumn of 2001 and the second phase in autumn 2002. A small third phase is underway and is expected to be completed in 2006. A large fourth phase, which would include a city ring, is still being investigated and debated before any political decision is made. A decision is expected in 2005.

The legislation regulating Ørestad and the Metro was accompanied by legislation regulating the Port of Copenhagen. The Port was authorized to continue its port activities and convert the previous Port land to new urban functions. Urban development has become an important task of the Port of Copenhagen. In addition, considerable cultural investment has been initiated in the form of spectacular new buildings along the waterfront: the Black Diamond of the Royal Library, a new playhouse for the Royal Theatre, and the Copenhagen Opera House. A new centre for fine arts education has been established at Holmen, a naval base until the late 1980s. Holmen has been further developed to become a new and interesting centrally-located district with low density housing. Many of the old, conservation-worthy buildings have been renovated and the green features have been sustained.

Finally, the government and the Folketing initiated numerous further transport investments, including a ring railway around the Cities of Copenhagen and Frederiksberg and extensive development and modernization of Copenhagen Airport, which was linked to motorways and railways as part of the fixed link with Sweden.

These governmental decisions contributed substantially to the creation of a new climate for business in the City of Copenhagen. In the 1970s and 1980s, investors, businesses, and building contractors perceived the City of Copenhagen as anti-business. This perception was partly related to the lack of planning; the City of Copenhagen only implemented its first comprehensive municipal plan in 1989. Investors wanted the investment security that a comprehensive plan could provide. However, from 1989, a new style of political leadership under a new Social Democratic Lord Mayor, together with extensive state investment, has contributed to a change in the investment climate in Copenhagen.

Greater Copenhagen and the City of Copenhagen were therefore fully able to exploit the economic boom in Denmark that began in 1994 and changed the pattern of regional development towards inner-city growth. Another prerequisite for this change was the extensive economic restructuring from manufacturing to services, which made available numerous sites for renewed urban development. Close cooperation between the state and the City of Copenhagen ensured that the necessary planning framework for regenerating and developing these sites was adopted.

The new opportunities for development in the Cities of Copenhagen and Frederiksberg combined with extensive state investment led relatively rapidly to considerable shifts in the pattern of location, despite the limited accessibility by car. One example is the extensive mergers in recent years between centrally-located law and accountancy firms. These mergers have led to substantial new construction on centrally-located sites on the waterfront. When similar mergers took place between centrally-located banks and insurance companies in the 1980s, there was an extensive move towards the suburbs.

The rents for office space also indicate the strong position of the traditional central business district in Copenhagen. Prime rents in the Copenhagen city centre are about €160–220 per m² and secondary office rents are €120–160 per m² (Sadolin & Albæk A/S, 2004). The highest rents are on the waterfront. Prime rents in suburban harbour areas north of the city centre are similar to the central harbour area. However, in secondary suburban locations, modern office space commands rents of about €135 per m²; office space of lesser quality is available for as little as €95 per m². The highest prime rent levels in suburban locations are €160 per m² in the northern fingers (Sadolin & Albæk A/S, 2004).

3.5
Regional planning strategies for locating workplaces

The deconcentration of buildings and workplaces in the 1960s, 1970s, and 1980s and the reconcentration in the 1990s were the result of market forces and specific political decisions and planning. Nevertheless, despite extensive regulatory authority, spatial planning has not been able to manage the envisaged construction and development as intended. Regional planning has been put in place to manage the deconcentration and reconcentration of buildings and jobs. Planning emphasized the development of dispersed secondary centres from the 1960s to the 1980s. In the 1990s, regional planning was designed to promote location near stations everywhere in Greater Copenhagen and to establish secondary centres in the City of Copenhagen (Figures 3.3 and 3.4).

Denmark's planning system[5] extensively decentralizes responsibility, practises framework management, and promotes public participation. The popularly-elected municipal councils have primary responsibility and considerable autonomy to determine their path of spatial development within the framework of regional planning established by popularly-elected regional councils. The legislative basis for regional planning was created in 1973 with special provisions for regional planning in Greater Copenhagen. Regional plans provide a binding framework for municipal planning. The organization of regional planning in Greater Copenhagen has been debated and revised at regular intervals. Many models have been used in the course of time: the Greater Copenhagen Council from 1974 to 1989; five county and city units from 1990 to 2001; and the Greater Copenhagen Authority from 2001 until its revocation in 2006.[6]

Denmark's state interests in spatial planning are largely attended to through regional planning. Until 1992, the state approved regional plans. From 1992, state approval was replaced by the authority of the Minister for the Environment to approve or veto plans. In Greater Copenhagen, the veto has been used to attempt to ensure a strict location policy that links urban development and the location of urban functions close to public transport nodes. Other examples are the protection of the green wedges between the urban fingers from any development for urban purposes and the delimitation of new urban zones for commercial purposes.

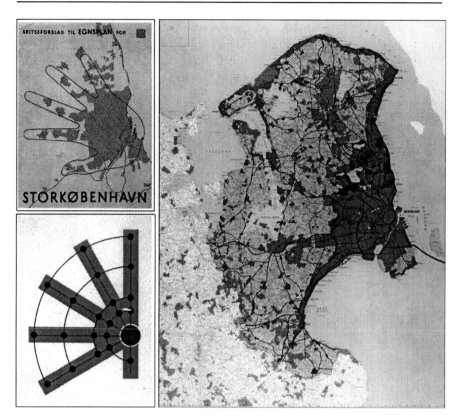

Fig. 3.3 Greater Copenhagen – the urban finger structure
Top left: The 1948 Finger Plan for Greater Copenhagen; bottom left: The 1989 Regional Plan for Greater Copenhagen: main planning principles for urban development and location strategy showing the best served stations at the railway lines (transport nodes). Right: Map of the Greater Copenhagen Area today showing the urban zones, areas for summer cottages (the north coast), and traffic infrastructure

Source: Hartoft-Nielsen, P. (2002a)

In Greater Copenhagen, regional planning started before it was authorized by national legislation. The finger plan for Greater Copenhagen was adopted in 1948 (Figure 3.3). The plan featured a principle for urban development that has been confirmed in later regional planning, namely that Greater Copenhagen should be developed in radial urban fingers alongside the suburban railway lines and with green wedges between the fingers to be maintained for recreational purposes. This structure is easy to recognize on a map or while travelling in Greater Copenhagen. The fingers have tended to become thicker than was originally envisaged, but the intention of avoiding uncontrolled urban sprawl was largely fulfilled in the subsequent six decades.

From 1948, the finger plan covered the Cities of Copenhagen and Frederiksberg and Copenhagen County, an area that is considerably smaller than that which is

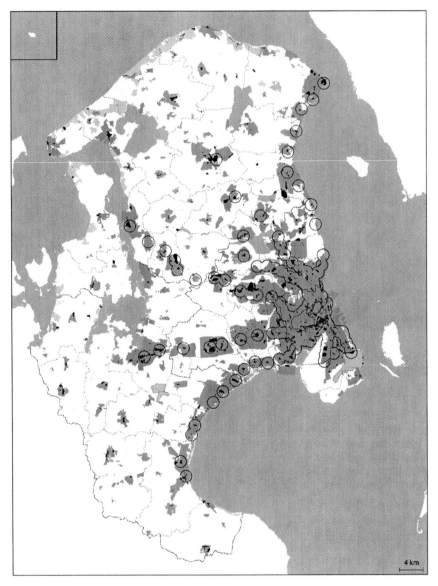

Fig. 3.4 Areas designated for offices in Greater Copenhagen

The map shows the location strategy for developing new areas for offices and services (1km circles around stations at the regional-, suburban- and metro-railways) and areas already designated for offices and services in the municipality plans (for instance Lautrupparken (Business Park) and Hoersholm Science Park located outside the circles). The grey areas are the urban zones

Source: Proposal for the 2005 Regional Plan for Greater Copenhagen

now referred to as Greater Copenhagen (Figure 3.3). The finger plan was based on a single-centre structure with the Copenhagen city centre as the only centre for general urban functions. Dwellings and locally-oriented workplaces were to be constructed near stations along the urban fingers. Public transport was oriented towards the city centre, and the maximum travel time to Copenhagen city centre was supposed to be no more than 30 minutes. Industrial workplaces in the suburbs were to be located in industrial districts at the root of each finger at the edge of the palm.

The City of Copenhagen did not have a comprehensive plan.[7] A General Plan was prepared in 1954, but individual plans for major projects were dominant in the 1960s and 1970s. There were plans for a major city annex (City Plan West) that would require the extensive demolition of dwellings in inner Vesterbro and the extension of the motorways to the Cities of Copenhagen and Frederiksberg, including motorways along the picturesque lakes bordering on the city centre and the central residential districts.

Citizens' groups strongly opposed the plans for motorway construction and the demolition and construction of offices. These proposed plans also blocked any decision on renewing the central residential districts and initiating the required improvement of the housing stock; decisions were consequently seriously delayed. The demolition and motorway plans and projects were abandoned in the mid-1970s, when growth stagnated and the state no longer reimbursed 85 percent of road investment in cities. This turnabout was fortunate for Copenhagen and created the basis for the development of many of the positive qualities that characterize the Copenhagen city centre today.

3.5.1
Planned secondary centres outside the cities of Copenhagen and Frederiksberg

In the meantime, new regional plans had been prepared that drew development away from the Cities of Copenhagen and Frederiksberg. In the 1960s, regional planning introduced a shopping centre next to the town of Lyngby, about 10 km from the city centre in one of the northern urban fingers (Figure 3.1). The intention was to complement a new shopping mall in the western finger 20 km from Copenhagen in the new town of Høje-Taastrup that was to include primary urban functions (Figure 3.1). Future urban growth was to be directed towards the two urban fingers towards the south and west; the two fingers were to be extended to the provincial towns of Roskilde and Køge (Figure 3.1). The attractive landscape in northern Greater Copenhagen was to be spared further urban development, and recreational functions were to be extended.

In the 1970s, regional planners maintained and extended the principle of secondary centres. The 1973 regional plan for Greater Copenhagen contained a new overall structure for urban development that fundamentally challenged the finger-city structure. Development was to be channelled away from the Cities of Copenhagen and Frederiksberg, since very strong urban growth was expected.

New primary regional centres and business nodes were to be developed as new towns at designated locations near the main transport nodes. Høje-Taastrup was still designated in the western finger in addition to one new node in each of the northern, north-western, and south-western fingers. The intention was for most urban growth to be associated with Ring 5, a transport corridor that was to link the new nodes at a considerable distance from central Copenhagen. The 1973 regional plan represented a clear break with the Finger Structure; the plan was later adopted by the Greater Copenhagen Council[8]. Economic development stagnated after the oil crisis in the 1970s, and, except for Høje-Taastrup, the nodes (and Ring 5) were largely abandoned.

3.5.2
Limited implementation of secondary centres

Secondary centres have only been established to a very limited extent, despite the deconcentration of workplaces until the 1980s and the clear intentions of regional planning. Secondary centres have mainly comprised shopping malls and have few office workplaces.

A new town has been established in Høje-Taastrup (Figure 3.1). Planning and development started in the 1970s, but the station at the centre of the town did not open until 1986. This station is very well served by public transport, including intercity, regional, and suburban trains. The station town of Høje-Taastrup is the site of many large office workplaces within the banking, insurance, and telecommunication sectors; they typically serve back-office functions. Most buildings have just two or three storeys; the building density in the station town is modest and it does not appear very urban. There are few dwellings, and the very few shops are all locally oriented. City 2, a large shopping mall, opened before the station and at some distance from it. The station complex and town centre have only 7125 of the 32,700 workplaces in the Municipality of Høje-Taastrup[9]. Thus, few workplaces are located centrally.

Lyngby has a shopping mall with a large department store and other facilities and is a well-developed commercial centre (Figure 3.1). The town centre around the station, the main street and the shopping mall, hosts only 9300 of the 31,900 workplaces in the municipality.[10] Lyngby hosts the Technical University of Denmark and numerous corporate headquarters, including IBM Denmark and some of Denmark's largest consulting engineering companies. With a few exceptions, the institutions and companies are dispersed in isolated enclaves far from the town centre and station, but close to the motorways in this area of natural beauty.

The five provincial towns in Greater Copenhagen also have no concentrated workplaces. Roskilde is one of the municipalities (with Ballerup, Høje Taastrup, and Lyngby) with the most workplaces (Figure 3.1). Roskilde accommodates the county administration, hospitals, and other regional functions. In the late 1970s, Roskilde University was built to relieve the University of Copenhagen. But Roskilde University is located about 3–4 km to the east of Roskilde. Most of its students live in the cities of Copenhagen and Frederiksberg. A station has since opened at the University, and a new urban area with 2400 dwellings is being developed. Later, two large national research institutes were established in Roskilde. They are about 6–7 km north of the town centre and isolated from both the town and the University. The town centre contains 6,500 of Roskilde's 31,000 workplaces.[11]

Despite the principles of regional planning, the state actively contributed to the establishment of the Hørsholm Science Park (now SCION DTU) for private and public research companies about 25 km from the Copenhagen city centre, close to the motorway but at some distance from a station (Figure 3.1). The Science Park has 70 companies with 2800 employees in such fields as biotechnology, pharmaceuticals, medical equipment, and energy.[12]

Another new business park is Lautrupparken in Ballerup; it is situated 15 km northwest of the Copenhagen city centre. Lautrupparken was set up by a municipality, in spite of the regional planning principles (Figure 3.1). The municipality bought the area in 1963, originally planning to construct dwellings there, but in 1971 it was designated for business purposes. This development took place a few years before the Greater Copenhagen Council was established and thus in a period of limited regional planning awareness. Lautrupparken is in one of the green wedges, isolated from centres, stations, and other urban functions. Both business parks therefore depend on car transport and are poorly served by public transport.

Lautrupparken has the largest concentration of office workplaces outside the Cities of Copenhagen and Frederiksberg. There are several company headquarters in the information technology, telecommunication, energy, biotechnology, banking, and insurance sectors. Lautrupparken is dominated by large units on large lots; there are 11,200 employees.[13] The business park's success has resulted from good accessibility by car and a green, well-planned site. At rush hour, severe congestion now builds up, undermining one of Lautrupparken's original attractions: accessibility by car. Alternatives to car transport are limited. The Municipality of Ballerup has 37,500 jobs within its boundaries – more than any other suburban municipality.

Despite the extensive deconcentration, there are thus very few large pockets of jobs outside the Cities of Copenhagen and Frederiksberg. The largest are at Lautrupparken, a green business park with low building density, and Copenhagen Airport. The planned secondary centres have been very limited in implementation; most are shopping centres. Jobs have been deconcentrated to many sites throughout Greater Copenhagen.

3.5.3
New location strategy in the 1989 regional plan
for greater Copenhagen

The Greater Copenhagen Council based the 1989 Regional Plan for Greater Copenhagen on the changed expectations for economic growth (Hovedstadsrådet, 1989). In approving the 1985 Regional Plan the state acquired a completely new regional plan with a general structure based on increasing the density of and refining the existing urban centres around the stations in the fingers and extensively utilizing other business sites and districts (Figure 3.3 and 3.4). The plan prohibited the designation of new areas for business far from stations.

This new policy was another attempt to get businesses to locate near stations. The general structure of the 1989 regional plan reintroduced and reinterpreted the finger structure. The urban fingers had been extended to the five provincial towns at the end of the railway lines. The single-centre structure was replaced by a multiple-centre structure including the sites near transport nodes: stations served by both radial railway lines and cross-cutting bus lines. Businesses can locate secondarily at sites around other railway stations. The centre structure is a hierarchical multiple-centre network between the urban centres near stations.

This location strategy attempts to bring about the location near stations of the urban functions that can utilize land intensively and the creation of extensive passenger transport for commuters and visitors. Examples include offices, densely-built housing development, leisure and cultural institutions, sports arenas, and shopping centres. The regional plan has binding guidelines stipulating that increases in building density and intensified use may only be carried out on sites near stations. The 1993, 1997, and 2001 regional plans confirmed this location strategy. These plans were drawn up after the five counties in the region abolished the Greater Copenhagen Council. The 2001 regional plans were handed over to the Greater Copenhagen Authority. The state played an important part in confirming the location strategy. The overall aim of this location policy is to direct workplaces towards station sites. One objective is to promote public transport at the expense of car transport. In addition, this policy aims to utilize transport investment optimally, to minimize the land designated for urban purposes and conserve the green wedges.

3.5.4
Limited implementation of the policy

Time inevitably passes between the introduction of a new comprehensive planning principle and its implementation. This interval was particularly likely to occur when the existing municipal and local plans were prepared in a period in which substantial growth was expected and on the basis of another planning principle that still allowed for considerable development. It needs to be taken into account in any evaluation of the policy promoting development near stations. Nevertheless, it must be said that the implementation of this policy has been very weak. For example, 1.6 million m^2 of floor space for office purposes was constructed in Greater Copenhagen from 1990 to 2001, but only about half of it was within 1 km of a public transport node or within 0.5 km of another station (Figure 3.5).

This situation represents a slight improvement in the amount of development near stations compared with the 1980s. Nevertheless, this improvement coincides with a shift towards development in the Cities of Copenhagen and Frederiksberg. The City of Copenhagen hosted 45 percent of office construction in Greater

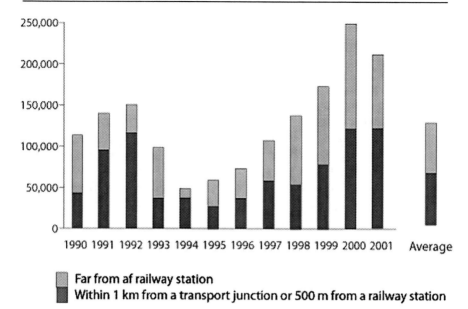

Far from af railway station
Within 1 km from a transport junction or 500 m from a railway station

Fig. 3.5 Office floor space constructed 1990–2001 in Greater Copenhagen
The diagram shows the total office floor space (sq.m.) constructed year by year from 1990 to 2001
distributed according to distance to a railway station. Source: Hartoft-Nielsen, (2002a, 2002b)

Copenhagen in the 1990s versus 20 percent in the 1980s. The development of office buildings in Greater Copenhagen has exploded in recent years and shifted even more towards the City of Copenhagen, with 60 percent of office construction in Greater Copenhagen within the City of Copenhagen in 2000 and 2001 (Hartoft-Nielsen, 2002a, 2002b).

Two thirds of new office construction in the Cities of Copenhagen and Frederiksberg are near a station versus 40 percent in the inner and outer suburban rings. The most recent proportion in the suburbs has declined further to 20 percent (Hartoft-Nielsen, 2002a, 2002b). The shift to construction in the Cities of Copenhagen and Frederiksberg inherently increases the percentage of construction near a station, since the density of stations is higher there than in the suburbs.

Lautrupparken – the Business Park in Ballerup 15 km northwest of the Copenhagen city centre – accounts for one third of the suburban office construction not in the vicinity of a station. A further third has been constructed in traditional industrial areas, despite the planning principle of maintaining low building density there. Most of the remaining third has been constructed outside urban areas, often adjacent to the beautiful landscapes that abound in the northern part of Greater Copenhagen (Hartoft-Nielsen, 2002a).

Office construction in Greater Copenhagen has averaged 135,000 m^2 of floor space annually since 1990, and total business construction has averaged 500,000 m^2: 40 percent within 1 km of a station, 30 percent 1–2 km from a station, and 30 percent more than 2 km from a station. For housing construction, 45 percent has been within 1 km of a station since 1990, ranging from more than 60 percent for apartment blocks to 20 percent for high-density low-rise housing (Hartoft-Nielsen, 2002a, 2002b). Thus, new construction has not brought workplaces closer to the stations. The overall distribution of workplaces, however, is influenced by events in existing buildings. The proportions of workplaces at various distances from a station remained relatively constant from 1990 to 2002, but declined somewhat for those close to a station and increased for those far away (Table 3.7).

The proportion of workplaces near a station declined in a period in which the policy was to increase this proportion. Currently, 28 percent of workplaces are within 0.5 km of a station and 60 percent within 1 km of a station (Figure 3.6). The shares are only high in the central cities. Forty-five percent live more than 1 km from a station (Figure 3.7).

3.5.5
Secondary centres in the cities of Copenhagen and Frederiksberg

Regional planning in the 1990s did not aim to relieve the pressure on the Cities of Copenhagen and Frederiksberg. The five county units were responsible for regional planning, so the Cities of Copenhagen and Frederiksberg were regional planning authorities. Market forces could therefore determine whether companies located in the centre or the periphery. Regional planning promoted renewed growth in central locations. The conversion of derelict and empty sites was to be encouraged. To protect the historic city centre and avoid automotive congestion in the rest of the city centre and the central residential districts, development is being promoted along the waterfront and in Ørestad (Figure 3.1). Three secondary centres in the City of

Table 3.7 Numbers of workplaces in Greater Copenhagen in 1990 and 2002 according to distance to a station (existing or politically decided stations for regional or suburban trains or Metro)

Distance to City Centre (km)	Workplace					
	1990		2002		Growth, 1990–2002	
	n	%	n	%	n	%
0.0–0.5 km	274,444	30.1%	272,314	28.4%	−2,130	−0.8%
0.5–1.0 km	296,107	32.4%	307,535	32.1%	11,428	3.9%
1.0–2.0 km	186,781	20.5%	202,436	21.1%	15,655	8.4%
> 2.0 km	155,823	17.1%	176,749	18.4%	20,926	13.4%
Total	913,155	100.0%	959,034	100.0%	45,879	5.0%

Not all workplaces have an exact address. The proportion of workplaces not included in this table for this reason comprised 4.5% in 1990 and 5.2% in 2002.
Source: Danish Centre for Forest, Landscape and Planning, calculated using a geographical information system from 100 m by 100 m grid data from Statistics Denmark.

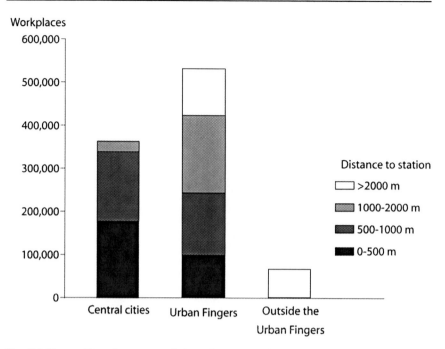

Fig. 3.6 Greater Copenhagen – workplaces by geographical unit and distance from railway station, 2002
The diagram shows the total number of workplaces in 2002 in Greater Copenhagen distributed according to urban segments and distance to a railway station

Copenhagen were identified in the 1989 Regional Plan for Greater Copenhagen. The site later named Ørestad was designated for internationally-oriented urban functions and business; the former naval base, Holmen, for nationally-oriented functions; and the northern part of the Harbour for regionally-oriented functions and business. The transformation and development of these sites has been taking place during the last decade. Ørestad and the harbour areas are still the most important sites for developing offices and workplaces in the City of Copenhagen; in general terms, however, the City of Copenhagen has adopted and implemented the location strategy of promoting workplaces near stations.

3.6
Barriers to the implementation of the location policy

Why has the implementation of the policy on locating near stations been so modest when Denmark's spatial planning system contains all the required instruments to ensure implementation? The reasons include:

- conflicts and the balance of power between the three administrative levels: state, county units, and municipalities

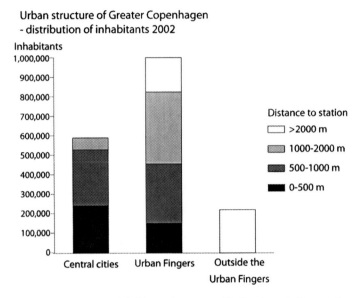

Urban structure of Greater Copenhagen
- distribution of inhabitants 2002

Fig. 3.7 Greater Copenhagen – inhabitants by geographical unit and distance from railway station, 2002
The diagram shows the total number of inhabitants in 2002 in Greater Copenhagen distributed according to urban segments and distance to a railway station

- conflicts between planning considerations and sectoral considerations
- conflicts between overall planning considerations and the interests of individual property owners
- developing existing urban sites often requires extensive conversion and is generally more difficult than greenfield development (Hartoft-Nielsen, 2002a).

Denmark's public sector is strongly decentralized. The municipalities have considerable power based on their substantial income from personal income taxes. County units are much weaker politically. State intervention in planning issues is considered unlawful and undesirable by local politicians and the Liberal party, the largest party in the Danish Parliament. Municipalities have generally avoided strict adherence to regional planning. They have been able to do so, because the political support at the regional level has been declining through municipal resistance. The policy of promoting location near stations has therefore been maintained through state intervention by veto. Municipalities do not have any sense of identification with the policy, and even the county units do not feel any greater sense of ownership of it. That having been said, one must concede that the current Chair of the Greater Copenhagen Authority, who is also the Mayor of the City of Frederiksberg, and the Lord Major of the City of Copenhagen both strongly support the policy. The municipal plan for the City of Copenhagen is an outstanding example of the general pattern of ignoring the location policy. Furthermore, the new Planning

Act coming into force in 2007 includes special provisions for spatial planning in Greater Copenhagen. These provisions include the maintenance and further development of the urban finger structure, protecting the green wedges, and promoting location near stations.

The resistance to the location strategy is manifold and is exemplified by the following quotations (Hartoft-Nielsen, 2002a):

The Minister for Finance responded as below to the pressure from municipal councils to oppose the policy of promoting location near stations in a letter to the Minister for the Environment in connection with the preparation of the 1993 regional plans:

> The proposed regional plan for Copenhagen County has aroused anger among all Social Democratic Mayors and municipal council spokespeople, because it prohibits business location more than 1 km from stations. My own Executive Board in the Glostrup Electoral District has asked me to emphasize the importance of the relaxation of this requirement. I hope that you can accommodate this.

The preface to the 1993 regional plan for Copenhagen County by the County Mayor makes clear the declining regional support:

> The County Council believes that the Minister for the Environment interpreted the "principle of promoting location near stations" too strictly in preparing the 1993 regional plans. The County Council has therefore adopted the following statement: "The location strategies should be reassessed in connection with the continuing regional planning efforts.... The basis should be that all urban areas in Copenhagen County are considered to be near stations."

Or, as the previous chair of the Greater Copenhagen Authority stated at several public meetings on the 2001 regional plan for Greater Copenhagen:

> Proximity to stations is a sensible principle for location. It should not however prevent development in other areas of the region.

The local politicians' failure to identify with the location policy has meant that the substantial development opportunities on sites distant from stations based on previous zoning have not been reduced as was desired. Consideration for the property owners affected has also been a factor. The policy has also met resistance in the wishes of many municipalities to convert and renew traditional industrial areas at a distance from stations. Pressure from property owners and developers has therefore caused many municipalities to interpret the planning stipulations very liberally.

In general, planning and the market may have interacted inappropriately (Hartoft-Nielsen, 2002a). Developers can reap substantial benefits by speculating against planning provisions. The greatest potential gains for developers can be gathered where the planning stipulations are changed or interpreted more liberally and where landowners are thus willing to sell at prices that do not reflect more intensive land use. The planning changes can include transferring land from a rural zone to an urban zone at the urban fringe or allowing the intensive use of sites previously zoned for low-density functions such as in traditional industrial or commercial districts. Before such conversion, land prices are low.

Sites with good accessibility by motorway or near attractive landscapes may be more lucrative for developers than sites already designated for office buildings with considerable building density. The price expectations of the owners of these latter sites, which may already have been capitalized, reduce the potential gains of developers and others. The prices and pricing mechanisms created by planning provisions on use and building density may therefore generate economic incentives for property owners, developers, investors, and others who can thwart the intentions of the planners. Ideas for projects may thus be proposed that municipalities may find difficult to reject or modify.

In addition, greenfield urban development is both less expensive and less complicated than development in existing urban areas, which may require complex conversion. In 2001, a government commission (Erhvervs- og Bypolitisk Udvalg, 2001) therefore put forward proposals for streamlining and promoting urban conversion through legislation. As a result of the change from a Social Democratic to a Liberal Party government, only a few of the commission's proposals have been implemented. Among these is a provision allowing noise limits to be exceeded for up to five years in areas designated for conversion in the municipality plans. The effects cannot yet be assessed, however. The commission's proposal that the municipalities should be given the right to order landowners in conversion areas to contribute to infrastructure investments was opposed by the government, because of the overriding priority of a tax stop.

Conflicts between planning considerations and sectoral considerations seem to be another important factor in derailing the policy of promoting location near stations. Even the actions of the state exemplify this. The state has been the main actor in the relatively strict implementation of the policy, but has nevertheless located some of its own institutions through exemption from the overall regional planning rules and forced location distant from stations for economic and other reasons. Furthermore, state sectoral authorities have tried to obtain the highest possible price for state land regardless of the location, which has led to demands for the intensive use of sites distant from stations. Government finance decisions may require a sectoral authority to manage to buy land and carry out construction with an unrealistically low budget or may require sectoral authorities to sell land at an unrealistically high price, given the current planning framework.

Other examples are a lack of, or a delay in, state investment in transport infrastructure. This bottleneck applied to the railway investment required to develop the south-western urban finger to the provincial town of Køge; development there began in the 1960s, but the railway did not reach Køge until 1983. A similar bottleneck affected the establishment of the secondary centre in Høje-Taastrup, which started in the 1970s, while the station was not completed until 1986. Developing the secondary centre in the City of Copenhagen, Ørestad, and the construction of the Metro mark a commendable change in the tradition; the Metroline opened just as the first building in Ørestad was built.

3.7
Effects of the deconcentration of workplaces

The location of urban functions and destinations affects transport and the environment. Decades of the deconcentration of workplaces have improved the overall spatial balance of workplaces and the workforce. However, total transport and its environmental impact have not been reduced. The residents of the central cities seem to have enjoyed an improved quality of life through the periods of deconcentration and reconcentration. The weak implementation of location strategy means negative effects on transport and quality of life.

Today, the total population is quite evenly distributed between the three spatial units (urban rings). Workplaces are still slightly more concentrated in the central parts of the region. The Cities of Copenhagen and Frederiksberg have 20 percent more workplaces than people in the workforce. The inner suburban ring has a surplus of jobs over employees of 16 percent, whereas the workforce in the outer suburban ring exceeds the number of workplaces by 28 percent.

The deconcentration of workplaces has substantially changed the commuting pattern. However, the better balance between the workplaces and the total workforce in the suburban municipalities has not reduced the proportion of long-distance commuters (defined as people living in one municipality and working in another), which is increasing steadily, as is the average commuting distance. For employees in offices in Greater Copenhagen, the average commuting distance in the mid-1990s exceeded 20 km; it was about 10 km in the mid-1970s (Hartoft-Nielsen, 2001a).

The current proportion of long-distance commuters in Greater Copenhagen is 60 percent. For example, the Municipality of Gladsaxe nearly balances workplaces and total workforce, but 70 percent of employed people living in Gladsaxe work elsewhere, and employees living outside Gladsaxe fill 74 percent of all jobs there. The Municipality of Glostrup has twice as many workplaces as employed people living there; 73 percent of the employed people living in Glostrup work elsewhere and employees living elsewhere occupy 87 percent of the workplaces in Glostrup. In the City of Copenhagen, the surplus of workplaces over employees declined from 144,000 in 1981 to 62,000 in 2002. In the same period, the number of people commuting into the Cities of Copenhagen and Frederiksberg only declined from 203,000 to 167,000 (18 percent), and the number of people living in the Cities of Copenhagen and Frederiksberg and working elsewhere increased from 59,000 to 105,000 (77 percent).

3.7.1
Negative effects on the pattern of transport

Changes in the commuting pattern are mainly brought about by an increasingly differentiated labour market and an increasingly specialized workforce. In addition, most households have more than one person employed. Nevertheless, the deconcentration of population and workplaces has contributed to increasing total transport and the share carried by the car. The increase in car use is related to the lack of success in managing the location of workplaces on the basis of the strategies used in regional planning.

Extensive studies of potential associations between housing location and transport behaviour (Hartoft-Nielsen, 2001b; Næss, 2003) have shown that daily transport and car use grow significantly with the distance of the dwelling from the Copenhagen city centre. This relationship also applies when socioeconomic factors, such as income, car ownership and the presence of children in the household, are controlled for. Residents of recently-built housing developments in the Cities of Copenhagen and Frederiksberg travel 20 km per day on average. Residents of recent housing developments with similar socioeconomic conditions located 25–30 km from the Copenhagen city centre travel about 40 km per day. The corresponding ratio for car transport alone is 2.5–3.0 (Hartoft-Nielsen, 2001b).

The deconcentration of workplaces has only increased total daily transport slightly. Extensive studies of potential associations between the location of workplaces and transport behaviour (Hartoft-Nielsen, 2001a) have shown that the average commuting distance in Greater Copenhagen is about 20 km. Location has little effect, but the commuting distance is slightly shorter in the Cities of Copenhagen and Frederiksberg and slightly longer in the suburbs. Car use and distances driven increase markedly, however, for employees working outside the Cities of Copenhagen and Frederiksberg. Cycling and public transport comprise a large proportion of transport for central locations. Some studies (Hartoft-Nielsen, 2001a, 2002a, 2004b) have shown that the distance from transport nodes significantly influences the choice of mode of transport.

Some studies (Hartoft-Nielsen, 2001a) show that 20–25 percent of employees drive to workplaces in the Copenhagen city centre; 40–50 percent to just outside the city centre; 40–60 percent to a nearby transport node in the suburbs; and 75–85 percent to a location at a distance from a station (Figure 3.8). The exact percentages within these ranges depend on such factors as the type of company and the composition of the personnel. Thus, locating office workplaces in the Cities of Copenhagen and Frederiksberg results in the least car driving by far; accessibility is poor by car and excellent by public transport and cycling comprises a large proportion of commuting. Even in winter, 30–40 percent of commuters cycle to office workplaces in the Cities of Copenhagen and Frederiksberg (Hartoft-Nielsen, 2003, 2004b).

People travelling to workplace locations near or far from suburban stations differ substantially in whether they use a car at all and how many kilometres they drive. Studies (Hartoft-Nielsen, 2002a) have shown that locating an office workplace near a suburban station reduces car driving by about 10 km per day. About 20–30 percent of employees who drive to their workplace when it is far from a station would choose public transport if the workplace were close to a station. These differences are assumed to result solely from voluntary shifts from car to public transport and are obtained by comparing suburban workplaces far from and near to a station

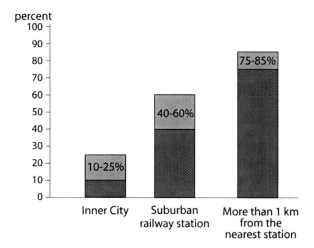

Fig. 3.8 Travel behaviour by employees in big office firms
The diagram shows the share of employees driving a car in daily commuting to firms with different locations in Greater Copenhagen. The exact percentages depend on such factors as the type of company and the composition of the personnel

Photo 3.1 "Even in winter, 30–40 percent of commuters cycle to office workplaces in the Cities of Copenhagen and Frederiksberg"
Source: Erik Petersen, Polfoto.

when both are readily accessible by car. The limited implementation of the policy of promoting location near stations in regional planning has therefore considerably increased car driving. The result is increasing congestion on the motorways in Greater Copenhagen during the rush hour and the declining competitiveness and deteriorating finances of public transport.

A recent survey of transport behaviour among the more than 400 employees of Ferring International (Hartoft-Nielsen, 2003, 2004b) indicated that developing Ørestad would help limit car driving in Greater Copenhagen. Ferring International was the first company to locate in Ørestad Centre at the new Ørestad Station, which is a transport node next to a motorway access road. The survey showed that the assumption that people want to drive is unfounded. When public transport is good and the walking distance from the station is short, many people avoid using a car. Most Ferring International employees are well paid and have a car. Nevertheless, 57 percent of employees living in Denmark use public transport and only 35 percent drive (nearly all employees living in Sweden take the train). The distribution by income shows that only the people whose annual household income exceeds €120,000 drive rather than use public transport. This pattern has been stable in surveys conducted over several years (Hartoft-Nielsen, 2003, 2004b).

3.7.2
Positive effects for residents of the cities of Copenhagen and Frederiksberg

Both the extensive deconcentration of workplaces from the 1960s to the 1980s and the reconcentration of workplaces in the 1990s positively influenced the quality of life of the residents of the Copenhagen city centre and the nearby densely populated districts. Development pressure in the Cities of Copenhagen and Frederiksberg was limited for decades. The strong public protest against the extension of the major arteries and motorways into the Cities of Copenhagen and Frederiksberg, comprehensive urban renewal, and office ghettos in inner Vesterbro was accepted politically. The expression of public feeling created the basis for the continuing development and planning of Copenhagen, with pedestrian streets and traffic-calming in the city centre, extended cycle paths, fewer parking spaces, and the improvement of many urban spaces. Cycling regained its major transport role in central Copenhagen. Despite economic growth and increased prosperity, the number of commuting drivers entering the City of Copenhagen remained below the 1970 level until the early 1990s.

The historic city centre has been maintained as a lively mixed-use district that is neither an office wasteland nor a museum. The central residential districts nearby have been renewed in a comprehensive effort to renovate the community environment with not only improved dwellings, but also improved courtyards, streetscapes, squares, and other urban spaces. This renovation has provided the Cities of Copenhagen and Frederiksberg with the opportunity to retain families with children and prosperous taxpayers who would previously have moved to the suburbs. The increasing population growth in the Cities of Copenhagen and Frederiksberg has been accompanied by a remarkable shift in the social composition of the residents. Two decades ago Copenhagen had many elderly residents, whereas today the number of elderly people has declined substantially and young people dominate.

Today, housing construction is an important aspect of the conversion of disused harbour and industrial sites, including the waterfront. The harbour entrance in central Copenhagen has recently been cleansed and the water is now suitable for swimming. Very popular swimming pools and beach parks have been created in the city centre. There is now vibrant urban activity throughout the Cities of Copenhagen and Frederiksberg. New recreational facilities have been created that are unique to the densely populated city centre, including some features that previously required a trip outside the city.

The long period of stagnation and decline in the 1970s and 1980s contributed to the creation of the basis for the later successful renovation of the city. Copenhagen was not overrun by motorways and office skyscrapers, as many other European metropolises were. Nevertheless, the renewed economic growth and reconcentration of workplaces was an important prerequisite for the many qualitative improvements achieved in Copenhagen in recent years.

The disadvantages of deconcentration include an increased average commuting distance for the residents of the Cities of Copenhagen and Frederiksberg: many

Photo 3.2 "The harbour entrance in the central Copenhagen has recently been cleansed and the water is now suitable for bathing"

people commute to other municipalities. The dispersed location of peripheral work-places far from any station has obliged many residents of the Cities of Copenhagen and Frederiksberg to buy a car. Even for affluent people, car ownership in the Cities of Copenhagen and Frederiksberg has been slight. One of the advantages of living centrally has been the opportunity to avoid car ownership without loss of mobility. Today, allocating scarce parking space in dense older districts of Copenhagen has become a planning problem.

3.7.3
Mixed effects for suburban residents

Much of the growth in jobs since the 1960s has been associated with the develop-ment of the welfare society. Thus, most suburban residents have taken advantage of the improved supply of services accompanying the deconcentration of work-places. Nevertheless, the proportion of suburban residents in the labour market who have taken advantage of the greater supply of workplaces close to home is much smaller. The labour market is strongly differentiated, and the average commuting distance has therefore increased. Suburban residents' most obvious advantage from the deconcentration of office workplaces is their improved car accessibility. But not everyone, however, has achieved this advantage. Trips taken against the predominant flow of traffic are rapid, but commuting to a workplace across the radial fingers or further inward on the fingers often means heavy rush-hour traffic. Public transport to workplaces outside the Cities of Copenhagen and Frederiksberg and to areas far from the stations in the urban finger in which people live is scarce. Establishing excellent public transport lines across the urban fingers is therefore one of the greatest planning challenges in Greater Copenhagen. The desired cross-border integration with the adjacent part of Sweden will also revive demands for a regional location policy that allows public transport to be a realistic commuting alternative to the car.

3.8
Conclusions

Urban development has been controlled in Greater Copenhagen through compre-hensive regional planning for nearly sixty years. The main principle – the Finger Plan – has been implemented, even though the urban fingers were thicker than intended. Regional Planning has thereby succeeded in creating a well-functioning urban region and preventing urban sprawl. In the 1960s, 1970s, and 1980s, regional planning sought to channel the deconcentration of regionally-oriented office and service workplaces to planned secondary centres. Developing new towns and urban districts was part of the strategy. The secondary centres outside the Cities of Copenhagen and Frederiksberg have not developed as planned, however. Those that have been developed have mainly become shopping centres. Workplaces were deconcentrated to many sites in Greater Copenhagen. A few business parks have been developed in the periphery, but office workplaces have also been located throughout small enclaves in urban areas or in traditional industrial areas, with a few along motorways and on relatively isolated sites with picturesque views. Densely built, mixed-use districts, office towns and centres are therefore virtually nonexistent outside the Cities of Copenhagen and Frederiksberg.

The 1989 Regional Plan for Greater Copenhagen reintroduced and reinterpreted the finger structure. Since 1990, the general location strategy has been to direct workplaces towards sites near train stations, thus creating a hierarchical multicentre network mainly within the existing urban fabric. In the early 1990s, firm political decisions were taken to revitalize and promote urban development in the central part of the region. These decisions included a fixed link to Sweden and a new urban development, Ørestad, located close to the city centre and Copenhagen Airport and served from the outset by a new Metro.

The political decision to revitalize the City of Copenhagen has been a success. The 1990s became a period of workplace reconcentration; after 15 years of stagnation, population and workplace growth returned to the region. The extensive deconcentration of workplaces from the 1960s to the 1980s and the reconcentration of workplaces in the 1990s positively influenced the quality of life of the residents of Copenhagen city centre and surrounding districts.

The policy of promoting development near stations has not been implemented as planned, particularly outside the central cities. Only half the total office floor space constructed in the 1990s in Greater Copenhagen was located within walking distance from a station. Studies have shown that locating firms near stations has a substantial impact on employees' travel behaviour. The weak implementation of the location strategy has increased car driving considerably and contributed to the congestion on the roads in Greater Copenhagen during the rush hour.

A time interval between the introduction of any new comprehensive planning principle and its implementation is to be expected. Several barriers to the implementation of the location policy can be identified. These include various conflicts: between the three administrative levels; between planning considerations and sectoral considerations; between overall planning considerations and the interests of individual property owners (including public ownership) and greenfield development. Although Denmark's spatial planning system seems to contain all the required instruments to ensure implementation, planning and the market may have been interacting inappropriately. Developers can reap substantial benefits by speculating against planning provisions.

The prices and pricing mechanisms created by planning provisions on use and building density may generate economic incentives for property owners, developers, investors and others that can thwart planning intentions. Ideas for projects may thus arise that municipalities may find difficult to reject or modify. This complex interplay between spatial planning and the property market is one of the challenges for regional planning in metropolitan areas and the drawing up of the spatial planning legislation.

In 2005, the Danish government adopted an administrative reform that will change the structure of local government substantially. The county units and the Greater Copenhagen Authority will be abolished in January 2007. Denmark's 271 municipalities will be reduced to 98. Land-use planning will be a matter settled between the state and the municipalities. Special provisions for spatial planning in Greater Copenhagen are incorporated in the new Planning Act. This also has provisions for the maintenance and further development of the finger structure, protection of the green wedges, and the location strategy promoting dense urban development near stations. The Act gives the Minister for the Environment the power to establish binding rules on the content of the planning in such matters as urban development and the location of urban functions in National Planning Directives for Greater Copenhagen.

The conflicts mentioned are inevitable. Regional planning strategies always operate in a political and economic space where conflicting interests obtain. A planning model with heavy regulation by the state should only be for the short term. Long-term solutions for the benefit of the entire Greater Copenhagen seem to require a popularly-elected regional council with a stronger tax base derived from personal income than the municipalities. Furthermore, the Danish Planning Act still needs better tools to promote the conversion and urban development of the existing urban areas.

Notes

[1] The main sources for this chapter are Hartoft-Nielsen, (2002a, 2004a). Planning history is also based on Rasmussen (1969) and regional planning documents. Since the mid80s the author has been working in the Spatial Planning Department, Ministry of Environment, with national interests in planning in Greater Copenhagen. When figures are not given a specific reference, the source is StatBank Denmark, Statistics Denmark.

[2] The City of Frederiksberg is enclosed within the City of Copenhagen and is thus very close to the Copenhagen city centre.

[3] Denmark adopted an administrative reform in June 2004 that will substantially change the structure of local government. The current 16 county units and Greater Copenhagen Authority are being abolished. Five new regional councils will mainly focus on hospital services. However, they will prepare regional development plans at a more comprehensive and strategic level than the present regional planning. The small municipalities will be amalgamated into larger units and will carry out more of the spatial planning tasks. Today's 271 municipalities will be reduced to 98. In Greater Copenhagen 50 municipalities will be reduced to 34. A new Planning Act was adopted in summer 2005 with special provisions on spatial planning in Greater Copenhagen.

[4] Hovedstadsregionens Statistikkontor (1999): "Arbejdspladser efter lokaliseringskategori" and HUR (Greater Copenhagen Authority, 2004): "Arealundersøgelse 2002".

[5] See note 3.

[6] See note 3.

[7] Only in 1989 the first comprehensive Municipal Plan for the City of Copenhagen was adopted.

[8] Existed from 1974 to newyear 1989/90 and was responsible for regional planning in Greater Copenhagen.

[9] Source: Danish Centre for Forest, Landscape and Planning, calculated using a geographical information system from 100 m by 100 m grid data from Statistics Denmark.
[10] See note 9.
[11] See note 9.
[12] See note 9.
[13] See note 9.

References

Erhvervs-og Bypolitisk Udvalg [The Industrial and Urban Policy Committee] (2001) *Betænkning*, Publication No. 1397. Ministry of the Environment and Energy and Ministry of Housing, Denmark

Hartoft-Nielsen P (2001a) Arbejdspladslokalisering og transportadfærd [Location of workplaces and transport behaviour]. Danish Centre for Forest, Landscape and Planning, Hørsholm (By- og Landsplanserien nr. 16)

Hartoft-Nielsen P (2001b) Boliglokalisering og transportadfærd [Location of dwellings and transport behaviour]. Danish Centre for Forest, Landscape and Planning, Hørsholm (By- og Landsplanserien nr. 15)

Hartoft-Nielsen P (2002a) Stationsnærhedspolitikken i hovedstadsområdet – baggrund og effekter [The policy of promoting development near stations in Greater Copenhagen – background and effects]. Danish Centre for Forest, Landscape and Planning, Hørsholm (By- og Landsplanserien nr. 18)

Hartoft-Nielsen P (2002b) Byudvikling i større byer – mulige konsekvenser for transport [Urban development in cities – potential effects on transport]. Danish Centre for Forest, Landscape and Planning, Hørsholm (By- og Landsplanserien nr. 17)

Hartoft-Nielsen P (2003) Metroens effekt på ansattes transportadfærd – virksomheder ved metroens første og anden etape – første, anden og tredje delundersøgelse [Effect of the Copenhagen Metro on the transport behaviour of employees at companies along the first and second phases of the Metro – parts 1–3]. Danish Centre for Forest, Landscape and Planning, Hørsholm (Arbejdsrapport nr. 47)

Hartoft-Nielsen P (2004a) Spatial deconcentration of workplaces and economic land use in Denmark. Case study analysis. Danish Centre for Forest, Landscape and Planning. WP1- Working report SELMA project, Copenhagen

Hartoft-Nielsen P (2004b) Metroens effekt på ansattes transportadfærd – virksomheder ved metroens første og anden etape – fjerde og femte delundersøgelse [Effect of the Copenhagen Metro on the transport behaviour of employees at companies along the first and second phases of the Metro – parts 4 and 5]. Hørsholm: Danish Centre for Forest, Landscape and Planning (Skov & Landskab Arbejdsrapport nr. 3)

Hovedstadsrådet [Greater Copenhagen Council] (1989), Regionplan 1989 [1989 Regional Plan]

Næss P (2003) Boliglokalisering, bilafhængighed og transportadfærd i hovedstadsområdet [Housing location, dependence on car transport and transport behaviour in Greater Copenhagen]. Byplan, no. 6

Rasmussen SE (1969) København: et bysamfunds særpræg og udvikling gennem tiderne [Copenhagen: the special characteristics and development of an urban community over time]. Gads Forlag, Copenhagen (2nd edition 1994)

Sadolin & Albæk A/S (2004) Copenhagen and Malmoe property market report 2004. Sadolin & Albæk A/S, Copenhagen

4 Economic deconcentration processes in mid-sized English cities: Deconcentrated outcomes and spatially differentiated impacts

Ian Smith

Cities Research Centre, University of the West of England, Bristol, Coldharbour Lane, Bristol BS16 1QY, United Kingdom

Abstract: The outcome of employment land policy in provincial English city-regions has been employment deconcentration, but the spatial impacts of this process of relative deconcentration have been complex. The capacity of the land-use planning system to manage the consequences of deconcentrated growth patterns is limited. The quality-of-life impacts of the changing geography of employment have been explored, using the labour market as the mechanism mediating impacts on metropolitan residents. The impacts vary spatially, with the urban fringe benefiting most and the central cities experiencing spatial polarization between those in employment and those who are not

Key words: Metropolitan governance, employment geography

4.1
Introduction

Recent processes of urban change and economic deconcentration can be understood in the context of the transition of the capitalist system (and its modes of regulation) from a Fordist to a post-Fordist economy. This is a transition whose ignition point is typically dated to the early 1970s. The deconcentrating city-region economy is associated with the broader process of metropolitanisation that the United Nations Human Settlements Programme (2004) identifies with four dimensions: spatial, social, institutional and economic. Contemporary urban economies are complex spatial systems of central cores, suburban employment centres, edge cities, clusters operating at various regional scales and home working that all impact on how city-regions function and on how they look and represented. The argument appears to be cities are doing well but that this has been at a cost of re-ordering the city-region spatial economy and the knock on effect is the impact on the quality of life in these city-regions.

This chapter explores empirically how the restructuring of the spatial urban economy has impacted on two provincial city-regions within Southern England over the last two decades of the 20th century. In particular the chapter will explain these particular instances of economic deconcentration and set out the impacts of deconcentration mediated through local labour markets on those who live in these city-regions. The final section of the chapter will outline the public policy implications of the spatially differentiated outcomes and impacts that have come in the

E. Razin et al. (eds.), Employment Deconcentration in European Metropolitan Areas, 89–114.
© 2007 *Springer.*

wake of spatial restructuring. These two affluent city-regions appear to have both the financial resources and political will to frame economic development in terms of sustainability arguments thereby minimising social and environmental impacts of economic development but that in practice have been unable to manage the externalities of economic deconcentration. These observations will be developed to demonstrate the limitations of land use planning to tackle difficult issues that need an integrated policy approach.

4.2
Theories of change and impact in metropolitan economic development

In simple descriptive terms employment has declined in large metropolitan areas in the UK (see Gillespie, 1999 or Bailey and Turok, 2000) whilst employment has grown in smaller towns and rural areas across the British urban system. On the whole over this period there is a shedding of jobs in manufacturing and major growth in private sector services with the differentials in jobs growth explained by strong performance in service employment. This pattern of employment shift has also been identified within both the North American (see McDonald and Prather, 1994 or Gordon and Richardson, 1996) and European urban systems (see Gaschet, 2002 for work on French cities). However this is a process that is not only being witnessed through whole urban systems but it is also evident in city-regions through the growth of polycentric urban regions (see Kloosterman and Musterd, 2001 or Kunzman, 1996) and in the case of North America edge cities (see Garreau, 1991) and suburban employment centres (see McDonald and Prather, 1994). It is this process that is taken as either the sprawl or deconcentration of economic land uses and hence of employment. The tendency to de-concentrate is not consistent across industries and this continues to be the case but the process of economic change that underpins deconcentration has meant that even industries that have traditionally chosen to locate within central cities are now moving to urban fringe and suburban locations (see for example Shearmur and Alvergne, 2002).

4.2.1
Explaining differential performance and economic deconcentration

In considering the way in which a city-region functions economically, it is important to consider two things. The first is to consider the whether some areas within city-regions are more economically successful than others (a potential outcome of deconcentration) and the second is to consider whether there are consistent processes that underpin differential economic performance between central areas and their urban fringes.

The evidence of differential economic performance within city-regions is clear. Deas and Giordano (2002) considered indicators of economic competitiveness covering the economic context (human capital), policy context (regeneration monies), state of the built environment (housing and roads) and social context for 17 British cities. This work revealed consistent pattern where urban fringes on the whole were performing better than their core cities in that they had a better set of urban assets and they had achieved higher levels of economic outcomes. This is work that stresses not only the importance of having a better set of assets but also stressed the important ability of being able to mobilise those assets. For the most part, urban fringes had more assets and were also the best at mobilising those assets but the authors were not able to establish a clear relationship between the performance of the core city and their respective suburbs. Voith (1998) has considered economic success in terms of income, house price and population change between central cities and their suburbs for a sample of US metropolitan areas and demonstrated that the economic fortunes of the suburbs and central areas are linked where the population of the central city exceeds 500,000 inhabitants. The evidence of differential performance suggests that whereas the relationship between a central city and its suburbs may not be consistent but that there may be reinforcing relationship of economic success at a particular scale or economic mass (see Rice and Venables, 2005 for exploration of economic growth and urban structure in the UK) and that there is a role for governance in terms of mobilising assets.

Whereas research has observed differential economic performance within city-regions and has put forward explanations relating to economic mass and governance, there is also a body of literature that considers the process of economic deconcentration. Within the British urban system, Gillespie has grouped explanations of deconcentration under four headings (1999: 18-22):

1. The relationship between employment uses and the urban populations who are either the labour force or the market for the goods and services produced. Thus deconcentration happens as businesses move to the suburbs and the urban fringe in pursuit of markets or workers;
2. The re-organisation of production chains and work enabled by information, communication and transport technologies freeing businesses from traditional location factors (technology mediated business activities). Deconcentration happens because businesses can organise themselves differently to take advantage of lower costs (either wages or premises);
3. Land and property supply creating differential opportunities for business location. Here deconcentration happens because of the workings of the property and land market allowing businesses to benefit from cheaper accommodation in the urban fringe; and,
4. Differing rates of entrepreneurship within sub-areas of city-regions leading to differential rates of job growth (business activities). Deconcentration happens because urban fringes are more economically dynamic locations than central city areas.

These explanations are all partial in that they can operate simultaneously with each explanation being relevant at different times and in different industries. Some are interdependent since the capacity of businesses to re-organise production depends on the capacity of either the development industry or the property sector to provide cheaper premises. However the combination of these processes leads to a differential map of agglomerative economy across a city-region that offers competitive advantage to successful industries (measured by their levels of employment) in locations outside of traditional city centre business districts so long as employers can mobilise these assets.

4.2.2
Local labour markets as mediation of social and environmental impact

Whereas researchers generally agree that there has been a level of deconcentration of employment out of central city centres to suburban centres (albeit that the patterns of movement and change are complex) and that the outcomes of these processes can be represented in terms of economic success, there has been limited work on assessing both the social and environmental impact of these changes. Garb et al (2004: 12) in reviewing the literature on the impact of non-residential sprawl on the quality of life of urban residents note that the spatial impacts of non-residential sprawl appear to be spatially selective and location specific. In this chapter the argument will concentrate on the way in which labour markets mediate the social and environmental impacts of spatial re-organisation in the urban economy.

Labour responds to employment opportunity in a number of ways:

- Those who are unemployed find employment;
- Those who are economically inactive become economically active;
- Those who travel further to get new work from where they currently live; and,
- Those who move house (migrate) into an area to gain access to employment opportunities.

Commuting patterns of labour respond to changes in employment opportunity. There has been significantly more work in relation to commuting patterns and the notion of wasted commuting engendered by decentralised patterns of employment (see for example Dubin, 1991 or Giuliano and Small, 1993) that suggests commuting should reduce with deconcentration if housing markets are operating efficiently. Urban economists point to the concept of 'wasted commuting' as indicative of the inability or unwillingness of workers to move house to be close to where they work. However, over the past 20 years it is clear that motoring costs have reduced in the United Kingdom relative to average earnings and relative to the use of public transport (Rogers and Power, 2000: 106). In contrast there is concern that the housing market within Great Britain has been able to offer the opportunity for workers to move closer to where they work even if household patterns of employment in dual earning household allowed this idea to have any sense (see Green, 1997). It is the patterns of commuting especially by the private car that can be associated with negative environmental impacts such as pollution (from exhaust fumes and noise) as well as problematic issues of congestion.

It is a combination of housing choices, choices in relation to transport and access to information about job opportunities (see Ihlanfeldt, 1997) that creates the spatial impact of employment opportunities within a city-region. It is differences in these factors that generate differing capacities of individual workers to react to the changing geography of employment. Hence some authors indicate that the social impacts of a changing geography of employment are evidence in higher levels of spatial inequality within city-regions (see Gottlieb and Lentnek, 2001) through social and spatial polarisation especially in relation to economic activity and unemployment rates.

4.2.3
Framing economic deconcentration with 'good governance'

The discussion above has already indicated that having economic assets such as a well trained labour force are not sufficient in and of themselves for an area within a city-region to succeed, urban areas also need to be able to mobilise what assets it has. Here it is the role of urban governance that becomes important in understanding both the differential economic performance of sub-areas in city-regions in general and of economic deconcentration in particular. Governance here will both incorporate the institutions and institutional structures that elaborate and implement public policy but also will include the policy interventions and policies that these structures formulate and put into play.

The relationship between 'good governance' and economic development is a theme that has been pursued by institutions associated with international development since the mid nineties. At the level of national policy-making, the United Nations is clear that "good governance is perhaps the single most important factor in eradicating poverty and promoting development" (UN Secretary General cited in Narang, 2005: 2). At the urban level as at the national level policy-makers such as the United Nations and the World Bank assert the importance of good governance to tackle development issues but the research evidence for such assertions at the metropolitan level are less clear. Harding (2005: 62) notes that the current conventional wisdom is that more responsive and integrated urban governance is the key to the pursuit and balancing of urban competitiveness (of which economic deconcentration may be one element) and social cohesion. One might equally add the enhancement of environmental capital to this mix. Re-phrasing this in the context of this chapter, better urban governance allows the successful balance between economic development and the social and environmental impacts of economic development. In this respect the OECD (2000) points to outdated and poorly adapted governance structures as a hindrance to tackling area-wide urban problems such as urban sprawl in metropolitan areas.

4.3
Two English city-regions

In order to explore the spatially differentiated impacts of the spatial re-structuring of employment within city-regions this chapter will consider two case studies for southern England: the city-regions of Bristol and Southampton (Figure 4.1). The economy of southern England and London has been subject to a long economic growth period through the nineties that has imposed economic development pressures on city-regions. Table 4.1 establishes some basic characteristics of the two case study city-regions in terms of residential population, jobs and economic value of production (as Gross Value Added or GVA). Bristol is a mid-sized city set in a wider area of nearly one million residents and over 400,000 jobs. Southampton is a small city set in a wider sub-region of around 800,000 inhabitants. In terms of inhabitants, jobs and economic value the City of Bristol dominates its sub-region to a greater degree than the City of Southampton.

Table 4.2 outlines the economic dynamic of both the central cities and the metropolitan areas as a whole for the late nineties and also establishes their relative success through the nineties again in relation to population size, the number of jobs in the urban economy and the value of economic production. It is interesting to

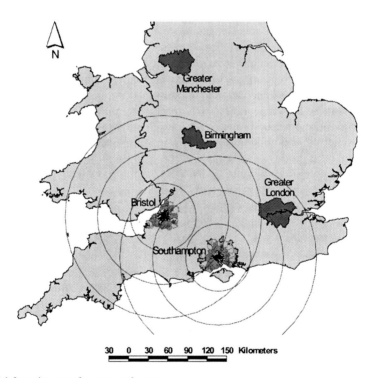

Fig. 4.1 Location map for case study areas

Table 4.1 Basic economic characteristics of city-regions

	Bristol urban area[i]		Southampton city-region[i]	
	City	City-region	City	City-region
Residential population (mid-year estimate), 1995[ii]	391,300	968,100	211,200	797,500
Number of jobs (total), 1995[iii]	209,973	423,469	103,267	321,192
Gross Value Added (GVA), 1995 (£ millions)[iv]	£5,142	£10,808	£2,710	£9,217[v]

Notes:
i. City-region figures include the central city and based on aggregating local authority areas and central city is the central local authority area
ii. Mid-year estimates from Office for National Statistics via NOMIS
iii. Jobs figures derived from Annual Employment Survey via NOMIS
iv. Gross Value Added (GVA) figures from Regional Trends
v. GVA estimate for Southampton city-region based on scaled estimate derived from figure for the County of Hampshire

Table 4.2 Economic change in case study city-regions

		Bristol urban area[i]		Southampton city-region[i]	
	England	City	City-region	City	City-region
Change in residential population 1995-2003[ii]	3.0%	0.1%	3.4%	4.7%	5.1%
Change in number of jobs 1995-2003[iii]	13.6%	10.1%	20.8%	7.8%	18.3%
Change in Gross Value Added 1995–2001[iv]	38.7%	45.1%	49.4%	26.0%	33.6%[v]

Notes:
i. City-region figures include the central city and based on aggregating local authority areas and central city is the central local authority area
ii. Mid-year estimates from Office for National Statistics via NOMIS
iii. Jobs figures derived from Annual Employment Survey via NOMIS
iv. Gross Value Added (GVA) figures from Regional Trends
v. GVA estimate for Southampton city-region based on scaled estimate derived from figure for the County of Hampshire

note that on the whole both city-regions have performed well in the second half of the nineties in terms of population, employment and economic production growth. Without exception on these three indicators the central city areas have performed less well than their city-regions as a whole implying that it has been areas around the central cities that have been performing better than the central urban cores.

Thus the two city-regions under scrutiny here are economically successful using economic indicators relating to economic output and employment. As economically successful places it is reasonable to assume that these are city-regions that should have access to the resources required to manage and mitigate the social and environmental externalities of growth and hence this is why they have been selected for study.

4.4
Differential economic change and impact

The next stage in the argument is to establish how the growth of these city-regions is rates are experienced differential across areas within the respective city-regions and by doing this establish the nature of economic deconcentration. The analysis will concentrate on three sub-areas of the city-region using a simple concentric model to explore changes relative the traditional city centre core of both city-regions: the central city centre; the central city suburbs (within a 5km radius of the city centre); and then an urban fringe extending up to 30km from the city centre that excludes (where feasible) other cities.

4.4.1
Jobs, premises and housing

Table 4.3 develops the picture set out in Table 4.2 by breaking down employment change in relation to sub-areas within each city-region and to broad definitions of economic activity. The table shows both the number of jobs by category of economic activity in 1991 and gives the percentage change in employment between 1991 and 2001. In both cases it was growth in producer services that accounted for the largest percentage growth in employment whilst retail and consumer services accounted for the largest number of jobs.

In both city-regions there is a spatially differentiated pattern to employment growth through the 1990s. In numeric terms the largest growth of employment has been located in the urban fringes that are already part of the built up area of the respective city-regions. Although it is important to note (as already noted from Table 4.2) that employment in the central city core also grew over this period thus we can only talk about relative employment deconcentration (rather than absolute deconcentration). The largest percentage change in employment is located in the rural areas of the urban fringe where growth in terms of the number of jobs has matched the growth of employment in the central city centre (around 20000 jobs in Bristol city-region and about 12000 jobs in Southampton city-region).

Considering employment in relation to the three classes of economic activity, the picture is one of strong relative deconcentration in both types of service activity (producer and consumer services) but there is a more complicated and unclear story within manufacturing and construction. Manufacturing employment has been in decline although employment in the construction industry has compensated for this loss in aggregate terms. The general trend for manufacturing in the UK through the

Table 4.3 Changes in total non-agricultural employment 1991–2001 by city-region sub-areas

	Manufacturing & construction[1]		Producer services[2]		Consumer services[3]		Total non-agricultural employment	
Bristol city-region	Jobs 1991–2001	% 1991–2001	Jobs 1991–2001	% 1991–2001	Jobs 1991–2001	% 1991–2001	Jobs 1991–2001	% 1991–2001
Central city	500	4.1%	13400	26.8%	3200	5.5%	21800	14.2%
Suburbs	−600	−6.1%	−900	−9.2%	8100	32.2%	6600	14.7%
Urban fringe	−3000	0.2%	18900	74.6%	40000	42.7%	51200	34.5%
Total city-region	−3150	0.1%	31300	41.5%	51300	30.3%	79500	25.9%
Rural areas in urban fringe	−600	−4.2%	11100	166.8%	9300	66.1%	20000	57.2%
Southampton city-region								
Central city	−400	−5.6%	6800	30.3%	4900	18.7%	11200	20.2%
Suburbs	−800	−8.3%	3000	53.7%	2700	9.8%	4900	11.4%
Urban fringe	4800	10.7%	14300	50.7%	31700	28.4%	50800	28.9%
Total city-region	3600	6.1%	24100	44.5%	39300	24.1%	66900	25.0%
Rural areas in urban fringe	300	7.5%	7500	185.0%	4300	30.6%	12100	54.8%

Notes:

1. Manufacturing & construction includes sections C (manufacturing), D (electricity, gas and water production), and E (construction) (SIC92)
2. Producer services include sections I (transport and communications), J (financial services), and K (business services) (SIC92)
3. Consumer services includes sections G (wholesale and retail), H (hotels and hospitality), L (public administration), M (education), N (health and social services), O (other services) and P (domestic employment) (SIC92)
4. All sections of the Standard Industrial Classification 1992 (SIC92) correspond to NACE rev. 1

Source: Census of Employment employee analysis 1991 and Annual Business Inquiry employee analysis 2001 via Nomis.

nineties has been one of decreasing employment although increasing manufacturing output. In these city-regions the employment change figures suggest that there is no clear deconcentration process within manufacturing and construction. It is likely that the deconcentration and re-structuring of manufacturing has more or less been completed prior to 1991.

However service sector employment growth has been an important feature of economic development through the 1990s. In both cases the urban fringe has been the dominant area in terms of employment growth although deconcentration has been rampant in relation to consumer services where employment growth in the urban fringe has been equal to 6-12 times the employment generated in the central city centre. In the case of producer services employment growth in the central city has more closely matched that in the urban fringe reflecting the long-standing preference of financial, business and property service companies to prefer central locations. In addition to the contribution of the urban fringe that is part of the contiguous built-up area, the rural part of the urban fringe has also seen large numbers of jobs created in both producer and consumer services. Here employment growth in numeric terms matches at least that of the central city and in the case of consumer services around Bristol is three times the growth of employment in the central area. This indicates that development may be jumping the constraining 'green-belt' around the existing built up area.

The feature that differentiates the two city-regions is that of the performance of the suburbs. In the case of Bristol there was employment decline in producer services and in the case of Southampton there was relatively poor performance in consumer service employment. These figures do not detract from the story of relative deconcentration but are likely to reflect the functional micro-geographies of the two city-regions and the choice of arbitrary concentric rings to explore these changes rather than a functional definition of suburbs versus central city and urban fringe.

Thus there is a clear deconcentration outcome of relative employment shift away from the traditional city centre areas. But the question arises as to whether this employment growth is growing in concentrated areas within the urban fringe or whether there is a more general dispersal outcome. The relative strength of fringe agglomeration versus employment dispersal can be gauged by considering measurements of relative entropy of economic activity. As a spatial distribution becomes more evenly spread the measure of relative entropy will approach a score of one whereas a highly concentrated spatial distribution of jobs (such as all jobs located in the central city) will have an entropy score that approaches zero. Table 4.4 sets out relative entropy measures for three areas of economic activity for 1991 and 2001. The calculation has been based on the ward geographies of the two city-regions and thus it is not possible to compare results between city-regions but because a consistent ward-geography has been used it is possible to compare results for the same city-region over time. Using these measures it is evident that of these economic activities, consumer services are the most dispersed and producer services are the most concentrated. This would be expected on the grounds that

Table 4.4 Relative entropy measures for employment by economic activity, 1991–2001

		Employment in			
		Manufacturing and construction[1]	Producer services[2]	Consumer services[3]	Total non-agricultural activities[4]
Bristol	1991	0.800	0.666	0.830	0.817
city-region	2001	0.855	0.707	0.865	0.846
Southampton	1991	0.811	0.704	0.839	0.830
city-region	2001	0.834	0.745	0.861	0.847

Notes:
1. Manufacturing & construction includes sections C (manufacturing), D (electricity, gas and water production), and E (construction) (SIC92)
2. Producer services include sections I (transport and communications), J (financial services), and K (business services) (SIC92)
3. Consumer services includes sections G (wholesale and retail), H (hotels and hospitality), L (public administration), M (education), N (health and social services), O (other services) and P (domestic employment) (SIC92)
4. Total employment exclude agriculture and fisheries due to unreliability of data-set
5. All sections of the Standard Industrial Classification 1992 (SIC92) correspond to NACE rev. 1
Source: Census of Employment employee analysis 1991 and Annual Business Inquiry employee analysis 2001 via Nomis.

consumer services tend to follow where people live whilst producer services have a preference for central areas. However all types of economic activity have shown a tendency to disperse through the 1990s with the tendency being slightly greater in the Bristol city-region.

Clearly the use of such broad categorisations of economic activity risks concealing the dynamics of sub-categories of activity and this appears to be the case for employment within distribution, hotels and catering (shopping and tourism activities). Despite the broad category of consumer services showing a general tendency for dispersal, the relative entropy score for employment within distribution, hotels and catering did not change through the nineties (remaining at 0.83) and yet employment growth in the urban fringes of both city-regions was between 55 and 63 percent. This would indicate a pattern of relative concentrated deconcentration (growth in existing fringe locations) whereas the general pattern of employment change across other sectors is more of increased dispersal and large increase in the fringes (dispersed deconcentration).

Using dissimilarity indices it is also possible to explore whether two given spatial distributions of employment are tending to co-locate. Table 4.5 sets out the dissimilarity indices calculated between the patterns of employment in the three broad classes of economic activity. The dissimilarity index reveals what percentage of employment in a given sector would need to move in order achieve an equal spatial distribution to its comparator. Thus an index of 50 would indicate that 50

Table 4.5 Dissimilarity indices by economic activity between 1991 and 2001

		Bristol city-region		Southampton city-region	
		Producer services[2]	Consumer services[3]	Producer services[2]	Consumer services[3]
1991	Manufacturing & construction[1]	56.24	54.71	48.30	47.04
	Producer services[2]		33.84		35.97
2001	Manufacturing & construction[1]	51.89	48.69	44.56	44.02
	Producer services[2]		35.04		32.48

Notes:
1. Manufacturing & construction includes sections C (manufacturing), D (electricity, gas and water production), and E (construction) (SIC92)
2. Producer services include sections I (transport and communications), J (financial services), and K (business services) (SIC92)
3. Consumer services includes sections G (wholesale and retail), H (hotels and hospitality), L (public administration), M (education), N (health and social services), O (other services) and P (domestic employment) (SIC92)
4. All sections of the Standard Industrial Classification 1992 (SIC92) correspond to NACE rev. 1
Source: Census of Employment employee analysis 1991 and Annual Business Inquiry employee analysis 2001 via Nomis.

percent of employment in that sector would need to re-locate in order to achieve parity. Table 4.5 reveals that there is a relatively close distribution of employment between both producer services and consumer services but a relatively different spatial pattern of employment with both these broad sectors and the manufacturing sector. Thus around 50% of manufacturing employment would need to re-locate to get a distribution similar to either of the service sectors whereas only around 35 percent of employment in producer services would need to move to get a distribution similar to that of consumer services. However through the nineties the distributions of manufacturing employment and service sector employment have become more alike. The net aggregate impact of spatial change is equivalent to 3 to 6 percent of employment in services moving to locations where manufacturing is already present (equivalent to between 5000 and 10000 jobs in each city-region).

4.4.2
Explaining deconcentration

Thus in terms of employment, the data suggests that there has been a generalised net dispersal of employment within these city-regions with the exception of retailing where there is a suggestion of concentrated deconcentration within the urban fringe. There are a number of potential explanations for this change (see above) that relate to the differential levels of business start ups between different locations, the differential opportunities for developers to create new commercial and industrial premises and the relationship between employment land uses and residential land use. We can review each of these issues in relation to secondary data.

Table 4.6 explores the relative rates of business registrations and de-registrations by area since 1980. Due to changes in the definitions of inclusion of businesses in this data-source the data-set needs to be split in 1994. However the basic data reveals that entrepreneurship measured by rates of business registration are higher in central cities than in their urban fringes. Yet the annual net change in the number of businesses (stocks) in the urban fringe of these two city-regions has consistently risen faster than the central cities. It is the rates of business de-registration (resulting from a business failure or re-location) relative to business registration that differentiates between the areas. Urban fringes are more conducive to businesses staying in business but are not more entrepreneurial locations.

The second explanation centres on the supply and availability of premises. Table 4.7 outlines changes in the stock of office space (for B1 business class) for the period 1984-2004. This is a form of development that is most likely to impact on producer services but will equally have an impact on consumer service activities. The table reveals a pattern of relative deconcentration of the city-region office stock over this period with a massive increase in the office stock in the fringes with only a modest rise in the amount of office space in the central city areas in both city-regions. In both cases there annualised rates of development were 90-100 percent higher in the fringe than in the central cities indicating that the development of new office space was clearly creating an opportunity for office-based economic activity in the fringes. The underlying story is the same for both city-regions: commercial office development has gone in parallel to employment

Table 4.6 Business registration and de-registration rates for VAT 1980–2003 across all economic activities

	1980–1993			1994–2003		
	Average registration rate per 100 existing businesses	Average de-registration rate per 100 existing businesses	Average year on year % change in stocks	Average registration rate per 100 existing businesses	Average de-registration rate per 100 existing businesses	Average year on year % change in stocks
Bristol (UA)	15.2	13.8	1.1%	12.0	10.8	1.1%
Bristol urban fringe	13.4	11.0	2.4%	10.2	8.8	1.6%
Southampton (UA)	15.7	15.7	0.2%	12.2	12.1	0.0%
South Hampshire	14.3	11.0	3.4%	10.2	8.4	2.0%

Source: VAT registration/deregistrations by industry data (DTI) via Nomis.

Table 4.7 Office development for commercial business uses 1984–2004 by city-region sub-areas

	Stock of office space ('000s sq m)		% Change in stock 1984–2004	Annualised net rate of change 1984–2004 (sq m)	Annualised rate of dev't 1990–2002 (sq m)[3]
	1984	2004			
Bristol (UA)	983	1088	10.7	5,200	19,100
Bristol urban fringe [1]	206	876	325.2	33,500	39,200
Southampton (UA)	285	445	56.1	8,000	18,100
Southampton urban fringe [2]	127	398	213.4	13,550	33,900

Notes:
1. Bristol urban fringe made up of South Gloucestershire, North and North East Somerset
2. Southampton urban fringe made up of Eastleigh, New Forest and Test Valley
3. Annualised rate for development is 1989-2001 for Bristol and 1990-2002 for Southampton
Source: Department of the Environment (1995), Office for the Deputy Prime Minister (2004).

deconcentration although based on this data it is not possible to indicate whether the development preceded the movement of employment or rather follows this trend.

Finally we can assess the impact of housing development. This is of particular interest because of its potential link with consumer services that we can hypothesise as following residential movements. The picture of housing development shows some common trends across the city-regions in Table 4.8. Here there is also a picture of relative deconcentration with the net rates of increase in the number of dwellings in the fringe being twice that of the central city areas. These figures of total dwellings based on the Census of Population are comparable to the figures of housing completions (based on development control monitoring). Here the annualised rates of housing completions match the net change in the housing stock with the exception of Southampton City where the implication is that there has been some re-development of the housing stock within the central area.

The development outcome in the city-regions points to a process of deconcentration both in terms of employment, office development and housing development. The plausible story behind this concentration is that consumer service employment is following residential development whilst producer service employment is following the availability of new office development. This office development is co-located with earlier phases of industrial development bringing the spatial distribution of services into line with that of the remaining manufacturing activities. The evidence does not suggest a deficit of entrepreneurialism between the central areas and the urban fringe (in fact the opposite seems to be true) but that businesses in the urban fringe are finding it easier to sustain themselves creating a marked differential in business survival rates. The aggregate deconcentration outcome is more extreme within the Bristol city-region than within the Southampton city-region. This would suggest that at least two of Gillespie's explanations hold up to scrutiny

Table 4.8 Housing development 1991–2003 by city-region sub-areas

	Number of dwellings		%Change 1991–2001	Completed dwellings[1]	Annualised dwellings completed[1]	Annualised per 10000 existing dwellings[1]
	1991	2001				
Bristol	162,501	169,675	4.4%	5479	685	42
Bristol fringe[2]	227,612	253,223	11.3%	20380	2548	112
Southampton	84,446	89,002	5.4%	4434	633	75
Southampton fringe[3]	229,730	256,094	11.5%	16287	2327	101

Notes:
1. period covered 1991-99 for Bristol and 1996-2003 for Southampton – these are statistics based on development control monitoring within respective city-regions
2. Bristol urban fringe made up of South Gloucestershire, North and North East Somerset
3. Southampton urban fringe made up of Eastleigh, Fareham, New Forest, Winchester and Test Valley
Source: Census of Population 1991 and 2001 (Office for National Statistics), Joint Strategic Planning and Transportation Unit and Hampshire County Council.

in these particular localities. However this chapter wants to develop a further understanding of what is going on and in particular in relation to how labour market characteristics have responded to these processes of economic deconcentration. However establishing these processes of deconcentration and describing the nature of the change is only the first aim of this paper, the second is to establish the social and economic impact of these changes. This issue will be addressed in the next section.

4.5
Social and environmental impacts through local labour markets

The main way in which the deconcentration processes indicated above impact on those living in the respective city-regions is through the local labour market. The main mechanisms by which changing employment patterns impact on local labour are:

- Improving physical accessibility to employment opportunities;
- Altering commuting patterns (generally assumed to be a reduction in commuting); and,
- Increasing levels of economic activity in resident population and decreasing levels of worklessness.

The aggregate pattern of housing development in Table 4.8 suggests that housing development had largely followed the pattern of employment growth noted in Table 4.3 (although without time series data it is not possible to demonstrate the sequence of events). Given that housing development and employment growth was largely similar in pattern, one would expect employment land uses to be more accessible in 2001 than for 1991. Table 4.9 explores this idea measuring the index of dissimilarity between the spatial patterns of where workers live in the city-region and where jobs are located. Using the index of dissimilarity across both city-regions for the spatial distribution of where workers live and where jobs are located it is evident from Table 4.9 that these spatial distributions have become more alike between 1991 and 2001. This indicates that land use planning has had an aggregate impact on the location of housing development and the development of employment land uses.

The consequence of that shift is witnessed in the accessibility figures in Table 4.9. Thus in 2001 some 16 percent of workers in the Bristol city-region

Table 4.9 Changing patterns of accessibility to employment sites 1991–2001

		Index of dissimilarity: workers and jobs	Percentage of the resident population living within the following distance of a major employment site		
			1 km	5 km	15 km
Central Bristol	1991		55.1%	100.0%	100.0%
	2001		68.8%	100.0%	100.0%
Suburban Bristol	1991		22.8%	100.0%	100.0%
	2001		24.0%	100.0%	100.0%
Fringe Bristol	1991		5.5%	53.3%	91.6%
	2001		7.2%	56.8%	92.8%
Bristol city-region	1991	41.4	13.4%	67.1%	94.2%
	2001	38.7	16.2%	69.3%	95.2%
Central Southampton	1991		52.3%	100.0%	100.0%
	2001		51.0%	100.0%	100.0%
Suburban Southampton	1991		21.2%	97.5%	100.0%
	2001		23.4%	100.0%	100.0%
Fringe Southampton	1991		5.9%	57.8%	87.2%
	2001		11.7%	71.9%	96.6%
Southampton city-region	1991	41.7	15.5%	71.8%	91.6%
	2001	38.6	21.8%	81.7%	97.8%

Notes:
1. indices derived from small area data aggregated to 1991 ward boundaries
2. major employment centre defined as a ward containing more than 5000 jobs
Source: Census of Employment employee analysis 1991 and Annual Business Inquiry employee analysis 2001 via Nomis.

and 22 percent of workers in the Southampton region were within one kilometre of a major employment centre (defined as a ward with more than 5000 jobs). This improved the theoretical accessibility of 45000 workers in Bristol and 87000 workers in Southampton. On the whole the principal beneficiaries of improved employment accessibility have been the working age residents of the urban fringe although 20000 workers from central Bristol benefited from employment generated in the southern central area of the city centre.

However in order to understand how the patterns of housing location for workers match up to employment opportunities, it is necessary to consider commuting patterns. Table 4.10 sets out patterns of commuting within the two city-regions firstly in relation to the number of person-kilometres travelled and in relation to the average commuting distance (as a direct line distance). The evidence of Table 4.10 confounds the aggregate observation of Table 4.9. Between 1981 and 2001, there has been a massive increase in the number of commuting kilometres travelled and in the average distance travelled for work despite the converging spatial distribution of housing and employment. Rather than using the opportunity of living closer to where they work, the workers of these city-regions have embraced mobility and commute further. These figures do not give any notion of how long commuting takes in terms of time but does offer insight into the energy cost of such movement. However, Gordon and Richardson (1997 and 1991) suggest in the context of the US that the de-centralisation of employment accompanied by appropriate suburbanisation should lead to the reduction of traffic congestion (measured in terms of travel time). Based on evidence from the US, Giuliano and Small (1993) indicate that if housing markets are operating efficiently there is scope for workers to reduce their commuting. The conclusion from this is that

Table 4.10 Commuting distances and commuting loads, 1981–2001

Origin of travel to work journey	Number of person-km travelled to work within city-region			Average commuting distance (km) for journeys within city-region	
	1981	2001	% change 1981–2001	1981	2001
Bristol city centre	105, 134	243, 830	131.9%	2.9	5.3
Suburban Bristol	242, 243	427, 025	76.3%	3.7	5.6
Urban fringe Bristol area	1, 360, 210	2, 810, 626	106.6%	6.2	8.0
Southampton city centre	34, 602	107, 704	211.3%	2.7	6.4
Suburban Southampton	237, 192	476, 528	100.9%	3.9	6.1
Urban fringe Southampton area	1, 009, 529	2, 982, 264	195.4%	5.9	8.1

Source: Census of Population 1981 (Census Interaction Data Service, MIMAS), Census of Population 2001, National Statistics (all Crown Copyright).

workers are choosing not to respond to the changing geography of employment and this might be explained relative to the high cost of housing, the low cost of mobility and the low priority placed on work-related reasons for moving house.

Given that the response of workers to the changing geography of employment has been to commute further, the question arises as to the impact of changing labour demand on the spatial distribution of employment-related disadvantage. Table 4.11 sets out the pattern of economic activity within the city-regions for the period 1981-2001. Overall the aggregate picture suggests that the population of economically active adults is growing both in the central city areas and in the city-region fringes with a stable population of economically active adults in the suburbs. The phenomenon that distinguishes the central city from the urban fringe is that in the central city the growth of the economically active population is broadly in line with population growth as a whole (generated by natural changes and patterns of migration) whilst in the urban fringe it only accounts for around half the growth of the economically active population. Thus within the urban fringe about half the growth in economically active adults is due to economically inactive adults becoming economically active.

Thus there is a plausible story of employment opportunity resulting from employment deconcentration attracting economically inactive residents in the urban fringe (especially women) into the formal labour market. But a question arises as to whether this generates polarisation in the city-region labour market. Table 4.12 uses indices of segregation to examine the relationship between those in employment, those seeking work and those who are economically inactive using indices of dissimilarity (developed by Duncan and Duncan, 1955) that measure the relative distribution of two distributions in space and indices of interaction (developed by Bell, 1954) that measure the likelihood of individuals from specified groups meeting. Duncan and Duncan's index of dissimilarity is interpreted as the

Table 4.11 Patterns of economic activity, 1981–2001

Sub-area within sub-region	Number of economically active resident population aged 16–74 years			Economic activity rates for residents aged 16–74 years	
	1981	2001	% Change 1981–2001	1981	2001
Central Bristol	44747	50811	13.6%	67.2%	66.5%
Suburban Bristol	79509	79605	0.1%	64.3%	66.9%
Urban fringe Bristol	304173	371482	22.1%	65.4%	70.3%
Bristol city-region	428429	501898	17.1%	65.4%	69.4%
Central Southampton	17403	22340	28.4%	66.5%	60.1%
Suburban Southampton	79538	80477	1.2%	66.0%	65.5%
Urban fringe Southampton	289394	364415	25.9%	65.2%	70.4%
Southampton city-region	386335	467232	20.9%	65.4%	68.9%

Source: Census of Population 1981, 2001 (Census Dissemination Unit, MIMAS)

Table 4.12 Indices of spatial segregation of labour market characteristics 1981–2001

		Index of dissimilarity between:			Index of interaction:	
		Those in employment and the unemployed ID(XY)	The economic inactive and those in employment	Unemployed and the economic inactive ID(YZ)	Within the un-employed yPy	Between the employed and the un-employed xPy
Central Bristol	1981	0.164	0.090	0.114	0.100	0.534
	2001	0.192	0.122	0.191	0.044	0.567
Suburban	1981	0.210	0.097	0.271	0.071	0.505
Bristol	2001	0.141	0.141	0.169	0.030	0.602
Fringe Bristol	1981	0.165	0.072	0.149	0.049	0.552
	2001	0.153	0.094	0.121	0.024	0.648
Bristol	1981	0.212	0.073	0.199	0.063	0.538
city-region	2001	0.178	0.103	0.137	0.028	0.626
Central	1981	0.102	0.058	0.044	0.092	0.544
Southampton	2001	0.126	0.211	0.085	0.032	0.469
Suburban	1981	0.078	0.028	0.090	0.059	0.527
Southampton	2001	0.073	0.113	0.125	0.029	0.597
Fringe	1981	0.151	0.069	0.152	0.046	0.563
Southampton	2001	0.144	0.095	0.135	0.021	0.652
Southampton	1981	0.173	0.062	0.172	0.054	0.552
city-region	2001	0.174	0.117	0.140	0.024	0.623

Notes: indices derived from small area data from the Census of Population 1981 and 2001 aggregated to 1991 ward boundaries – data sourced from the Census Dissemination Unit.

percentage of population group that would need to be relocated in order to achieve a similar spatial distribution to the comparator group. The index can vary from zero to one with the larger the value of the index, the greater the dissimilarity in spatial distribution between the groups.

Calculating these indices both in relation to the city-region as a whole and by sub-areas within the city-region one can start to capture some diverging labour market dynamics within the city-regions with regards to the spatial distributions of economic activity. Thus whereas the overall distribution of those in employment and those seeking employment became more similar between 1981 and 2001, once the city-region is broken down into sub-regions it becomes clear that there is some level of segregation within the central city areas with a further process of increasing segregation between the unemployed and the economically inactive. This data would suggest that labour market polarisation is not a general process across the whole city-region but is witnessed in specific areas of the city that are masked by taking a sub-regional overview.

The key spatial patterns at the level of the city-region is the increasing similarity of spatial distributions between both those seeking employment and both those in employment and those who are economically inactive with part of this explained by the decreasing numbers of those seeking employment. Hence in 1981 within the Bristol city-region an unemployed resident had a 6 percent probability of living next door to someone else who was unemployed but by 2001 there was only a 3 percent probability of this being true. However there appears to be some divergence in the spatial patterns of those in employment and those who are economically inactive. In the case of the Southampton city-region in 1981, some 6 percent of those in employment would need to move to 'match up' the spatial distribution of those in employment with that of economically inactive residents but by 2001 this figure had risen to nearly 12 percent. This indicates that the spatial distributions have become less alike over this period.

Thus the overall pattern of impacts from employment deconcentration point to some theoretic benefits of the spatial patterns of employment and housing with some evidence of spatial polarisation in the central city areas of these city-regions combined with an increasing environmental cost associated with lengthening commutes across the whole city-region. Residents within the city centre now commute as far as suburbanites in these two city-regions despite the proximity to the central business district. Table 4.13 summarises the observed changes that have been contemporary to the deconcentration of economic activity within these city-regions. These are summarised in relation to the sub-areas of the city-region and are indicated against four 'quality of life' issues and the main policy sector under which the 'quality of life' issue is usually is tackled.

On these four issues residents in the urban fringe have clearly benefited the most in terms of increased potential access to employment, economic activity rates and decreased spatial polarisation in relation to the unemployed (although there has been increasing segregation in relation to the economically inactive). However residents pay for this through increased commuting and the environmental pollution that commuting by private car brings. Suburban dwellers appear to have

Table 4.13 Summary of social and environmental impacts associated with economic deconcentration

		Impact on issue in:		
Quality of life issue	Main policy sector relevant to issue	central city	suburbs	Urban fringe
Spatial access to employment opportunity	Land use planning	☺	☹	☺☺
Economic activity rates	Economic development, education and skills	☹	☹	☺
Spatial polarisation of labour market	Welfare, education and skills	☹☹	☹	☺
Commuting as pollution proxy	Transport planning, energy	☹	☹	☹

a fairly neutral outcome of employment deconcentration with the exception of the pollution effects of increased commuting. In the central city area there is a process of polarisation whereby the average potential earnings increase but more residents experience exclusion from the labour market and income poverty. Again city centre residents are commuting further.

These are complex issues that cover a range of policy sectors. Clearly there has been a broadly positive economic impact of economic deconcentration (as one element of economic re-structuring in these city-regions) but that the social and environmental consequences of economic deconcentration have been less well managed. In the next section the chapter will explore the institutional dimension to economic deconcentration.

4.6
Metropolitan governance and deconcentration

Urban governance is the fourth dimension of metropolitanisation. The conventional wisdom for metropolitan areas suggests that in order to achieve a blend of economic growth with social cohesion and environmental enhancement, urban governance needs to deliver an integrated policy response. Table 4.13 has indicated the principal policy sectors that relate to four quality of life outcomes associated with the geography of employment. In public policy terms, land use planning has been reasonably successful in these city-regions in achieving a better balance between the spatial distribution of housing and employment sites in aggregate terms albeit that this spatial re-organisation has resulted in a pattern of relative dispersed deconcentration of economic activity. A priori the deconcentration of development does not lead to a city-region that is more wasteful of environmental resources since for example the deconcentration of employment may lead to a net reduction in commuting distances. However in these city-regions there has been a massive increase in commuting with little indication of labour markets adjusting spatially as workers move house to reduce commuting costs. We can conclude that the English planning system can get housing to be built in proximity to employment sites but it is unable to get workers to live closer to where they work.

One of the characteristics of joined up urban governance could be the formulation of policy and plans that create a discourse of being joined up either in terms of policy sectors or in terms of the metropolitan territory. We can explore whether there is an integrated inter-sectoral discourse of policy-making by considering the territorial coverage of plans and strategies relating to the policy sectors outlined in Table 4.13. The main finding of Table 4.14 is the complete fragmentation of policy space across these two city-regions. The issue of territorial fragmentation has become more problematic through the nineties with local government re-organisation in 1996-97 that has further fragmented local policy responses in relation to land use planning, transport and education. As a non-statutory local government function the delivery of economic development strategies has always relied on partnerships such that the situation post 1997 is not any more muddled than before 1997. It is thus of little surprise that there have not been integrated city-region wide responses to the impacts of economic deconcentration in these city-regions through the nineties. Clearly fragmented governance does not unduly impact on economic development and aspects of land use planning such as the allocation of employment and housing land for development in the urban fringe have shaped the pattern of economic deconcentration. However the evidence of the social and environmental outcomes of economic deconcentration suggests that a more integrated response is required to tackle 'quality of life' issues.

The apparent lack of joined up (in the territorial sense) policy-making as evidenced in Table 4.14 goes part of the way to explain the inability of metropolitan governance to achieve social and environmental outcomes consistent with sustainability despite achieving relatively positive economic outcomes. As most of these plans and strategies espouse the aim of achieving forms of development that optimise economic, social and environmental outcomes (under the heading of being more sustainable) this is a notable failure of metropolitan governance in England. This is particularly acute given the notion of the ecological and environmental impacts of cities extend way beyond existing local authority boundaries. There is an absence of coherence and holism (using the language of the OECD principles of metropolitan governance) and the outcomes achieved indicate a lack of sustainability that is symptomatic of a failure of governance. Thus fragmented governance may permit the deconcentration of employment land uses but it does not facilitate the management of the consequences of this deconcentration.

Table 4.14 Institutional dimension of managing economic deconcentration outcomes and impacts

Policy domain	When applicable	Bristol city-region	Southampton city-region
Land use planning	Pre-1997	One strategic, six local plans	One strategic, six local plans
	Post 1997	One strategic partnership of four local authorities, four local plans and one set of regional guidance	One strategic partnership by three local authorities, six local plans and one set of regional guidance
Transport Planning	Pre-1997	One transport plan	One transport plan
	Post 1997	Four local transport plans	Two local transport plans
Education and skills	Pre-1997	One education authority, one learning and skills council	One education authority, one learning and skills council
	Post 1997	Four education authorities and one learning and skills council	Two education authorities and one learning and skills council
Economic development	Pre-1997	One sub-regional strategy with partial local strategy coverage	One sub-regional strategy with partial local strategy coverage
	Post 1997	One regional strategy, four local strategies	One regional strategy, six local strategies

However joining up policy at the metropolitan scale is only one dimension of 'good' governance. Work by the OECD and World Bank (e.g. Kamal-Chaoui, 2003 or Huther and Shah, 1998) has attempted to capture other dimensions including transparency, accountability and participation. The question arises as to the degree these dimensions of governance might have shaped employment deconcentration in these city-regions. In terms of these case studies the discussion here will concentrate on three issues in particular: the emergence of economic development partnerships, the participation of interest groups in policy formulation and the relationship between central and local government on planning issues.

Since 1997 there has been a growth in partnerships across these city-regions. In terms of economic development both city-regions are covered by partnerships that incorporate the private sector (both from the development industry as well as broader representation across these sub-regional economies). These partnerships have been active in developing sub-regional visions for their respective city-regions and have found a role in the recent rounds of strategic planning but for the bulk of this period economic development partnerships have played a negligible role in shaping the patterns of development seen on the ground. These are arrangements that have increased the level of engagement of private sector actors but have not increased the accountability or transparency of governance arrangements in their respective city-regions.

Both city regions have been compelled by central government to act in partnership to develop sub-regional land use planning. This institutional arrangement was imposed with the re-organisation of local government in 1997. These partnerships of local authorities have driven one round of structure planning in the city-regions but this arrangement has been consistently incapable of resolving difficult issues such as the allocation of housing development across their respective city-regions to the satisfaction of central government. Again this is an arrangement that has had a negligible impact on the management of the consequences of deconcentration. These arrangements have also placed local policy-makers in conflict with the wishes of central government. Consistently the aims and objectives of local policy-makers have been to restrict economic and housing development arguing that rampant development ruins the competitive assets of these city-regions (in terms of their quality of life). However, Central Government has been keen to promote economic and housing development in southern England wherever 'market-based' actors desire development in these city-regions because they are seen as the economic drivers for wider regional and national economic spaces.

Participation has been a concern of land-use planners through this period. The evidence is that community groups have become increasingly organised as they have come to understand the planning system. Thus community groups have engaged with strategic land use plan-making through the various public inquiries and examinations in public but mainly playing the role of trying to prevent development (especially housing). However the bulk of public engagement focuses on the prevention of specific projects rather than on the strategic shape of the city-region. This public opposition may have resulted in some contrary outcomes such as the development of Bristol's regional airport (and potential site for employment expansion) in the city's greenbelt and pushing housing development outside of the first ring of urban authorities to a second ring of local authorities. Hence what participation that has been generated has not been harnessed into the creation of a strategic vision to take either city-region forward.

Thus overall the failure of metropolitan governance must extend to the failure to create a coherent public policy position on managing and shaping the consequences of economic development as well as the failure to generate a transparent and accountable institutional structure (either through partnerships or through the constitution of a new body) that has the capacity, vision and legitimacy to stand up to central government. However, despite the failure or absence of effective metropolitan governance, it should still be noted that these city-regions as a whole have performed relatively well in terms of economic outcomes. One can certainly question the notion that good governance is necessary for good economic performance at least over the time-span of a decade. There are two points to note here. The first is that the development process can be slow to respond to changing policy frameworks. Thus developers may sit on planning permissions for five to ten years before implementing them especially if one takes into consideration the interaction of the policy framework with the business cycle of the economy. Any change in policy arrangements may not see changes on the ground for a decade and hence the impact of ineffective metropolitan governance may only be witnessed in the following business cycle. Thus the development trends of the nineties were a result of governance arrangements in the 1980s and not those of the 1990s. Secondly the failure of metropolitan governance may play out mainly in the ability of metropolitan areas to equitably share out the benefits of economic development since metropolitan governance is largely unable to positively influence local economic development (although it may have the capacity to have a negative impact).

4.7
Concluding comments and prospects for change

These case studies have revealed processes of relative employment deconcentration within these city-regions over a twenty year period. These are processes that have been broadly positive for their city-region economies but the consequences for urban sustainability are generally poor. The process of deconcentration can be explained in relation to the availability of premises (generally new premises) and the better survival rates of businesses in the urban fringes. The lack of ability to harness economic growth to improve social and environmental outcomes for the city-region as a whole can be put down to a failure of metropolitan-wide governance although it should be noted firstly that the institutional arrangements that have been in place have not prevented a broadly positive set of economic outcomes and secondly that the spatial distribution of social and environment benefits and costs has been spatially (and socially) uneven.

There are prospects for change although there is little prospect of this change being rapid on the ground. There is a resurgence of interest in sub-regional planning associated with changes in the English planning system and there has been a greater attempt to at least join up the strategic policy positions of regional bodies in England. It is less easy to see how the joining up of public policy will play out at the city-region or sub-regional level. The notion of the city-region has re-emerged on the agenda of the Labour administration that came to office in May 2005 but there is little clarity about how this will be developed. However since 2000 efforts to join up local public policy has focussed at the level of local authority areas through the implementation of local strategic partnerships mainly but not exclusively located in the 88 most deprived local authority areas. Evidently these do not cover metropolitan areas and are severely under-resourced in relation to the problems they are attempting to tackle. Even if new forms of metropolitan and strategic governance, it is also unlikely to be seen on the ground before the end of the next business cycle. A less charitable interpretation of these changes is that they are merely part of a thirty year cycle of government re-interpreting what has been tried (and failed) before (in this case re-interpreting debates from the late 1960s and early 1970s of functional urban regions and local government reform). Thus the immediate prospects for resolving the spatially differentiated impacts of on-going economic deconcentration across city-regions are unclear although there are some emerging prospects for the reform of metropolitan governance. It is always best to travel hopefully.

References

Bailey N, Turok I (2000) Adjustment to job loss in Britain's major cities. Regional Studies 34(7):631–653

Bell W (1954) A probability model for the measurement of ecological segregation. American Sociological Review 32:357–364

Deas I, Giordano B (2002) Locating the competitive city in England. In: Begg I (ed) Urban competitiveness: policies for dynamic cities. Policy Press, Bristol

Dubin R (1991) Commuting patterns and firm decentralisation. Land Econ 67(1):5–29

Duncan OD, Duncan B (1955) A methodological analysis of segregation indices. American Sociological Review 41:210–217

Garb Y, van Kamp I, Kuijpers M, Quředníček M, Sýkora L (2004) Quality of Life Indicators. Report for Work Package 2 of the SELMA project

Garreau J (1991) Edge city: life on the new frontier. Doubleday/Anchor, New York

Gaschet F (2002) The new intra-urban dynamics: suburbanisation and functional specialisation in French cities. Pap Reg Sci 81:63–81

Gillespie A (1999) The changing employment geography of Britain. In: Breheny M (ed) The people: where will they work? Report of TCPA research into the changing geography of employment. TCPA, London

Giuliano G, Small KA (1993) Is the journey to work explained by urban structure? Urban Studies 30(9):1485–1500

Gordon P, Richardson HW (1997) Are compact cities a desirable planning goal? J Am Plann Assoc 63(1):95–106

Gordon P, Richardson HW (1996) Employment decentralisation in US metropolitan areas: is Los Angeles an outlier or the norm? Environ Plann A 28:1727–1743

Gordon P, Richardson HW (1991) The commuting paradox: evidence from the top twenty. Journal of the American Planning Association 57(4):416–420

Gottlieb PD, Lentnek B (2001) Spatial mismatch is not always a central-city problem: an analysis of commuting behaviour in Cleveland Ohio and its suburbs. Urban Studies 38(7):1161–1186

Green A (1997) A question of compromise? Case study evidence on the location and mobility strategies of dual career households. Regional Studies 31(7):641–657

Harding A (2005) Governance and socio-economic change in cities. In: Buck N, Gordon I, Harding A, Turok I (eds) Changing cities: rethinking urban competitiveness, cohesion and governance. Palgrave Macmillan, Basingstoke

Huther J, Shah A (1998) Applying a simple measure of good governance to the debate on fiscal decentralisation, Working Paper 1894, the World Bank

Ihlanfeldt KR (1997) Information of the spatial distribution of job opportunities within metropolitan areas. J Urban Econ 41:218–242. In: Wassmer RW (ed) (2000) Readings in urban Economics: issues and public policy. Blackwells, Oxford

Kamal-Chaoui L (2003) Metropolitan governance in OECD countries. A paper presented at the OECD-Busan seminar on Policy Challenges in Metropolitan Regions in Busan, Korea (July 2003)

Kloosterman RC, Musterd S (2001) The polycentric urban region: towards a research agenda. Urban Studies 38(4):623–633

Kunzman KR (1996) Euro-megalopolis or themepark Europe? Scenarios for European spatial development. International Planning Studies 1(2):143–163

McDonald JF, Prather PJ (1994) Suburban employment centres: the case of Chicago. Urban Studies 31(2):201–218

Narang S (2005) Disaggregating governance indicators: why local governance is important and how it can be measured. A paper presented to the technical workshop on governance indicators, April 20-22 New Delhi, India

OECD (2000) The reform of metropolitan governance. OECD Observer Policy Brief, October 2000, sourced at www.oecd.org

Rice P, Venables AJ (2005) Spatial determinants of productivity analysis for the regions of Great Britain. London School of Economics working paper.

Rogers R, Power A (2000) Cities for a small country. Faber and Faber, London

Shearmur R, Alvergne C (2002) Intra-metropolitan patterns of high-order business service location: a comparative study of seventeen sectors in Ile-de-France. Urban Studies 7:1143–1163

United Nations Human Settlements Programme (2004) The state of the World's cities 2004/2005: globalisation and urban culture. Earthscan, London

Voith RA (1998) Do suburbs need cities? J Reg Sci 38(3):45–64. In: Wassmer RW (ed) (2000) Readings in urban Economics: issues and public policy. Blackwells, Oxford

5 The Spanish way to economic deconcentration: A process of several speeds

Manuel Valenzuela[1], Carmen Vázquez[2], Antonio J. Palacios[1] and Ángel Jodra[1]

[1] *Department of Geography, Madrid's Autonomous University, Cantoblanco, 28049 Madrid, Spain*
[2] *Department of Geography and Planning, Faculty of Humanities, University of Castilla-La Mancha, Avd. los Alfares 44, 16002 Cuenca, Spain*

Abstract: In this chapter we describe how Spanish metropolitan areas still display a strong monocentric pattern, although familiar market processes of employment deconcentration are in play, frequently assisted by public policies and initiatives. Until recently, Spanish cities have undergone mainly residential deconcentration processes. The two case studies – Madrid and Valladolid – show that urban planning has encouraged this market-led process through built-up area reassessment techniques. During the 1990s, two main confluent variables played major parts: (1) the huge price increases of real estate in central areas; (2) the deliberate regional political decision to spread economic activities, even those traditionally linked to the city core such as offices, retail, and even public services. The land-use policy of regional governments and the development of new transport infrastructures contribute to a gradual erosion of the existing monocentric spatial structure

Key words: Employment deconcentration, monocentric spatial pattern, regional planning, Madrid, Valladolid

5.1 Introduction

Until recently, metropolitan areas located in Mediterranean Europe have usually been charged with unplanned deconcentration, resulting from loose management practices and low levels of enforcement of laws and regulations. However, Spanish and Italian case studies reveal a different reality. Although the familiar landscape of employment deconcentration can be observed at some suburban locations, metropolitan areas in both countries seem to have retained a strong monocentric employment distribution. In Spain's growing metropolitan areas, employment has not so far followed the marked residential deconcentration. In fact, Spanish cities are competing with cities in Poland and the Czech Republic to attract or take over industrial production sites from West European companies (Krätke, 2001). In the two Italian metropolitan areas (Rome and Chieti-Pescara) described in another chapter of this book, central cities and city centres have retained their dominance in commerce, leisure, and office employment. Are planning regulations in these countries more effective than could have been hoped for here? Are market pressures for employment deconcentration weaker than expected, because of demographic decline, or of being at an earlier phase of metropolitan development, or because

115

E. Razin et al. (eds.), Employment Deconcentration in European Metropolitan Areas, 115–144.
© 2007 *Springer.*

of specific values and tastes that affect business location decisions? To ascertain these issues in the Spanish case, we have analysed two case studies: Madrid and Valladolid metropolitan areas.

The profile of the process of urbanization in the last few decades in Spain differs markedly from that operating in other West European countries. The difference derives from a trend of urban concentration starting later, with a pattern in favour of the very few cities to which much of the demographic and economic flows were directed. It must be borne in mind that until the 1950s the urbanization rate was around 41 percent: that figure represents a typically rural habitat. From the 1950s onwards, a great part of the rural population has been channelled towards the major industrial cities (mostly Barcelona, Bilbao, and Madrid) giving as a consequence a yearly urban population growth rate of around 3.1 percent through the 1960s and 1970s; in both decades the urban population increase was about 34 percent. At the end of the 1970s, the urban population exceeded the rural population by 50 percent: the greatest concentration of population was in the big cities and the metropolis.

However, through the 1980s and 1990s, urban population growth decreased (Precedo, 1996), although levels remained higher than in those countries that have finished their urban transition. In fact, in Spain the increase in the more developed urban systems with an industrial background was smaller, whereas growth in the semi developed cities was more rapid. Even so, the growth of the biggest cities is still exceeding that of the overall urban and total population; the process of urban concentration is still in place.

In this context, the metropolitan areas of Madrid and Valladolid both still display a strong monocentric pattern, although familiar market processes of employment deconcentration are at play, frequently assisted by public policies and initiatives. Until recently, Spanish cities have mainly undergone residential deconcentration processes. Nevertheless, employment deconcentration is also at play, affecting the inner areas. These could become dependent on advanced tertiary activities, exclusive retail and luxury shops, and high standard housing as a result of the loss of their more traditional activities. Changes in lifestyle and high levels of motorization influence these new spatial patterns.

The two case studies – Madrid and Valladolid – show that urban planning has encouraged this process through built-up area reassessment techniques. In parallel, newly-built-up areas in peripheral states, whether developed spontaneously or through planning, have driven deconcentration, normally without taking account of the local labour market specificities. During the 1990s, two main confluent variables played major roles: (1) the huge price increases of real estate in central areas; (2) the deliberate Madrid regional political decision of spreading economic activities more widely, even those traditionally linked to the city core such as offices, retail, and public services. These include advanced producer services, business parks, universities, and cultural facilities. A gradual erosion of the existing monocentric spatial structure has been brought about by the regional government land-use policy and the development of new transport infrastructures: the regional railway, subway, ring roads and airport enlargement.

Employment opportunities in both Madrid and Valladolid are highly concentrated within the central city, especially in Valladolid where economic deconcentration processes are in their infancy. The deconcentration of employment and the resulting changes in economic land use has not led to the emergence of local employment sub-markets in the suburban rings in either Madrid or Valladolid. Consequently, the amount of commuting is increasing tremendously in a multi-directional pattern (not only inwards and outwards), even though the Madrid urban core continues to be the main commuting destination and the central city of Valladolid dominates even more.

The discussion in this chapter concentrates on how regional and urban planning has influenced economic deconcentration in the context of a market-led process focused on a services sector characterized by huge price increases of real estate in central areas, the search for an appropriate environment for employees in the context of new life styles, and the restructuring of big companies (merging processes) in the framework of globalizing European markets. We start with a brief presentation of the regulation framework and continue with the case studies' definition of boundaries. We then describe the design of the analysis, paying particular attention to some methodological issues. In section 4, we present the case studies profile. The prime focus in section 5 is the process of employment deconcentration as it applies in both case studies. Finally, our main conclusions are presented in section 6.

5.2
The regulation framework: Town and Country planning and specialized planning determining the deconcentration processes in Spain

The metropolitan legal foundations were established after the Civil War, during the 1940s and 1950s, when some urban agglomerations received *Big City* status[1]. These were Madrid, Barcelona, Valencia, and Bilbao. But that is not to say that there was a clear planning scheme or a real metropolitan government. After 1956, the legal shifts of Spanish urban planning have been subject to constant review (1975, 1990, 1998), but no specific metropolitan regulation was ever approved. Only Madrid and Barcelona acquired a Metropolitan Plan, supported in the case of Madrid by a Capital Status Act enacted by Parliament. In 1963, in accordance with Madrid's exceptional status, a Master Plan that included a specialized authority (COPLACO) to put it into effect was drawn up and enacted.

The arrival of democracy and the shaping of the new Autonomous Community structure forced a general discussion on the metropolitan areas and their possibilities of self-government. Paradoxically, the decentralization pattern represented by the Autonomous Communities had a negative effect on the survival of the metropolitan authorities with urban planning scope. The view was taken that these institutions were no longer appropriate in a decentralized context; a few years later, the Metropolitan Planning structure of Bilbao (1980), Valencia (1986) and Barcelona (1987) disappeared. Before it was dissolved (July 1983), the Metropolitan Authority of Madrid (COPLACO) transferred its planning responsibilities to the Madrid Autonomous Community.

The current legal framework, and specifically the 1985 Local Government Act, allows Autonomous Communities to create local institutions in their own territory embracing a set of municipalities. The three possibilities mentioned in the Act are: the region, the metropolitan area, and the municipal commonwealth. The metropolitan areas are local institutions integrated by the municipalities of big urban agglomerations. Their urban settlements maintain economic and social relations that oblige the joint planning and coordination of services, public works, and urban amenities. Responsibility for the metropolitan areas lies within the Autonomous Communities, which can create, modify and suppress them through legislation. The Local Government Act bases the creation of the metropolitan institutions on two main needs: joint planning for wide, complex territories that exceed the municipal boundaries; the management of services and works appropriate to the metropolitan scale.

The Autonomous Communities have scarcely developed the possibilities of the metropolitan areas. However, in some cases the autonomous legal framework dealing with local government refers explicitly to the metropolitan institutions. The most meaningful example is that of Catalonia with the Local Government and Municipal Act of Catalonia (8/1987), which prepares for the possibility of creating Metropolitan Authorities.

Spain has recently entered the stage in the process of urbanization that is marked by a general dispersion of the cities into their surrounding territories and the reinforcement of the metropolization processes. Once the economic crisis of the first part of the 1990s had been overcome, Spanish cities of any size entered a stage characterized by weak demographic growth and extensive spatial sprawl. The results of this situation are complex and include: the emergence of technological and business parks as tools of urban marketing for the competition between cities; the reorganization and modernization of the infrastructure (roads, railroads, harbours, airports, and so forth); and the consolidation of new central areas devoted to tertiary sectors such as shopping and leisure centres, mostly located in the metropolitan periphery.

The case of Valladolid was quite different; this and the surrounding municipalities have never been considered as a metropolitan area, nor have they been regulated through a Metropolitan Plan. Each municipality has remained as an independent body for administrative matters, including planning. Only recently (1998) has a territorial sub regional division (designated 'Valladolid and the surrounding area') been approved with the support of the Town and Country Planning Guidelines for the whole Castilla y León Region.

5.3
Definition of boundaries and description of methods used in the case studies

In Madrid, we have followed the administrative-functional boundaries. The Madrid municipality is divided into two well-defined areas: urban core, including six inner central city districts surrounded by the first highway (M-30); and the outer central city with the remaining fifteen peripheral districts of the Madrid municipality.

Outside the Madrid municipality, two rings have been defined: the inner and outer suburban rings (Figure 5.1). The inner ring's boundaries are those established when the Metropolitan Area was created in 1963 along the lines of the American Standard Metropolitan Statistical Areas. The Metropolitan Area was extended during the 1970s to incorporate a total of 26 municipalities. In the 1990s, the former new town of Tres Cantos also attained municipal status. The current 27 municipalities belonging to the inner suburban ring were governed by a specialist metropolitan authority (COPLACO) responsible for the urban and territorial planning scheme. After the establishment of autonomous status in 1983, the metropolitan ring was eliminated as an administrative entity, even though scholars and practitioners continue to refer to it as the functional territorial unit where the advanced processes of multifunctionalization operate. We assert that the economic deconcentration in this ring achieved the most outstanding results during the 1990s.

From the point of view of this research, the outer suburban ring is considered to be the familiar rural-urban fringe: urban functions (residence, manufactory, retail, leisure) coexist with rural activities, retaining some rural population. The characteristic that therefore better encapsulates the qualities of this outer suburban ring is the mixture of functions and the process of change affecting all the territorial aspects (functional, morphological, and social). The two kinds of deconcentration are proceeding at a different pace: residential deconcentration underwent a high growth rate during the 1990s; economic deconcentration fell behind, except in the southeast corridor (in the direction towards Valencia road) and in the southwest corridor (in the direction towards Toledo).

Valladolid has not yet become a true Metropolitan Area, since the main conditions for that status have not been fulfilled, including the demographic conditions (most of the surrounding municipalities do not reach 10,000 inhabitants) and the socio-economic conditions (the economic and labour flows are very low). The only aspect indicative of the metropolization process is the residential deconcentration from the central city to the municipalities nearby; people are looking for cheaper housing prices and better living and environmental conditions.

Consequently, the boundaries taken for this case study are those established for planning purposes in the Town and Country Planning Guidelines approved by the

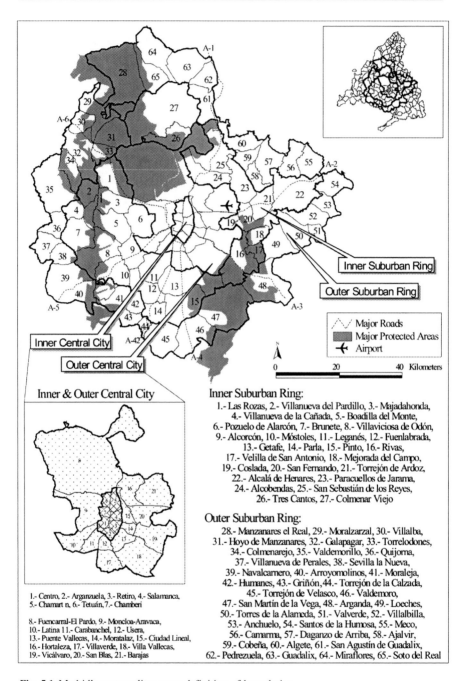

Fig. 5.1 Madrid's metropolitan area: definition of boundaries

Inner & Outer Central City

1.- Centro, 2.- Arganzuela, 3.- Retiro, 4.- Salamanca,
5.- Chamart n, 6.- Tetuán, 7.- Chamberí

8.- Fuencarral-El Pardo, 9.- Moncloa-Aravaca,
10.- Latina 11.- Carabanchel, 12.- Usera,
13.- Puente Vallecas, 14.- Moratalaz, 15.- Ciudad Lineal,
16.- Hortaleza, 17.- Villaverde, 18.- Villa Vallecas,
19.- Vicálvaro, 20.- San Blas, 21.- Barajas

Inner Suburban Ring:
1.- Las Rozas, 2.- Villanueva del Pardillo, 3.- Majadahonda,
4.- Villanueva de la Cañada, 5.- Boadilla del Monte,
6.- Pozuelo de Alarcón, 7.- Brunete, 8.- Villaviciosa de Odón,
9.- Alcorcón, 10.- Móstoles, 11.- Leganés, 12.- Fuenlabrada,
13.- Getafe, 14.- Parla, 15.- Pinto, 16.- Rivas,
17.- Velilla de San Antonio, 18.- Mejorada del Campo,
19.- Coslada, 20.- San Fernando, 21.- Torrejón de Ardoz,
22.- Alcalá de Henares, 23.- Paracuellos de Jarama,
24.- Alcobendas, 25.- San Sebastián de los Reyes,
26.- Tres Cantos, 27.- Colmenar Viejo

Outer Suburban Ring:
28.- Manzanares el Real, 29.- Moralzarzal, 30.- Villalba,
31.- Hoyo de Manzanares, 32.- Galapagar, 33.- Torrelodones,
34.- Colmenarejo, 35.- Valdemorillo, 36.- Quijorna,
37.- Villanueva de Perales, 38.- Sevilla la Nueva,
39.- Navalcarnero, 40.- Arroyomolinos, 41.- Moraleja,
42.- Humanes, 43.- Griñón, 44.- Torrejón de la Calzada,
45.- Torrejón de Velasco, 46.- Valdemoro,
47.- San Martín de la Vega, 48.- Arganda, 49.- Loeches,
50.- Torres de la Alameda, 51.- Valverde, 52.- Villalbilla,
53.- Anchuelo, 54.- Santos de la Humosa, 55.- Meco,
56.- Camarma, 57.- Daganzo de Arriba, 58.- Ajalvir,
59.- Cobeña, 60.- Algete, 61.- San Agustín de Guadalix,
62.- Pedrezuela, 63.- Guadalix, 64.- Miraflores, 65.- Soto del Real

Regional Parliament in 1998. The areas considered are (Figure 5.2):

- Central city: Valladolid municipality.
- Inner suburban ring: twelve municipalities bordering the Valladolid municipality.
- Outer suburban ring: the other ten municipalities from the inner ring to the outer
  border of the planning territory defined by the guidelines mentioned above.

The two case studies analysed involve data sources for economic and employment
deconcentration that differ in scope and quality. Madrid has a rich data
resource through the information provided by the Statistical Institute of Madrid's
Autonomous Community, but Valladolid lacks a counterpart institution and consequently access to comparable data has been difficult. In addition to the analysis

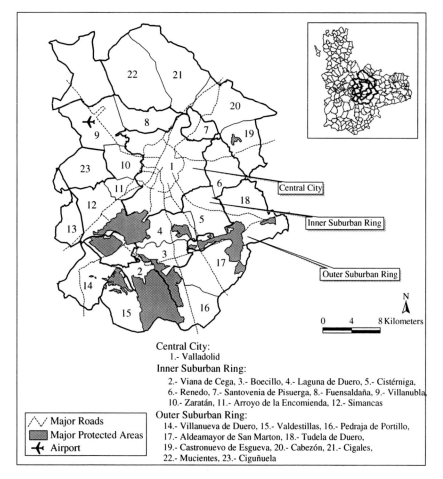

Central City:
  1.- Valladolid
Inner Suburban Ring:
  2.- Viana de Cega, 3.- Boecillo, 4.- Laguna de Duero, 5.- Cistérniga,
  6.- Renedo, 7.- Santovenia de Pisuerga, 8.- Fuensaldaña, 9.- Villanubla
  10.- Zaratán, 11.- Arroyo de la Encomienda, 12.- Simancas
Outer Suburban Ring:
  14.- Villanueva de Duero, 15.- Valdestillas, 16.- Pedraja de Portillo,
  17.- Aldeamayor de San Marton, 18.- Tudela de Duero,
  19.- Castronuevo de Esgueva, 20.- Cabezón, 21.- Cigales,
  22.- Mucientes, 23.- Ciguñuela

/\\/ Major Roads
▨ Major Protected Areas
✈ Airport

Fig. 5.2 Valladolid's urban agglomeration: definition of boundaries

of the population census, the evaluation of economic and employment deconcentration in Madrid's case has been based primarily on the analysis of the Local Workplaces Directory (1998, 1999, 2000 and 2001), the most fruitful resource for this topic. In the case of Valladolid, the lack of a comparable data source has obliged us to use the available data on employees and enterprises of the Social Security Affiliation for the period 1999–2000.

In order to operationalize the employment density analysis, we superimposed on the whole study area of the administrative and land-use layers a geometric network comprising a number of rings drawn at regular intervals from the city centre (10 km. in both case studies). Later, we split these rings into the sectors and wedges structured by the main transport highways that contribute to the distribution of economic activities over the territory in the Madrid case and a compass rose composition for Valladolid. The challenge was to identify meaningful location patterns by means of a pie-ring chart. As far as mixed uses are concerned, we have tried to verify the degree to which two or even three economic uses coexist within the same ring/wedge. The level of mixed use was calculated by measuring the relative employment specialization by economic branch and combining and comparing these so as to identify the dominant economic activities/employment. To arrive at a meaningful result, we applied a simple, straightforward methodology:

• An activity is considered to have significant weight in a specific activity in a spatial sector when it exceeds 16.6 percent (one sixth of 100 percent) of total activity.
• When several activities reach this weight in the same sector, it is considered to be multifunctional.
• When the percentage of the employees in a spatial sector who work in a specific activity exceeds the threshold of 33.2 percent, we conclude that the sector specializes in that activity.

5.4
Case studies profile

The Madrid Autonomous Community is located in the core of the peninsula and covers a surface of $8,030.1 \text{ km}^2$. The Community encompasses 179 municipalities, including Madrid — the capital of both the state and the Autonomous Community. Madrid's profile is that of a great metropolis, accommodating more than 5 million inhabitants (2001) within the metropolitan area, creating a boundary effect against the surrounding provinces and regions in economic and labour terms and in demographic and residential sprawl.

The Madrid municipality is the eighth largest city in Europe; it is a major financial and economic centre, well equipped with advanced services. Madrid has a vibrant cultural, leisure, and nightlife scene. In 1995, 53 percent of the Region's theatres and cinemas, 69 percent of libraries, and 73 percent of the museums and cultural centres were located in Madrid. Many international congresses, conferences, and exhibitions are held there.

During the last decade, new organizational forms within the productive system have forced a number of changes that can be summed up as follows:

- Peripheral expansion: The built-up area keeps expanding; this process is associated with the increasing motorization rate.
- Displacement of central activities (industry, commerce, offices etc) towards peripheral locations, generating an important flow of mobility for work, leisure, and tourism, which leads to an increase of employment.

The decentralization processes that have been going on since the 1970s are varied in nature although related to a great extent to the residential market. The considerable increases in housing prices inside the central city have resulted in the following: the appearance of satellite towns around the city and its metropolitan periphery; the conversion of former secondary residences, mostly located in the north and northwest side of Madrid municipality close to the Sierra of Guadarrama; the consolidation of former low-density urbanizations scattered throughout the territory; and, importantly in relation to our project, the attraction of economic activities and therefore of employment resulting from the move from central to more peripheral locations or to in situ-growth.

Nowadays, there is a tendency for activities to spread into the metropolitan periphery (second and third ring) at distances between 20 and 30 km from the central city. This tendency applies particularly to advanced services, financing, marketing, legal assistance, and so forth, even though considerable expansion of these activities towards certain peripheral districts has been observed since the mid 1990s. The commercial sector is one of the most outstanding in the economy of Madrid, especially the new commercial and leisure complexes (hypermarkets, commercial and leisure parks) that have generated new consumption spaces around the main communication routes.

Bearing in mind this economic and functional background, Madrid can be considered the most suitable laboratory for the study of such processes that go beyond the purely administrative boundaries. These processes can be seen in the neighbouring provinces of Guadalajara, Toledo, and Segovia (Angelet Cladellas, 2000; Celada Crespo and Méndez, 1994; Galve Martín, 1992). For the purposes of this project, we analysed 66 municipalities in total.

Valladolid, located in the northern sector of the Spanish *Meseta,* has been the capital of the Castilla y León region since 1983. The city is the tenth in terms of population size; it is classified within the Spanish urban system as a regional metropolis. During the last few years, Valladolid has become consolidated as an important urban centre within its region, thanks to its excellent geographical position, its urban hierarchy, and its industrial and economic services background. The current phenomenon of urban sprawl is easy to identify. Valladolid has spread over the territory, even though the city itself has been predominantly residential following the search for new residential lifestyles (de las Rivas, 1998: 219–221). Within the framework of this project we have analysed the 23 municipalities included in the "Town and Country Planning Guidelines of Valladolid and Surroundings" (Alonso, 1993).

5.5
Employment deconcentration

5.5.1
Madrid's employment deconcentration

Unlike Valladolid, Madrid has developed since the late 1980s through uncontrolled growth, a speculative process in which the management of public administration has failed to keep up with the physical and economic growth. In spite of the fact that during the last 15 years Madrid has undergone substantial economic growth, non-residential deconcentration processes follow a widely-spread spatial pattern. Some differences can be observed when considering the three main sectors: industry, new commercial developments, and offices.

With respect to the industrial sector, most authors agree that industrial firms started to disappear from Madrid's central city ten years ago as a result of technological innovations, lack of adequate premises, environmental requirements (migration of graphic arts, reprography, car repair garages, and so forth to the first ring), and the pressures of highly competitive residential land uses (Pardo, 2004).

The decline of industrial employment has run parallel to the employment growth within the tertiary sector; the closing and migration of old industrial premises is closely connected with land-use re-classification projects. The preferred location destinies have tended to be the southern metropolitan municipalities and the Henares' corridor within the first and second suburban rings (Celada Crespo, 1998; Celada Crespo, 1999; López de Lucio, 1999; Méndez, 1997). The underlying reasons for this trend seem to be lower land prices and the targeting of the southern metropolitan area as Urgent Re-industrializing Zones. Some deconcentration processes have crossed the border of the region to profit from EU and regional subsidies. The array of activities within the new industrial developments can hardly be called truly industrial processes; we find storage premises, logistic areas, car concessionaires, furniture showrooms, and so forth. Some firms search out strategic locations; logistic enterprises accumulate round an airport, for example. From the geographical point of view, experts have failed to discover why some municipalities are more appealing than others when their background conditions are similar.

Turning to new commercial/leisure complexes, deconcentration trends have run parallel to the extensive communication infrastructure layout (Méndez & Ondátegui, 1999). Here, when considering the reasons underlying the locations of new shopping/leisure malls, authors' opinions divide according to two contradictory theories. Do these facilities follow residential developments or do they deconcentrate, seeking high-accessibility locations in a context of improved transportation across long distances and a growing preference for suburban and rural living? Within Madrid central city, processes such as these have led to the disappearance of traditional little shops in favour of big supermarkets and discount chains and a greater specialization of commerce.

Tertiary activities, particularly offices, display selective location preferences in the context of significant geographic movements of people and jobs. Besides the CBD, which accommodates prime headquarters, most firms move to the north highway, the northwest corridor, and two business parks in the northeast (Alcobendas and San Sebastián de los Reyes) and the Juan Carlos I's Fairground park close to the airport city complex (Carrera Sánchez, 1995; Méndez & Ondátegui, 1999). The office market in the periphery, which has been booming during the last five years, has forced prices down and led to the displacement of offices to the first ring.

The Spanish companies that have featured most actively in the real-estate disinvestment belong to the banking and energetic sector and, to a lesser degree, to insurance services and the pharmaceuticals sector. All have benefited from the current buying frenzy on the Spanish office market, especially in the city of Madrid. The massive sale of real estate in the current decade has had a clear motivation: the capital appreciation associated with property. The increase in property prices has allowed companies to accumulate capital; although the buildings are out of date, the big companies possess the best and most central properties in the cities in which they are located, a fact that reflects their financial power. The four enterprises that disposed of most real estate between 2000 and 2004 -BBVA, SCH, Telefonica and Endesa – obtained more than one billion euro in capital appreciation. These figures prove the good yields of the real-estate business in the last few years, yields which the stock markets have not matched. Considering only the 20 most active companies in the displacement of their headquarters and other offices, the economic volume that they have handled exceeds 4,500 million euro. But at the moment of confronting their real-estate strategy, the opportunities left open to these companies have been diminished to two. The first option is to regroup the staff distributed in different locations in a unique new construction, provided with the most modern facilities and placed in the periphery of the city, in property that is either owned or rented (Photo 5.1). The second option is to continue to use the same office block, but sell the property and lease it back from the new owner; the office block can be in the downtown area or in the periphery.

In general terms, all researchers agree about the poor level of planning coordination across and within sectors and at different government levels, except for the public transport policies within the Madrid region (Valenzuela, 1994). The different policies have been developed in watertight compartments. Regional and local government authorities usually differ in their strategy, the former trying to reach territorial balance, the latter to expand. Only shopping malls, universities, and hospitals seem to have coordinated their strategies with transport infrastructures.

Comparing population and employment growth in the late 1990s, the dissimilarity of the trends in both dimensions is clear. The Outer Suburban Ring leads the population growth in the functional metropolitan area (Table 5.1 and Figure 5.3) while the central city maintains a remarkable level of employment growth even though top place belongs to the Inner Suburban Ring.

Photo 5.1 Santander Holding Bank city's aerial photography

The correlation between population growth and local employment reinforces the idea of a more segregated housing location pattern in contrast with a dispersed local employment pattern. In the case of Madrid, the highest population increases appear in the outer ring, mainly in the west/northwest, south, and northeast, while employment spreads out following a more gradual profile and favouring the inner

Table 5.1 Madrid's population breakdown by functional areas, 1991–2001

Areas	1991	1996	2001	1991–2001	
					Percent
Inner Central City (*)	990,679	915,318	931,432	−59,247	−6
Outer Central City (*)	2,019,813	1,951,532	1,972,444	−47,369	−2.3
Inner Suburban Ring	1,582,077	1,709,956	1,906,360	324,283	20.5
Outer Suburban Ring	172,657	232,592	325,592	152,935	88.6
Total	4,765,226	4,809,398	5,135,828	370,602	7.8

Source: Statistical National Institute and Madrid Autonomous Statistical Institute.
(*) 2001 cell contains data for the year 2000.

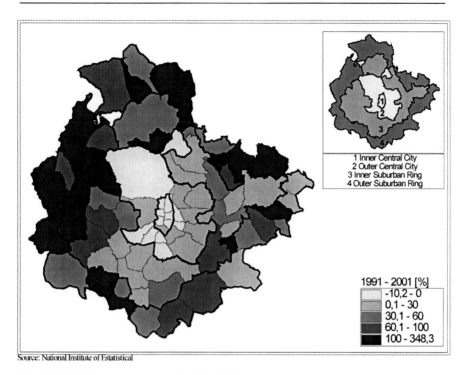

1 Inner Central City
2 Outer Central City
3 Inner Suburban Ring
4 Outer Suburban Ring

1991 - 2001 [%]
-10,2 - 0
0,1 - 30
30,1 - 60
60,1 - 100
100 - 348,3

Source: National Institute of Estatistical

Fig. 5.3 Madrid – population growth, 1991–2001

suburban ring. There, not only companies, but also public and private institutions (universities, hospitals, and so forth) have settled during the last decade. The number of companies settled in some municipalities within the inner suburban ring grew by more than 200 percent during the decade (Villanueva del Pardillo 704.8 percent; Las Rozas de Madrid 309.6 percent; Rivas-Vaciamadrid, 258.9 percent; Villanueva de la Cañada, 231.7 percent). A complementary correlation between the location of local employment and residents in work in the Madrid metropolitan area also confirms this hypothesis. People look for high-quality residential areas far from the metropolitan core; rapid job deconcentration, particularly from the city to the inner ring, still fails to catch up with the remarkable suburbanization of population to the outer ring. So, while the dependence on the employment of residents in the inner rings is decreasing, those living in the outer municipalities contribute to the commuting problems.

In the Madrid Metropolitan Area, both the core and the outer central city have registered a decrease of population, the highest in the whole metropolitan area. In the inner-outer central city, some districts lost more than 10 percent of their population in 10 years; in fact, except for the east/southeast of the municipality, the whole built-up area has undergone a density decrease. The Madrid inner ring has had a general increase of population (11.5 percent in the last 5 years), led mainly by the west side of the ring. Growth in the outer suburban ring has been even faster (40 percent in the last 5 years) as a result of the urban sprawl processes based on a low-density typology of detached and semi-detached housing developments.

The urban deconcentration in Madrid remains mostly residential and consequently the Metropolitan Area shows an unbalanced employment/population relationship. The only areas with a clear labour surplus are the city's urban core together with some of the outer ring municipalities. Those districts with a balanced relationship are situated mainly in the Outer Suburban Ring. The employment evolution between 1990 and 2001 in the Madrid functional area has undergone a deconcentration process favouring the municipalities located on the west side and some scattered municipalities in the northeast and southeast (Figure 5.4). The analysis of deconcentration trends on a ring scale point to a similar process for employment growth, although the outer ring has played a more active part during the last decade. In contrast, the employment evolution in the central city stagnated during the same period.

Nevertheless, in 2001, the Madrid municipality still accounted for 66.5 percent of the total employment; in second place was the inner ring (27.8 percent). With

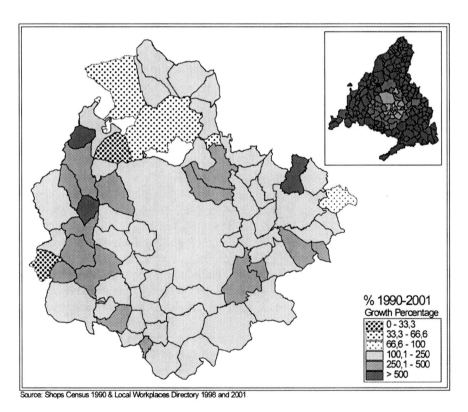

Source: Shops Census 1990 & Local Workplaces Directory 1998 and 2001

Fig. 5.4 Madrid – employment evolution, 1990–2001

Table 5.2 Madrid's employment breakdown by economic sectors, 1990–2001

Spatial unit	Year	Total employment		Retailing/consumer services		Manufacturing/ construction		Producer services	
		Absolute	Share in percent	Absolute	Share in percent	Absolute	Share in percent	Absolute	Share in percent
CBD/centre	1990	669,014	47.3	404,521	48.6	83,483	26.6	180,853	67.7
of central city	2001	690,978	41.1	323,441	41.7	99,748	24.9	266,570	58.3
Rest central	1990	399,999	28.3	244,683	29.4	102,098	32.5	53,218	19.9
city	2001	427,132	25.4	197,004	25.4	109,860	27.4	119,937	24.0
Inner	1990	286,503	20.3	157,803	19.0	99,125	31.5	29,296	11.0
suburban ring	2001	467,694	27.8	217,492	28.0	147,067	36.6	102,872	20.6
Outer	1990	58,762	4.2	25,434	3.1	29,501	9.4	3,713	1.4
suburban ring	2001	94,401	5.6	38,440	5.0	44,692	11.1	11,108	2.2
Total	1990	1,414,278	100	832,441	100	314,207	100	267,080	100
urbanized area	2001	1,680,205	100	776,377	100	401,367	100	500,487	100

Source: Madrid Autonomous Statistical Institute.

only 5.6 percent of the employment, the outer ring was less relevant in employment terms (Table 5.2). In contrast, the employment growth has favoured the inner suburban ring, where the growth of employees in the period 1990–2001 reached 63.2 percent. The growth was concentrated in a few municipalities (Villanueva del Pardillo, Villalba and Camarna).

Of course, Madrid offers a wide range of employment opportunities. The activity rates during the 1990s show an expanding economy; Madrid and all the municipalities included in the inner ring have increased their activity rates by at least five points; the increase has been ten points or more in some cases more distant from Madrid. The increase in activity rates during the period 1991–2001 in the outer ring is even more striking, with gains of over 15 points in all the municipalities and exceeding 30 points in some cases. Population growth in this ring during the last decade has been relatively high, even exceeding 100 percent; most of the new residents are young professional couples living in owner-occupied houses.

When comparing the functional zones described, only the Madrid Urban Core has an employment surplus; the values in the outer Madrid districts are below average, while the local employment-local working population relationships in the suburban rings are balanced (Figure 5.5). At the municipal level, in the Madrid Metropolitan Area the municipalities with a labour surplus are located in a northeast-southwest arch belonging to the east inner ring and south outer ring sectors. Other than in four of the Madrid districts, an exceptional surplus index (more than 2) is only found in some municipalities of the outer ring bordering the industrial "Henares' Corridor".

In general terms, the employment density in the Madrid metropolitan area displays a clear spatial pattern that follows a decreasing clockwise sequence (Figure 5.6). The northern and northeast wedges show the highest employment densities; the former is linked to Madrid's CBD. A few inner and outer suburban

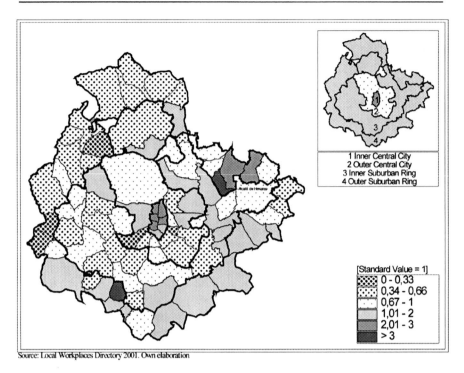

Source: Local Workplaces Directory 2001. Own elaboration

Fig. 5.5 Madrid – local employees/local working population, 2001

municipalities have business and science parks, together with universities and administration and public services. In this case, the employment distance decay model appears to apply. The latter fits the well-known Henares' industrial axis.

The two southeast wedges have also reached high employment densities; both accommodate working-class districts and a number of industrial and logistic municipalities along the Valencia and Andalusia' main transport axes. The next three wedges follow a decreasing pattern of dominant residential specialization combined with public and private services to the local and metropolitan population. Only the more distant municipalities in the south-west wedge contradict the distance decay model due to the settlement of some industrial and service companies currently together with the opening of a big leisure and commercial centre (Xanadú complex in Arroyomolinos).

The retail employment density replicates the decreasing clockwise sequence (Figure 5.6). The north and northeast wedges have the highest values through the presence of Madrid's districts and large retail and wholesale areas along the Henares' axis. Outside the Madrid municipality, the highest values per sector appear in the north and southeast, the former including big shopping malls in the municipalities of Alcobendas and San Sebastián de los Reyes, and the latter in that of Rivas-Vaciamadrid.

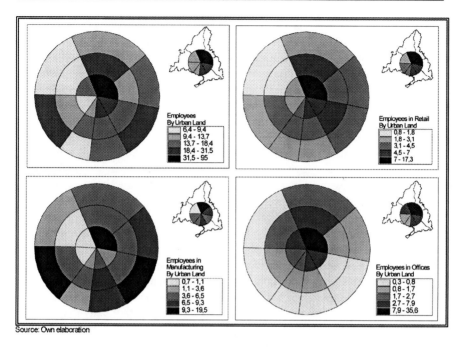

Fig. 5.6 Madrid metropolitan area – employment density, 1998

The northern wedge has the highest relative figures for manufacturing employment density, followed by the northeast and south (Figure 5.6). The figures for the north and northeast are both boosted by the weight of Madrid's districts. In fact, all the wedges except the northwest display medium-to-high manufacturing employment densities. However, an analysis by sector reveals the important role of the outskirt municipalities in the southeast (Arganda, Campo Real) and southwest (Arroyomolinos, Cubas de la Sagra, Griñón, Humanes de Madrid, Moraleja de Enmedio). The results in both these cases confirm the hypothesis that no productive space may be identified in the region as an industrial district in its full sense, although a series of territorial industrial groupings with the character of local productive systems has appeared. The most consolidated areas in this respect are centred around Fuenlabrada-Humanes de Madrid and Arganda del Rey; these areas could eventually become an "emerging industrial district", although the relatively recent development has not yet led to a bond between the productive and social aspects (creation of an industrial atmosphere, generation of innovation, consolidation of local institutions, and so forth) that characterises a district.

The spatial pattern of office employment density replicates the location trends of advanced tertiary services within the Madrid metropolitan area (Figure 5.6). The highest density values are found in the northern and northeast wedges; the former faithfully follows the distance decay model. The poorest densities appear on the southwest side of the metropolis. In general terms, the whole of the south has undergone a relative deprivation compared with the north. The two main transport highways to the Basque Country in the north and Galicia in the northwest have become key infrastructures in developing business and science parks. Here, banking, telecommunication and building companies have recently settled. This deconcentration model also correlates with the land prices spatial pattern: in other words, wherever new office developments appear prosperous low-density residential areas also contribute to the urban sprawl. Blue collar activities in the manufacturing sector are excluded.

The level of mixed use has been calculated by measuring, combining, and comparing the employment density by economic sector. We have avoided comparison with only residential uses since our focus is on economic rather than residential deconcentration. The methodology applied includes the selection of two different quantitative thresholds: the first (16.6 percent) defines a minimum economic presence by sector and the second (33.2 percent) identifies the dominance of an economic category.

The results can be seen in Figure 5.7. A preliminary breakdown by economic category highlights the strong concentration and segregated spatial pattern of manufacturing and, to a lesser extent, retail, while transport and public services are scattered throughout the whole metropolitan region. The spatial pattern confirms the statements previously made: industrial employment is mainly located in the southeast and southwest, but always in the sectors furthest from the metropolitan centre. On the other hand, retail employment is located mainly in the most distant

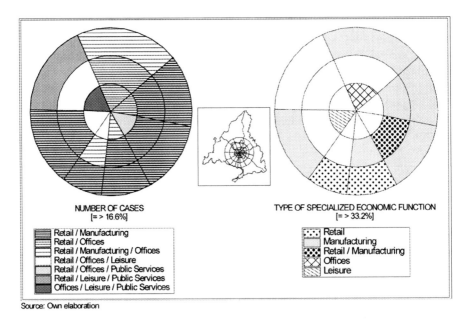

NUMBER OF CASES
[= > 16.6%]

Retail / Manufacturing
Retail / Offices
Retail / Manufacturing / Offices
Retail / Offices / Leisure
Retail / Offices / Public Services
Retail / Leisure / Public Services
Offices / Leisure / Public Services

TYPE OF SPECIALIZED ECONOMIC FUNCTION
[= > 33.2%]

Retail
Manufacturing
Retail / Manufacturing
Offices
Leisure

Source: Own elaboration

Fig. 5.7 Madrid – economic functions mixed uses, 2002

southern locations. The concentration rates for office employment are lower, but with a clear spatial pattern: the northern wedge has the strongest impact in Madrid's northern districts. Comparative figures for leisure employment are greatest in the northwest wedge and southwest Madrid's districts.

In summary, the assessment of economic mixed use confirms the hypothesis of a distant ring of manufacturing activities; these are more strongly affected by deconcentration processes, which tend to locate in the southeast and southwest as well as in the north-northeast. In general terms, this location pattern does not contradict the Madrid metropolitan area's traditional functional structure. On the contrary, the pattern is reinforced by the dispersal of the manufacturing activities. Deconcentrated retail activities have also moved to the south, while offices and leisure facilities are at the threshold of deconcentration processes, with the former moving to the prosperous north-northwest.

The highly concentrated and segregated spatial pattern of manufacturing and a lower level retail is worthy of note; transport and public services are scattered throughout the metropolitan region; concentration rates in office employment are not as high, but have a clear spatial preferences for the northern wedge. The bigger values for leisure jobs are concentrated in the northwest wedge.

5.5.2
Valladolid's employment deconcentration

The Valladolid municipality accounts for 86.4 percent of the total employment. This share represents a leading position in the labour market; in second place comes the inner ring (11.1 percent). The outer ring, with only 2.5 percent of the employment, is not relevant in employment terms (Table 5.3). In contrast, employment growth in the inner suburban ring rose by 29.4 percent in the period 1999-2001, with the growth concentrated in a few municipalities (Arroyo de la Encomienda, Boecillo and La Cistérniga).

The 2001 activity rates can be seen to be much lower in the Valladolid case (53.3) than in the inner ring municipality, largely because these have become dormitory towns (Arroyo de la Encomienda, 68.3). In contrast, activity rates in the outer ring municipalities are lower, because of their semi rural profile.

Valladolid, the capital of a less-well-developed inland region, is a more planned city than Madrid; public involvement in its growth has traditionally been substantial. Since the 1950s, Valladolid has been linked to car industries (Renault, Iveco, Michelin). Factories (mainly those with obsolete facilities) and logistic and distribution premises (Centrolid) are now leaving for cheaper industrial developments within the metropolitan area. Most of the economic activities are still located in the central city (approximately 90 percent), including a sector of prestigious office headquarters and Boecillo's Technological Park. This has been a successful model of "concentrated deconcentration" developed by regional administration; it has been devoted to the settlement of information and communication technology firms (Vodafone, Telefonica, for example).

Table 5.3 Valladolid's employment breakdown by economic sectors, 1999–2002

Spatial unit	Year	Total employment		Retailing/consumer services		Manufacturing/ construction		Producer services	
		Absolute	Share in percent	Absolute	Share in percent	Absolute	Share in percent	Absolute	Share in percent
CBD/centre of	1999	119,694	88.9	58,335	91.5	36,361	86.3	23,801	89.2
central city +	2002	130,943	86.4	65,084	89.3	36,436	83.0	28,249	86.6
Rest central city									
Inner suburban	1999	11,847	8.8	4,218	6.6	4,599	10.9	2,599	9.7
ring	2002	16,876	11.1	6,395	8.8	6,020	13.7	4,003	12.3
Outer suburban	1999	3,030	2.3	1,202	1.9	1,174	2.8	277	1.0
ring	2002	3,764	2.5	1,439	2.0	1,443	3.3	380	1.2
Total urbanized	1999	134,571	100	63,755	100	42,134	100	26,677	100
area	2002	151,583	100	72,918	100	43,899	100	32,632	100

Source: Ministry of Employment and Social Affairs.

The municipality of Valladolid views the deconcentration of non-residential activities towards the metropolitan area as a threat and has classified new industrial land within the last Structural Plan to reduce economic deconcentration. Companies have moved not only to metropolitan municipalities, but also to other provinces. Large shopping/leisure malls have also been built within the metropolitan area, forcing the closure of traditional small shops. Schools and education facilities have also deconcentrated in line with the residential deconcentration.

The new town and country planning guidelines for the territory surrounding Valladolid are an attempt to resolve the lack of coordination between the Valladolid central city and the metropolitan municipalities. This planning tool has, however, encountered opposition from the municipalities, who consider that it violates municipal autonomy. Valladolid lacks a metropolitan authority to coordinate the territorial planning of the different municipalities. Consequently, new informal and illegal developments have been allowed in the surrounding municipalities, which depend on Valladolid central city to guarantee basic supplies (water, electricity, sewerage, waste disposal).

The factors underlying non-residential deconcentration processes are mainly economic, including urban land prices and land availability and current industrial zone congestion within the central city. Good locations and accessibility plus public subsidies (the Technological Park of Boecillo) have contributed to the success of some deconcentration processes (concentrated deconcentration model) towards the inner suburban ring.

Comparing population and employment growth from the late 1990s, some kind of similarity can be found at the metropolitan level (Figure 5.8). Population growth is most concentrated in the Inner Suburban Ring, which is followed by the Outer Ring and then the Central City (Table 5.4). In contrast, the highest employment growths have favoured both rings, mainly in the southern sector. Valladolid's central city has at best stagnated during the last decade, while the inner suburban

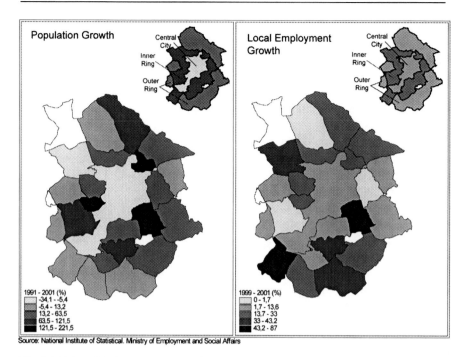

Source: National Institute of Statistical. Ministry of Employment and Social Affairs

Fig. 5.8 Valladolid – Population growth (1991–2001) and local employment growth (1999–2001)

ring has taken over the highest population growth (44.2 percent in the last 5 years). The outer suburban ring has recently experienced a population rise (13.4 percent in the last 5 years), a figure reflecting dynamics far below those of the inner ring.

The spatial pattern for Valladolid differs markedly from that of Madrid. Valladolid is an urban agglomeration in which the recent suburbanization of population has favoured the inner suburban ring, while the bypass and road network has supported the deconcentration of jobs and economic activities far away from the central city. Poor historical data series (1998–2002), hardly lead us to expect some kind of employment deconcentration in favour of the first suburban ring, since

Table 5.4 Valladolid's population by functional areas, 2001

Areas	1991	1996	2001	1991–2001	
					Percent
Central City	330,700	319,805	316,580	−14,120	−4,3
Inner Suburban Ring	24,122	30,588	44,123	20,001	82,9
Outer Suburban Ring	13,399	15,753	17,868	4,469	33,4
Total	368,221	366,146	378,571	10,350	2,8

Source: Statistical National Institute.

most of the outer municipalities are really rural-urban areas. As the percentages of new employment contracts for the period 1998–2002 show, the rates for the Valladolid municipality lag behind the increases in the other rings. The increase in employment contracts in Valladolid was only 15 percent compared with 55 percent in the inner suburban ring and 57 percent in the outer suburban ring, even though the contracts signed during this period in Valladolid municipality amount to 88.4 percent against 9.6 percent in the inner ring and 2 percent in the outer ring.

A slightly more favourable image of the employment deconcentration process can be obtained from information on workers affiliated to Social Security for the period 1999–2002. The Valladolid municipality holds a clear first position with 66.1 percent of the affiliation gains in absolute numbers (11,269 affiliated increment); the figures for the inner and outer rings are 29.5 percent and 5,036 affiliation gains and 4 percent and 746 gains respectively.

In contrast, the increment percentages of the three sectors in the same period were 9.41 percent in Valladolid, 29.8 percent in the inner ring, and 19.75 percent in the outer ring. A preliminary conclusion can therefore be drawn: The economic model in Valladolid is still highly concentrated and the process of deconcentration is only just starting with selective results in certain municipalities.

Our main findings can be summarized dealing with three economic sectors: manufacturing, retail and offices. Valladolid preserves a prominent position in industrial employment with 87.4 percent of the total, since most of the industrial land on offer is still in the central city, where the biggest industrial estates are located (Avance del Plan Industrial, 2002). On other hand, employment gains also take place in the inner periphery in those municipalities with urbanized land available (La Cistérniga, Santovenia) or even a technological park (Boecillo). These areas are all located in the eastern arch of the Valladolid agglomeration (Figure 5.9). Together, they account for 90 percent of the industrial employment increase in the whole ring. That is concentrated deconcentration. But even the poor industrial employment gain in the outer ring seems to be linked to the proximity of those municipalities in the eastern arch but with other patterns of physical location (road strips, scattered). The three municipalities with gains of over 25 employment places are located in the northeast and southwest sectors of the outer ring.

Assuming that the best data source for the whole period (1990–2000) refers to the generation of industrial employment, we can state that deconcentration processes are still at an early stage. Valladolid city has acquired more than 69 percent of new industrial employment during the last decade. Consequently, the employment deconcentration process in this case is at an early stage, and the inner suburban ring has hardly benefited, with only 22 percent of the total. As far as the spatial pattern is concerned, the industrial deconcentration is mostly located in the eastern arch of the metropolitan area. That it dates from the second half of the 1990s is evidence of how recent is the generation of the new employment in the southern area of the inner and outer ring. Similar early deconcentration processes can be identified in most of the economic sectors; even the outer ring can lead the

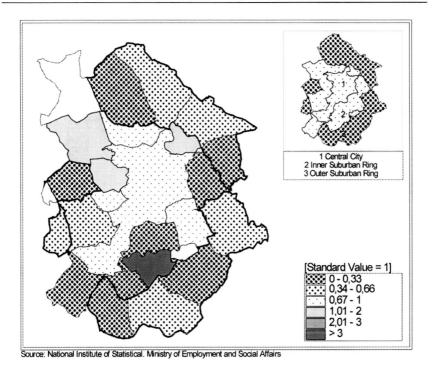

1 Central City
2 Inner Suburban Ring
3 Outer Suburban Ring

[Standard Value = 1]
0 - 0,33
0,34 - 0,66
0,67 - 1
1,01 - 2
2,01 - 3
> 3

Source: National Institute of Statistical. Ministry of Employment and Social Affairs

Fig. 5.9 Valladolid – local employees/local working population, 2001

percentage increase in employment, bearing in mind that its departure point was very low.

Some preliminary findings dealing with the deconcentration spatial pattern can be put forward, while bearing in mind that, in our approach, employment is related to urban land (which is not equivalent to the built-up area) and that data is only available for one year (1998). The results of the density approach related to urban land surface show that the central city density is over four times that of the rings (28.8). By sectors, the highest density values are found for the southern part of the inner ring, where some industrial estates are located (La Cistérniga and Boecillo) (Figure 5.10).

As expected, the highest retail densities are in the central city, where 88.7 percent of the retail employees and 63.1 percent of the urban surface are concentrated. Of the ring sectors, only one has a medium-high density value: the outer sector of the north-western ring, where the airport and new retail structures are located (Figure 5.10). The relatively high densities result from the reduced urban land surface rather than the number of employees. A third density level with medium-low densities can be observed in the eastern half of both rings. At wedge level, a clockwise density decline occurs, ranging from the highest values in the north-east to the lowest in the north-western corner.

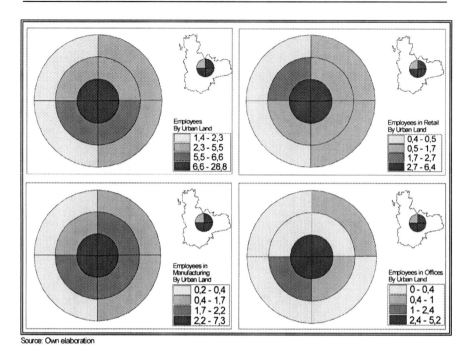

Fig. 5.10 Valladolid – employment density, 1998

In manufacturing, the highest density values are once again in the central city; translated into relative figures, the shares are 88.7 percent of the employment and 63.1 percent of the urban surface. With five fewer density points, three inner ring sectors belong to the medium-high interval. The largest peripheral estates are located in these sectors (Santovenia, La Cistérniga, Boecillo). The lower density values can be seen in the outer and western sectors (Figure 5.10). In terms of wedges, the highest density is also located in the north-eastern corner of the diagram, where several dynamic municipalities other than Valladolid are located (Santovenia, Cigales, for example). The density values of the next clockwise sectors are slightly lower (5 and 4.7), but still much higher than the next (north-western) sector, again at the bottom of the economic activity deconcentration.

The primary position of the central city in the office sector is shown by both absolute and relative values in employees (17,035) and in urban surface, even if the density in lower than in the others considered (5.2). With respect to offices, only the south-western inner ring sector has any relevance; there the Boecillo Technological Park is located, with 1,538 employees and a density of 2.4. Only the inner eastern sector reaches a density rate of 1; there, the only true dormitory town is located (Laguna de Duero). No other sector in the compass rose diagram exceeds the density rate of 1 (Figure 5.10). In terms of wedges, surprisingly similar densities are shown in three sectors with values between 3 and 4. As in other activity sectors, the lowest value is located in the north-western wedge (0.8), a figure that stresses the poor employment opportunities.

Valladolid hardly has a CBD, but there is an area of high economic concentration associated with ring one. Its only connections with what should be the CBD are the roads leaving the Central City; with the only high-density values along them, mostly in industrial employment. The mononuclearity of Valladolid is even more striking than in Madrid; no suburban centre has become a truly multifunctional city; even the larger centres are dormitory towns or low-density settlements.

The last investigation of economic deconcentration in the Valladolid case was to assess the multifunctional degree at sector level for the year 2002 using employment information for the six economic sectors chosen. As shown in Figure 5.11, the mixture of uses covers a wide range of combinations in both peripheral rings. The chart is divided into twelve radial-concentric sectors, half with no clear specialization (mostly the inner ring); the only exceptions are the manufacturing specialization of the north-eastern ring and the leisure specialization of the outer western arch. The pie chart suggests the main conclusion: the multifunctionallity reaches the maximum in Valladolid municipality; concerning the inner suburban ring the economic activity mixture affects to some activities depending on their situations. Finally, the situation in the outer suburban ring is similar, but the proximity can affect more and scattered functions even if the decentralization process is less developed.

Recently, a new strategy of municipal competitiveness has appeared among metropolitan municipalities. Bearing in mind that urban planning is under the

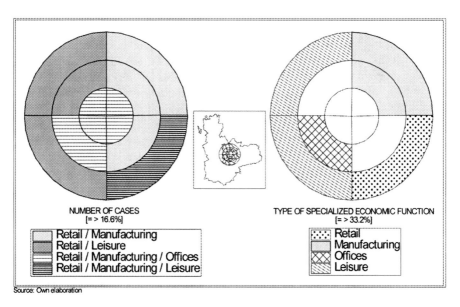

NUMBER OF CASES
[=> 16.6%]
Retail / Manufacturing
Retail / Leisure
Retail / Manufacturing / Offices
Retail / Manufacturing / Leisure

TYPE OF SPECIALIZED ECONOMIC FUNCTION
[=> 33.2%]
Retail
Manufacturing
Offices
Leisure

Source: Own elaboration

Fig. 5.11 Valladolid. Economic Functions Mixed Uses (2002)

governance of regional and local administration (public administration controls land-use classification and the location or facilities), the statement that the private sector provides the demand and the public sector the supply seems to approximate to reality. Real-estate developers, shopping/leisure malls and hotel companies are moving out of the Valladolid municipality while the central city is struggling to retain these activities. Private agents are directed by economic conjuncture and profitability criteria (land prices, communications and accessibility, workforce), so they deconcentrate commercial and leisure activities; also the closeness to other related companies (within the car sector), and a pleasant environmental location play a part.

Reactions about the extent to which an attempt has been made to coordinate policies both across and within sectors, and at different government levels, are discouraging. Some scholars stress that there is a strategy to deconcentrate population, but not services. Valladolid lacks a relation between territorial and sectoral policies. Coordination, collaboration, and cooperation are empty concepts; only water and waste disposal rate coordination efforts. Small municipalities within the metropolitan area, all of which want to grow, spoil valuable landscapes or develop without previously solving the problem of water supply. Sectoral policies determine different trends, while transport policies favour deconcentration processes. Environmental policies seek to limit deconcentration. However, environmental policies sometimes contribute to the ejection of pollutant industries. Valladolid must now adapt 166 factories to meet the new European Directive and the new Environmental Protection Act. Some of the factories will be able to adapt, but some will have to move. In the case of Valladolid, in future high speed trains will have big impacts and consequences. The building of underground urban infrastructures will also favour new economic and residential development. Ambitious infrastructure policies could be said to favour deconcentration, even indirectly. New residential developments force the development of new facilities and services.

However, other scholars (López de Lucio, 1999) surmise that economic activity lacks the circumstances and incentives to deconcentrate, so the lack of reaction of public administration can be considered a negative policy. Spanish municipalities lack the economic resources to play a part within these policies. Only regional and central government authorities are able to build new economic developments. When local administrations took on territorial planning, they did not receive a proportional budget. So, in order to attract economic activities, they offer low taxes and cheap services.

5.6
Conclusions

The processes of the metropolitan decentralization of both housing and employment and their effect on traffic congestion as well as other negative environmental impacts have provoked debate in recent literature. According to some authors, the duration and distance of commuting increase in the course of time and decrease when there is a territorial balance in the distribution of housing and workplaces. Unfortunately, the mononuclear profile of both Madrid and Valladolid and the centripetal traffic network subject to increasing car ownership among employees have favoured congestion and higher pollution (Naredo, 1999).

We have described recent trends in the decentralization of employment and housing in the metropolitan areas of Madrid and Valladolid and put forward some preliminary conclusions concerning their relationship with the quality of life. The results of our analysis show a clear tendency of decentralization towards the respective suburban areas, although jobs located outside the central cities area are still far below the percentages shown in other towns and cities. This decentralization generates a high increase in the demand for inter-municipality mobility. In both cases, the process described shows the lack of efficient planning at the metropolitan or regional level to find a better adjustment in the territorial assignation of employment and housing by subordinating local planning to these supra-municipal objectives. Local planning has mainly pursued housing-related aims, while the location of companies appears to obey different criteria. These are some of the factors that help distort the local markets for land, housing, and transport, and help explain the peculiarity of the process described over the growing imbalance in the territorial designation of employment and housing.

During the period considered (1990–2004), some fundamental changes have occurred in the national governance structure affecting the legal set-up of land use and planning. In 1990, following the 1956 and 1975 Acts, parliament approved the third Planning Act as a planning regulation scheme for the whole country. However, during the 1980s Spain had become one of the most politically-decentralized countries in Europe; seventeen regional governments were fully competent to deal with town and country planning regulations. Consequently, some regional governments appealed to the Constitutional Court against the 1990 Planning Act. Judgement in their favour was given in 1997. Two-thirds of national legislation has been declared unconstitutional. Since that time, the opportunities for the central government authorities to regulate urban development and curb urban sprawl have reduced their scope to those aspects of planning dealing with economic dimension of land use; all other aspects have been left in the hands of regional governments. Considering the impact of the law on economic deconcentration processes, it must be emphasized that one of the core legal principles is that all land is considered developable unless it is subject to some kind of protection (ecological or agricultural values). This new status opens up opportunities to future widening of the urban built-up area, mostly in suburban areas, provided that both public and private actors are allowed to develop land. In any case, the municipalities are responsible for adapting their urban planning scheme to the legal framework created by the regional and national powers.

Until now, the deconcentration processes in both Madrid and Valladolid have been mainly residential and only partly economic. Both cities have kept the highest concentration of employment opportunities in the central city, especially in the

Valladolid case, where economic deconcentration processes are at an early stage. The deconcentration of employment and the resulting changes in economic land use has not led to the emergence of local employment sub-markets in the suburban rings in either Madrid or Valladolid. Consequently, there has been a tremendous increase in commuting in a multidirectional sense, even though the Madrid urban core continues to be the main labour-force-flow destination; the labour leadership of Valladolid central city is even stronger.

In the Madrid case (5,133,401 inhabitants in 2001), public administration is responsible for economic deconcentration through urban planning; regional administration gives final approval to all the municipal structural plans. But it is the private sector that leads the process. Indisputably, economic agents are the leaders of deconcentration processes. All the companies look for profitability and the improvement of communications. Every economic agent tries to maximize the benefits, even in the case of private-public negotiation. Small enterprises (<5 employees) are in the habit of staying in the central city, while medium-size companies (5–20 employees) move to grow, and big enterprises deconcentrate because of economic profitability (low salaries, land prices gap, innovative technologies, and so forth). Industrial factories benefit from deconcentration; they leave obsolete locations and enter new premises while gaining from the land value gap. Land speculation is thought to be one of the principal reasons behind moving out.

Up to now, in the Valladolid case, employment deconcentration is just beginning, spreading economic activities almost exclusively towards the inner ring. Even so, last year's information on new employment contracts seems to point to a change of tendency towards a more balanced relationship among the three areas; anyway deep differences in municipal activity deconcentration have to be highlighted. Industrial companies look for locations with low land prices and good accessibility. If an enterprise has a lot of employees, it must look for a location close to good transport connections. Middle-sized industries deconcentrate mainly because of land scarcity in the central city. Nevertheless, some big industries in Valladolid have not deconcentrated. Small industrial enterprises have deconcentrated preferably towards Santovenia and transport companies towards La Cistérniga. On the other hand, tertiary activities remain concentrated.

Unlike Madrid, Valladolid (378,571 inhabitants in 2001) displays a much more planned urban evolution. Because of its excellent accessibility Valladolid was selected as "development centre" in the context of Franco's Regional Development Programme during the 1960s. This political decision brought important economic benefits to Valladolid in terms of industrial activities diversification. In Valladolid, both Spanish and foreign first-rank enterprises have established important industrial factories in metallurgy, automobiles, pharmaceuticals, machinery, agro-industry, and so forth. On the other hand, the Valladolid municipality has considered the deconcentration of non-residential activities towards the metropolitan area to be a threat and it has classified new industrial land within the last Structural Plan in order to avoid economic deconcentration. However, while key experts agree that the region suffers from a public-subsidy approach to the economy in order to create new jobs, except from the case of the Technological Park, it is in fact quite difficult for public investment to determine economic activities. Concerning local policies, every municipality is trying to attract investors, Valladolid central city regards metropolitan municipalities as competitors, but the scarcity of industrial and residential land at available prices has forced the sprawl of industry and residential developments.

Note

[1] After the Civil War, urban planning regulations in the period 1940–1950 promoted the annexation of small bordering municipalities by the four big Spanish cities. This was the case for the Urban Planning Act of Madrid (1944), that for Great Bilbao (1945), Great Valencia (1946), and Barcelona (1953).

References

Alonso LF (Dir) (1993) Estructura territorial y ordenación de Valladolid y su entorno. Documento de síntesis. Valladolid en la encrucijada. Valladolid, Junta de Castilla y león, Consejería de Medio Ambiente y Ordenación del Territorio

Angelet Cladellas J (2000) La descentralización del empleo y de la residencia en las áreas metropolitanas de Barcelona y Madrid. Urban 4, primavera:124–144

Avance del Plan Industrial (2002) Ayuntamiento de Valladolid, Working Paper

Carrera Sánchez C (1995) Crecimiento diferencial y localización selectiva del sector terciario en la Comunidad de Madrid. Anales de Geografía de la Universidad Complutense 15: 205–220

Celada Crespo F (1998) Industria y reestructuración territorial en la Comunidad de Madrid. Situación, Serie Estudios Regionales, 285–304

Celada Crespo F (1999) Los distritos industriales en la Comunidad de Madrid, Papeles de Economía Española, Economía de las Comunidades Autónomas 18:200–211

Celada Crespo F, Méndez R (1994) Difusión metropolitana de la industria y efecto frontera en la Comunidad de Madrid, Economía y Sociedad 11 December, 197–217

Galve Martín A (1992) Dinámica industrial en el eje y márgenes del Corredor del Bajo Henares. Anales de Geografía de la Universidad Complutense de Madrid 11:181–204

Krätke S (2001) Strengthening the Polycentric Urban System in Europe: Conclusions from the ESDP. European Planning Studies 9(1):106–1116

López de Lucio R (1999) La nueva geografía de la producción y el consumo: reestructuración industrial, ejes terciarios y nuevas centralidades. In: Madrid 1979-1999, Madrid, Gerencia Municipal de Urbanismo, 185–224

Méndez R (1997) Tendencias de localización industrial y nuevos espacios productivos en la Comunidad de Madrid. In: El futuro de la industria en la Comunidad de Madrid, Instituto de Estadística de la Comunidad de Madrid, Consejería de Hacienda, Asociación madrileña de Ciencia Regional, 241–276

Méndez R, Ondátegui J (1999) La estructura territorial de las actividades económicas y la renta. In: García Delgado JL (ed) Estructura Económica de Madrid, Editorial Civitas, 135–179

Naredo JM (1999) Sobre la insostenibilidad de las actuales conurbaciones y el modo de paliarla, Dirección General de la Vivienda, la Arquitectura y el Urbanismo, Ministerio de Fomento

Pardo Abad CJ (2004) Vaciado industrial y Nuevo paisaje urbano en Madrid. Antiguas fábricas y renovación de la ciudad, Madrid, Ediciones La Librería, colección Estudios

Precedo Ledo A (1996) Ciudad y desarrollo urbano. Síntesis, Madrid

Razin E (1998) Policies to control urban sprawl: planning regulations or changes in the 'Rules of the game?' Urban Studies 35(2):321–340

de las Rivas Sanz JL (1998) Directrices de Ordenaci ón Territorial de Valladolid y Entorno, Valladolid, Junta de Castilla y León, Consejería de Medio Ambiente y ordenación del Territorio

Valenzuela M (1994) Madrid: Capital city and metropolitan region. In Clout H (ed) Europe's Cities in the Late Twentieth Century. Utrecht-Amsterdam, The Royal Dutch Geographical Society, 51–69

6 The Italian way to deconcentration.
Rome: The appeal of the historic centre.
Chieti-Pescara: The strength of the periphery

Armando Montanari[1], Barbara Staniscia[2], Simone Di Zio[2i]

[1] *Facoltà di Scienze Manageriali, Università degli Studi "G. d'Annunzio", Viale Pindaro 42, 65127 Pescara, Italy*
[2] *DEST – Università degli Studi "G. d'Annunzio", Viale Pindaro 42, 65127 Pescara, Italy*

Abstract: In this paper we deal with the topic of deconcentration in two Italian metropolitan areas: Rome, the capital city; and Chieti-Pescara, a medium-sized urban area. The paper reveals the particular patterns of deconcentration in those areas, exemplifying the Italian approach to deconcentration. These metropolitan areas show that deconcentration is an undesired phenomenon; enterprises choose peripheral areas for their lower costs on the real-estate market and for better accessibility; central locations are still favoured by the ICT sector and the front office functions in the tertiary sector; and deconcentration is showing an upward trend

Key words: Deconcentration, sprawl, Rome, economic dynamics, locational choices

6.1
Introduction

Italy is characterized by cities with outstanding historic, architectural, cultural, and environmental elements in the centres of the areas that determine their development. As such a historic centre, Rome has a value beyond price, and it exerts a force of attraction, a centripetal force.

Post-modern society does not simply demand spaces, but quality spaces. These can be provided by valuable centres or first-class peripheries. Further case studies would be necessary to establish its legitimacy, but the claim can justifiably be made that the centres of Italian cities are attractive when they are of high value. In contrast, the peripheries are a simple expedient resulting from the lower purchase and rental costs of land and property and the presence of a satisfactory infrastructural network. The peripheries constitute a second-best. The Italian way is, therefore, an undesired, but inevitable deconcentration.

How does Italian deconcentration differ from the other European cases?

Borsdorf and Wimmer (2005: 86) have described European cities as: "cities circled by a bacon ribbon – a belt of wealthy communes: wealthy because of the high-standing equipment with retail trade, industrial sites or education and health infrastructure. New installations in the sectors of trade, industry, research, education and leisure even look for more peripheral locations in areas which until recently could be characterized as totally rural."

E. Razin et al. (eds.), Employment Deconcentration in European Metropolitan Areas, 145–178.
© 2007 *Springer.*

Those cities that have experienced the processes of deconcentration present some common (although not necessarily coexisting) characteristics: (i) many European cities have a polycentric structure, where population and enterprises are equally distributed in the city centres and in the suburbs (Dieleman & Faludi, 1998; Bontje, 2004). These multiple centres are not in a hierarchical relationship and they form a polynucleated city, which is sometimes the result of the overlapping of several cities. This is the case for many areas in the Netherlands; (ii) in many European cities, specific policies to favour deconcentration or to discourage its effects in terms of sprawl are put into effect. Razin (1998: 321) stresses that: "urban sprawl is widely acknowledged as an undesirable form of development, due to its economic, social and environmental disadvantages. Attempts to control urban sprawl are frequently based on land-use plans at the national, regional and metropolitan levels." Simmons, Jones and Yeates (1998), with reference to the retail sector, highlight two different kinds of policy: the first are directly linked to deconcentration and refer in particular to transport and land use; the second kind has an indirect effect on deconcentration, since these policies are linked to the economic sector (through legislation establishing the maximum size of stores and their opening hours, for example). These policies imply that public actors envisage deconcentration as in need of their control or guidance; (iii) some European cities are in such an advanced stage of deconcentration, there is a trend in the opposite direction: that of reconcentration. Lowe (2005) presents the case of Southampton and shows how public players are implementing policies favouring retail reconcentration. These policies are linked to the need for the urban regeneration of city-centres, often abandoned because of their degradation resulting from the presence of old industrial plants and warehouses. These characteristics are discussed in the final section to illustrate how Italian deconcentration differs from other European processes (according to the results obtained in relation to our case studies).

A theoretical reference for deconcentration in Italy could be a reinvention of the 'push and pull' theory on a local scale. On a global scale, that theory was used to explain human mobility (Claval, 2002). But, whereas in that case the theory is considered obsolete (Ishikawa & Montanari, 2003), it can still be deemed valid for the mobility of enterprises, at least for Italian firms, which move on a metropolitan scale, slowly and with difficulty, feeling the effects of rigidity and inelasticity, linked to the actions of market forces and to the action (or non-action) of public players. These combined actions constitute the 'push' and 'pull' factors in the metropolitan mobility of Italian enterprises. The historic and environmental heritage constitutes the exogenous variable in this system. The examples of Italian deconcentration analysed in this chapter are the metropolitan areas of Rome and Chieti-Pescara.

A significant fact in the history of the deconcentration of Rome's metropolitan area is that the Municipality of Fiumicino was part of the Municipality of Rome until the beginning of the 1990s, when it became administratively autonomous following a public referendum. This new administrative status granted the municipality complete autonomy in the management of certain areas suitable for development that had, until then, been blocked by a larger-scale management perspective. Fiumicino's autonomy, given particular significance by the presence of the international airport of the same name, gave the go-ahead to an extensive process of spatial deconcentration of economic land use along the axis between Rome and the airport, the results of which will only become clear in quantitative terms at the end of this decade. In this case, the presence of a vast, as yet unexplored, archaeological zone containing the Imperial Ports of Claudius and Trajan is seen as an element not of containment of the process of deconcentration, but rather of its qualitative enhancement ('pull' factor).

The Chieti-Pescara metropolitan area is smaller in size and is spatially organized in an archipelago-system. The metropolitan area is characterized by the presence of medium-sized cities and small towns. This area is distinguished by an evident vitality and by interesting developments in the business services and ICT sectors. Until the first half of the 1990s, this territory was one of the Objective 1 EU Structural Funds areas.

In Section 6.2, we consider the national context of policies (or their lack) related to residential and economic deconcentration and the dynamics of the 'push' and 'pull' factors in the main sectors of economic activity; in section 6.3, we describe the methodological apparatus for the definition of the metropolitan areas, the data used, and the choice and interpretation of the indices and indicators; in section 6.4, we discuss residential deconcentration; in section 6.5, we report our quantitative analysis of the deconcentration of economic activities; in section 6.6, we consider some qualitative aspects of non-residential deconcentration in the Municipality of Rome; section 6.7 concludes the chapter.

6.2
Italian deconcentration between push and pull factors: Market forces vs public policies

Since the beginning of the 1970s, there has been a phenomenon of residential deconcentration in Italy, partly as a result of an explicit national policy and the creation of a network of physical infrastructures. During the 1970s, there was a demographic recovery of the peripheral areas. This recovery concerned 59 percent of the Italian municipalities and all the Italian regions. The population increase was limited in the large towns (with more than 50,000 inhabitants) and almost all the large cities (more than 200,000 inhabitants) suffered population losses (Montanari & Staniscia, 2003). At the same time, small villages and mid-sized towns started to grow, especially those close to the large metropolitan areas: between 1971 and 1981, municipalities with less than 5,000 inhabitants registered a population increase of 6–10 percent. This increase occurred for several reasons. Equipping peripheral areas with infrastructures, both in physical terms and in services, played an important part. However, changes in production schemes and the passage from Fordism to post-Fordism were the decisive reasons.

The counter-urbanization and spatial deconcentration processes cannot therefore be interpreted in just one manner. In the north-west, this deconcentration process was essentially the result of the expulsion of the active population from large firms and consequently from the large cities. On the other hand, in the Third Italy, productive dynamism brought about by the flexible production scheme created new employment in the peripheral areas (Vandermotten et al., 2004). In the south of Italy, the recovery of small and medium-sized municipalities seems to have been linked to the return of emigrants discharged from industry who, thanks to public transfers and their former gains, could return and engage in new economic activities, especially in the building and services sectors.

The urban crisis was also caused by urban congestion problems and by the diseconomies derived from a low urban quality of life, with intense traffic, lack of schools, hospitals, and green areas, and very high housing costs (Dematteis, 1995). The inadequate guidance of the process did not help reducing the imbalance. In particular, the problems linked to the chaotic urbanization process of the previous years were not resolved. The dysfunctions related to urban congestion were merely transferred to a different scale.

During the 1970s, Italy experienced the beginning of the process of the decline of the Fordist model, which favoured the following processes: (i) a deconcentration trend from the 'central city' to the 'periphery' in the major urban settlements in the north-west, resulting from a change in the urban policy at the local level; (ii) a deconcentration trend from the north to the south of the country, resulting from a specific regional policy and a differential in labour costs and social conflicts; (iii) the restructuring of the productive sectors and the establishment of new enterprises in the centre and in the north-east. More recently, the process of de-industrialization and the introduction of IT have contributed to the change in the major Italian cities. Empty areas were created when obsolete industrial plants were abandoned and by the necessity of the deconcentration of the major public infrastructures that were later filled with tertiary services. This de-industrialization applied to the early industrial cities of north-west Italy.

The non-residential deconcentration process is a consequence of a national spatial organization based on a system of regulation and not on the promotion of a process of local development. Infrastructure policies and regional policies were, until the 1960s, of exclusively national competence; since then, they have become a competence of the EU. Regions have been the administrative units with planning power since the 1970s. In the application of their policies, they basically maintained the characteristics of the national approach towards regulation, even though, in some cases, positive signs for local development can be found in the effects of the regional policies coordinated by the EU. At the local level, municipalities have planning power through the instrument of the City Master Plan.

Italian deconcentration is influenced, but not determined, by 'push' and 'pull' factors. 'Push' factors are the result of programming and planning policies executed in urban areas where economic activities have reached a state of maturity, some-times even becoming saturated, and in which there is a requirement to push non-qualifying firms out of the centre. 'Pull' factors are the result of policies implemented in fringe areas, characterized by a system of economic activities still in the early phases of development and growth and in which there is a demand for expansion.

The core and peripheral areas of the Rome metropolitan area operate in a 'push' and 'pull' relationship, also on the basis of property values. The core is selective in keeping firms which can afford the high purchase or letting costs for property that result from the lack of space and its high value in the centre. The peripheral areas become involved in the expansion and development of economic activities that are no longer able to grow within the core of the metropolitan area. Bear in mind that Rome holds second place to Verona in the growth rate of economic activities in Italy. Policies of the 'pull' type are exemplified by those implemented in the territorial pacts[ii] in Latium. The actions of the municipalities that carry out attraction policies are of two types: passive, pure investment attraction through the granting of concessions and services; active, the selection of investments which are qualified and qualifying and which form part of an overall development project.

By reinterpreting the 'push-pull' theory from the viewpoint of non-residential deconcentration, we can say that firms are repelled or attracted by positive or negative factors respectively which include the following: (i) unavailability/availability of good infrastructures of physical access and transport; (ii) absence/presence of spaces; (iii) high/low purchase costs of land and property letting; (iv) absence/presence of material and immaterial services; (v) negative/positive quality of the natural, social and cultural environment (Montanari & Staniscia, 2006). To different extents, these factors can be influenced by the programming and planning policies of the public actor at both a local and a supra-local level. It is important to stress that the non-action of the public actor also has an involuntary influence on these factors. In the case of non-residential deconcentration, public policies prove not to be neutral.

The empirical evidence of the Italian case demonstrates that the first to carry out deconcentration was the industrial sector, since it felt the effects, before the other sectors did, of the problems linked to the lack of space, the inadequacy of infrastructures resulting from the increased mobility of merchandise, and the need for the control and containment of the resulting pollution.

After industry, the commercial sector is the next to move. When this sector leads deconcentration, we enter into the second phase of the process. Deconcentration choices made by the commercial, leisure, and entertainment sectors take into consideration the consumers: the potential catchment area, in other words. There is a strong link with the population and with the other sector structures. The 'push' and 'pull' policies that affect enterprises are therefore less efficient here than in the industrial sector, since they cannot produce change in the catchment area. Indeed, the elasticity of consumer demand is linked to consumer preferences and to the human mobility on the territory that are finite and constrained by costs. The most efficient public policies in this case are those concerning revenue and services to the population and to enterprises. Non-residential deconcentration policies, on the other hand, work on a micro-area level insofar as they can condition location choices on sites that are very close to each other.

We learn from the literature that the ICT and business-services sector is spatially concentrated, especially in the large metropolitan areas (Lethiais et al., 2003). The example of Silicon Valley clearly demonstrates the importance of the external network economies and technological externalities, which are a source of innovation. Silicon Valley also plainly shows the existence of positive retroactions that lead to a process of endogenous growth, which strengthens the power of attraction of one region to the disadvantage of others. There are also positive externalities derived from the reduction of certain costs, such as through the sharing of telecommunications infrastructures, external economies for commercial aims, and the positive dynamics of social interaction. The analyses of industrial districts and their notions of agglomeration economies, learning processes, *filières,* and proximity can also be mentioned here (Becattini, 1991).

The Silicon Valley model is well-known: a large firm initiates the process and others follow. The same example has been encountered in Paris with the Silicon Sentier, which was set up by Yahoo. Of great importance to the ICT sector is the presence of urban amenities, which aid the development of creative capital and favour a highly-specialized local job market. The ICT and business services sector sees its firms distributed throughout both the Central Business District (CBD) and the suburban areas (Shearmur & Alvergne, 2002). Growth there is quicker, but that is not to say that the CBD is in decline. Indeed, there is a locational difference between the higher and lower rank services within this type of sector. Employment within the CBD tends to be associated with higher salaries and front-office functions; suburban employment tends to be characterized by lower incomes and retail and back-office functions. One of the reasons for the suburban growth in this type of sector is the fact that the CBD does not have a sufficient quantity of buildings to meet the requirements of this growth.

While the deconcentration of economic activities responds to both a 'push' and a 'pull' logic, the deconcentration of administrative activities reacts solely to a 'push' logic, put into effect by the entity which has the power to decentralize. Traditional public services (schools, hospitals, post offices, and telecommunications) do indeed follow population mobility to guarantee essential services. These public services to people track residential deconcentration very closely. This deconcentration concerns both the consumers and the employees who, however, do not have the political weight that the public actor has. The Italian cases show that the public actor follows population mobility with infrastructures, creating new ones where deemed necessary, but fails to remove the structures that are no longer required, even when they have become inefficient, so strong is the pressure from the associations representing the employees to keep employment in the places where it has been traditionally guaranteed. Public services therefore constitute an extremely rigid supply.

6.3
Research design

Italy is divided into regions, provinces, and municipalities. The metropolitan areas are constituted by an aggregation of municipalities (Nuts 4 and Nuts 5) belonging to different provinces (Nuts 3). The territory of the metropolitan areas is, therefore, sub-provincial and inter-provincial. Metropolitan areas in Italy are defined by Act 142/1990. This Act does not provide general criteria for determining the metropolitan areas; it simply provides a list of 12 municipalities (Turin, Milan, Venice, Genoa, Bologna, Florence, Rome, Naples, Bari, Cagliari, Catania, Palermo) that are considered to be the main cities for the 12 metropolitan areas which have to be defined. The national legislation therefore transfers to the regional governments the power of defining the territories included in the 12 metropolitan areas without setting strict criteria of inclusion/exclusion.

In the case of the metropolitan area of Rome (RMA), the definition provided by IRSPEL (1991) has been adopted in the present chapter[iii]. The municipalities included in the RMA are shown in Figure 6.1. The RMA has been divided into four parts: the 'core', 'central city', 'inner suburban ring', and 'outer suburban ring'.

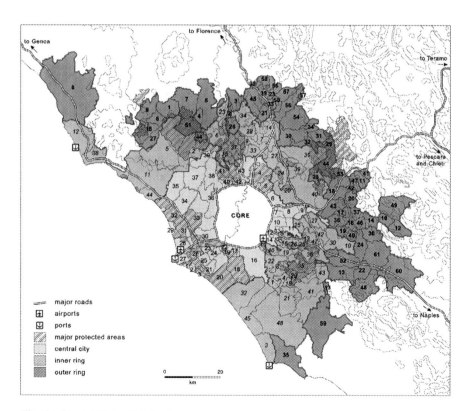

Fig. 6.1 Rome Metropolitan Area

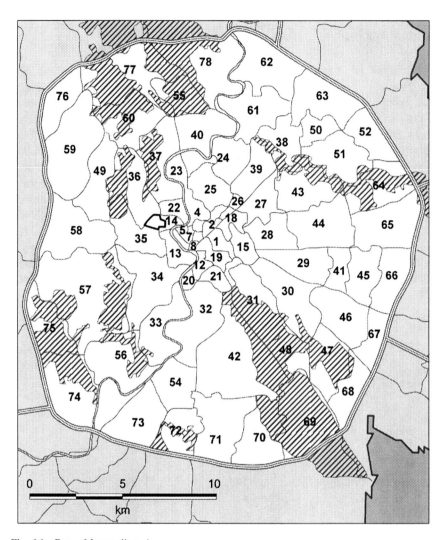

Fig. 6.1a Rome Metropolitan Area, core

CORE: (Rome) 1-Monti, 2-Trevi, 3-Colonna, 4-Campo Marzio, 5-Ponte, 6-Parione, 7-Regola, 8-Sant'eustachio, 9-Pigna, 10-Campitelli, 11-Sant'angelo, 12-Ripa, 13-Trastevere, 14-Borgo, 15-Esquilino, 16-Ludovisi, 17-Sallustiano, 18-Castro Pretorio, 19-Celio, 20-Testaccio, 21-San Saba, 22-Prati, 23-Flaminio, 24-Parioli, 25-Pinciano, 26-Salario, 27-Nomentano, 28-Tiburtino, 29-Prenestino-Labicano, 30-Tuscolano, 31-Appio-Latino, 32-Ostiense, 33-Portuense, 34-Gianicolense, 35-Aurelio, 36-Trionfale, 37-Della Vittoria, 38-Monte Sacro, 39-Trieste, 40-Tor Di Quinto, 41-Prenestino-Centocelle, 42-Ardeatino, 43-Pietralata, 44-Collatino, 45-Alessandrino, 46-Don Bosco, 47-Appio Claudio, 48-Appio-Pignatelli, 49-Primavalle, 50-Monte Sacro Alto, 51-Ponte Mammolo, 52-San Basilio, 53-Giuliano-Dalmata, 54-Europa E.U.R., 55-Tor Di Quinto, 56-Portuense, 57-Gianicolense, 58-Aurelio, 59-Trionfale, 60-Della Vittoria, 61-Val Melaina, 62-Castel Giubileo, 63-Casal Boccone, 64-Tor Cervara, 65-Tor Sapienza, 66-Torre Spaccata, 67-Torre Maura, 68-Capannelle, 69-Torricola, 70-Cecchignola, 71-Fonte Ostiense, 72-Torrino,

In the case of Chieti-Pescara (CPMA), the 'functional' criterion adopted is based on a socio-economic approach. This metropolitan area includes the municipalities that are more active from an economic point of view, municipalities belonging to the same productive system, referred to a reticular logic rather than to a spatial contiguity. The result is a 'network' of municipalities, all belonging to the same Consortium for Industrial Development, all insisting on a homogeneously planned and managed territory, as shown in Figure 6.2. For our purposes, we divided the CPMA into three parts: 'central city'; 'inner suburban ring'; 'outer suburban ring'.

The data used for the analysis of residential deconcentration in the RMA and CPMA were taken from the 1991 and 2001 censuses carried out by Istat (various years – a). The analysis is based on the change in the number of residents during the census years 1991 and 2001 at the municipal level. For the Municipalities of Rome and Fiumicino, given their size and complexity, sub-municipal units and toponymic sub-divisions were used. The analysis of migration is based on the

---

Fig. 6.1a 73-Tor Di Valle, 74-Magliana Vecchia, 75-La Pisana, 76-Ottavia, 77-Tomba Di Nerone, 78-Grottarossa. REST OF CENTRAL CITY: (Rome) 1-Lido Di Ostia Ponente, 2-Lido Di Ostia Levante, 3-Lido Di Castel Fusano, 4-Marcigliana, 5-Tor San Giovanni, 6-Settecamini, 7-Acqua Vergine, 8-Lunghezza, 9-San Vittorino, 10-Torre Angela, 11-Borghesiana, 12-Torrenova, 13-Torre Gaia, 14-Casal Morena, 15-Aereoporto Di Ciampino, 16-Castel Di Leva, 17-Vallerano, 18-Castel Di Decima, 19-Tor De' Cenci, 20-Castel Porziano, 21-Castel Fusano, 22-Mezzocamino, 23-Acilia Nord, 24-Acilia Sud, 25-Casal Balocco, 26-Ostia Antica, 30-Ponte Galeria, 33-Castel Di Guido, 36-Casalotti, 37-Santa Maria Di Galeria, 38-La Storta, 39-Cesano, 40-La Giustiniana, 41-Isola Farnese, 42-Labaro, 43-Prima Porta, 44-Polline-Martignano. (Fiumicino): 27-Isola Sacra, 28-Fiumicino, 29-Fregene, 31-Maccarese Sud, 32-Maccarese Nord, 34-Torrimpietra, 35-Palidoro.
INNER RING: *1-Albano Laziale, 2-Anguillara Sabazia, 3-Anzio, 4-Ariccia, 5-Bracciano, 6-Campagnano Di Roma, 7-Capena, 8-Castel Gandolfo, 9-Castelnuovo Di Porto, 10-Cave, 11-Cerveteri, 12-Civitavecchia, 13-Colonna, 14-Fiano Romano, 15-Formello, 16-Frascati, 17-Gallicano Nel Lazio, 18-Genzano Di Roma, 19-Grottaferrata, 20-Guidonia Montecelio, 21-Lanuvio, 22-Marino, 23-Mazzano Romano, 24-Mentana, 25-Montecompatri, 26-Monte Porzio Catone, 27-Monterotondo, 28-Morlupo, 29-Nemi, 30-Palestrina, 31-Palombara Sabina, 32-Pomezia, 33-Riano, 34-Rignano Flaminio, 35-Rocca Di Papa, 36-Rocca Priora, 37-Sacrofano, 38-Santa Marinella, 39-Sant'angelo Romano, 40-Tivoli, 41-Velletri, 42-Zagarolo, 43-Lariano, 44-Ladispoli, 45-Ardea, 46-Ciampino, 47-San Cesareo, 48-Aprilia.* OUTER RING: 1-Bassano Romano, 2-Calcata, 3-Faleria, 4-Monterosi, 5-Nepi, 6-Oriolo Romano, 7-Sutri, 8-Tarquinia, 9-Vejano, 10-Affile, 11-Anticoli Corrado, 12-Arcinazzo Romano, 13-Artena, 14-Bellegra, 15-Canale Monteranno, 16-Capranica Predestina, 17-Casape, 18-Castel Madama, 19-Castel San Pietro Romano, 20-Ciciliano, 21-Civitella San Paolo, 22-Colleferro, 23-Filacciano, 24-Genazzano, 25-Labico, 26-Magliano Romano, 27-Manziana, 28-Marcellina, 29-Monteflavio, 30-Montelibretti 31-Montorio Romano, 32-Moricone, 33-Nazzano, 34-Nerola, 35-Nettuno, 36-Olevano Romano, 37-Pisoniano, 38-Poli, 39-Ponzano Romano, 40-Rocca Di Cave, 41-Roviano, 42-Sambuci, 43-San Gregorio Da Sassola, 44-San Polo Dei Cavalieri, 45-Sant'Oreste, 46-San Vito Romano, 47-Saracinesco, 48-Segni, 49-Subiaco, 50-Torrita Tiberina, 51-Trevignano Romano, 52-Valmontone, 53-Vicovaro, 54-Fara In Sabina, 55-Forano, 56-Montopoli Di Sabina, 57-Poggio Mirteto, 58-Stimigliano, 59-Cisterna Di Latina, 60-Anagni, 61-Paliano.

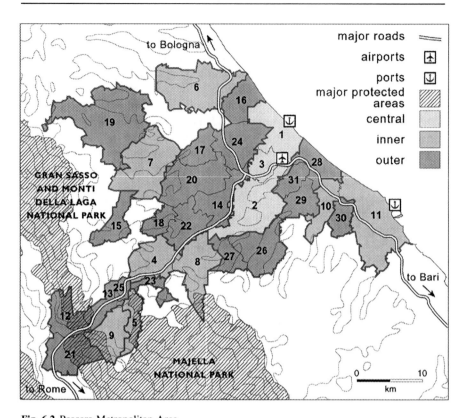

Fig. 6.2 Pescara Metropolitan Area
CENTRAL CITY: 1-Pescara, 2-Chieti, 3-San Giovanni Teatino. INNER RING: 4-Alanno, 5-Bolognano, 6-Citta' S. Angelo, 7-Loreto Aprutino, 8-Manoppello, 9-Tocco Da Casauria, 10-Miglianico, 11-Ortona. OUTER RING: 12-Bussi Sul Tirino, 13-Castiglione a Casauria, 14-Cepagatti, 15-Civitaquana, 16-Montesilvano, 17-Moscufo, 18-Nocciano, 19-Penne, 20-Pianella, 21-Popoli, 22-Rosciano, 23-Scafa, 24-Spoltore, 25-Torre De' Passeri, 26-Bucchianico, 27-Casalincontrada, 28-Francavilla Al Mare, 29-Ripa Teatina, 30-Tollo, 31-Torrevecchia Teatina.

yearly migratory rate taken from data provided by the Municipal General Registry Offices, for the period 1992-2000.

The data used for the analysis of the non-residential deconcentration relate to the number of jobs registered during the Census in the years 1991 and 2001, carried out by Istat (various years – b). The economic sectors considered are: (i) Industry: number of jobs in enterprises' local units from the NACE[iv] sectors C (mining and quarrying), D (manufacturing), E (electricity, gas and water supply), F (construction); (ii) Commerce: number of jobs in enterprises' local units from the NACE sectors G (wholesale and retail trade; repair of motor vehicles, motorcycles and personal and household goods); (iii) Services: number of jobs in enterprises' local units from the NACE sectors H (hotels and restaurants), I (transport, storage and communication), J (financial intermediation), K (real estate, renting and business administration), L (public administration and defence; compulsory social security), M (education), N (health and social work), O (other community, social and personal service activities), P (private households with employed persons), Q (extra-territorial organizations and bodies); (iv) Institutions[v]: number of jobs in institutions' local units from the C to Q NACE sectors.

Since deconcentration is a complex phenomenon there is no single indicator, so the analysis in question was conducted on the basis of a joint interpretation of different statistics. The variations of density between 1991 and 2001 were calculated, together with the percentage variations in relative importance that each sub-area experienced within the metropolitan area as a whole. In addition, the spatial correlation structure of the variables analysed was investigated for the period 1991–2001. With regard to the metropolitan area of Rome, we could calculate a deconcentration indicator which works out the distance of each area (municipality or toponymic sub-division) from the centroid of the core. If we indicate the geographical centroid of the core by C, we can calculate the distances between the centroid of each area and point C. This distance squared gives a weighting factor than can be used in the following index:

$$K(s) = \sum_{i=1}^{N} \alpha_i(s) \cdot d_i^2 \tag{1}$$

where N=231 is the total number of areas and $\alpha_i(s)$ represents the employment density of the sector (s) in the i area. The index $K(s)$ provides a measure of the employment density in the sector (s), weighted by the distance squared from the centre of the metropolitan area (STRATEC, 2003). This weighting means that an increase in the number of jobs in a municipality on the fringes of the metropolitan area will cause a higher increase in the index than an equal increase in the number of jobs in a central zone.

Since we are particularly interested in the comparison of the years 1991 and 2001, we rescaled $K(s)$ with regard to 1991 to obtain the following relative index, which we call the Weighted Density Index:

$$\hat{K}(s) = \frac{K(s)_{2001} - K(s)_{1991}}{K(s)_{1991}} \tag{2}$$

A value $\hat{K} > 0$ indicates deconcentration, while for $\hat{K} < 0$ we can say that inverse phenomena prevail. Clearly, a positive value of $\hat{K}$ is a necessary, but insufficient condition to claim that deconcentration has taken place in the metropolitan area. It is therefore necessary to evaluate this index together with other indicators of deconcentration.

In this sense, and in order to have further elements to assess the phenomenon of deconcentration, it is useful to calculate the spatial correlation structure of the data.

There are various indices, but the most widely-used is Moran's I Index (O'Sullivan & Unwin, 2003; Bailey & Gatrell, 1995), which is formulated as follows:

$$I = \frac{n}{\sum_{i=1}^{n} (y_i - \bar{y})^2} \frac{\sum_{i=1}^{n} \sum_{j=1}^{n} w_{ij} (y_i - \bar{y}) (y_j - \bar{y})}{\sum_{i=1}^{n} \sum_{j=1}^{n} w_{ij}} \tag{3}$$

This is a case of *spatial autocorrelation,* since the I Index concerns the correlation between values of the same variable in various spatial locations. The variable y_i expresses employment density in the sector considered in the area i, while $\bar{y}$ is the mean relative to the area as a whole. This index is based on the notion of spatial contiguity, expressed in the matrix of weights **W,** the elements of which, w_{ij}, represent a measurement of the spatial proximity of the areas A_i and A_j. Of the various ways in which it is possible to define the matrix **W,** the simplest is to consider two areas adjacent to each other if they have a border in common. The weights will be $w_{ij} = 1$, if area i and area j are adjacent to each other; otherwise, $w_{ij} = 0$.

A phenomenon is considered spatially autocorrelated if its manifestations are affected by the proximity of the territorial units. In particular, a variable presents a positive autocorrelation ($I > 0$) if the values obtained in nearby units resemble each other and a negative autocorrelation ($I < 0$) if the opposite is the case.

Moran's I Index is a global autocorrelation index, which takes into account the whole area under study. This index therefore restores a single value for the entire metropolitan area, and tells us whether or not the data are auto-correlated. By comparing the index values for the two years considered, we could deduce whether a sector in the metropolitan area was moving towards a situation of greater or less homogeneity in its spatial distribution.

We calculated local statistics to see where anomalous interactions occurred. The *Local Indicator of Spatial Association* (LISA) provides a measure of the degree to which particular municipalities (or toponymic sub-divisions) present values similar to (or different from) those of nearby areas (Getis & Ord, 1992). A significantly high value of Moran's local index in an area indicates that the nearby areas have similar values (whether high or low). A significant negative value indicates that the nearby areas have dissimilar values. This index facilitates the identification of clusters of municipalities characterized by similar values (whether high or low) in the employment density of a sector. Alternatively, the index identifies areas with high values surrounded by areas with low values, and vice versa. Furthermore, comparing the results for 1991 and 2001 indicates whether such clusters have changed, or whether they have moved into different zones of the metropolitan area.

In addition to Moran's global index and the local statistics, deconcentration is also assessed through the separate analysis of the correlation structures of the metropolitan areas' four sub-areas (core, rest of central city, inner suburban ring, outer suburban ring). Four different index values can be calculated: one for each sub-area. The comparison of the values for 1991 and 2001 within each sub-area is of greater interest than the comparison of the index values among the four sub-areas. Obviously, the results must be interpreted together with the other above-mentioned statistics.

A drop in the I index in a sub-area in which there has been a fall in the number of jobs indicates a lessening of the correlation structure as a result of a scattered reduction. Vice versa, the reduction in some municipalities with high values can lead to a levelling-out of data, with a resulting increase in the spatial correlation. So if, for example, between 1991 to 2001 the correlation structure in the core and the rest of the central city weakened (I decreased), while in the inner and outer rings it strengthened (I increased), and if contextually there was a drop in the number of jobs in the centre and an increase in the inner and outer rings, deconcentration would be inferred.

6.4
Residential deconcentration

Between 1981 and 1991, a phenomenon of territorial deconcentration of population occurred in Italy. All the municipalities with more than 20,000 inhabitants registered a decrease in population; the drop was higher than 10 percent for the municipalities with more than 500,000 inhabitants. However, this phenomenon of deconcentration was accompanied by a new tendency: new forms of urban polarization. The traditional 'core-periphery' scheme was replaced by a new 'network' scheme with strong links at several points. A new term has been found to describe this phenomenon, namely 'scattered town' (città diffusa) (Montanari & Staniscia, 2003). During the 1990s there was a slackening of internal and external movements of native-born Italians and an increase in migratory flows from abroad. At this point Italy confirmed its status of an 'immigration' country (Montanari & Cortese, 1993). Taking into account the urban dynamic, it can be said that: "in recent years the migration loss of the provinces with a very high population density intensified without an indication of a clear move to the small city stage" (Bonifazi & Heins, 2001).

During the period 1991–2001, the core of the metropolitan area of Rome registered a loss in population of 2.16 percent, while in the rest of the central city there was an increase of 22.87 percent (Figure 6.3). In the period 1992–2000, the migratory rate in the Municipality of Rome was negative (on average −2.5 per thousand per year). The Municipality of Fiumicino underwent a considerable high positive migratory rate (on average +20.4 per thousand per year). Fiumicino's administrative autonomy enabled the demand for construction settlements along the Rome-airport axis to be met, a demand that Rome's large municipal administration, which managed those spaces within the ambit of a more complex area, would have found difficult to fulfil. Indeed, in the metropolitan area of Rome, a growing need for housing has emerged, despite the demographic reduction, because of the changed organization of nuclear families with a decreasing numbers of components, and because of a lack of public initiative in the reuse of buildings.

In the inner ring, the population increased, particularly in the most southern municipalities. Overall, the area registered an increase of more than 100,000 units in the period considered. The migratory rate in the inner ring was positive and

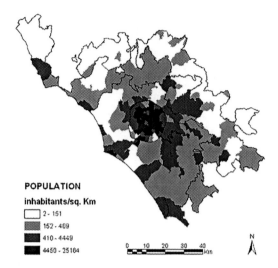

Fig. 6.3a Rome Metropolitan Area: population density, 2001

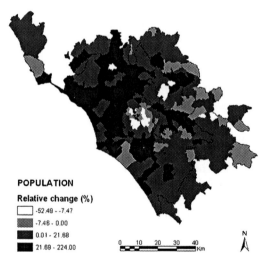

Fig. 6.3b Rome Metropolitan Area: population – relative change, 1991–2001
Data source: Istat, various years – a

particularly high (> +25 per thousand per year) in a few of the municipalities surrounding the Municipality of Rome. The total average yearly migratory rate was +15.5 per thousand.

In the outer ring there was a slight increase in population in the northern and southern parts and a loss in population in its eastern part. A total increase of almost 19,000 residents was registered in the period under consideration. In the outer ring there was a weak positive migratory rate in the majority of the municipalities, with some exceptions of high positive migratory rates in the northern part. The average yearly migratory rate was +8.7 per thousand.

The central city of the Chieti-Pescara metropolitan area registered a loss in population owing to a decrease in the two main cities (Pescara and Chieti). The net loss was about 8,000 inhabitants, or −4.15 percent. The coastal municipality experienced a negative migratory rate (−4.6 per thousand per year), the highest negative peak in the whole metropolitan area. In the internal municipalities the rate was positive. The total average yearly migratory rate was −1.8 per thousand.

The inner ring registered a weak increase in population as a result of the strong increase in the northern coastal municipality. The final result was an increase of around 2,000 units, or +3.68 percent. The migratory rates in the coastal communes were positive and high, reaching their peak in the northern coastal municipality (+15.2 per thousand per year). The other communes registered a weak positive migratory rate, with the most internal municipality as the only exception. The total average yearly migratory rate was +6.5 per thousand.

In the outer ring there was a significant increase in population; the rise was particularly high in the two coastal municipalities and in those surrounding the central city. The total increase was of more than 12,000 inhabitants: +8.78 percent. The outer ring registered a generalized positive migratory rate with the most internal communes as the only exceptions. The coastal municipalities and those surrounding the central city registered the highest positive peaks. The total average yearly migratory rate was +9.1 per thousand.

6.5
Employment deconcentration: A quantitative analysis of the metropolitan areas of Rome and Chieti-Pescara

Figure 6.4 shows the density of jobs in the four productive sectors in the metropolitan area of Rome. The core appears to dominate in all sectors. Moving from this premise that stresses the strong power of attraction of the central areas, the situation in the metropolitan area can be analysed by using a combination of indices and indicators that can better identify and represent the dynamism of the system. The quantitative analysis of the employment deconcentration has been carried out for each sector of economic activity and for each sub-area, using the following indices and phenomena:

(a) for the metropolitan area of Rome: (i) the weighted density index for the entire metropolitan area in the years 1991 and 2001; (ii) the change in the number of jobs in the sector during the period 1991–2001 for the entire metropolitan area (Figure 6.5); (iii) Moran's global index relative to the entire metropolitan area in 1991 and 2001; (iv) Moran's local index in 1991 and 2001; (v) the change in the number of jobs in the sector during the period 1991–2001 in the sub-areas (Table 6.1); (vi) Moran's index for each sector in the years 1991 and

2001 in each sub-area (Figure 6.6); (vii) the change in the percentage value of each sub-area in each sector during the period 1991–2001 (Table 6.1);

(b) for the metropolitan area of Pescara: (i) the change in the number of jobs in the sector during the period 1991–2001 for the entire metropolitan area (Table 6.2); (ii) the change in the number of jobs in the sector during the period 1991–2001 in the sub-areas (Table 6.2); (iii) the variation in the percentage composition of the relative importance of each sub-area in each sector during the period 1991–2001 (Table 6.2).

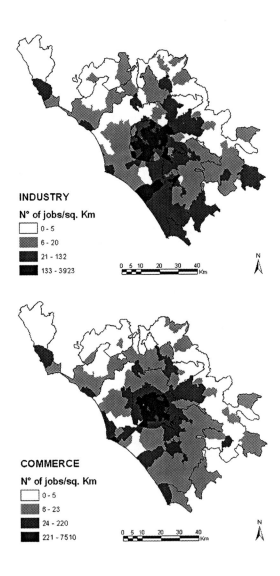

INDUSTRY

N° of jobs/sq. Km

- 0 - 5
- 6 - 20
- 21 - 132
- 133 - 3923

0 5 10   20   30   40 Km

N

COMMERCE

N° of jobs/sq. Km

- 0 - 5
- 6 - 23
- 24 - 220
- 221 - 7510

0 5 10   20   30   40 Km

N

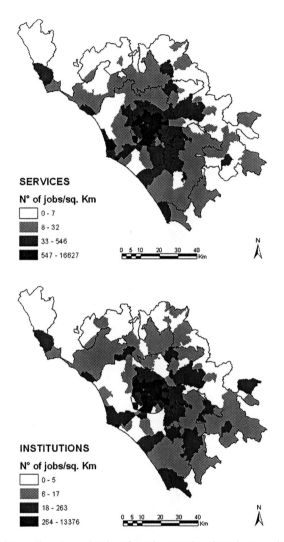

Fig. 6.4 Rome Metropolitan Area: density of employment in selected economic sectors, 2001
a. Industry
b. Commerce
c. Services
d. Institutions

Data source: Istat, various years – b

6.5.1
A sectoral analysis of the deconcentration process in the Rome metropolitan area

6.5.1.1
The industry sector

The weighted density index in the industry sector at metropolitan level in the period 1991–2001 was negative (−0.079), which at first glance indicates a process of concentration in the sector. When compared with the values in the other

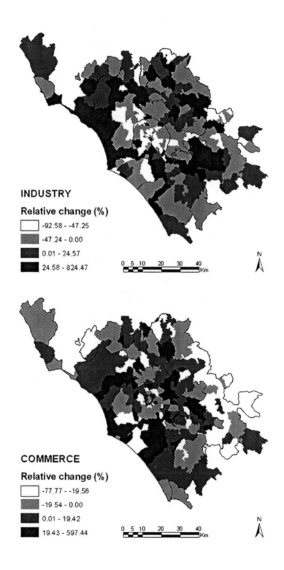

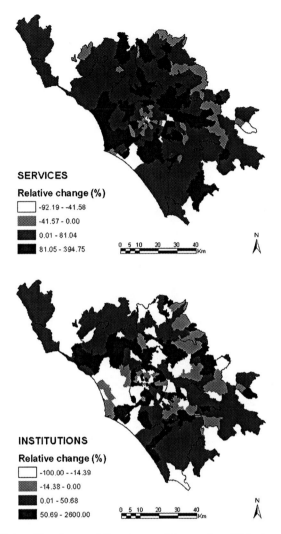

Fig. 6.5 Rome Metropolitan Area: relative change of the number of jobs in selected economic sectors, 1991–2001;
a. Industry
b. Commerce
c. Services
d. Institutions

Data source: Istat, various years - b

sectors, the industry sector was the lowest. Between 1991 and 2001, the number of jobs in the sector registered in the whole of the metropolitan area fell by −9.13 percent, the only negative value found when compared with those relative

Table 6.1 Rome Metropolitan Area: employment change by sector according to functional areas, 1991–2001

	Land area	Public institutions				Industry				Commerce				Services			
	Sq.km.	2001	1991–2001 change (%)	1991 % of total urbanized area	2001 % of total urbanized area	2001	1991–2001 change (%)	1991 % of total urbanized area	2001 % of total urbanized area	2001	1991–2001 change (%)	1991 % of total urbanized area	2001 % of total urbanized area	2001	1991–2001 change (%)	1991 % of total urbanized area	2001 % of total urbanized area
Core	344	244150	0.9	77.5	75.1	110100	–9.0	49.6	49.6	139589	–3.3	65.5	62.4	327458	–7.1	77.7	68.2
Rest of Central city	1154	22976	23.3	6.0	7.1	23510	–19.6	12.0	10.6	29674	27.1	10.6	13.3	63911	65.8	8.5	13.3
Inner suburban ring	2126	43521	14.7	12.2	13.4	62998	–7.3	27.9	28.4	43198	7.7	18.2	19.3	72028	44.5	11.0	15.0
Outer suburban ring	2170	14533	7.3	4.3	4.5	25185	–2.4	10.6	11.4	11333	–10.0	5.7	5.1	16769	32.3	2.8	3.5
Total urbanized area	5794	325180	4.2	100	100	221793	–9.1	100	100	223794	1.5	100	100	480166	5.8	100	100

Source: Istat (various years – b).

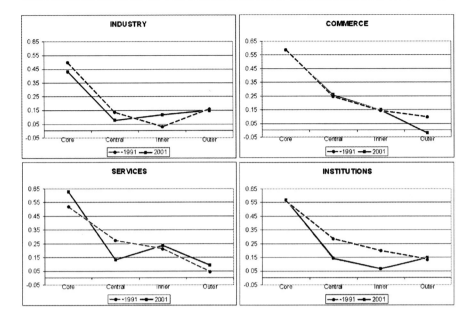

Fig. 6.6 Moran Indexes
Data source: authors' own calculation

to the other sectors. Moran's Index, calculated for the entire area, fell from 0.625 to 0.573 between 1991 and 2001.

With reference to Moran's local index, it can be noted that, whereas in 1991 there was a cluster of high values and, therefore, an industrial concentration in the southern part of the metropolitan area, in 2001 the cluster had dispersed, which helps explain the decrease in the global I index.

In analysing Moran's index in the industry sector within each individual sub-area, an increase was only registered in the inner ring during the period 1991–2001; this rise indicates an increase in the spatial correlation resulting from an increase in employment density in the north-western part of this sub-area. In this zone in 1991, however, employment density was much lower than that registered in the rest of the inner ring. The reduction in the index of all the other sub-areas was in line with the overall decrease in the number of jobs in the sector, which occurred in a scattered manner, thereby bringing about a reduction in spatial correlation.

We can state on the basis of the previous considerations and the analysis of data presented in Figure 6.5a and in Table 6.1 that there is a slight tendency towards deconcentration in the industry sector and that, against a background of an overall decrease in jobs, increases are registered in some municipalities in different zones of the metropolitan area, particularly in the outer ring.

Table 6.2 Chieti-Pescara Metropolitan Area: employment change by sector according to functional areas, 1991–2001

	Land area	Public institutions				Industry				Commerce				Services			
	Sq.km.	2001	1991–2001 change (%)	1991 % of total urbanized area	2001 % of total urbanized area	2001	1991–2001 change (%)	1991 % of total urbanized area	2001 % of total urbanized area	2001	1991–2001 change (%)	1991 % of total urbanized area	2001 % of total urbanized area	2001	1991–2001 change (%)	1991 % of total urbanized area	2001 % of total urbanized area
Central city	111	19214	−3.2	70.3	70.4	18691	−7.6	47.5	44.9	14322	0.3	58.8	57.4	27136	18.0	70.5	66.1
Inner suburban ring	333	2615	−7.0	10.0	9.6	8446	5.0	18.9	20.3	3365	11.0	12.5	13.5	4394	38.2	9.7	10.7
Outer suburban ring	534	5467	−1.6	19.7	20.0	14524	1.8	33.5	34.9	7251	3.9	28.7	29.1	9537	48.0	19.8	23.2
Total urbanized area	978	27296	−3.2	100	100	41661	−2.1	100	100	24938	2.7	100	100	41067	25.9	100	100

Source: Istat (various years – b).

6.5.1.2
The commerce sector

The weighted density index in the commerce sector at metropolitan level in the period 1991–2001 is 0.032: a positive, but relatively low value. This is explained by the fact that the most significant decreases in the number of jobs in the period 1991–2001 were concentrated on the eastern edge of the metropolitan area, while the most intense increases accumulated in the central city. These two effects compensated for each other and caused the resultant weighted density value. The variation in the number of jobs in the sector during the period 1991–2001 in the entire metropolitan area was 1.55 percent, a positive but low value, and the lowest registered increase compared with those relative to the other sectors. The values of Moran's global index in the two years considered were both significant at 0.693 and 0.685 respectively, which indicates a slight decrease in spatial correlation in this sector. In examining the distribution of values of Moran's local index, a cluster of high values can be clearly seen within the core in 1991. In 2001, the same cluster is reduced in size, but remains the only one to be detected.

By analysing Moran's Index in the sector in each individual sub-area, it could be observed that the index values calculated for the four sub-areas decreased as we move from the core towards the outer ring, both in 1991 and 2001. This decrease indicates a progressive reduction in the homogeneity of spatial diffusion in this sector as we move outwards. In comparing these two years, however, it can be noted that in the core, in the rest of the central city, and in the inner ring, the values did not vary whereas those in the outer ring fell. This result indicates that the variations in the first three sub-areas did not change the spatial correlation structure, whereas in the outer ring the above-mentioned decrease (−9.98 percent) concentrated in a single zone led to a reduction in the index.

We can conjecture a slight local deconcentration in the commerce sector, with a movement of enterprises from the core to the rest of the central city, on the basis of the previous considerations and the analysis of data contained in Figure 6.5b and in Table 6.1. The ring road no doubt represents a key element in this movement. This deconcentration has occurred in a scattered manner following the spatial opportunities given to enterprises by the presence of the ring road entrances and exits.

6.5.1.3
The services sector

The weighted density index value in the services sector at metropolitan level in the period 1991–2001 was 0.169; it relates to an increase in employment density in this sector in the peripheral zone of the metropolitan area. Analysing the employment variations in this sector over the entire metropolitan area from 1991 to 2001 reveals an increase of 5.84 percent, the highest for all the sectors considered. Moran's global index changed from 0.59 in 1991 to 0.71 in 2001. These values, both significant, indicate an increase in spatial correlation which, given the increase in this sector over the entire metropolitan area, implies a spatial homogeneity within the area.

By investigating the values of Moran's local index, a cluster of high values can be noted in the core similar to those relative to the commercial sector, and two low value clusters in the outer ring, more precisely in the north and north-east. This structure remained almost unvaried from 1991 to 2001.

Analysing Moran's index in each sub-area reveals an increase in the core against a reduction in the rest of the central city during the period 1991–2001. The spatial correlation structure within the inner and outer rings remained more or less unaltered, despite the registering of a slight increase. By interpreting these results together with the employment variations in each sub-area, we can conclude that, whereas the spatial correlation structure in the core strengthened, the increase in the number of jobs in the rest of the central city led to a situation of lower spatial homogeneity in the sector. On the basis of the previous considerations and the analysis of data represented by Figure 6.5c and Table 6.1, we can confirm that in the services sector there has been a deconcentration process that involved a movement from the core towards the rest of the central city. This case is one of small-scale, local, scattered deconcentration.

6.5.1.4
The institutions sector

The weighted density index related to the period 1991–2001 yields a value of 0.179, the highest of all four sectors considered; this is the first indication of deconcentration in the sector. No doubt this is the result of the consistent increase in employment density in some of the peripheral municipalities and the decrease in various areas which, on the other hand, are very close to the barycentre of the core. In the overall metropolitan area, employment in institutions rose by 4.23 percent during the period 1991–2001.

Considering the increase in jobs over the entire metropolitan area, the values of Moran's global index for the years 1991 and 2001 (0.65 and 0.67 respectively) indicate a significant positive spatial correlation in the institutions sector that persisted during the period considered. The values of Moran's local index show that the situation in this sector is very similar to that in the services sector. There is a cluster of high values in the core and two low-value clusters in the north and north-eastern parts of the outer ring. This structure remained fairly stable during the period 1991–2001.

While the core and outer ring values of Moran's I varied very little, the index decreased in the rest of the central city and the inner ring. Since the latter two sub-areas registered an increase in the number of jobs, this variation was probably concentrated in single zones and this concentration produced a reduction in the spatial correlation. On the basis of the above and the analysis of data contained in Figure 6.5d and Table 6.1, we can conclude that a slight, scattered decon-centration from the core towards the rest of the central city and inner ring took place in the period 1991–2001 in the institutions sector. This deconcentration can be linked to the administrative decentralization process that has taken place in Italy since the beginning of the 1990s.

6.5.2
A sectoral analysis of the deconcentration process in the Chieti-Pescara metropolitan area

6.5.2.1
The industry sector

During the period 1991–2001, a decline of 2.06 percent in the number of jobs was registered in the sector in the entire metropolitan area. This drop was the result of a reduction in the number of jobs in the central city (−7.56 percent), partly compensated by an increase in both the inner and outer rings (+4.97 percent and +1.77 percent respectively). These variations correspond to a change in the role played by the three sub-areas within the area. The central city, which accounted for 47.54 percent of jobs in 1991, only accounted for 44.86 percent of them in 2001, whereas the inner and outer rings shifted from 18.92 percent to 20.27 percent and from 33.55 percent to 34.86 percent respectively.

In short, we can conclude that in the metropolitan area of Chieti-Pescara, during the period considered, there was a process of deconcentration in the industry sector that involved both the inner and outer rings. Although numbers were significant in relative terms, only a few jobs were involved in this process.

6.5.2.2
The commerce sector

During the period 1991–2001, the sector registered a positive variation in the entire metropolitan area (+2.67 percent). This variation is particularly evident in the inner ring (+11.02 percent), but is also to be seen in the outer ring (+3.91 percent) and in the central city (+0.29 percent). Such an increase spread out in this way corresponds to a slight reduction in relative importance of the central city in terms of employment (the central city accounted for 58.79 percent of jobs in 1991 and 57.43 percent in 2001) and to an increase in the relative importance in employment terms of the inner ring (from 12.48 percent to 13.49 percent) and the outer ring (from 28.73 percent to 29.08 percent). In short, a slight deconcentration can be detected in this sector, in particular from the central city towards the inner ring.

6.5.2.3
The services sector

During the period 1991–2001, a significant positive variation in the number of jobs (25.88 percent) was registered in the entire metropolitan area. This variation was the result of an increase in all three sub-areas; it was particularly evident in the outer ring (+47.98 percent) and the inner ring (+38.18 percent), and was also significant in the central city (+17.99 percent).

These variations correspond to a change in the relative importance of each sub-area: there was a reduction in the importance of the central city (in 1991 it accounted for 70.50 percent of the total number of jobs, but only 66.08 percent in 2001) and a corresponding increase in the importance of the inner ring and, above all, the outer ring (the latter accounted for 19.76 percent of jobs in 1991 and 23.22 percent in 2001). In short, it can be said that there has been a process of deconcentration in the services sector, even though the central city continues to hold a significant share of the total number of jobs.

6.5.2.4
The institutions sector

During the period 1991–2001, there was a general contraction of the sector in the metropolitan area (−3.24 percent of jobs). This contraction was particularly marked in the inner ring (−7.01 percent) and in the central city (−3.17 percent). The relative importance of these sub-areas did not undergo significant variations; the highest, relative to the outer ring, was less than 2 percent in relative terms. There does not appear to have been a process of deconcentration in this sector.

6.5.3
A global analysis of the process of deconcentration in the Rome and Chieti-Pescara metropolitan areas

Deconcentration has been considered in this research (i) as a comparison of two steady states in two different historic moments (comparison of the relative importance of each sub-area at time t0 and time t1 throughout the metropolitan area) and (ii) as a movement, positive or negative, of firms within each sub-area during the period of time considered (comparison of the changes in terms of numbers of jobs registered in each sub-area during the period of time t0–t1).

In analysing the metropolitan area of Rome (Table 6.1), we can conclude that, considering deconcentration as a comparison of two steady states, during the period 1991–2001, the core lost relative importance (its importance in terms of the number of jobs in the entire metropolitan area fell from 69.9 percent to 65.65 percent) to the advantage of the rest of the central city (the importance of which rose from 8.92 percent to 11.2 percent) and of the inner ring (rising from 15.92 percent to 17.73 percent). These figures indicate a small scale deconcentration that occurred particularly between the core and the rest of the central city, an area which is strongly marked by the presence of the ring road.

This claim is strengthened when the variations in terms of numbers of jobs are taken into consideration: during the period 1991–2001, the core lost 4.48 percent of jobs, while there were increases of 27.62 percent in the rest of the central city and 13.2 percent in the inner ring respectively. The outer ring, which also registered an increase, stabilized with lower values. In all sectors except industry, the rest of the central city was the most dynamic sub-area, followed by the inner ring.

That said, this is a tendency which does not question the core's supremacy in holding the highest number of jobs which, in 2001, still accounted for 65.65 percent of jobs in the entire metropolitan area, with particularly high peaks in the services and institutional sectors. This figure confirms the metropolitan area of Rome as a strongly centralized, monocentric area.

In analysing the metropolitan area of Chieti-Pescara (Table 6.2) and interpreting deconcentration through a comparison of two steady states, during the period 1991–2001 the central city apparently suffered a slight loss of relative importance (its importance in terms of the number of jobs in the entire metropolitan area fell from 60.50 percent to 58.77 percent), to the advantage of both the inner and outer rings. This result indicates a light deconcentration that is confirmed, and even emphasized, by the trends in progress: the growth rate in the inner and outer rings was much higher than that of the central city (in the first two cases it exceeded 10 percent, whereas in the latter it barely rose above 2 percent).

Deconcentration during the period 1991–2001 was on a small scale, but it could intensify during the next few years if the trends were to continue. With the exception of the institutional sector, the central city is always the area with the lowest growth rate. The metropolitan area of Chieti-Pescara, therefore, is characterized by an external dynamism in a state of positive vitality.

6.6
Focus on the municipality of Rome: Some qualitative reflections about employment deconcentration

Rome is the largest municipality in Europe: its inhabited surface area amounts to a little less than that of Greater London and is almost double that of the Parisian territory within the Petite Couronne. This size is largely responsible for the fact that, despite the Act L. 142/1990 cited above, the metropolitan area of Rome never took off as a supra-municipal government unit. But apart from its large size, there is also a peculiar spatial distribution of the buildings within the municipality: large empty spaces alternate with large built-up spaces; light and shade effects create spatial discontinuity. This feature led to Rome being described as a city-archipelago (Marcelloni, 2003: 31). The vacant, non-built-up areas cover 73 percent of the territory; in Amsterdam and Paris these zones account for just 23 percent of the total (Marcelloni, 2003). These voids in Rome are often farmland (paradoxically, Rome is the largest farming municipality in Italy) or areas that have a high environmental, historic or cultural value. There are a few spaces in areas no longer used by factories, insofar as Rome has ever been an industrial city. Indeed, traditionally industry was located along a few road axes along which small and medium-sized enterprises grew up, certainly not large scale industry. The developed city, therefore, consists of residential-style buildings with some dedicated to commerce and services activities.

A characteristic of the Municipality of Rome is the large number of green spaces, archaeological sites, parks and natural reserves. This environmental system is constituted by the preservation of 82,000 hectares, 64 percent of the entire municipal territory. The city has traditionally been characterized by a public transport network on inadequate tracks. The underground railway system has only 2 lines, covers just 37 linear kilometres, and has 49 stations, all of which are within the ring road. This poor coverage is aggravated by the fact that, between 1981 and 1991, the residential population abandoned the areas within the ring road and moved towards the metropolitan belt, but the number of jobs in the centre has remained high: approximately one million people work within the ring road, with 800,000 of them in the services sector. This phenomenon of residential deconcentration and disproportionate economic deconcentration has provoked congestion and pollution. During the rush hour 5.6 million trips are made within the municipality; private transport accounts for 67 percent of the total; the rate of motorization is 0.5, one of the highest in the world (Los Angeles is 0.6; Paris is 0.3) (Marcelloni, 2003).

In the last few years, there has been a tendency to renovate peripheral buildings and existing spaces. In addition to this medium-term planning, the mid 1990s saw the creation of infrastructures and interventions for the celebration of the Holy Year in the Millennium of 2000, with the arrival of approximately 20 million pilgrims. This special year, with the urgency typical of such big events, fostered this new cultural tendency in some cases, but obstructed it in others. The new City Plan of 2003 envisaged the renovation of the areas concerned through housing renewal and the provision of new services and infrastructures. These should lead to an improvement in the environmental and living conditions of the residents and should enable the creation of new employment basins that will help reduce the pressure on the city centre. Policies are clearly aimed at a polycentric city with some peripheries that can become new centres: the City Plan identifies 18 new urban and metropolitan centres. The underlying aim is the revitalization of the peripheries through "city's injections administered to non-cities, a distribution of central city values throughout the suburbs" (Marcelloni, 2003: 132). The undertaking consists of finding peripheral locations in the municipality, not outside it, integrated into the network through the mobility system.

The situation in the main economic sectors has the following features:
(i) Industry developed, although with limited dimensions, as a result of the city's tertiary vocation, both in the areas expressly indicated in the City Plan[vi], and outside them. The areas explicitly assigned in the planning document of 1963 are along the main road axes (Tiburtina, Salaria, axis towards Pomezia where funds from the 'Cassa per il Mezzogiorno' were available), on the fringes of the core marked by the ring road and on the edges of the central city, delimited by the municipal administrative boundaries. Unplanned productive nuclei have emerged on both the fringes of the planned industrial areas and at some distance. These nuclei sprang up from the 1970s on, because of the lack of equipped areas and also as a consequence of the inadequate economic and legal conditions necessary

for proper settlement. The 1990s were characterized by the attempts, not always successful, to transform industrial areas from simple enterprise sites into complexes offering services to firms through the creation of technological poles[vii].

(ii) The situation in the commerce and leisure sectors is highly diversified. Although there are significant examples of deconcentration (large hypermarkets are located along the ring road, particularly along the tract between the exit of the A25 highway and the exit of the A1 highway; some business parks and entertainment centres are located along the Rome-Fiumicino road axes) we must stress that there is a solid leisure, entertainment and commercial structure in the historic centre. This is contained in the area bound by the Via Condotti, the Via Nazionale, and the Esquilino quarter (Figure 6.1, core, tsd n. 1–15). A virtual axis of commercial concentration passes through the historic centre in a north-west/south-east direction. The extreme north-west, beyond the Tiber, is represented by the Prati quarter (Figure 6.1, core, tsd n. 22); the south-east extremity crosses the Aurelian walls, passes beyond Piazza S. Giovanni and continues to the Appia Nuova road (Figure 6.1, core, tsd n. 19-31-47-48). Beyond this axis a few other centres[viii] have emerged. The area comprising the historic centre and the other centres is characterized by shops with small amounts of floor space (up to 250m^2). In the Municipality of Rome, these represent 61 percent of the total floor space and 95 percent of the total number of firms. Medium-sized floor spaces (between 250 and 2500m^2), represent 29 percent of the total surface area. Large floor spaces (above 2500m^2), represent 10 percent of the total surface area. The medium and large floor spaces are mostly located along the ring road and the main road axes (Cassia, Casilina, Collatina, Prenestina, Tuscolana, Laurentina). In particular, a quadrant has emerged in the area to the south-east of the Municipality, contained between Via Tiburtina and Via Tuscolana (Figure 6.1, core, tsd n. 28-29-30-41-44-45-46-47-64-65-66-67-68), where over half the hypermarkets (floor space > 2500m^2) are located. There are not very many in Rome (16, in contrast with 38 in Milan); the supermarkets (between 500 and 2500m^2) are well represented (406, compared with 333 in Milan). It appears that there is a trend towards an increase in large floor space outlets; the number rose by 2 percent between 1998 and 2002 (Comune di Roma, 2002). We refer as an example to the recent settlement in the zone of Anagnina (Figure 6.1, core, tsd n. 68) with Ikea's surface area of 13,000m^2. That having been said, the Municipality of Rome still remains characterized by extreme vitality in the historic centre, and an open-air, continuous and gigantic natural shopping centre.

(iii) A phenomenon similar to Silicon Sentier in Paris occurred in Saxa Rubra in Rome, (Figure 6.1, core, tsd n. 62–78), where RAI (Italian national public broadcasting) created a broadcasting centre. As a result of the restructuring of its activities, a centre of cinematographic, video, and entertainment activities was created at Cinecittà (fig 1, core, tsd n. 67). Excite is a good example of the importance of urban amenities in the ICT sector in Rome. The multinational has a small firm in the capital located within the Aurelian Walls in an historic villa near the Thermal Baths of Caracalla (Figure 6.1, core, tsd n. 21). The image the company wanted to project determined the choice of the location; this was also chosen because an aesthetically-pleasing physical environment would hopefully encourage employees to remain in the workplace longer and to work creatively. An example similar to La Défense in Paris can be found in Rome in the EUR district, where there is a concentration of firms from the ICT and business services sector (Figure 6.1, core, tsd n. 54). This area, which was developed in the 1940s in the southern part of the core, should have hosted the 1942 Expo; the development was completed in 1960 on the occasion of the Olympic Games, to accommodate the headquarters of public offices. From the 1980s onwards, prestigious multinationals located their headquarters for Europe and Italy there. EUR represents an example of deconcentration in concentration. The district is located on the fringe of the core, close to the ring road and yet near the centre. The district represents a city within the city through its architecture and spatial organization. Within the district there is a centre and a suburb; the location of firms in one or the other corresponds to their financial capacity and their image requirements. In the EUR district, centrality and suburban features can therefore be found that characterize the ICT and business services sector.

(iv) The Municipality of Rome has already started to reuse and renovate abandoned areas in the core through town planning instruments. In the Ostiense area (Figure 6.1, core, tsd n. 32), the demolition of redundant industrial buildings has made way for the third university. This regeneration operation in the Ostiense district is continuing with the Campidoglio Due (Capitol Two) project: the administrative decentralization of the municipal offices in three buildings to be located in the area. Other interventions have been planned for the district of Esquilino (Figure 6.1, core, tsd n. 15) and the new Fiorentini (Figure 6.1, core, tsd n. 28) located along the Tiburtino axis. Further important deconcentration projects planned by the Municipality of Rome are those of the Magliana (fig 1, core, tsd n. 74), with the creation of a music centre, and the transfer of the LUISS University, one of the capital's private business schools, together with the relocation of the Fiera di Roma (Rome Fair) from its traditional place along the axis that joins the historic centre to the EUR district (via Cristoforo Colombo) (Figure 6.1, core, tsd n.54), to the locality of Ponte Galeria on the Rome-Fiumicino axis (Figure 6.1, rest of the central city, tsd n. 30).

6.7
Conclusions and discussion

The phenomena of deconcentration observed in the two metropolitan areas, slight though they may be, appear to be the result of market forces and the public players' unconscious actions or failures to act. Indeed, no specific policy of deconcentration has materialized. The few cases of deconcentration that have arisen are rather the results of the 'spontaneous' dynamics of the enterprises involved, the opportunities the territories offer, and the capacity of the enterprises to choose their location.

In the areas where processes of deconcentration have taken place, the effect on the environment and the quality of life has often been negative, largely because of the lack of an adequate system of infrastructures and services. Furthermore, the interaction between economic deconcentration and residential deconcentration is still rare and unplanned.

With regard to the specific cases studied, we can see that the Municipality of Rome presents an urban model that developed around a high-value centre with several peripheral areas that deteriorate increasingly the further they are from the centre. This situation creates serious problems for environmental quality (air pollution and noise) and for the quality of life for both residents and commuters. People spend much of their daily time budget on house-work-services trips, because many of the services did not follow population mobility.

In order to counteract these problems, in 2003 the Municipality of Rome presented a new City Plan based on a new polycentric model of development. The main objective of this plan is the organization of a network city incorporating many centres that will replace those now in existence. The limitations of this process are that the City of Rome can only operate within its boundaries that are part of Rome's 'functional' metropolitan area.

In the case of Chieti-Pescara, the hilly part is characterized by residential areas and the accommodation of administrative services. Because of its morphology, access by car is difficult and public transport is inefficient. The valley settlement has a grid road system; the traffic on it, essentially private cars, creates serious problems of air pollution, noise, and congestion.

It should be noted that, if the environmental quality of the City of Chieti is in line with the Italian average, that of the City of Pescara is way below it. The values related to 'environmental pressure', 'environmental quality', and 'environmental management' are particularly low. This situation is the result of the pressure of population and economic activities in this municipality and, until recently, the city's poor planning.

Deconcentration in Italy, as it emerges from the case studies, does not seem to be particularly evident as a phenomenon, nor does it seem to be one that is particularly felt by the private operators and even less by the public players. Not having assumed significant proportions during the decade considered, deconcentration did not create any overwhelming problems in environmental or social respects. In the future, this result should be considered a competitive advantage in Italian urban areas and public actors should feature deconcentration judiciously in their urban management policies.

Many of the findings indicate that, in the case of Rome, the deconcentration process could assume more significant characteristics during the next two decades when projects are implemented to transfer certain important public buildings to the periphery. The lack of a metropolitan administration, however, threatens the effectiveness of planning, the capacity to use the territory efficiently, the potential of governance, and therefore the protection of environmental integrity and quality of life.

In highlighting the main characteristics of the deconcentration process in Italy with reference to the three aspects listed in the introduction, we can assert that: (i) the metropolitan areas analysed illustrate a small scale deconcentration and the Rome metropolitan area exemplifies the dominance of the city centre. Such a city centre strongly attracts enterprises that later abandon it for economic expediency. Many enterprises that can afford high costs continue to prefer central locations, while new peripheral locations are close to infrastructural axes. Good accessibility and low costs for purchasing and renting land and property are the most important determinants of deconcentration in the areas studied; (ii) in the cases analysed there are no specific policies dealing with deconcentration; it is not even perceived by public authorities to be a problem. The State has no planning power in Italy; planning is the task of the municipalities, but these administrative units are too small and are incapable of managing such a complex phenomenon. The Municipality of Rome is very large; as a result, it may be possible for the deconcentration process to be guided in the future through the creation of 'new centralities'. If it is to be effective, the Municipality will have to relate its activities to those of the neighbouring municipalities, such as Fiumicino; (iii) the areas analysed are in the initial stage of the deconcentration process; they are very far from the processes of reconcentration, since their city centres have not been abandoned; they, indeed, remain very dynamic, even in modifying their functions.

A trend towards more intense deconcentration can be expected in the future for both metropolitan areas. The need is recognized for adequate public policies at the appropriate levels of government, that is, on the metropolitan scale.

Notes

[i] Although this chapter is the result of a joint collaboration by the three authors, Montanari coordinated the research, Di Zio wrote paragraphs 6.3, 6.5.1.1, 6.5.1.2, 6.5.2.1, 6.5.2.2, and Staniscia wrote the rest of the text. Di Zio prepared the figures using the Geographical Information System (GIS).

[ii] The territorial pacts are specific intervention methodologies for local development of the territory implemented in Italy from the beginning of the 1990s. For an account of a comparable instrument adopted by the EU, see Staniscia, 2003.

[iii] This definition of the RMA is based on an appropriate consideration and combination of the following variables (IRSPEL, 1991, p. 17): (a) economic activities: daily average flow of people for work reasons from/to Rome; (b) social services: daily average flow of people for study reasons from/to Rome, daily flow of people attending courses in high schools from/to Rome, yearly flow of people hospitalised in the Roman hospitals; (c) cultural links: number of second homes occupied by residents in the Municipality of Rome, changes in residence from/to Rome during the period 1976/1981, changes in residence from/to Rome during the period 1987/1988; (d) territorial characteristics: accessibility level of Rome, measured by transportation costs.

[iv] Nomenclature statistique des activités économiques dans la Communauté Europeénne – Statistical classification of economic activities in the European Community

[v] The fundamental difference between an enterprise and an institution is that an enterprise is a "juridical-economic unit which produces goods and provides services destined for sale and that, on the basis of current legislation, is able to distribute profits to the proprietors, either private or public. The managing body is represented by one or more people, on an individual or associate basis, or by one or more juridical people. Enterprises include: individual enterprises, partnerships, capital companies,

cooperatives, special municipal, provincial or regional firms. Self-employed and freelance workers are also counted as enterprises" (Istat, various years - b), whereas an institution is a "juridical-economic unit whose main function is to produce goods and provide services which are not destined for sale and/or to redistribute revenue and wealth, and whose principal resources are constituted by obligatory withdrawals made by families, enterprises and non-profit institutions or by transfers without security (a fondo perduto) received from other public administration institutions. Examples of public institutions are: harbour authorities, Chamber of Commerce, Municipality, Ministry, Province, Region, public university, etc." (Istat, various years - b)

[vi] Roma-Sulmona, Tor Sapienza, Tor Cervara, Salaria, Acilia, Castel Romano, Flaminia, Tiburtina, Magliana, Santa Palomba, Torre Maura, Pantano di Grano

[vii] Examples include the scientific and technological park in the Tiburtina industrial zone; the research area at Tor Vergata; the technological industrial park and the creation of structures for techno-scientific and training activities at Castel Romano; the BIC in the locality of Morena.

[viii] To the north-east of Via Alessandria, the zone included between Piazza Bologna and Tiburtina, the area near Piazza Sempione and the district of Montesacro; to the south-west, the area behind the Vatican and along the Trastevere axis, up to Piazza della Radio.

References

Bailey TC, Gatrell AC (1995) Interactive spatial data analysis. Longman, Harlow

Becattini G (1991) The industrial district as a creative milieu. In: Benko G, Dunford M (eds) Industrial change and regional development. The transformation of new industrial spaces. Belhaven Press, London, pp 102–116

Bonifazi C, Heins F (2001) Dynamics of urbanisation in Italy. In: IUSSP-International Union for the Scientific Study of Population, XXIV General Population Conference, proceedings, Salvador-Brazil

Bontje M (2004) From suburbia to post-suburbia in the Netherlands: potentials and threats for sustainable regional development. J Housing Built Environ. 19:25–47

Borsdorf A, Wimmer H (2005) The European city: a phase-out model; challenges for European urban policy and research in the 21st century. Paper presented at the conference: The role of urban research in the 7th framework programme, http://www.mep.tno.nl/super/, 31/05/2005

Claval P (2002) Reflections on human mobility at the time of globalization. In: Montanari A (ed) Human mobility in a borderless world? Vol I IGU. Home of Geography Publication Series, SGI, Rome, pp 47–68

Comune di Roma (2002) Verso il nuovo piano regolatore. Le aree commerciali. Working paper.

Dematteis G (1995) Le trasformazioni territoriali e ambientali. In: AAVV, Storia dell'Italia Repubblicana. La trasformazione dell'Italia. Sviluppo e squilibri, Vol. 2*. Einaudi, Torino, pp 659–709

Dieleman F, Faludi A (1998) Polynucleated metropolitan regions in Northwest Europe: theme of the special issue. European Planning Studies 6(4):365–377

Getis A, Ord JK (1992) The analysis of spatial association by use of distance statistics. Geogr Anal 24:189–206

IRSPEL (1991) Studi sulla città metropolitana di Roma. Working paper, Rome

Ishikawa Y, Montanari A (2003) The new geography of human mobility - inequality trends? Vol IV IGU. Home of Geography Publication Series, SGI, Rome

ISTAT (various years – a) Censimento Generale della Popolazione e delle Abitazioni. Istat, Rome

ISTAT (various years – b) Censimento Generale dell'Industria e dei Servizi. Istat, Rome

Lethiais V, Rallet A, Vicente J (2003) TIC et réorganization spatiale des activités économiques. Introduction. Géographie, Economie, Société 5(3–4):275–285

Lowe M (2005) The regional shopping centre in the inner city: a study of retail-led urban regeneration. Urban Studies 42(3):449–470

Marcelloni M (2003) Pensare la città contemporanea. Il nuovo piano regolatore di Roma. Laterza, Roma-Bari

Montanari A, Cortese A (1993) Third world immigrants in Italy. In: King R (ed) Mass migrations in Europe. The legacy and the future. Belhaven Press, London, pp 275–292

Montanari A, Staniscia B (2003) Changing patterns & new migration trends in Italy. In: Ishikawa Y, Montanari A (eds) The new Geography of human mobility - inequality trends? Vol IV IGU. Home of Geography Publication Series, Rome, pp 141–167

Montanari A, Staniscia B (2006) Types of economic deconcentration in European Urban Space. Magnitude, physical forms, sectoral composition and governance context. Die Erde 137 (1–2): 135–153

O'Sullivan D, Unwin DJ (2003) Geographic information analysis. John Wiley, NY

Razin E (1998) Policies to control urban sprawl: planning regulations or changes in the rules of the game? Urban Studies 35(2):321–340

Shearmur R, Alvergne C (2002) Intrametropolitan patterns of high-order business service location. A comparative study of seventeen sectors in Ile-de-France. Urban Studies 39(7):1143–1163

Simmons J, Jones K, Yeates M (1998) The need for international comparisons of commercial structure and change. Prog Plann 50(4):207–215

Staniscia B (2003) L'Europa dello sviluppo locale. I patti territoriali per l'occupazione in una prospettiva comparata. Donzelli, Roma

STRATEC SA (2003) SCATTER. Sprawling Cities And TransporT: from Evaluation to Recommendations, Project funded by the EC, Contract number EVK4-CT-2001-00063, http://www.casa.ucl.ac.uk/research/scatter.htm, 27/09/2005

Vandermotten C, Van Hamme G, Medina Lockhart P, Wayens B (2004) Migration in Europe. The four last decades Vol V IGU. Home of Geography Publication Series, SGI, Rome

7 Deconcentration in a context of population growth and ideological change: The Tel-Aviv and Beer-Sheva metropolitan areas

Eran Razin and Arie Shachar

Department of Geography, The Hebrew University, Jerusalem 91905, Israel

Abstract: Employment deconcentration in Israel's Tel Aviv and Beer Sheva metropolitan areas is assessed in the context of rapid demographic growth, land scarcity, an ideological shift from welfare state to neoliberal values, and an erosion of policies to protect agricultural land. The study reveals rapid employment deconcentration, including retail and increasingly office activities, in the economically-prominent Tel Aviv metropolis. Deconcentration has been much weaker in Beer Sheva, where the major issue is to promote economic growth. The Israeli case is far from a *laissez-faire* regime, but parallels can be drawn between the transformations in Israeli and post-Communist European metropolitan areas. Israeli planning is unable to influence significantly the deconcentration from Tel Aviv's core to its suburbs, but seems to be somewhat effective in limiting scattered patterns of deconcentration

Key words: Employment deconcentration, sprawl, Tel Aviv, Beer Sheva

7.1
Introduction

Market forces and policy interventions that determine patterns of deconcentration of economic activities in Israel's metropolitan areas are unique in several respects. First, pressures of demographic growth in Israel are far greater than those in demographically stagnant Europe, resembling more North American trends. Rapid demographic growth in Israel takes place in the context of a fairly developed economy, in terms of patterns of production and consumption, implying relatively high consumption of space by workplaces and high spatial mobility of individuals. Hence, demographic growth potentially creates substantial deconcentration pressures. However, Israel lacks the abundance of land that characterizes North America, thus high land prices could constrain excessive American-style sprawl. Scarce open space could also boost the support for public intervention to control sprawl.

Second, Israel has a tradition of centralized planning – although within a democratic framework. This is partly attributed to British colonial roots of its planning and local government legislation and to the socialist roots of state founders, but can also be related to causes frequently argued to promote centralism in the Netherlands – perhaps the most centralized European welfare state. These causes include extremely scarce land reserves, high densities and external threats that promote collective action (the conflict with the Palestinians and Arab neighbours in the

179

E. Razin et al. (eds.), Employment Deconcentration in European Metropolitan Areas, 179–207.
© 2007 *Springer.*

case of Israel, and the threat of the sea in the Netherlands). Nevertheless, Israeli political culture differs fundamentally from the Dutch one. Political decision-making in Israel lacks both Dutch tradition of consensus after deliberation, and a tendency to accept the central state as a fair broker. Moreover, substantial informal political decentralization did take place in Israel, and decision-making powers are practically less centralized than formal legal and bureaucratic structures suggest (Kalchheim, 1980; Dery, 2002; Razin, 2004).

Finally, a marked ideological shift has occurred in Israel in recent decades. Socialist, collective ideals lost grounds in favour of greater individualism and American-type emphasis on markets and competition. This transition, somewhat resembling more radical transformations that took place in post-communist countries such as the Czech Republic, Hungary and Poland, had a profound influence on Israel's land policy, and could have influenced markedly the deconcentration of economic activities. Welfare state and public sector reforms, undertaken in Israel in the context of the security and economic crisis of the early 2000s, have been influenced by American neo-liberal ideologies. However, with Israel's political culture and ideological foundations so different than those of the United States, one could argue that implementation largely followed the much more centralized Thatcherian legacy of privatization and reduction of the public sector, tending to bypass local government (Razin and Hazan, 2007).

The aim of our paper is to identify and interpret patterns of deconcentration of economic activities in Israel's metropolitan areas, to discuss factors that explain these patterns, particularly the role of the processes mentioned above and the changing balance between market forces and public intervention in the Israeli context.

We focus on the Tel Aviv and Beer Sheva metropolitan areas – metropolitan areas that represent two extremes. The Tel Aviv metropolitan area (TAMA) – Israel's dominant economic and cultural heart – is the wealthiest region in Israel's space economy, although characterized by substantial disparities. The Beer Sheva metropolitan area (BSMA) – located in Israel's semi-arid and arid southern periphery – is Israel's poorest and smallest metropolitan area.

Our paper demonstrates that a most substantial process of deconcentration of economic activities has occurred in Israel's major metropolitan area, triggered by demand and supply factors that represent market forces, public policy shifts and erosion of central control. We also demonstrate the unique nature of deconcentration in a small and peripheral metropolitan area, where growing intra- and inter-regional disparities are a major concern, rather than urban-environmental concerns, such as preserving open space. We emphasize that public intervention to control sprawl did not cease, although transformed – previous checks on metropolitan expansion based on a firm policy to preserve agricultural land replaced by efforts to strengthen national and district planning and by legal battles initiated by NGOs, at the background of growing judicial activism. Deconcentration processes in Israel share some common attributes with transformations that have occurred in post-communist metropolitan areas in central Europe, but have not become similar to those of the politically decentralized United States.

The study of the TAMA includes data of Labor Force Surveys and Censuses of Population and Housing held by Israel's Central Bureau of Statistics. Such data could not be used for the BSMA, because of poor quality of data on places of work for this metropolitan area. Data on retail floor space in the Tel Aviv metropolis was received from Czamanski Ben Shahar and Co. Ltd. – a leading consulting firm that specializes in retail location. Additional material surveyed included national, metropolitan and district planning documents, relevant decisions of Israel's Land Administration, research, documents and articles published in national and local newspapers. Interviews were conducted with bureaucrats (mainly from planning departments) and politicians in the Tel Aviv and Beer Sheva metropolitan areas.

The chapter begins with a review of factors that influence suburbanization and deconcentration in Israel's metropolitan areas, followed by a discussion of suburbanization processes in the TAMA and the BSMA. A detailed examination of employment deconcentration in the TAMA is then presented, followed by a shorter qualitative account of these trends in the BSMA. Conclusions sum up major trends and comment on Israeli lessons on the balance between market forces and planning regulations.

7.2
The context: Suburbanization and deconcentration in Israel's metropolitan areas

The Tel Aviv Metropolitan Area (TAMA) is the core region of Israel, containing more than 40 percent of Israel's population and producing about 45 percent of its GDP. Secondary metropolitan areas include the national capital of Jerusalem, which grew to become a metropolitan area of significant size after 1967, and Haifa. More recently, a fourth metropolitan area has evolved – the Beer Sheva Metropolitan Area (BSMA) (Figure 7.1). While the TAMA and Haifa Metropolitan Area are in a mature stage in their development process and are structured in the well-known pattern of a metropolitan region, BSMA is still in its early stages of development and thus lacks some of the basic features of a metropolitan area. Jerusalem is a special case, being contested by two national groups that are struggling for territorial control over the city and its region. Therefore its development has been heavily influenced by geopolitical considerations and has produced quite a unique and convoluted structure for a metropolitan area.

The metropolitan character of Israel's spatial organization is a new phenomenon in the national context of development. For nearly 100 years after the beginning of the Jewish national revival in Palestine the basic orientation of Jewish society was towards rural development. In the first few years following the founding of the State of Israel in 1948, hundreds of rural settlements were established in all parts of the country, almost all of which were of a communal

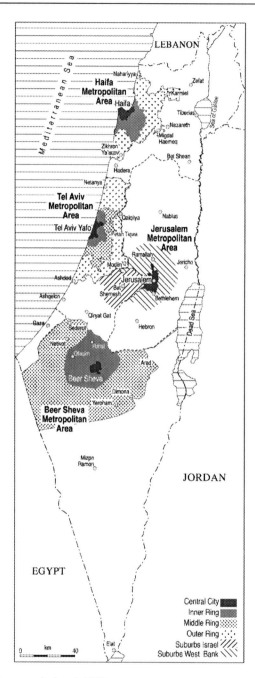

Fig. 7.1 Metropolitan areas in Israel, 2003

Note: Tel Aviv, Haifa and Beer Sheva – Central Bureau of Statistics definitions. Jerusalem – authors' definition.

or cooperative nature (kibbutzim and moshavim). At the same time, the State began to support the establishment of new towns, mainly in the peripheral areas of the country. The establishment of new towns in the periphery was done under the national meta-goal of population dispersal and given high priority on the national agenda. Despite this ideological and policy background, economic and social processes produced a national landscape that did not fit the basic ideological-political premises defined and successfully executed until the 1970s. Agglomeration processes produced a significant concentration of economic activities in the metropolitan areas, thus causing them to expand and grow steadily up to their present day hegemonic position. The process was accentuated by the decline and crisis in the agricultural sector, which allowed the spread of urban settlements at the fringe of the metropolitan areas to encroach deeply into agricultural lands. The fast metropolitanization process received formal recognition by the national planning authorities in the National Outline Plan of 1992 (NOP31), based on the four metropolitan areas. This realization was confirmed and deepened in the most recent national outline plan (NOP35), approved in 2005, which for the first time defined a meta-goal of reorganizing and streamlining the future development of the four metropolitan areas. Thus, the transformation from a rural development ideology based on a strong communal orientation into a metropolitan society based on a strong partnership between public and private investments took close to a century occur. During most of this period urbanization processes, and later on metropolitanization processes, were much more effective in creating the national landscape than the prevailing ideology and most planning regulations.

Major processes that contributed to metropolitan expansion in Israel, since the 1990s, can be divided into demand-driven and supply-driven factors. A first demand-driven factor consisted of rapid population growth, particularly the immigration of nearly one million immigrants from the former USSR between the autumn of 1989 and 2001. Israeli population grew by 48% between 1989 and 2003, from 4.56 million to 6.75 million.

Growing popularity of low-density neighbourhoods (Gonen, 1995) has been a second demand-driven factor. The Israeli middle-class tended to concentrate in apartment buildings until the late 1970s, but increasingly opted afterwards for the new Israeli dream of a single-family house, a semi-detached house or a townhouse with a backyard and a red roof. This shift of preferences has been a product of both Anglo-Saxon cultural/lifestyle influences and the rising standards of living.

A third demand-driven factor concerned local government finance. Local governments have become increasingly dependent on self-generated revenues since the mid- 1980s, thus fiercely competing over commercial and industrial land uses, considered to be profitable from the point of view of the local tax base (Razin, 1998, 2004; Ben-Elia, 2000). The development of numerous industrial parks, retail centers and office buildings has been encouraged by local authorities as a result of what has been termed in the United States "fiscal zoning". Residential development has been encouraged as well, in some cases, for its development fees, particularly on privately owned agricultural land where substantial betterment levies could be collected from its rezoning (50% of the increase in value of rezoned land). Large dwellings of high standards have been preferred by local authorities, in order to minimize future welfare expenditures. Rural regional councils that hold most open space in the metropolitan fringe within their jurisdictional boundaries have largely ceased to operate only as loose federative organizations of rural-cooperative settlements and assumed new tasks that required additional resources. Thus, they have also increasingly engaged in fiscally oriented development of residential, commercial and industrial land uses.

A final demand-driven factor concerned shopping preferences. North American style shopping malls and big-box retail centers have become extremely popular in Israel, since their successful arrival in the mid 1980s. Planned shopping centers have offered the convenience of good access to private automobiles, including parking (usually free), and an air-conditioned environment – an asset in the long summer months. Large-scale big-box retail centers located in metropolitan fringe locations, either on rezoned agricultural land or in suburban industrial zones. Retail centers located in metropolitan fringe locations, particularly those located within the jurisdictional areas of regional councils had an additional advantage: an easier ability to open for business on Saturdays (the Jewish Sabbath), due to lower friction with religious population. Growing problems of terror and insecurity in the early 2000s, associated with the Israeli-Palestinian conflict, gave planned shopping centers an additional advantage: a guarded and more secure environment.

Supply-driven causes for metropolitan expansion have first included the removal of barriers to rezone agricultural lands in the early 1990s (Razin, 1996, Feitelson, 1999). The Commission for the Preservation Agricultural Land – the most powerful tool of Israel's Planning Administration between the late 1960s and 1990 – lost much of its power, and even more crucial were the decisions of Israel's Land Administration, from 1992 onwards, that enabled lessees of government-owned agricultural land to profit from its rezoning. This shift was associated with the long-term crisis in agriculture, as well as with the pressures of mass-immigration and the ideological change in rural-cooperative kibbutzim and moshavim. Ideological arguments favouring the privatization of publicly owned land became more common (Biran, 2000), and the rise of neo-liberal ideologies might have created a less favourable environment for public intervention to control sprawl.

Other supply-driven factors included the removal of barriers for the establishment and expansion of non-agricultural, non-cooperative exurban settlements (Newman and Applebaum, 1992), and the political, economic and ideological crisis and transformation in kibbutzim and moshavim. These cooperative settlements have largely ceased to act as watch dogs of agricultural land and have become increasingly interested in real estate profits from the rezoning of agricultural land into residential or business land uses. Moreover, particularly within moshavim, unused farm structures were leased (largely illegally) to retail, wholesale, warehousing, office and small manufacturing enterprises. This phenomenon increased immensely the availability of space for businesses in metropolitan fringe locations, bypassing the need for planning approvals and adding to the leapfrogging nature of this development.

In addition, the role of technological improvements in promoting employment deconcentration should not be understated. These refer in particular to telecommunication technologies that make it easier to office activities and to various computer-related enterprises to disperse, and to investment in the suburban road network that gradually erodes the accessibility advantage of the inner parts of the metropolitan areas. The completion of toll highway no. 6 in 2004, which practically serves as a beltway along the eastern boundary of the Tel Aviv metropolitan area, and associated investment in suburban highways, have practically reduced the location advantage of the city of Tel Aviv. Location near the Ayalon highway that crosses the city of Tel Aviv from north to south seems to have lost its advantage as the most accessible location in Israel for car-oriented travel.

All the above factors taken into account, one should not ignore the still powerful factors that act to check deconcentration processes in Israel. These include scarcity of land that leads to high land prices, and a still relatively powerful planning establishment at the state level (Alterman, 2002). The Planning Administration of the Ministry of Interior is the seat of the two upper tiers of Israel's hierarchical statutory planning system: the National Council for Planning and Construction and the six District Committees for Planning and Construction. Only the lower level is largely in the hands of local authorities. As a response to the practical collapse of the old planning doctrine – of population dispersal and preservation of agricultural land – the Planning Administration embarked during the 1990s in a new round of national and district plans, emphasizing the metropolitan scale, the extreme land scarcity and the need to curb leapfrog development in rural areas.

"Green" and social justice lobbies have also assumed a considerable influence (although constrained by the fact that the public agenda tend to be dominated by issues associated with Israeli-Palestinian relations), increasingly engaged in legal battles challenging illegal construction on open space that was disregarded or even backed by local authorities, as well as public decisions that seemed to contradict principles of justice. An unprecedented ruling was given by the High Court of Justice in 2002, in an appeal of the Democratic Mizrahi Coalition – an NGO lobbying for social justice and the rights of the poorer segments of Israeli society. Based on principles of distributive justice, the court revoked Israel's Land Administration policy to provide generous compensation to agricultural lessees of rezoned land owned by the public, based on the value of the land after rezoning (Barak-Erez, 2004).

7.3
The Tel-Aviv and Beer Sheva metropolitan areas: Attributes and suburbanization processes

7.3.1
Tel Aviv metropolitan area (TAMA)

The boundaries of the metropolitan areas in Israel are determined by the Central Bureau of Statistics before each national census and are updated according to the geographical reality of the time. In early periods, the contiguity of the built up area was the main consideration in establishing the boundaries of the metropolitan area. In the 1995 census this criterion was dropped altogether and the main criterion applied was of the metropolitan area as a unified labor market. The application of this criterion meant the inclusion of a number of rural regional councils within the metropolitan area. Many of the rural settlements in these councils had lost their agricultural base and became suburban dormitory settlements. The 1995 delimitation defines the TAMA as the combined area of Tel Aviv district and Central district. To the south the Ashdod area was included within the metropolitan area. There are indications that the spillover of metropolitan development beyond the existing boundaries might necessitate the updating of the boundaries of the metropolitan area for the next national census scheduled for 2008.

According to the present definition of the metropolitan area, the central city of Tel Aviv-Yaffo had, at the end of 2004, a population of 371,000; the inner ring had 805,000 inhabitants; the middle ring had a population of 941,000; and the outer ring had a population of 869,000, bringing the total population of the TAMA to about three million inhabitants.

The city of Tel Aviv-Yaffo is the core area of the TAMA. Tel-Aviv was established in 1909 as a garden suburb to the ancient city of Yaffo. Since its establishment, the city of Tel-Aviv comprises the core of the metropolitan area being the largest concentration of employment and the main economic and cultural hub of the TAMA. The municipalities around Tel-Aviv, such as Ramat Gan, Bene Beraq and Herzeliyya, started as agricultural settlements and through a fast urbanisation process became regarded, already in the 1950s, as the inner ring of the TAMA. Through a strong industrialization process, the veteran settlements such as Petah Tiqwa, Rishon LeZiyyon and Kefar Sava created the middle ring of the metropolitan area.

From the 1980s, a wave of suburbanization created an overspill of development beyond the middle ring represented by the establishment or growth of small to middle size towns such as Rosh HaAyin, Yavne, Shoham and Modiin. Most of this urban development was planned, initiated and executed by various government authorities. This is an example of 'induced suburbanisation' at its prime. During the same period the largest of the new towns of Israel, the port city of Ashdod, became part of the labour market of the Tel Aviv region. Another part of this overspill has been of spontaneous suburbanization of rural settlements. The fast growth of suburban communities was enhanced by the growing number of private vehicles and the continuous decline of the agricultural base of many of the rural settlements in this area. This phase of strong suburbanization and significant expansion of the labour market created the outer ring of the TAMA (Figure 7.1).

The analysis of population dynamics in the TAMA by rings enables the identification of the 'expansion wave' – the most rapidly growing ring – over the last 40 years since the first population census in 1961 (Figure 7.2). At the beginning of the 1960s, the population living in the core city of Tel Aviv-Yaffo was dominant and accounted for 37 percent of the total population of the metropolitan area (as defined today). The inner ring had 29 percent, the middle ring 21 percent and outer ring 13 percent of the population of the TAMA. Reviewing the situation after 44 years, we can notice that towards the end of 1990s the expansion wave moved into the outer ring. The relative share of population in the various rings changed dramatically: most updated population estimates (2004) show that the highest relative share moved into the middle ring. The share of population in the core was down to 12.4 percent, in the inner ring the share was 27.0 percent, in the middle ring it was up to 31.5 percent and in the outer ring it was up to 29.1 percent. It can be concluded that the dynamics of population in the TAMA has followed the well-known spatial-demographic model of concentric wave expansion: the Van den Berg *et al.* (1995) metropolitan development model.

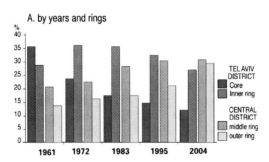

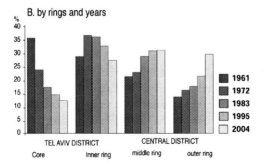

Fig. 7.2 Population of the TAMA by ring (1995 boundaries), 1961–2004

7.3.2
Beer Sheva Metropolitan Area (BSMA)

The city of Beer Sheva and its surroundings were defined as a metropolitan area as part of the preparation of a master plan for the Beer Sheva region at the beginning of the 1990s. It has to be emphasized from the outset that the BSMA is in a very early stage of development. The central city of the BSMA in its modern form is about 55 years old and the urban settlements surrounding it are even younger. Another unique feature of the BSMA is the fact that the entire settlement system is located within an arid or semi-arid region. A main economic base for urban development in this arid region is the utilization of natural resources such as potash, phosphates, bromide, and natural gas. Another source of employment is the operation of obnoxious facilities such as the central dump for solid waste located north of Beer Sheva and the central industrial zone for dangerous chemicals south of Beer Sheva. Facilities which had to be placed in remote areas as far as possible from the main concentration of population in Israel were also located in the region of Beer Sheva, such as a nuclear facility operating east of Beer Sheva. The unique conditions of an arid region, relatively rich with mineral resources and remote from the main concentration of population, can explain the basic spatial pattern of dispersal of employment within the BSMA.

The delineation of the BSMA was based almost exclusively on the pattern of economic interactions between the city of Beer Sheva and the urban settlements surrounding it. There was even a normative-symbolic motivation in defining a metropolitan area around Beer Sheva, the capital of the Negev, which was to "elevate" it as an integral part of the metropolitan system of Israel.

Much of the residential and non-residential development in "suburban" Beer Sheva did not reflect, until the 1990s, suburbanization and deconcentration processes, but location decisions largely unrelated to metropolitan dynamics. The growth of new development towns in the Beer Sheva region, the growth of the Arab-Bedouin population in Beer Sheva's surroundings, and the development of large out-of-town complexes of heavy chemical industries, mineral-extracting plants and the Nuclear Research Center, were all major engines of growth in suburban space, but did not consist of any movement of population and businesses from central parts of the "metropolitan area" to its outer parts.

The core of the BSMA is the city of Beer Sheva, established by the Turkish authorities at the beginning of the 20th century as a desert outpost with the aim of controlling the nomad population roaming in the desert. It remained a small town until 1948 when a large number of Jewish immigrants were settled around the site of the Turkish town. Becoming the capital of the Negev meant the establishment of governmental and public services in Beer Sheva serving the entire population of the Negev (the desert that comprises the southern part of Israel). In addition to the service function, the central government channelled large amount of public support in order to build up a strong regional industrial base. Many of those employed in the new mineral-extracting and processing plants made Beer Sheva their home. Towards the end of the 1980s, the population of Beer Sheva crossed the 100,000 mark. Then in the 1990s it grew very rapidly because of the large influx of immigrants from the former Soviet Union who found there housing at relatively easy terms. Beer Sheva reached the population of 180,000 in the early 2000s and is still growing vigorously.

The inner ring of the BSMA is made up of urban settlements of three types: a) Three suburbs established to the north of Beer Sheva by families who left Beer Sheva in the pursuit of a suburban way of life, low densities, and urban amenities of high quality. b) The town of Ofakim, established at the beginning of the 1950s as a service center for some rural settlements, but functioning as a struggling industrial town. It has at present about 23,000 inhabitants and is strongly connected to the Beer Sheva labor market. c) Bedouin towns and rural settlements. The largest of these Bedouin towns is Rahat to the north of Beer Sheva, with a population of 36,000. Many of Rahat's inhabitants are employed in Beer Sheva and in many of the industrial plants of the region. To the south, the inner ring includes the largest industrial zone of dangerous chemicals – Ramat Hovav – which is a source of tremendous ecological problems. The entire population of the inner ring amounts to about 176,000 persons in 2002.

The outer ring is comprised of five weak Jewish towns established in the 1950s and 1960s: Arad, Dimona, Yerucham, Netivot and Sederot. Unemployment in these new towns is quite high and the socioeconomic status of their populations is rather low. Beer Sheva serves all of these urban settlements and there is an extensive network of commuting between these towns and the central city as well as towards the large industrial plants of the region. Within the western – less arid – sector of the outer ring, there is an extensive rural population. In the eastern sector of this outer ring, there is a large Bedouin population, many of them in informal settlements. The total population of the outer ring is around 134,000. The total population of the BSMA, comprised of the central city and the two rings, is fast approaching the half a million mark.

The distribution of population in the BSMA by rings changed considerably between 1990 and 2002. The share of the core decreased from 44 percent of the total to 35 percent, whereas the fastest growth occurred in the inner ring moving from 21 percent to 34 percent. The outer ring declined slightly from 35 percent to 31 percent. The rapid growth of the inner ring was caused by two completely different processes: the first is an overspill of Jewish population from Beer Sheva to new suburban communities. The second process is the sedentarization of some of the Bedouin population and their very high natural growth rate, reflected in the fast growth of quasi-urban and informal settlements. The location of the crest of the "expansion wave" in the inner ring is typical of a metropolitan area in its early stage of development.

The main reason for the relative decline of the outer ring is the very low rates of population growth in the Jewish towns. Out of the five towns at the outer ring, four suffered from a negative migration balance – Dimona, Arad, Yeruham and Sederot – and only one – Netivot – kept a positive migration balance in

2002, albeit a very small one. In-migration to the outer ring comprised mainly of
new immigrants who recently arrived in Israel.

7.4
Accelerating deconcentration of employment in the TAMA

7.4.1
Trends of deconcentration

The proportion of jobs in the city of Tel Aviv, out of the total number of jobs
in the metropolitan area, has declined steadily. High rates of job growth in the
metropolitan area during the 1990s were associated with a new wave of job deconcentration out of the city of Tel Aviv. Job growth was most remarkable in the
middle and outer rings (Table 7.1; Figure 7.3). Deconcentration has accelerated
after 1995 and by the early 2000s nearly one half of all jobs in the Tel Aviv
metropolis was in the middle and outer rings (more than one half if the city of
Ashdod is included). Although rates of population growth have been particularly
high in the middle and outer rings in recent decades, growth rates of the number of

Table 7.1 Employment in the Tel Aviv metropolitan area by rings, 1970–2003

	1970	1980	1989	1990	1995	2000	2001	2003
	Number of employed persons – place of work (% of the metro area)							
The City of Tel Aviv	49.2	39.6	38.0	37.7	34.6	31.6	30.4	29.3
Inner ring	18.8	21.0	23.6	24.5	24.9	22.9	22.5	22.4
Middle and outer rings	32.0	39.4	38.4	37.9	40.5	45.5	47.1	48.3
Total metro	100	100	100	100	100	100	100	100
Total metro (thousands)	480.7	587.4	683.0	707.2	949.1	1065.4	1091.1	1124.9
	Number of employed persons – place of work (% of Israel – total)							
Total metro (excluding Ashdod)	49.9	46.8	46.8%	47.4	48.2	48.0	48.1	48.3
	1971–1980	1981–1989	1990	1991–1995	1996–2000	2001–2003		
	Percent annual growth							
The City of Tel Aviv	−0.15	1.21	2.58	4.29	0.50	−0.73		
Inner ring	3.15	3.03	7.58	6.43	0.59	1.14		
Middle and outer rings	4.16	1.41	2.02	7.48	4.78	3.86		
Total metro	2.02	1.69	3.54	6.06	2.34	1.83		
Israel – total	2.68	1.71	2.13	5.69	2.45	1.61		

Source: Central Bureau of Statistics, Labor Force Survey (annual publications)
Tables 7.1–7.4 do not include the City of Ashdod, located in the Southern District, but within
the outer ring of the Tel Aviv metropolis.
The labor force survey data includes only the civilian labor force, and does not include Palestinians
residing in the Palestinian territories and working in Israel.

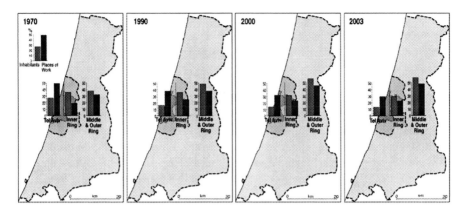

Fig. 7.3 Population and employment in the TAMA, 1970-2003

jobs in these rings were even higher since the 1990s. Thus, remarkable suburbanization of population was accompanied in the 1990s and 2000s by an even more
remarkable suburbanization of jobs.

Obviously, the city of Tel Aviv had many more jobs than employed residents
(Table 7.2). The inner ring (the rest of the Tel Aviv District) was at the other
extreme, characterized by substantially more employed persons residing in this
ring than jobs located in the ring. Proximity to job opportunities within the city of
Tel Aviv could explain the low ratio of jobs per employed residents in the inner
ring. Nevertheless, this ratio in the inner ring was gradually rising, as a result of
limited population growth and spillover of economic activity from employment
cores within Tel Aviv. In the middle and outer rings, a U shaped curve can be
identified (Table 7.2). The number of employed persons residing in these outer
rings grew more rapidly than the number of jobs until 1990, but the trend was
reversed in the 1990s – the number of jobs in the middle and outer rings now grew
more rapidly than the number of employed residents. In the 1960s and 1970s such
a low dependency reflected limited links with the Tel Aviv economy, whereas

Table 7.2 Employed persons in sub-areas of the Tel Aviv metro (place of work) versus employed
persons residing in the sub-areas (place of residence), 1970–2003

	1970	1980	1990	1995	2000	2001	2003
The City of Tel Aviv	1.61	1.98	2.13	2.07	2.10	2.02	1.99
Inner ring	0.53	0.55	0.67	0.76	0.76	0.77	0.81
Middle and outer rings	0.86	0.84	0.79	0.84	0.85	0.88	0.88
Total metro	0.97	0.96	0.98	1.02	1.02	1.02	1.03

1 = Number of employed persons in the area (place of work) equals number of employed persons
residing in the area.

since the 1990s the renewed low dependency reflected rapid deconcentration of jobs within the metropolitan area.

A more detailed analysis of data files of the 1983 and 1995 Censuses of Population and of the 2001 Labor Force Survey shows that major employment concentrations out of the city of Tel Aviv in 1983 were the city of Petah Tikva (a large regional city that fully became a suburb of Tel Aviv in the 1960s) and the city of Ramat Gan (an inner suburb, whose office complex forms an integral part of the metropolitan CBD), followed by Holon (an inner suburb with a large industrial zone) and Netanya (a regional city considered as an outer suburb of Tel Aviv since the 1990s). Each had between 6.2 percent and 4.5 percent of the places of work in the Tel Aviv metropolis in 1983, compared to 42.6 percent in the city of Tel Aviv.

Employment distribution in the TAMA according to the basic components of the metropolitan structure – rings and sectors – is presented in Figure 7.4. The highest concentration of workplaces is still in the core area of the TAMA, the city of Tel Aviv-Yaffo, but the share of employment in the core area has declined

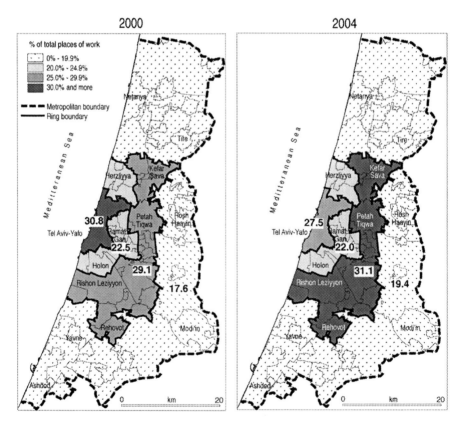

Fig. 7.4 Places of work in the TAMA, 2000–2004

systematically from 30.8 percent in 2000 to 27.5 percent in 2004 of the total employment in the TAMA. The inner ring had remained stable with 22.5 percent of the total number of workplaces in both 2000 and 2004. The middle ring included 29.1 percent of employment in 2000, increasing to 31.1 percent in 2004. The outer ring still has the lowest share of employment in the entire metropolitan area, but this share grew steadily from 17.6 percent in 2000 to 19.4 percent in 2004. Thus, the main bulk of employment is moving slowly from the inner parts of the metropolitan area to the outer parts. In fact, this pattern of change resembles the pattern of changes in the population distribution, reflecting both a cause and effect process where population is following the deconcentration of employment and, at the same time, new places of work are established near new suburban residential areas.

The decline in the proportion of jobs within the city of Tel Aviv was not accompanied by the emergence of a particularly prominent employment node in a particular suburban node. The proportion of jobs in the inner suburbs of Ramat Gan and Holon even declined slightly between 1995 and 2001. The proportion of jobs in the outer suburbs of Petah Tikva and Netanya grew somewhat, and several new employment nodes grew substantially in the outer suburbs: Rishon Letsion, Ashdod and Herzeliyya. Deconcentration of employment was thus associated with the growth of new suburban nodes, rather than with growing prominence of existing ones. Except for Rishon Letsion and Ashdod, job growth between 1983 and 2001 was most rapid in suburban locations that were minor employment centers in 1983.

Figure 7.5 presents the places of residence of those employed in the various rings of the metropolitan area in 1999. The four maps show a strong correspondence between place of work and place of residence. Of those working in the core – the city of Tel Aviv – 33.5 percent reside in the core. Moving out of the core to the subsequent rings, there is a declining gradient of the percentage persons living in the rings and working in the core. Of the persons employed in the inner ring more than 60 percent live in the same ring. In the middle ring the proportion of persons living and working in the same ring is even higher reaching about 66 percent. For those working in the outer ring the proportion of those living in the same ring is the highest: 77 percent. Thus, the correspondence between place of work and place of residence becomes more marked as we move to the outer parts of the metropolitan area.

7.4.2
Industrial variations

The economy of the city of Tel Aviv has been increasingly dominated by financing and business services, whereas manufacturing in the city declined rapidly and continuously. Similar processes have occurred in the inner ring although financing and business services have been less prominent in the inner ring than in the city. The most remarkable trend in the middle and outer rings was the practical collapse

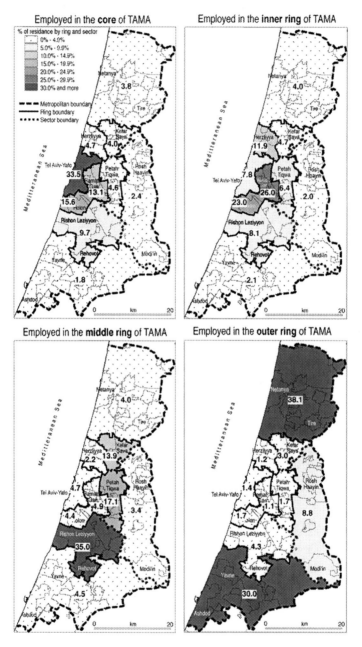

Fig. 7.5 Places of residence of those employed in each ring of TAMA, 1999

of employment in agriculture. In contrast, jobs in commerce have become more prominent, particularly since the 1990s.

An examination of the geographical distribution of major economic branches (Table 7.3) reveals striking deconcentration of commerce from the city of Tel Aviv to the outer suburbs. The proportion of jobs in commerce, restaurants and hotels in the city of Tel Aviv has sunk from 60 percent in 1970 to around 30 percent in 2000. The share of the middle and outer rings grew at a particularly rapid pace between 1995 and 2000. Detailed data on retail trade clearly demonstrates that rapid deconcentration from Tel Aviv in the 1990s was indeed deconcentration and not reconcentration in a small number of suburban locations.

Financing and business services have been the most concentrated economic branch within the Tel Aviv metropolis as a whole. They have also been the economic activities most concentrated in the city of Tel Aviv. However, a most remarkable process of job deconcentration in this branch – particularly from the city to the middle and outer rings – has occurred, accelerating since the mid 1990s. Whereas Tel Aviv was extremely prominent in financing and business services in 1983, with another concentration of a significant size only in adjacent Ramat Gan, by 2001 new concentrations have emerged. In addition to the strengthened concentration in Ramat Gan, new concentrations in the outer rings included Petah Tikva, Herzeliyya, Rishon Letsion, Netanya and Raanana. Financing and business services were a prominent sector only in Tel Aviv in 1983, being significant also

Table 7.3 Employed persons in the Tel Aviv metropolitan area by place of work and selected economic branches (old classification), 1970–2000

	Manufacturing					Commerce, restaurants, hotels				
	1970	1980	1990	1995	2000	1970	1980	1990	1995	2000
% of the metro area										
The city of Tel Aviv	46.2%	30.9%	28.1%	26.5%	20.6%	60.0%	52.1%	44.9%	37.6%	30.9%
Inner ring	21.0%	25.9%	27.9%	26.3%	23.8%	18.3%	22.0%	26.3%	27.7%	23.8%
Middle and outer rings	32.8%	43.1%	44.0%	47.2%	55.6%	21.7%	25.9%	28.8%	34.7%	45.3%
Tel Aviv metro – total	100%	100%	100%	100%	100%	100%	100%	100%	100%	100%
% of Israel – total										
Tel Aviv metro – total	56.7%	52.3%	49.2%	46.8%	44.1%	56.0%	52.5%	53.0%	53.8%	50.6%

	Transport, storage, communications					Financing, business services				
	1970	1980	1990	1995	2000	1970	1980	1990	1995	2000
% of the metro area										
The city of Tel Aviv	62.9%	47.5%	42.0%	40.2%	33.8%	81.5%	68.8%	64.6%	53.8%	46.8%
Inner ring	9.1%	11.9%	15.2%	19.3%	18.1%	10.3%	15.6%	19.0%	22.3%	23.1%
Middle and outer rings	28.0%	40.5%	42.7%	40.5%	48.1%	8.2%	15.6%	16.3%	24.0%	30.3%
Tel Aviv metro – total	100%	100%	100%	100%	100%	100%	100%	100%	100%	100%
% of Israel – total										
Tel Aviv metro – total	45.6%	44.8%	47.6%	51.0%	52.6%	66.4%	66.3%	65.2%	61.0%	62.4%

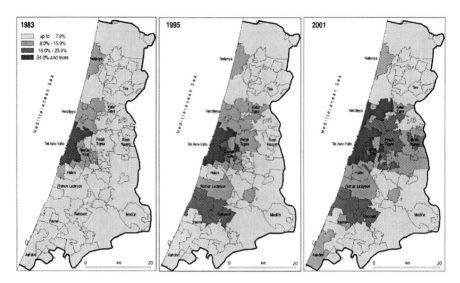

Fig. 7.6 Places of work in the TAMA – percentage in financing and business services, 1983-2001

in adjacent Ramat Gan and Givatayim (Figure 7.6). By 2001 it was as prominent in the job market of several suburban cities as in Tel Aviv. Herzeliyya (Kipnis and Noam, 1998) and Raanana – two northern suburbs – seem in particular to emerge as locations where a substantial proportion of jobs is in this sector, thus resembling the share of this sector in the economic structure of Tel Aviv and Ramat Gan (Figure 7.6). In transport, storage and communications, jobs have increasingly concentrated in the Tel Aviv metropolis, but deconcentrated substantially within the metropolitan area, particularly towards the middle and outer rings.

An examination based on a new, more detailed, classification of economic branches (Table 7.4) reaffirms evidence on significant deconcentration of manufacturing, wholesale and retail trade, transport and communications, business services and even banking, insurance and financial institutions. Various public services were the only major branches in which the city of Tel Aviv did not lose ground since 1995.

Suburbanization of manufacturing is expected, because this land-use usually cannot compete with rents paid by commercial and office uses in inner city locations. Some deconcentration of retail is also expected, given the deconcentration of population. However, the pace of retail deconcentration from Tel Aviv to the middle and outer rings of the metropolis between 1995 and 2003 was most remarkable and indicates that the city of Tel Aviv has largely lost its position as the commercial center of the metropolis. Finally, the marked deconcentration of jobs in business services and even in banking and finance is the most worrying process from the point of view of Tel Aviv. These sectors are the leading economic activities in the city (Kipnis, 1998), given substantial agglomeration economies that have limited their dispersal in the past. However, their recent deconcentration

Table 7.4 Employed persons in the Tel Aviv metropolitan area by place of work and selected economic branches (new classification), 1995–2003

	Manufacturing			Wholesale, retail trade, automobile repairs			Accommodation services and restaurants		
	1995	2000	2003	1995	2000	2003	1995	2000	2003
% of the metro area									
The city of Tel Aviv	26.5%	20.6%	18.8%	35.1%	28.5%	23.8%	45.7%	38.7%	39.7%
Inner ring	26.3%	23.8%	21.2%	30.1%	24.1%	25.2%	19.6%	22.6%	20.8%
Middle and outer rings	47.2%	55.6%	60.0%	34.8%	47.4%	51.0%	34.7%	38.7%	39.5%
Tel Aviv metro – total	100%	100%	100%	100%	100%	100%	100%	100%	100%
% of Israel – total									
Tel Aviv metro – total	46.8%	44.1%	44.1%	57.3%	54.1%	53.8%	44.6%	41.7%	44.4%

	Transport, storage and communication			Banking, insurance, financial institutions			Business services		
	1995	2000	2003	1995	2000	2003	1995	2000	2003
% of the metro area									
The city of Tel Aviv	39.9%	33.5%	27.2%	61.1%	59.8%	55.4%	51.2%	42.4%	39.3%
Inner ring	19.2%	17.9%	19.3%	20.2%	21.2%	21.3%	23.3%	23.8%	22.0%
Middle and outer rings	40.9%	48.6%	53.5%	18.7%	19.0%	23.3%	25.5%	33.8%	38.7%
Tel Aviv metro – total	100%	100%	100%	100%	100%	100%	100%	100%	100%
% of Israel – total									
Tel Aviv metro – total	50.8%	52.4%	52.9%	68.6%	69.1%	70.3%	58.9%	61.1%	62.1%

hints that agglomeration economies offered by the city of Tel Aviv are either losing significance or that similar economies are increasingly available in selected suburban locations that are on their way to become "mini-edge cities".

7.4.3
Commuting patterns

Data on commuting patterns (not presented) indicates that commuting from inner ring sub-areas to the city of Tel Aviv became less and less prominent between 1983 and 2001, because of job deconcentration. However, the proportion of those commuting to Tel Aviv among employed persons residing in the middle and outer rings did not decline and in some cases even grew slightly between 1983 and 1995, probably because of the growing integration of the middle and outer rings in the metropolitan economy. Nevertheless, job deconcentration has lead to a reversal of this trend and the tendency of middle and outer rings residents to commute to the city of Tel Aviv slightly decreased between 1995 and 2001. Among those working in the city of Tel Aviv, an increasing proportion came from the middle and outer rings and from out of the metropolitan area. As expected, females tend much more than males to be employed in their area of residence, i.e. to commute shorter distances. This lower tendency of females to commute long distances did not diminish at all between 1983 and 2001, and even grew in some locations.

7.4.4
The distribution of floor space for economic uses

Data on floor space for economic land uses (not including public administration) is in line with employment data. The proportion of floor space in the city of Tel Aviv and in the inner ring in 1995 (Table 7.5). was slightly lower than the proportion of jobs located in the city and the inner ring (Table 7.1). In contrast, the middle and outer rings included 51 percent of metropolitan floor space, although containing only 40 percent of jobs in the metropolitan area in that year. These differences reflect variations in land prices. Higher land prices lead to higher land use intensity in the dense inner parts of the metropolis, in terms of jobs per square meters.

Inclusion of approved plans and plans in the process of approval by the planning commissions in 1995, hints at most substantial future deconcentration of economic land uses into the outer rings of the Tel Aviv metropolis (Table 7.5). Indeed, employment data for the period 1995–2003 indicates that deconcentration has accelerated substantially, despite of the slowdown in the economy through most of these years.

The substantial downturn in the real estate market in the years 2001–2003 has affected more significantly rents for office space in Tel Aviv than office space in major suburban concentrations, such as Raanana, Petah Tikva, Airport City (near Ben Gurion Airport), Nes Ziyyona and Rehovot. Indeed new office parks at the above suburban locations – many of them officially established as high technology industrial parts – have been aggressively soliciting tenants from Tel Aviv, Ramat Gan and Herzeliyya, offering lower costs and convenient car accessibility. Although their advantage in basic rent has been eroding, due to the rapid decline in rents within Tel Aviv, the overall package still remained attractive

Table 7.5 The Tel Aviv metropolis – built up and planned floor space (in square meters) for businesses, offices and manufacturing land uses, 1995

	Economic land uses		Existing and planned economic land uses	
	Square meters	Percent	Square meters	Percent
The City of Tel Aviv	6,216,000	31.5	10,225,500	17.0
Inner ring	3,413,023	17.3	8,364,000	13.9
Middle and outer rings	10,083,200	51.2	41,542,400	69.1
Total	19,712,223	100.0	60,131,900	100.0

Source: Metropolitan Planning Team (1998) *Principles of Development Policy for the Tel Aviv Metropolitan Area, Volume B.*
Data is based on local property tax files and on information provided by city engineers.

due to lower local taxes, maintenance fees and parking costs. Those attracted to suburban locations have been largely large corporations, each occupying substantial office space, whereas small-scale office activities still tend to remain in the older more central locations, due to their dependence on varied external services still not fully available in suburban locations.

7.4.5
The suburbanization of retail: Planned shopping centers

The deconcentration of retail, particularly into planned car-oriented shopping malls and big-box retail centers (power centers), stands at the heart of the controversy over sprawl of economic land use, although the deconcentration of office space could have even more far-reaching implications on the vitality of central cities and on commuting and transportation implications of sprawl.

The first "American style" shopping mall in Israel opened in Ramat Gan in 1987. Its huge success has lead to the transformation of the geography of retail in Israel within a few years. Construction of numerous shopping malls was later on followed by a growing popularity of power centers – shopping centers oriented towards big box retail and discount stores. Rents at traditional CBDs/commercial streets fell sharply and many of them have turned to specialize in inexpensive merchandize.

Our data confirms that planned shopping centers of various types are indeed a suburban phenomenon. By 2003, retail floor space in planned shopping centers in the middle and outer rings of the Tel Aviv metropolis reached 740,000 square meters (Table 7.6), compared to only 350,000 square meters in planned shopping centers in the central city and the inner ring. Another new phenomenon – the conversion of farm structures into non-agricultural businesses – added another estimated 130,000 square meters of retail floor space in the middle and outer rings.

Table 7.6 Retail floor space (square meters) in planned shopping centers in the middle and outer rings of the Tel Aviv metropolis by type of center and type of local authority, 2003

Type of local authority	Type of center			Total
	Neighborhood center	Shopping mall	Power center – big box/discount retail	
City	46700	384035	178900	609635
Local council (up to 20,000 inhabitants)	5300	0	35000	40300
Rural regional council	8000	11400	71200	90600
Total	60000	395435	285100	740535

Source: Data of Czamanski Ben Shahar and Co. Ltd., Haifa.
Floor space in square meters includes only retail space, excluding restaurants, cinemas, services and corridors. However, it includes retail space not in use.

Table 7.7 Retail floor space (square meters) in the TAMA by type, 2003

	Core and inner ring	Middle and outer ring (excluding Ashdod)	Total
Planned shopping centers	350,000	640,000	990,000
Out of planned centers	750,000	800,000	1,550,000
In the rural sector	0	130,000	130,000
Total	1,100,000	1,570,000	2,670,000

Source: Data of Czamanski Ben Shahar and Co. Ltd., Haifa.
The Table presents rough estimates of net retail floor space.

The largest concentration of retail space in planned shopping centers was built in the suburban city of Rishon Letsion (141,900 square meters net retail space by 2003). Rishon Letsion explicitly aspired to turn its western industrial zones into retail and business complex that would rival those in the city of Tel Aviv. However, it has become instead one of two main examples in Israel for intense competition in which each new shopping mall, larger and more glamorous than its older competitors, leads to the decline and even collapse of older malls, established only a few years earlier. Indeed, the northern and southern suburbs of Tel Aviv have become prime cases of intense competition among developers and among local authorities over retail development. Major players in the north were the cities of Herzeliyya, Raanana, Kefar Sava, Netanya, and Hof Hasharon regional council. Major players in the south were Rishon Letsion, Nes Ziyyona, Rehovot, Ashdod, Qiryat Ekron and adjacent regional councils. The latter have an advantage in some cases in space-consuming power centers that can open in Saturdays and also compete through numerous businesses established in unused farm structures. Over-investment in planned shopping centers has, thus, become a worry not only of land use planners and environmentalists, but also of business consultants who are concerned particularly by vast over investment in power centers that can lead to wide-scale collapse in the retail sector (Czamanski Ben Shahar and Co., 2003).

Whereas total retail floor-space in traditional street locations (including industrial zones) is still larger than total floor-space in planned centers established since the mid 1980s, the gap is very narrow in the middle and outer rings (Table 7.7) and in a few years more retail space will be located in planned centers that have a major role in accelerating deconcentration. Even in the core and inner ring of the metropolis, about one third of retail space is already in planned shopping centers.

7.5
Deconcentration of employment in the BSMA in a context of economic weakness

The peripheral Beer Sheva region suffers from economic weakness, also reflected by fiscal weakness of its local authorities. Soft demand for business land uses is a result of the lack of substantial high-technology industry, large-scale office functions, and logistics. Its economy thus depends on manufacturing, public services and some retail/services/tourism businesses. Land values are low throughout the region and do not act as a significant driving force of deconcentration.

The geography of employment in the Beer Sheva region is characterized primarily by large out-of-town concentrations of mineral extracting plants and of environmentally hazardous industries and facilities. The location of those has been determined by mineral extraction and by the need of hazardous facilities to locate far from built-up areas. Thus, outward commuting (much of it paid and organized by the large employers) has been prominent in this region for many decades.

Data on manufacturing employment in the BSMA in 1996 and 2001 is available from a biennial survey of industry in the Southern District of Israel, carried out by the Negev Center for Regional Development, Ben-Gurion University of the Negev. Total manufacturing employment in 1996 was 15,409 of which 27 percent were located in the city of Beer Sheva, 14 percent in the inner ring and 59 percent in the outer ring. In 2001 the total manufacturing employment grew to 19,933: the core increased its share to 29 percent, the inner ring grew to 21 percent, while the share of employment in the outer ring declined to 50 percent of the total. Manufacturing in the outer ring is based mainly on the processing of natural resources, apparently not growing in terms of employment. Manufacturing in the core and the inner ring are based more on the manufacturing of goods, receiving a boost by 'A' priority zone incentives (subsidies to finance industrial investment) granted to the city of Beer Sheva in the 1990s. Previously such incentives were granted only to the vicinity of Beer Sheva but not to the city itself (Gradus *et al.*, 1993).

The city of Beer Sheva's local economic base has largely reflected the city's stable central place function. It has included public facilities that serve the much of Israel's southern region, such as the Soroka hospital and the Ben Gurion University of the Negev, as well as commerce – constrained before the 1990s by the limited purchasing power of the population. Office activities were constrained by the dominance of Tel Aviv – most headquarters of corporations operating in the Beer Sheva region, as well as business services serving these corporations, have been located in the Tel Aviv area.

The geography of retail in Beer Sheva was completely transformed since the 1990s. The old CBD and local neighborhood shops finally gave in to new planned shopping centers – first to an indoor shopping mall and than to a large big-box retail power center, as well as to other commercial facilities in the city's industrial zones. In Beer Sheva, this shift is considered most welcome. The old CBD was regarded to be unattractive and unfit for its function and the shift finally gave Beer Sheva retail services at par with those offered in the large metropolitan areas. All planned shopping centers are so far within city boundaries, thus the local tax base has not suffered and access to local residents has not been adversely affected.

However, the next phase of retail and business development in the Beer Sheva region is expected to include deconcentration beyond Beer Sheva's municipal boundaries. This is a market led process augmented by initiatives of local authorities that could be expected to trigger central city-suburban competition. Initiatives for the deconcentration of economic activities heavily depend on exploitation of accessible sites in suburban space, such as major junctions.

Growth took place also in Beer Sheva's office sector. Government district offices moved to new modern buildings, a first hotel of a reasonable standard was finally built and the office complex to the northeast of the historical CBD finally took off. A new industrial park in the adjacent exurban municipality of Omer forms, however, substantial competition to Beer Sheva and its local tax base, because it aims at the very few high technology enterprises in the region as well as offering office space.

Much of Beer Sheva's surroundings consist of dusty desert environment that is not considered as prime open space worthy of preservation. Sprawl is thus less an issue of environmental concern, except for problems of proximity to hazardous and polluting industries. However, sprawl in this region could pose dilemmas that concern inequalities and social justice, particularly as higher income population and businesses, attractive from the point of view of the local tax base, increasingly concentrate in exurban municipalities and in rural regional councils.

Our survey indicates that initiatives for the development of economic land uses, which imitate inter-municipal competition for business land uses in the Tel Aviv region, proliferate in the Beer Sheva region. However, on the ground, development is limited. The initiatives in the Beer Sheva region tend to be public – of local authorities that subsequently attempt to market projects to the private sector. This is unlike the Tel Aviv metro where effective response to opportunities created by the private sector can suffice in attractive locations.

Our survey also indicates that the "human factor" – capacity and character of mayors – are most significant in local government performance, even more crucial in small and medium sized municipalities. There is a substantial problem of administrative-political culture of local government in the Beer Sheva region. Rural regional councils and middle-class exurban settlements are an exception. Indeed, the only successful high-technology park (in practice, more an office park) is an initiative of the mayor of exurban Omer. These realities pose a dilemma. Deconcentration of economic activities into rural and exurban space exacerbates disparities, but rural and exurban leaders have been so far the more effective public agents of development in the Beer Sheva region.

Inter-municipal cooperation in the development of economic land uses emerges in the Beer Sheva region mainly due to central government pressure, and fears that without such cooperation the plan for an industrial/business park would not be approved. A planned "industrial" park on a strategic junction on the Beer Sheva-Tel Aviv highway, to be developed and managed jointly by the Bene Shimon regional council, the Bedouin city of Rahat and the exurban local council of Lehavim, is such an example. Jewish-Arab cooperation, as in the above example, is viewed most positively by public policy, and inter-municipal cooperation in the development of industrial parks is also viewed as a policy tool to concentrate development and reduce sprawl. However, this planned industrial park could compete with the city of Beer Sheva over retail and other attractive business land uses, rather than serving manufacturing initiatives oriented to the nearby Bedouin city. The high dependence on the central government for planning approvals and financial assistance presents a particular problem in the Beer Sheva region, in a period of shrinking public budgets, when central government policies also tend to be inconsistent and unstable, due to rapid turnover of governments and ministers.

7.6
Conclusions

7.6.1
Major trends of deconcentration

Our study demonstrates that places of work in Israel increasingly concentrate in the Tel Aviv metropolis, as the functional boundaries of this metropolis expand. Within the Tel Aviv metropolitan area, economic activities in manufacturing, retail, high-technology industries, warehousing and entertainment/recreation functions have deconcentrated rapidly, whereas office deconcentration has been in a more initial stage.

Job deconcentration in the Tel Aviv metropolis is particularly from the city of Tel Aviv to the outer rings of the metropolitan area. Cities within the inner ring frequently cannot offer competitive land prices and also lack accessibility advantages of either the city of Tel Aviv or the outer suburbs. Proximity to major highways and highway junctions is a major location consideration for economic activities in the outer rings. Logistics (warehousing) tends in particular to seek proximity to major highways, but retail establishments, offices and entertainment functions can be expected to follow. Remarkable suburbanization of population to the outer rings has thus been accompanied by even more remarkable suburbanization of jobs, thus the dependency of residents of the outer rings on employment in the metropolitan core is decreasing.

The recent deconcentration of retail and of financing and business services from the city of Tel Aviv to the outer suburbs is a particularly significant phenomenon. Tel Aviv is losing its position as the retail hub of the metropolis and its unique agglomeration economies in finance and business services could be eroding as well. The fiscal soundness of the Tel Aviv municipality has not been negatively affected so far from accelerated suburbanization of economic activities, because accelerated suburbanization of population have helped to maintain a very high ratio of business per residential land uses (nearly 80% of Tel Aviv's property taxes comes from non-residential property). Tel Aviv remained attractive for high socioeconomic status population, out-migration from the central city has not been associated with an increasing concentration of poor immobile population in the city – a fact that also contributed to maintain the fiscal strength of the city.

Employment deconcentration from Tel Aviv does not seem to be associated with the formation of one or few prominent employment nodes in the suburbs.

This is particularly true in retail. In advanced business services and associated activities, a northern suburban node may be emerging in Herzeliyya-Raanana, characterized by a concentration of jobs in white-collar occupations that attract highly educated segments in the labor market. However, a node in the south – Nes Ziyyona-Rehovot – and new competitors to the east also gain strength.

Rural regional councils are frequently accused of unfair competition that undermines the tax base of adjacent cities and encourages scattered patterns of deconcentration. The advantage of the regional councils is based on abundance of land, lower rents, easier ability of retail establishments to open on Saturdays, tendercy to informally accept illegal establishment of businesses on rural land and to grant permits to establish businesses using extensively the 'exceptional usage' controversial tool (Han, 2004). Nonetheless, most deconcentrated economic activities do locate in urban local authorities. Retail, office and entertainment establishments move to industrial areas within suburban cities, using the same 'exceptional usage' tool (Goldfisher, 2004). In fact, some new industrial parks approved by planning authorities never host any manufacturing or warehousing and are immediately developed for big box retail and alike. Moreover, stricter policies of the district planning committees in the early 2000s make it increasingly difficult to gain approval for rezoning agricultural land in rural regional councils, particularly to industrial and commercial land uses.

Over-investment in retail in the outer suburbs leads to intense competition and could lead to crisis conditions. A major issue likely to emerge, both in public policy and among business decision-making, is how to revive declining commercial centers, both unplanned and planned. In contrast, there still seems to be a substantial potential for the deconcentration of office space, encouraged by improved road infrastructure in suburban areas. Such a process could have grave consequences on the economic vitality of the city of Tel Aviv. Tel Aviv can either opt at a political strategy of trying to block through the national planning system initiatives to establish and expand office parks in the outer rings, or attempt to focus on specific niches in which it can develop long-term competitive advantages. The development of light and suburban rail systems could somewhat slow down deconcentration processes but can hardly be expected to have a major impact.

The peripheral metropolitan area of Beer Sheva demonstrates a case in which until recently suburban development of housing and economic activities did not represent deconcentration processes. Beer Sheva also represents a case in which deconcentration does not necessarily present an environmental or urban planning problem. Indeed, the transformation of the retail scene from unplanned CBDs to planned shopping centers actually seems to have given a boost to the urban economy and to the quality of life. Deconcentration could exacerbate socio-spatial disparities, when retail and offices leave the central cities, particularly to more affluent exurban and rural local authorities. Competition over meager investment in the Beer Sheva region depends much more on central government assistance and on effective local leadership, which is more likely in the more economically sound local authorities. Inter-municipal cooperation could offer a substantial advantage under these circumstances, in promoting development, rationalizing spatial development patterns and reducing disparities, but is very difficult to achieve.

7.6.2
Market forces versus planning regulations – Israeli lessons

The Israeli case reveals powerful market forces, originating in demographic and economic growth, as well as in ideological change, that have led to a remarkable ongoing process of deconcentration of economic activities in the dominant Tel Aviv metropolis. The private sector (land owners, lessees of government owned land, developers and a variety of businesses) and competing local authorities have been the prime agents of this deconcentration process. Political decentralization and a right-wing ideological shift have worked together to weaken planning controls that restrained this process in the past.

Deconcentration has been much weaker in the peripheral Beer Sheva metropolitan area, where growing intra-regional disparities could emerge as the most problematic aspect of deconcentration. The major issue on the agenda in the periphery concerns needed public action to promote economic growth rather than to control its spatial development. It should be noted that Israel's northern periphery could display somewhat different attributes, being more environmentally sensitive and displaying greater complexities associated with Jewish-Arab relations, potentially influencing patterns of deconcentration.

However, the Israeli case is far from representing anything close to a laissez faire regime. It is far from American realities, in which local governments hold most land use planning powers, and local politics tends to be dominated by business interests, although in many aspects it has moved in the direction of the American model. Central government agencies in Israel have not given up powers or ceased to intervene in land use planning. Rather, the nature of central intervention seems to have changed, becoming more pluralist, with the central government itself frequently acting as several uncoordinated stakeholders, and decisions being exposed to diverse pressures. The Planning Administration has reacted to intensified pressures on the planning system by an intensive effort to strengthen national and district planning. Another channel of public action, employed in particular by NGOs engaged with civil rights, social justice and environmental concerns, has utilized growing judicial activism to influence public decisions through lawsuits and appeals to the High Court of Justice.

It is possible to draw quite a few parallels between processes of deconcentration in Israeli metropolitan areas and those in post-communist European metropolitan areas. A prominent feature in Israel between the 1950s and early 1970s was the construction of large immigrant neighborhoods at the edge of suburban cities and towns. A marked transition occurred in the late 1970s and the 1980s, when a flow of middle class population into low density suburban and exurban localities commenced. This shift resembles somewhat an even more radical transition that has occurred since the late 1990s in post-communist metropolitan areas such as Prague

(Sykora *et al.*, 2000), in which suburban locations, previously dominated by high-rise residential estates have become the destination for the middle class attracted to low-density housing. However, in post-communist Europe, deconcentration of economic activities – big box retail, warehousing and alike – preceded suburbanization of the middle class, being financed by foreign capital when the vast majority of the middle class still could not afford low density suburbanization. In Israel, deconcentration of economic activities followed an earlier process of residential suburbanization. The political-ideological transition in post-communist Europe was much more dramatic than in Israel, purchasing power in post-communist metropolitan areas is still generally much lower than in Israel, but the resemblance is quite marked, also in the prevalent political culture.

In sum, Israeli planning does not seem to be able to halt, or influence in any visible way, the deconcentration of economic activities from Tel Aviv's core to it suburbs. However, it seems to be effective to a growing extent in limiting scattered patterns of deconcentration. The real test to the power of the emerging new planning regime will nonetheless come when Israeli real estate market – stagnant between 1996 and 2005 – heats up again.

References

Alterman R (2002) Planning in the face of crisis, land use, housing, and mass immigration in Israel. Routledge, London

Barak-Erez D (2004) Distributional justice in Israel's land: after the High Court ruling on agricultural land. HaMishpat 18:54–63 (Hebrew)

Ben-Elia N (2000) The fiscalization of local planning and development. The Floersheimer Institute for Policy Studies, Jerusalem (Hebrew)

Biran SF (2000) Property rights, old and new, the proposal for social privatization in Israel. Hakibbutz Hameuchad, Tel Aviv (Hebrew)

Czamanski Ben Shahar and Company Limited (2003) The writing on the wall: the retail system before crisis. Haifa (unpublished) (Hebrew)

Dery D (2002) Fuzzy control. Journal of Public Administration Research and Theory 12:191–216

Feitelson E (1999) Social norms, rationales and policies: reframing farmland protection in Israel. Journal of Rural Studies 15:431–446

Goldfisher Z (2004) Non-industrial land use in industrial zones: market forces or public directing? Karka 58:16–24 (Hebrew)

Gonen A (1995) Between city and suburb, urban residential patterns and processes in Israel. Avebury, Aldershot

Gradus Y, Razin E, Krakover S (1993) The industrial geography of Israel. Routledge, London and New York

Han I (2004) Non-conforming use of open agricultural areas. The Jerusalem Institute for Israel Studies, Jerusalem (Hebrew)

Kalchheim C (1980) The limited effectiveness of central government control over local government. Planning and Administration 7(1):76–86

Kipnis BA (1998) Spatial reach of office firms: case study in the metropolitan CBD of Tel Aviv, Israel. Geografiska Annaler 80B:17–28

Kipnis BA, Noam T (1998) Restructuring of a metropolitan suburban industrial park: case study in metropolitan Tel Aviv, Israel. Geografiska Annaler 80B:215–227

Newman D, Applebaum L (1992) Recent exurbanization in Israel. In: Golani Y, Eldor S, Garon M (eds) Planning & housing in Israel in the wake of rapid changes, R&L Creative Communications, Tel Aviv, pp 313–321

Razin E (1996) Rapid development and restructuring of fringe areas: the Tel Aviv metropolis. In: Davies RJ (ed) Contemporary city structuring - international geographical insights, Society of South African Geographers, Cape Town, pp 451–466

Razin E (1998) Policies to control urban sprawl: planning regulations or changes in the "rules of the game". Urban Studies 35:321–340

Razin E (2004) Needs and impediments for local government reform: lessons from Israel. Journal of Urban Affairs 26:623–640

Razin E, Hazan A (2007) Local government amalgamation in Israel: towards the modernization of local government? In: Evans M, Wollmann H, Lazin F, Hoffmann-Martinot V (eds) Reform and democracy in local government of countries in transformation, Lexington Books, Lanham, MD

Sykora L, Kamenicky J, Hauptmann P (2000) Changes in the spatial structure of Prague and Brno in the 1990s. Acta Universitatis Carolinae Geographica 35(1):61–76

Van den Berg L, Van der Meer J, Pol P (1995) Audit of European policies on metropolitan cities. Euricur, Erasmus University, Rotterdam

8 Sprawling post-communist metropolis: Commercial and residential suburbanization in Prague and Brno, the Czech Republic

Luděk Sýkora and Martin Ouředníček

Charles University, Faculty of Science, Dept. of Social Geography and Regional Development, Albertov 6, 128 43 Prague 2, Czech Republic

Abstract: In this chapter, we review the development of suburbanization in Prague and Brno metropolitan areas in the Czech Republic with particular attention paid to specific features of suburbanization in post-communist cities. Residential deconcentration brought about the spatial redistribution of the population within metropolitan areas while the overall population stagnated. The suburbanization of non-residential functions in the form of out-of-town greenfield developments has been more dynamic, influenced by the massive inflow of foreign investments expanding on new markets. Employment in core cities is shrinking while it is expanding in suburban areas, particularly in retail, warehousing, and — in Brno— also in the industrial sectors.

Key words: Suburbanization, post-communist city, urban change, Prague, Brno

8.1
Introduction: Conditions for suburbanization in the Czech Republic

Suburbanization is the dominant process that is changing the spatial organization of post-communist cities and their metropolitan areas. Despite the brevity of the period from the beginning of the transition, suburbanization has already dramatically reshaped the physical morphology, functional land-use pattern, and socio-spatial structure. The process deserves attention not only as the subject of our interest in the transformation of urban areas, but also because suburbanization brings irreversible changes into settlement patterns and produces economic, social, and environmental consequences that will influence our society for several future generations (TCRP, 1998).

This chapter presents an overview of the development of suburbanization in the Prague and Brno metropolitan areas in the Czech Republic. Particular attention is paid to specific features of suburbanization in post-communist cities. We first outline the specific conditions for suburbanization in the context of settlement structure and the transition from a centrally-planned to a market economy. We begin our report of suburbanization in Prague and Brno with an introduction to these metropolitan areas and their spatial structure and follow with an account of the main aspects and trends of recent residential and non-residential suburbanization. Detailed analyses of the deconcentration of the population and employment are given.

E. Razin et al. (eds.), Employment Deconcentration in European Metropolitan Areas, 209–233.
© 2007 *Springer.*

The Czech Republic and the metropolitan areas of Prague and Brno are very special cases within the context of this book. In post-communist areas, the radical change of urban structures through suburbanization started only recently. During Communism and central planning, there was a strong preference for the concentration of investment and development into major urban centres and within their territories to high-density residential housing estates and industrial zones at the edge of cities (Musil & Ryšavý, 1983). The hinterland of large urban centres has received minimum investment and was characterized by stagnation and even decline, the concentration of people of lower socioeconomic status, and agrarian and associated industrial production.

It should, however, be noted that Czech cities and their surrounding areas experienced suburbanization in the interwar period of the 1920s and 1930s (Ullrich *et al.*, 1938). At that time, residential areas were springing up around railway stations on rail tracks radiating in all directions from central cities. These well-established residential settlements are now some of the most prestigious and sought-after addresses in the metropolitan regions. Such a development was observed in Prague and other smaller Czech cities as it was elsewhere in the region in Budapest or Tallinn, for instance (Berényi, 1994; Tammaru, 2001). At that time, spatial deconcentration did not include economic functions.

The character of urbanization is strongly shaped by historically-developed settlement patterns. The Czech Republic has a very dense network of small settlements. While the urbanization included the concentration of population and jobs to selected places, suburbanization does not mean a spatial expansion of cities into an unsettled hinterland, but rather to areas that have already been settled and used for a considerable time. Furthermore, besides the decentralization within the metropolitan areas, when compared with the overall country settlement and regional development, a continuing concentration into metropolitan areas can be seen. This is especially strong concerning employment, particularly in the service sector.

Suburbanization as experienced in the United States and West European countries did not develop in the post-Second World War period. The urbanization pattern in Communist countries was characterized by the concentration of investments and growth into medium and large cities and within their territories into large housing and industrial complexes at their urban edges. Suburbanization in the western sense has not developed (Enyedi, 1996: 117; Enyedi, 1998: 15). Szelényi (1996) uses the concept of under-urbanization to describe how the growth of the urban population was lower than the growth of jobs in the urban industrial and tertiary sector. Consequently, a sharp rise in commuting from the urban hinterland substituted for urban growth via residential suburbanization. A straightforward comparison of the spatial structures of capitalist and communist cities can reveal important differences in the character of the built environment, land-use patterns, and socio-spatial structures. The main differences are in the central cities and the suburban areas.

The spatial structure of cities and their metropolitan areas has gradually changed in the course of time. The relatively smooth process of urban change can sometimes be interrupted by periods of radical spatial restructuring influenced by turbulent developments in society. One recent example of such change is the urban transformation in post-communist societies. With the decentralization of decision-making in a market economy, conditions become more favourable for the development of spatial deconcentration.

8.2
Prague and Brno metropolitan areas

Prague and Brno are the country's two major metropolitan areas. They have the best preconditions for the development of suburbanization. The process is developing in both these regions, although differing in extent and dynamics. With a population of 1.2 million, Prague is the country's largest city and its capital. It is a dominant centre in the Czech settlement and regional systems, not only because of its population size, but also because it accommodates most of the government institutions and economic control and command functions. Prague is the gateway to the country for foreign investors (Drbohlav & Sýkora, 1997). It is situated in the middle of Bohemia, the western part of the Czech Republic (Figure 8.1).

Brno is the country's second largest city; it is sometimes considered as the "capital" of Moravia, the eastern part of the country. With nearly 400,000 inhabitants, as a settlement centre it ranks second in the national urban hierarchy.

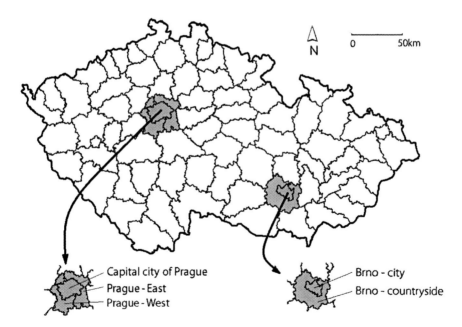

Fig. 8.1 Location of the case study areas within the territorial structure of districts

Brno is the seat of the Supreme Court; the city hosts the most important trade fairs in the country and is a major centre of university education.

Metropolitan regions do not exist as independent administrative units in the Czech Republic. They consist of core cities and a large number of smaller municipalities ranging from villages of a few hundred inhabitants to small towns with a population in tens of thousands. There is no single officially declared delimitation of a metropolitan area. In this chapter, we use the term *metropolitan area* (MA) to refer to a core city and the adjacent districts (Figure 8.1). This description allows us to use statistical information that is only available at the district level for the analysis of employment deconcentration. The Prague Metropolitan Area (PMA) covers an area of 1666 square kilometres and has 1.35 million inhabitants living in the city of Prague and the two surrounding districts of Prague-East and Prague-West. The Brno Metropolitan Area (BMA; 1338 sq. km) consists of the two districts of Brno-city and Brno-countryside with a total population of 535,000 people. Basic data from the 2001 Census are presented in Table 8.1.

The analysis of the spatial deconcentration processes within the metropolitan areas is based on their division into four main zones: (1) centre; (2) inner city; (3) first (inner) suburban zone; (4) second (outer) suburban zone (Figure 8.2). The subdivision of the Prague and Brno metropolitan areas respects urban morphology and takes into account the boundaries of local government territorial units. Both Prague and Brno are municipalities. Therefore, from the point of view of local government, their rights and responsibilities are on the same level as those of the small municipalities around them. They are, however, municipalities of a special kind and can be divided (at their own discretion) into boroughs, each with its own elected local government. The spatial delimitation of metropolitan zones uses borough and municipal boundaries. The suburban zone is delimited as the area outside the compact city and within the metropolitan area. The administrative boundary of a Czech city extends far beyond its compact built-up area; the city's administrative territory contains part of the suburban zone. Therefore, the suburban

Table 8.1 Prague and Brno - basic data from Census 2001 (1.3.2001)

Region	Area (sq. km)	No. of municipalities	Population	Density of population
Prague				
City	496	1 (57)*	1169106	2357
Hinterland	1170	171	179150	153
Total PMA	1666	172 (228)*	1348256	810
Brno				
City	230	1 (29)*	376172	1636
Countryside	1108	137	159169	144
Total BMA	1338	138 (166)*	535341	400

Note: * number of boroughs in the cities of Prague and Brno

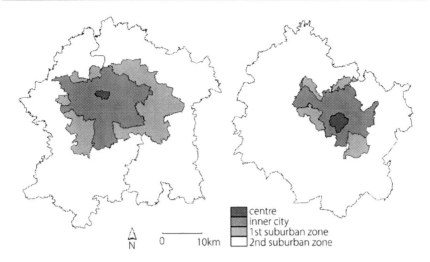

centre
inner city
1st suburban zone
2nd suburban zone

0   10km

Fig. 8.2 Zones of Prague (left) and Brno (right) metropolitan areas

zone in a metropolitan area consists of a zone within the administrative boundary of the core city together with areas outside it. We use the city administrative boundary as the division line between the first and second or the inner and outer suburban zones. The second (outer) suburban zone is defined as the districts around the core city (or municipalities within these districts). In the case of Prague, there are two districts Prague-West and Prague-East; in the case of Brno, there is the Brno-countryside district.

The division of city territory into centre, inner city, and inner suburban zone reflects the historical development of the intra-urban spatial structure. Both cities have medieval cores in which government and commercial functions are now concentrated; these cores play the role of a city centre. A historic core/city centre is encircled by an inner city made up of densely-built-up residential neighbourhoods and old industrial zones dating from the industrialization and rural-to-urban migration of the 19th century. In the inter-war period of the 1920s and 1930s, low-rise and low-density residential areas consisting of detached and terraced single-family houses were constructed around the inner city in both cities. During the communist period, zones were constructed consisting of housing estates with high-rise prefabricated apartment blocks and new industrial districts spatially separated from the residential areas. In both cities, these zones form compact built-up areas. We separate the essential city centres from the rest of what is termed the inner city and consists of a heterogeneous urban environment. Beyond the compact city, but still within the administrative boundaries, is a zone characterized by a rural landscape with small villages and agricultural land. This zone is now the subject of intensive transformation through both residential and non-residential suburbanization; we define the area as the first (or inner) suburban zone.

In our analyses, we depend on two levels of metropolitan territory division. The first is a rough division between the core city and the surrounding districts. This division is used in the analysis of employment deconcentration, since the data are only available at the district level. Unfortunately, the developments in the inner suburban zone are then not depicted. The second division provides a more detailed spatial distribution of the lowest tier of administrative areas in the Czech Republic, namely the municipalities in the city hinterlands and the boroughs within the core cities.

8.3
Suburbanization in Prague and Brno

Although the main trends in intra-urban change have been similar, post-communist urban restructuring has been more dynamic in Prague than in Brno. In both cities, the most important processes of urban change since the beginning of the post-communist transition have been the commercialization of the historic cores and adjacent areas of the inner cities, the commercial and residential suburbanization in the outer city and urban hinterland, and selective revitalization in inner city areas (Sýkora *et al.*, 2000). While most of the 1990s were characterized by a huge investment inflow to city centres to bring about their commercialization and physical upgrading, suburbanization has been the most dynamic process changing metropolitan landscapes since the late 1990s (Sýkora, 1999).

Until the mid 1990s, residential suburbanization was only marginal, restricted by the population's limited purchasing power. During the second half of the 1990s, residential and commercial suburbanization developed quickly in the outer parts of Prague and Brno and the adjacent zone of their metropolitan regions. By the turn of the century, commercial suburbanization had become the most important process of urban change in both cities. New residential districts and reconstructed village properties have been accompanied by new shopping centres, hypermarkets, warehousing, and industrial properties. Importantly, while in the West residential suburbanization preceded non-residential deconcentration, commercial developments are currently changing suburban areas of post-communist cities more radically than the suburbanization of homes. Grimm (1995), Nuissl and Rink (2003), and Lisowski and Wilk (2002) have observed this reversed sequence for Leipzig and Warsaw respectively.

Residential suburbanization takes several forms. There are districts of speculative housing development. Developers also acquire land, add infrastructure, and sell plots for housing construction, often on a turn-key basis. Both forms create new residential districts for prosperous owner occupiers. These estates are usually spatially attached to existing settlements. There are also some individual developments that transform existing villages. Households purchase vacant lots within villages and build new homes; or they purchase existing properties that they then reconstruct and expand, or demolish them and replace them with new luxurious homes. The suburban zone is now acquiring a better-educated population with high incomes (Ouředníček, 2003). Suburban settlements with emergent residential districts consist of two distinct types with contrasting populations: prosperous newcomers versus the lower income, less well-educated, indigenous inhabitants of the former rural villages. In general, residential suburbanization is changing the spatial distribution of the population according to socioeconomic status. It contributes to a reversal of the traditional sociospatial pattern of the socialist city in which the socio-economic status of the residents declined with distance from the centre. Residential suburbanization is more developed around Prague than Brno or other smaller cities and towns. This is the result of a higher share of households with high incomes and a larger total number of such households in Prague Metropolitan Area. The process is spatially very selective. New districts of suburban housing emerge in areas with a good physical environment (such as the south-east of Prague and north of Brno) and transport connections to the city centre. During most of the 1990s, the development of residential suburbanization was very slow, limited by the population's limited purchasing power. However, with the increasing prosperity, particularly of the Prague population, and with the introduction of mortgages supported by a state subsidy, more dynamic development of suburban family housing started at the turn of this century.

While there is a tradition of residential suburbanization predating the Second World War, non-residential suburbanization is a completely new and very recent phenomenon in the Czech Republic. While residential suburbanization is driven by the investments of Czech households, the motor for non-residential suburbanization is the demand of international firms expanding onto Czech markets. After a few years of experience, we can observe that non-residential suburbanization has had more important impacts on the transformation of outer urban areas. Commercial projects are concentrated in complexes built along major highways and at important transport intersections. In Prague, another important location factor is the underground transport system extending to the city outskirts. Non-residential developments include retail, warehousing, and distribution and, in Brno, industry. The deconcentration does not involve offices unless they are an integral part of a retail or warehousing facility.

8.3.1
Residential deconcentration

During the communist period, there was some deconcentration of population within urban areas, although it was quite different in nature from the developments in Western cities. Almost all the houses and apartments constructed by the state were built on housing estates with large prefabricated apartment blocks at the edge of cities. These areas were characterized by high densities; they were linked by public transportation to the city centre and other places with a concentration of jobs. The construction of housing estates could be seen as a continuation of urbanization through compact urban morphology and high density construction.

The situation changed with the transition and the reestablishment of the market economy. The private ownership of land and houses formed necessary preconditions on the supply side. The growth in the prosperity of some segments of the population in large cities and their preference for suburban living created a demand for the development of residential suburbanization. This demand was further accelerated with the establishment of a mortgage system that included state financial contributions to mortgages used to finance newly-built housing.

The suburbanization process in Prague and Brno has not been as intensive as it was after the 2nd World War in North America or Western Europe. There is a general decrease of population in the Czech Republic and a stagnation of population in the metropolitan areas (Table 8.2). The deconcentration of population has occurred mainly though the spatial redistribution of the population within metropolitan areas with declining central and inner cities and growing suburban areas (Ouředníček & Sýkora, 2002). This process of residential suburbanization started to develop from the beginning of the 1990s. However, from the late 1990s, residential suburbanization gained a new dynamic that can be seen in particular around Prague and, to a lesser extent, in the metropolitan areas around Brno. This spurt is mirrored in the dynamics of population change observed when the periods 1991–96 and 1996–2001 are compared (Table 8.2).

Detailed representations of population growth and decline in Prague and Brno metropolitan areas according to municipalities and boroughs show that, while

Table 8.2 Population in Prague and Brno metropolitan areas and their respective zones in 1991–2001

Area	1991	1996	2001	2001/91	1996/91	2001/96
Prague						
Centre	42590	37953	34581	81.20	89.11	91.12
Inner city	1065401	1058771	1018396	95.59	99.38	96.19
First suburban zone	106183	108229	116129	109.37	101.93	107.30
Second suburban zone	167421	167721	179150	107.01	100.18	106.81
Prague City	1214174	1204953	1169106	96.29	99.24	97.03
Prague Metropolitan Area	1381595	1372674	1350257	97.73	99.35	98.37
Brno						
Centre	78631		67395	85.71		
Inner city	295730	387570*	293528	99.26	103.03*	97.06*
First suburban zone	13935		15249	109.43		
Second suburban zone	156189	157042	159169	101.91	100.55	101.35
Brno City	388296	387570	376172	96.88	99.81	97.06
Brno metropolitan area	544485	544612	535341	98.32	100.02	98.30
Czech Republic	10302215	10309137	10230060	99.30	100.07	99.23

Notes: Data from Census (March 3rd, 1991 and March 1st, 2001) and population register (December 31st, 1996).
* In 1996, data are available only for Brno city as one spatial unit.

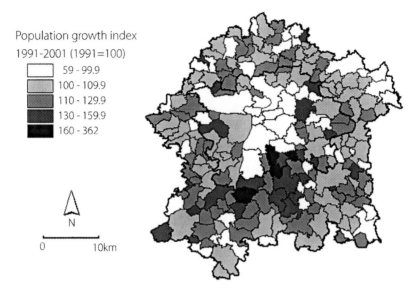

Population growth index
1991-2001 (1991=100)

☐ 59 - 99.9
▨ 100 - 109.9
▨ 110 - 129.9
▨ 130 - 159.9
■ 160 - 362

N

0   10km

Fig. 8.3 Population change in the boroughs (city parts) and municipalities of Prague Metropolitan Area in 1991–2001

declining in most units in the inner city, the population is increasing in the majority of the suburban (outside the compact city) boroughs and municipalities (Figures 8.3 and 8.4). The patterns of growth in Prague and Brno and within their metropolitan areas differ. Growth is concentrated in areas with the best natural environment and good transport accessibility. The population of some municipalities in Prague MA doubled in the period 1991–2001, while around Brno growth was quite modest. According to Mulíček and Olšová (2002), most of the new residential construction and population growth in Brno has taken place in the outer areas of the city of Brno that still lie within the administrative boundary (that is, within the first suburban zone), with only some municipalities beyond the Brno administrative boundary registering growth.

A more precise method of evaluating population deconcentration is to divide the total population increase into its migration and natural change components. The whole of the metropolitan areas and all their zones are affected by natural population decrease, with the greatest decline in the city centres. Migration is the key factor that contributes to the spatial redistribution of population and can indicate suburbanization and population deconcentration trends. During the 1990s, the inner cities started to lose population by migration, while city hinterlands became the most important destinations of migrants (Figure 8.5). At present, city centres and inner cities are losing population by natural decrease and migration, while both suburban zones are gaining population through migration. The rate of growth is especially strong in areas located just outside the city's administrative boundaries. Prague's second suburban zone now has the highest rates of net migration registered in the whole Czech Republic during the last forty years.

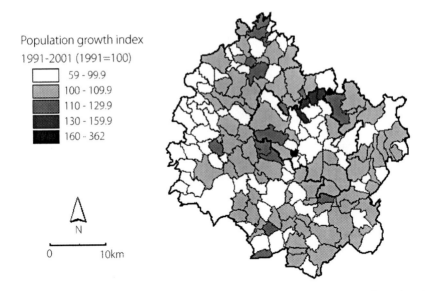

Fig. 8.4 Population change in city parts and municipalities of Brno Metropolitan Area in 1991–2001

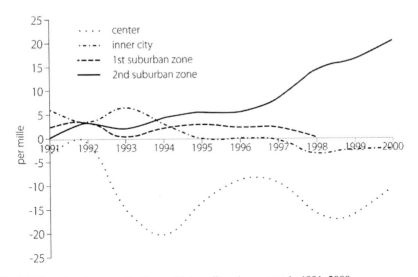

Fig. 8.5 Net migration rates for Prague Metropolitan Area zones in 1991–2000

8.3.2
Non-residential deconcentration

The non-residential deconcentration within Prague and Brno metropolitan areas is a very recent phenomenon; it started in the second half of the 1990s. However, the growth of new economic activities and jobs in suburban locations has been quite rapid, in particular around Prague. This section provides an account of the economic restructuring in the metropolitan areas of Prague and Brno, and the spatial implications, with the emphasis on the decentralization tendencies.

The economic change through the first two-thirds of the 1990s was directed by government reforms such as privatization and the consequent economic restructuring of the original domestic enterprises. This restructuring has only had indirect effects on spatial reconfiguration through the differences in restructuring in particular areas. New employment growth was concentrated in financial intermediation and other business services (especially in Prague, associated with its role as the command and control centre and gateway to the country), retail (in all larger towns and cities, associated with low levels of retail supply under Communism), and hotels and restaurants (in Prague, associated with the growth of tourism). Most of these jobs were concentrated in the city centres; some new jobs were associated with real-estate development or redevelopment (mainly offices, but also hotels, retail or multipurpose centres) and consequent land use changes affecting central cities (Sýkora, 1998). In this period, there were a few cases of the relocation of production facilities from central parts of cities to the city outskirts (such as the printing house Labe-Vltava-Press from downtown Prague to the suburban borough Uhříněves) or outside metropolitan areas (various industrial branches).

The situation changed towards the end of the 1990s with the development of new economic activities located in new suburban locations. This change was largely fuelled by the inflow of foreign direct investments; economic activities in retail, warehousing and distribution, and industries were particularly affected. The late 1990s and early 2000s were characterized by a massive expansion of new retail operations to the Czech Republic. Hypermarkets and do-it-yourself (DIY) stores in big-boxes and later whole retail parks composed of a shopping mall with a variety of entertainment and retail facilities such as DIY and factory outlets rapidly changed the outer areas in the larger Czech cities. These facilities were mostly built on greenfield areas at suburban locations or on the edge of the compact city. There are also, of course, examples of inner city malls, but the majority of new retail emerged in outer city locations. These new facilities offer a relatively large amount of new jobs and have substantially influenced the pattern of commuting for people employed in retail. New warehousing and distribution facilities have been concentrated in industrial and logistic parks developed on greenfield areas, usually outside the city's administrative boundaries.

Industrial employment has suffered a major decline, particularly in the cities. The development of employment in the manufacturing sector was given a new momentum by the inflow of the foreign direct investment attracted by a stabilized domestic economic and political situation, a skilled and cheap labour force, and adequate infrastructure. Many towns and cities affected by the decline in employment set up new industrial zones on greenfield sites located at the edge of existing urban areas, usually in locations with good transport accessibility. Through the newly-established organization CzechInvest, the Czech government attracted foreign direct investments into the country and supported selected local governments in their preparation of new industrial zones. Consequently, there has been a reindustrialization involving the creation of new manufacturing jobs in the suburban locations of many towns and cities.

Retail has been the major force behind non-residential deconcentration. New suburban retail developments have emerged around virtually all the cities and towns with a population over 50,000 (Smolová & Szczyrba, 2000). There are several edge-of-city and suburban locations with new retail and wholesale facilities in Prague and its hinterland (see Figure 8.6). Some of these areas also accommodate warehousing. The most important shopping areas are at Zličín (west), Černý Most (north-east), Průhonice/Čestlice (south-east), Letňany (north), and Štěrboholy (east) (Pommois, 2004). All of them contain a shopping mall, at least one hypermarket, a DIY (do-it-yourself) or furniture stores and other facilities. These areas can be divided into two types according to their location: Zličín, Černý Most, Letňany, and Štěrboboly are located just at the edge of a compact built-up area adjacent to the inner city and the suburban zone. This type certainly contributes to the spatial deconcentration of retail within the city. However, it is questionable whether this type of location forms part of the suburbanization process. The location of these consumption places within the metropolitan area can be seen as the result of a long-term strategic vision that placed them between the large pool of an inner-city population with huge consumption power and the new suburban residential areas with growth potential and a smaller number of people, but with high incomes. Two of these new shopping areas, Zličín and Černý Most, are located on the last stops of the underground: they are well served by the inner city public transportation. The other two, Letňany and Štěrboholy, are currently served by buses while the new underground line towards Letňany is under construction. These access factors contribute to their perception as edge-of-city rather than suburban places.

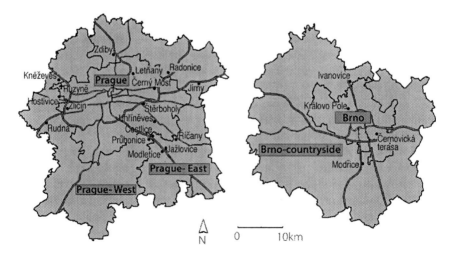

Fig. 8.6 Locations of places mentioned in the text

Průhonice/Čestlice zone exemplifies another type of location (Photos 8.1 and 8.2). This zone emerged out of Prague on the territory of two adjacent municipalities located on both sides of the major D1 highway that connects Prague with Brno. The zone is at some distance from the edge of the compact city. There is a hypermarket with a small mall, an independent shopping mall, a cash-and-carry hypermarket, a DIY store, a furniture store, and other specialized shopping facilities ranging from electronics to sports equipment, clothing to luxury lights. There are also some factory outlets and wholesale facilities. Furthermore, the territory next to the retail section accommodates a large segment of warehousing. Currently, an aqua-park is under construction, adding a leisure and entertainment element. This whole area is situated at the beginning of a major ribbon development along the national highway D1 linking Prague with Brno. The ribbon contains some other shops (from footwear and china to gardening tools) and includes some large industrial/logistic zones on the next highway exit at Říčany.

This huge concentration is a prime example of non-residential suburban development and metropolitan deconcentration. In the section devoted to employment deconcentration, we draw on the case of Průhonice/Čestlice and Říčany as examples of changes in employment in the period 1991–2001. Beside these major retail locations, there are many independent stores, usually DIY, cash&carry, and hypermarkets in big-boxes located in the outer areas of inner city or just at its edge, usually in places with good accessibility by private car.

Brno saw the opening of the first Czech hypermarket in 1996 (Globus). It is located in Ivanovice, at the northern edge of the city, just outside the compact city. The hypermarket is now accompanied by a DIY store. Since that time, a new and now dominant retail zone has been developed in the southern part of the city, next to the junction of two major highways. This retail zone contains shopping malls, hypermarkets, DIY and furniture stores, and other facilities (Mulíček 2002; Strategie pro Brno 2003; Photo 8.3). The huge concentration in one spot is the result of the market competition and location strategies of competing firms bringing together an agglomeration of economic activities and at the same time increasing the distance between services and customers. Some argue that these firms produce the advantage of bigger choice in one place. This concentration was strongly influenced by specific local factors, namely the highway junction and the availability of large plots of land.

While until recently most retail turnover was concentrated in city centres and inner-city shopping areas, a large proportion of shopping is now moving to the suburban zone. In Prague, the first suburban shopping zone opened in the mid-1990s; since 1997, the growth of suburban retail parks and zones has been rapid, with several main concentrations developed outside the compact-city area. Similarly, there has been a massive explosion of suburban retail in Brno, with one large shopping area south of the city. This development has caused a radical transformation in the spatial pattern of shopping and travel. In Prague, half the retail turnover was concentrated in the city centre in 1989. In 1998, the hypermarket was the first shopping place for 4 percent of Czechs; two years later, in 2000, the hypermarket

Photo 8.1 Průhonice/Čestlice business zone

Source: Geodis Brno, 2002

Photo 8.2 Průhonice/Čestlice business zone on D1 Highway approaching Prague from south-east

Author: Jana Temelová, 2004

was the first shopping place for 20 percent of Czechs and 25 percent of Prague inhabitants. Most new retail space in shopping malls, hypermarkets, and big box do-it-yourself stores are located in out-of-city areas and the urban population travel to them for shopping and entertainment by private car.

Warehousing and distribution is another vital component of the recent suburban development, especially in the Prague metropolitan area. Prague is well situated in the middle of the Bohemian basin: that is, it is a place from which the rest of the western part of country can be served. Prague and its vicinity is also an

Photo 8.3 Olympia Shopping Park, Brno

Source: Geodis Brno, 2002

area of major junctions, with motorways going in all directions. At the same time, Prague and the Central Bohemian region are huge markets with many consumers with above-average consumption power. Last but not least, the proximity of the headquarters of major international as well as many domestic firms and government offices contribute to the attractiveness of this location.

In and around Prague, the major logistic parks are located on major highways, the outer city-ring-road, and in the vicinity of the international airport Ruzyně. All the new major areas are in the 2nd suburban zone or even beyond it, outside Prague's administrative boundary.

Photo 8.4 Warehousing area around D1 Exit Říčany/Jesenice

Source: Geodis Brno, 2002

Two major logistic parks have been developed to the east and west of the city. First, along the major country highway D1 connecting Prague with Brno, there is an extensive ribbon development starting with a retail outlet near Průhonice and continuing with warehousing and distribution facilities organized in parks or even as independent buildings. Beside the Průhonice/Čestlice zone (discussed in the retail section), there are three major clusters of warehousing and distribution around the exit to Říčany and Jesenice (Jažlovice Industrial Zone, Říčany Logistic Park and Modletice cluster, Photo 8.4). There are further warehousing and distribution facilities on the following exits.

Second, there is a large warehousing and distribution park containing several premises in Rudná, west of Prague on the D5 highway to Pilsen and Bavaria (Photo 8.5). There are also some single buildings at the junction of the D5 highway and the outer city-ring-road (on both sides of the Prague administrative boundary). The large retail concentration at Zličín at the edge of Prague is also on this highway. Northpoint Distribution Park is currently under development on D8 highway to Dresden in Germany near Zdiby at the northern part of Prague Metropolitan Area. There are some smaller new warehousing and distribution locations. Tulip Park, near Hostivice in Prague-West, is capitalizing on the proximity of the outer city-ring–road; the park is located between the international airport Ruzyně and the D5 highway to Germany. Airport Logistic Park, as the name suggests, is located next to the airport, on the territory of Kněževes municipality just outside the city's administrative boundary on the R7 highway heading north-west of Prague. Two other warehousing locations are situated on the highway to the north-east (R10 to

Photo 8.5 Rudná warehousing and distribution park on the D5 highway

Source: Geodis Brno, 2002

Mladá Bosleslav and Liberec) at Radonice and east (D11 to Hradec Králové and Pardubice) at Jirny. In Brno, there is a new warehousing and distribution area: Central Trade Park Brno, located in Modřice, south of the centre and close to the area of large retail concentration.

Both Prague and Brno have industrial zones located in their outskirts. These areas are now undergoing a transformation, influenced by the general economic restructuring. The transformation often includes the takeover by new firms of existing building and their reconstruction and extension. In addition, new premises are built on empty lots within these industrial zones or in adjacent areas. An example of a newly-built industrial property is the Labe-Vltava Press printing house in Uhříněves, which now accommodates economic activities formerly located on Venceslas Square in the centre of Prague. This printing house is an example of relocation and the direct deconcentration of economic function from the city centre to the inner suburban zone. Another example is the relocation of the former ČKD (now Siemens) factory from the inner city area Smíchov to the edge-of-city location at Zličín, next to the retail area described above. The situation in Brno is quite different, with the establishment of new zones for production activities. The first, Czech Technology Park, is located in the northern part of the inner city (Královo Pole), next to the campus of Brno Technical University. The Park contains both office and production facilities. The Technology Park is an example of spatial deconcentration within the city's compact built-up area and does not contribute to suburbanization. An example of suburban non-residential deconcentration is the Brno Industrial Zone Černovická terasa, established by the city government with central government support on a greenfield site in the south-east of the city, within the inner suburban zone. This new production/industrial site together with the distribution/warehousing Central Trade Park Brno Modřice and a huge concentration of retail outlets has created a new large non-residential suburban belt along the south-eastern edge of Brno.

The industrial zones are the major difference between Prague and other cities and towns in the Czech Republic. Although Prague accommodates the command and control function (offices), the major distribution hub (logistic, distribution and warehousing), and a huge regional market (retail), new industry tends to develop elsewhere. This concentrates around other towns, where government authorities have prepared service plots in industrial zones and attracted foreign investors through cheap land and labour. Brno cannot aspire to become another command and control centre. It does, however, have the ambition to attract routine manufacturing and high-value-added production and services to the Czech Technology Park. The park has not generated many new jobs, however, as it is focused on high-value-added and capital-intensive rather than labour-intensive production. The city of Brno has therefore also developed a new suburban greenfield industrial zone to attract manufacturing production and provide employment opportunities for people with traditional industrial skills.

8.3.3
Employment deconcentration

In this section, we document the changes in the distribution of jobs between the core city and the remaining suburban parts of the metropolitan areas, referring in particular to the economic sectors according to the NACE classification. There are two sources of information about employment and the spatial distribution of jobs: the population censuses; and the registers of the numbers of employees. We have drawn on the Censuses of 1991 and 2001 and from the registry of employees available from the annual reports of the Czech Statistical Office. Unfortunately, the registry only covers about two thirds of the jobs in the country and the criteria for the inclusion of employees changed several times during the 1990s. The Census data, the alternative source, has available the number of economically active people living in a particular geographic area and the number of people commuting out of and into the area according to NACE sectors.

The number of jobs in the whole country declined between 1991 and 2001 by 10.8 percent. There are only two geographic areas where the number of jobs increased: Prague metropolitan area and the Mladá Boleslav district (the location of the Volkswagen-Škoda car-production plant). Between 1991 and 2001, the share of the total number of jobs in the country increased by 15 percent in Prague MA and 4 percent in Brno MA (Table 8.3). These figures clearly

Table 8.3 Number of jobs in the metropolitan areas and their share of total jobs in the Czech Republic

	1991 No of jobs	2001 No of jobs	1991 Share on CR	2001 Share on CR	2001/1991 Change in the share
Prague city	723349	734724	13.61%	15.50%	113.91%
2nd suburban zone	62842	73875	1.18%	1.56%	131.83%
PMA	786191	808599	14.79%	17.06%	115.34%
Brno city	245755	228494	4.62%	4.82%	104.27%
2nd suburban zone	57265	52687	1.08%	1.11%	103.18%
BMA	303020	281181	5.70%	5.93%	104.06%

show a major difference in the dynamics of the two metropolitan economies. The growth rate in the Prague hinterland was 32 percent compared with 14 percent in the city itself. These figures include the suburban growth within the city's administrative boundary. The contrast between the jobs growth in the compact city and the suburban zone would therefore be much sharper. In Brno MA, the city's share of the country's total pool of jobs increased slightly faster than did the hinterland's share. Economic deconcentration in Brno MA is not very pronounced; furthermore, most of it is realized inside the city's administrative boundary.

What is the spatial distribution of jobs within the Prague and Brno Metropolitan Areas and how did it change between 1991 and 2001? Prague city has the dominant position in its metropolitan area accounting for over 90 percent of all jobs (Table 8.4). In 2001, 14 percent of all metropolitan jobs were in the city centre, 70 percent in the inner city, 7 percent in suburban areas within the city limits and 9 percent in the suburbs outside the city. Similarly in the Brno area, the city is dominant, accounting for 81 percent of metropolitan jobs. However, the Brno proportion is slowly changing. Between 1991 and 2001, the hinterland of Prague increased its share of jobs in the whole MA by 14 percent, while the city's share declined slightly (Table 8.5).

Which economic sectors contributed most to the differential growth in the cities and their suburban hinterland? In Prague, compared with the city, growth in the suburban zone has been remarkable in (F) construction, (G) wholesale and retail and (I) transport, storage, and communications. The growth in Brno was mostly in (F) construction, while the increase in (G) wholesale and retail was also high in the city. Transport, storage and communications (I) did not increase significantly. These data, however, do not take into account the growth in suburban areas inside the city's administrative boundary. If this growth was included, the difference would be more pronounced.

The economic deconcentration is spatially very selective. It is bringing about rapid and enormous changes in particular locations and zones, while other parts

Table 8.4 Share of the total number of jobs in metropolitan areas according to zone and economic branch (NACE)

NACE sectors	All sectors	A+B	C–E	F	G	I	M+N	H+J+K+L+O
1991								
Prague city	91.94%	1.48%	18.66%	11.01%	12.96%	8.10%	15.27%	24.46%
2nd suburban zone	8.06%	1.47%	2.57%	0.55%	0.77%	0.35%	0.81%	1.55%
Total PMA	100.00%	2.95%	21.23%	11.57%	13.72%	8.45%	16.08%	26.00%
2001								
Prague city	90.83%	0.46%	11.15%	8.39%	11.34%	8.77%	10.38%	40.34%
2nd suburban zone	9.17%	0.33%	2.33%	0.94%	1.47%	0.67%	0.69%	2.74%
Total PMA	100.00%	0.79%	13.48%	9.33%	12.81%	9.44%	11.07%	43.08%
1991								
Brno city	81.14%	1.87%	27.59%	9.69%	7.41%	5.89%	13.39%	15.30%
2nd suburban zone	18.86%	3.42%	8.06%	1.04%	1.50%	0.86%	1.84%	2.15%
Total BMA	100.00%	5.29%	35.65%	10.73%	8.90%	6.75%	15.23%	17.45%
2001								
Brno city	81.23%	0.77%	16.68%	9.33%	10.08%	5.99%	12.23%	26.14%
2nd suburban zone	18.77%	1.28%	6.85%	2.11%	2.14%	1.07%	1.89%	3.43%
Total BMA	100.00%	2.05%	23.54%	11.44%	12.23%	7.06%	14.12%	29.57%

Note: A+B – agriculture, forestry, fishing; C-E – total industry; F – construction; G – wholesale and retail; H – hotels and restaurants; I - transport, storage and communications; J – financial intermediation; K – real estate; renting and business activities; L – public administration and defence; M – education; N – health and social work; O – other communal, social and personal services.

of suburban areas are untouched. The aggregated data for the whole districts do not allow us to see this spatial variation. Furthermore, the most radical impact of employment decentralization concerns suburban municipalities, where new development takes place. We have selected three municipalities beyond the southeast edge of Prague's administrative boundary to illustrate the local impacts of employment deconcentration. There has been a remarkable growth in the number of jobs in all three municipalities (Table 8.6). However, their different situation is revealed in the variety of local outcomes of non-residential suburbanization.

Čestlice and Průhonice are neighbouring municipalities. Since 1997, a new commercial zone has been built on their territory. While, in 1991, Čestlice was an agricultural village from which most economically active people had to commute, Průhonice was a thriving suburb oriented to weekend recreation and tourism and with more jobs on offer than the number of economically active residents. By 2001, the situation had already become dramatically different, especially in Čestlice, with nearly four times as many jobs as there were economically active residents; 61 percent of the jobs were in wholesale and retail. The new retail and warehousing

Table 8.5 Change in the share on the total number of jobs in metropolitan areas

	All sectors	A+B	C–E	F	G	I	M+N	H+J+K+L+O
2001/1991								
Prague city	98.80%	30.74%	59.77%	76.15%	87.55%	108.30%	67.99%	164.95%
2nd suburban zone	113.69%	22.73%	90.49%	169.88%	191.90%	189.58%	85.64%	177.31%
Total PMA	100.00%	26.75%	63.49%	80.63%	93.37%	111.68%	68.88%	165.68%
2001/1991								
Brno city	100.12%	41.28%	60.47%	96.28%	136.14%	101.65%	91.34%	170.89%
2nd suburban zone	99.50%	37.32%	85.01%	202.40%	143.23%	125.24%	102.66%	159.57%
Total BMA	100.00%	38.72%	66.02%	106.57%	137.33%	104.65%	92.71%	169.50%

Table 8.6 Change in employment of selected municipalities 1991–2001

Municipality	Population	Economically active (Ea)	Employed (Emp)	Emp/Ea
1991				
Čestlice	405	226	62	0.274
Průhonice	1589	914	958	1.048
Říčany	10650	4259	3698	0.868
2001				
Čestlice	405	241	934	3.876
Průhonice	1948	1089	2197	2.017
Říčany	10876	5838	6301	1.079

zone also contributed markedly to the change in the structure of employment in Průhonice increasing the share of jobs in retail and wholesale from 8 percent to 33 percent. There was also growth in manufacturing jobs in Čestlice and transport and communication in Průhonice. The place became a strong suburban commuting target from Prague and the surrounding suburban municipalities for work in retail and warehousing facilities. Říčany is a small suburban town that has been losing its role of local centre since the 1960s. It lies in the shadow of Prague, to which many people used to commute. However, with the transition to a market economy, this town started to benefit from the vicinity of Prague and the processes of deconcentration. On municipal territory, but outside the town itself, however, two logistic and warehousing parks were established, thereby adding further to the employment.

Since most jobs are located in central cities, there is a high level of centrality in both Prague and Brno Metropolitan Areas. This centrality has recently been challenged by newly-established jobs in the newly-constructed suburban retail, warehousing, and industrial zones. The new suburban employment is clustered in just a few areas, challenging the former dominant concentration in the central city. A polynuclear pattern with strong dominance by the city centres is emerging in metropolitan areas. In most instances, the new areas are at the edge of the existing compact city, maintaining the continuity in urban expansion into the hinterland. However, there are also leapfrogging areas offering new jobs. The former compact city, with a continuous built-up area, is being transformed into a less continuous pattern with spatial fragmentation in the outer parts. It is possible that, in a few decades, the new suburban nuclei of economic activity will develop into large centres of employment (edge cities). In the long term the location of such new areas is strategic, since they are often placed between the existing city's huge population pool (labour supply, consumption power) and the expanding population in the new suburban areas. The spatial pattern of the metropolitan area could become polynuclear, with the strength of urban and suburban centres more evenly matched. The central city and the edge cities will, however, differ importantly in the composition of jobs, with specialized advanced services offering well-paid occupations in the centre and less-well-paid jobs in basic consumer and producer services (and industries) in the new suburban centres. Bearing in mind the residential pattern and the socio-spatial structure, a spatial mismatch between jobs and residences can be seen to emerge.

8.4
Conclusions and discussion

Suburbanization has only developed in Czech metropolitan areas as an important process of metropolitan change since the second half of the 1990s. The suburbanization of non-residential functions, particularly of retail and warehousing, has been more dynamic and influential than residential deconcentration. This situation is quite specific to a post-communist city, which in this respect differs from the common sequence familiar in North America and Western Europe.

The residential suburbanization has not been fostered by a large migration of population to metropolitan areas and a fast expansion of homes to the hinterland of the cities. The overall population stagnated and the deconcentration happened mainly though the spatial redistribution of the population within metropolitan areas. While the central and inner cities declined, there was a population increase in the suburban areas. In 2001, 22 percent of the population in Prague MA and 33 percent of the population in Brno MA lived in a suburban zone. However, most of these people were not typical suburban residents and the settlements are not the products of recent suburbanization. The dense settlement network around cities has its roots in the middle ages. Most suburban inhabitants still belong to a rural population. The original employment in agriculture has diminished over the past five decades and people have become dependent on industrial and service jobs in cities. The social status of this population is below average in the context of metropolitan areas. The true new middle-class suburbanites only settled these areas in the 1920 and 1930s and then again in the last few years. The overall presence of this middle-class is, therefore, not very strong. However, some municipalities have been significantly affected by suburbanization, where new residents already account for a substantial part of the population and in some cases even the majority.

Employment deconcentration is a completely new and very recent phenomenon. There has been a rapid growth of new economic activities and jobs in suburban locations, in particular around Prague and to a lesser extent also around Brno. Employment in the core cities of Prague and Brno metropolitan areas is shrinking, while it is expanding in suburban areas. This general employment deconcentration is also important in terms of its structural shift in employment composition. In particular, the growth in the suburbs is in the retail, wholesale, and storage sectors, while the decline in the cities is the result of deindustrialization. The spatial deconcentration of employment has not concerned advanced services or office jobs.

The extent, form, and functional composition of suburbanization in Prague and Brno differ. The metropolitan area of the capital city of Prague is the wealthiest region in post-communist Europe and residential suburbanization is driven mainly by the prosperity of its population. Commercial suburbanization has developed in retail and distribution, serving booming local markets and located in the very centre of the country. Residential suburbanization around Brno is less marked. The major difference from Prague is the development of new industrial zones and individual production plants in the Brno suburban areas. While Prague is the country's major command and control centre, Brno's economic development depends strongly on reindustrialization. In both cases, a majority of commercial facilities has been developed through the inflow of direct foreign investments; the development has been realized on out-of-town greenfields. However, the distinctive character of these two metropolitan economies has strongly affected the outcomes of suburbanization.

Suburbanization has made a major impact on the quality of life in metropolitan areas. The compact character of former socialist cities is being changed through rapid commercial and residential suburbanization taking the form of unregulated sprawl. Non-contiguous, leap-frog suburban sprawl has more negative economic, social, and environmental consequences than more concentrated forms of suburbanization. The societal costs of sprawl are well-known from North America and Western Europe; now sustainable metropolitan development in the Czech Republic is threatened. This threat concerns not only residential estates, but also new commercial facilities. For instance, the suburbanization of retail facilities has completely reshaped the pattern of travel for shopping. At present, suburban hypermarkets and shopping malls cater for a large share of shopping. Many of these locations are not served by capacity public transportation and people travel to them from the inner city by car. Another major impact of suburbanization is in the spatial mismatch in the distribution of jobs in metropolitan areas. Suburban employment is in retail, warehousing, and distribution, with low-paid jobs taken by people from the inner city and the surrounding region. In contrast, the suburban areas are now becoming the homes of prosperous people who commute to their office jobs in central and inner cities. There is, therefore, a spatial mismatch developing between the location of jobs and residences, contributing to an increase in travel in metropolitan areas, with consequent effects on the quality of life and the environment. The outcomes of rapidly-developing suburbanization in terms of spatial distribution of people and their activities in metropolitan areas form conditions that will influence the life of society for several generations. Patterns of urbanization in metropolitan areas will therefore become important targets of urban and metropolitan planning and policies that intend to keep a more compact urban form.

Acknowledgements

The authors acknowledge the support provided by the EU 5th Framework Programme, project no. EVK4-2001-00163 SELMA "Spatial Deconcentration of Economic Land Use and Quality of Life in European Metropolitan Areas" and by the Ministry of Education, Youth and Sports of the Czech Republic, project no. MSM0021620831 "Geographic Systems and Risk Processes in the Context of Global Change and European Integration."

References

Berényi I (1994) Transformation of the urban structure of Budapest. GeoJournal 32(4):403–414
Drbohlav D, Sýkora L (1997) Gateway cities in the process of regional integration in Central and Eastern Europe: the case of Prague. In: Migration, free trade and regional integration in central and eastern Europe. Verlag Österreich, Wien, pp 215–237
Enyedi G (1996) Urbanization under socialism. In: Andrusz G, Harloe M, Szelenyi I (eds) Cities after socialism. Blackwell, Oxford, pp 100–118
Enyedi G (1998) Transformation in central European postsocialist cities. In: Enyedi G (ed) Social change and urban restructuring in central Europe. Akadémiai Kiadó, Budapest, pp 9–34
Grimm F (1995) Return to normal – Leipzig in search of its future position in Central Europe. GeoJournal 26(4):319–335
Lisowski A, Wilk W (2002) The changing spatial distribution of services in Warsaw. European Urban and Regional Studies 9(1):81–89
Mulíček O (2002) Suburbanizace v Brně a jeho okolí [Suburbanization in Brno and its hinterland]. In: Sýkora L (ed) Suburbanizace a její sociální, ekonomické a ekologické důsledky. Ústav pro ekopolitiku, o.p.s., Praha, pp 171–182
Mulíček O, Olšová I (2002) Město Brno a důsledky různých forem urbanizace [The city of Brno and the consequences of varied forms of urbanization]. Urbanismus a územní rozvoj 5(6):17–21
Musil J, Ryšavý Z (1983) Urban and regional processes under capitalism and socialism: a case study from Czechoslovakia. International Journal of Urban and Regional Research 7(4):495–527

Nuissl H, Rink D (2003) Urban sprawl and post-socialist transformation: the case of Leipzig (Germany). UFZ-Bericht Nr. 4/2003

Ouředníček M (2003) Suburbanizace Prahy [Suburbanization of Prague]. Sociologický časopis 39(2):235–253

Ouředníček M, Sýkora L (2002) Současné změny v rozmístění obyvatelstva a v sociálně prostorové struktuře Prahy [Contemporary changes in the spatial distribution of population and socio-spatial structure of Prague]. Demografie 44(4):270–272

Pommois C (2004) The retailing urban structure of Prague from 1990 to 2003: catching up with the western cities? European Spatial Research and Policy 11(1):117–133

Smolová I, Szczyrba Z (2000) Large commercial centres in the Czech Republic – landscape and regionally aspects of development (contribution to the study of the problematic). Acta Universitatis Palackianae Olomoucensis Geographica 36:81–87

Strategie pro Brno (2003) Obchod a město: Regulace nebo liberalizace? [The Strategy for Brno, Retail and the city: regulation or liberalisation?] Available on http://www.brno.cz/toCP1250/strategie/obchod.pdf

Sýkora L (1998) Commercial property development in Budapest, Prague and Warsaw. In: Enyedi G (ed) Social change and urban restructuring in central Europe. Akadémiai Kiadó, Budapest, pp 109–136

Sýkora L (1999) Changes in the internal spatial structure of post-communist Prague. GeoJournal 49(1):79–89

Sýkora L, Kamenický J, Hauptmann P (2000) Changes in the spatial structure of Prague and Brno in the 1990s. Acta Universitatis Carolinae Geographica 35(1):61–76

Szelényi I (1996) Cities under socialism – and after. In: Andrusz G, Harloe M, Szelenyi I (eds) Cities after Socialism. Blackwell, Oxford, pp 287–317

Tammaru T (2001) Suburban growth and suburbanization under central planning: the case of Soviet Estonia. Urban Studies 38(8):1341–1357

Transit Cooperative Research Program (1998) TCRP Report 39. The Costs of Sprawl – Revisited. National Academy Press, Washington, DC

Ullrich Z, Bocková A, Dellin A, Hauner ES, Král J, Machotka O, Mertl J, Souček J, Turčín R, Voráček J (1938) Soziologische Studien zur Verstädterung der Prager Umgebung. Revue Sociologie a sociální problémy. Prague

9 The impact of retail deconcentration on travel to hypermarkets in Prague

Yaakov Garb[1]

Blaustein Institutes, Ben-Gurion University of the Negev, Sede Boqer Campus, Midreshet Ben-Gurion 84990, ISRAEL and Institute for Transportation and Development Policy (New York)

Abstract: This chapter provides the first comprehensive examination of the impact of retail decentralization on shopping travel and visitation patterns in post-communist Prague. Based on surveys of the current and prior shopping patterns reported in 2001 by shoppers in four recently opened hypermarket malls, the analysis shows how the transition to hypermarkets has affected shopping behaviour, and provides a detailed picture of current shopping trips, including an estimate of their contribution to total travel, and a multivariate analysis of the factors shaping trip length, mode, and frequency. The policy implications of these findings within the broader Central-European context are discussed

Key words: Retail, deconcentration, hypermarket, post-communist cities

9.1
Introduction

The first form of deconcentration in the wake of the political transition in the Central European countries (CEC) was the rapid exodus of retail from the traditional city core. Under the previous regime, retail was limited, government owned, and centralized not only spatially (in city centres of the larger cities) but also administratively. Stock, management, pricing, staff, and so forth were all centrally controlled. Beginning in the mid 1990s, however, and within less than a decade, a substantial portion of retail purchases was taking place in hundreds of hypermarkets. These are large (sales space of over 2500 m^2), modern, and highway-dependent malls. Many of them were located at the edge of or even outside the municipal boundaries of major CEC cities; almost all of them were leased by foreign owners to large West European retail chains. This revolution in retail format, scale, ownership, and location has become emblematic of the transition from Socialism in the CEC.[2] Unlike the more familiar pattern in developed countries, in central Europe 'big box' shopping was at the leading edge of deconcentration, preceding rather than following residential and job sprawl.

This chapter provides the first comprehensive examination of one key aspect of this revolution: its impact on shopping travel and visitation patterns. These have traditionally been a major concern with respect to retail deconcentration; the chapter places them on a firm empirical footing with particular respect to the Central European setting. Surveys of the current and prior shopping patterns reported by

E. Razin et al. (eds.), Employment Deconcentration in European Metropolitan Areas, 235–264.
© 2007 *Springer.*

shoppers in four Prague malls, both inside and outside the city boundaries, provide detailed insight into this key element of retail deconcentration. The survey reported here was conducted in the first malls established in Prague about 3-4 years after they opened. Thus, prior (pre-mall) shopping patterns were still relatively fresh in people's memories and were captured in these surveys. In this way, we are able to see in detail how the transition to hypermarkets has affected shopping behaviour.

Examination of the consequences of the transformation of retail is important in itself, as an important component of urban change in post-socialist cities is thereby illuminated. Furthermore, such an examination can not only help us understand past impacts in the CEC, but also anticipate future impacts as retailers move from the major cities (where retail markets are becoming saturated) to the smaller towns with fewer than 100,000 inhabitants, which are the new target of the large retail chains. This analysis of impacts is also relevant for other post-socialist cities to the south (the Balkans) and the east (Russia), where a similar process is taking place, albeit more slowly. (At the end of 2004, Russia had only 0.2 hypermarkets per million inhabitants, several orders of magnitude lower than the Czech Republic's 16 per million (PMR Publications, 2004)).

Current changes in shopping facilities and patterns in response to 'big box' projects in Asia, Latin America, Africa, and elsewhere render the lessons of Central Europe's 'flash malling' useful for transition countries globally. CEE retail patterns are also of interest to urban scholars in Western Europe and North America; the drastic and rapid retail revolution in the CEC provides hindsight into processes that occurred in developed economies in a more subdued form over a longer period. The CEC also provide models of some relatively sustainable niches of retail visitation retained in its cities, which are relatively compact and well served by transit (Garb & Dybicz, 2006).

9.2
The rapid malling of central Europe

After the Second World War, in countries under Soviet influence, the existing retail sector was systematically dismantled and reconstructed according to Marxist-Leninist ideologies and economic priorities (Michalak, 2001). As with other aspects of the economy, the retail sector became state-owned and controlled in most aspects: location, price, purchasing and stock, and staffing (Michalak, 2001). By the end of the 1980s, for example, 80 percent of stores – accounting for over 95 percent of turnover – were state owned (Michalak, 2001: 488). Almost all higher-order retail was located in the centres of the main CEC cities, which were compact and well served by public transport (subway, tram, and bus).[3] Other locations (smaller towns, villages, and even the massive housing estates established in 'suburban' locations around the main CEC cities) had only very basic shops.[4] The provision of goods and foodstuffs at factories, through 'grey' retailing, and through self-sufficient production supplemented the formal retail market, which was notorious for its limited quality and range.

Immediately after the transition, CEC countries had almost no modern retail and certainly no large-format out-of-town stores. In the following few years of initial transformation towards a market economy, retail went through a brief and dynamic stage of local ownership, although somewhat differently in each country. The state-owned retail enterprises were privatized to local CEE ownership on the one hand, and all kinds of *ad hoc* informal retailing sprang up on the other. Very soon, however, large West European retail chains sensed the opportunities in the region. At the time they were experiencing difficulties in their home markets through increased retail competition, market saturation, and zoning regulations that hindered the establishment of new hypermarket facilities. In the mid 1990s, hypermarkets accounted for between 22 percent (Norway) and 70 percent of market share (in France and the UK), whereas in Central Europe there were no hypermarkets. Thus, a highly developed, (even saturated) and also highly capitalized hypermarket system moved into virgin territory in Central Europe; the results were explosive.

In the Czech Republic, for example, the number of hypermarkets rose from practically zero in the mid 1990s to over 150 a decade later (Figure 9.1); the Czech Republic now leads Central Europe in hypermarket penetration. The percentage of modern retailing in hypermarket format rose rapidly from zero, soon reaching almost 50 percent (Dries et al., 2004). The share of foreign ownership in the top 50 retail trade companies rose from under 20 percent in 1993 to 80 percent in 2001 and has continued to rise. Thus, hypermarket retail is now entirely dominated by multinationals (some key players are the German Metro/Makro, the British Tesco, and the French Auchan and Carrefour); domestic chains have survived to a somewhat greater extent in Hungary and Poland.

The entry of these multinational companies into Central Europe was facilitated by the logistic convenience of their geographic proximity, coupled with their cultural similarities with Western Europe, which led to a fluent working relationship of CEE stores with their West European headquarters. At the same

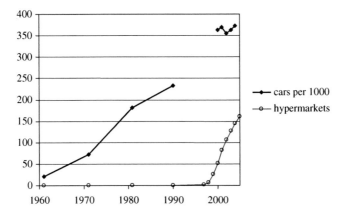

Fig. 9.1 Growth of motorization and hypermarkets in the Czech Republic[5]

time, the prospect of these countries joining NATO and then the European Union reassured Western investors of the likelihood of political stability and a rise in purchasing power. The hypermarkets were unstoppable: a key characteristic of socialist economies was the limited range and amount of commodities, and the great difficulties in obtaining even these, so the modernization of retail was symbolically the leading edge of the new political and economic freedoms.

Given central Europe's compact cities, excellent urban public transport, and predominantly urban customers, market forces alone might have encouraged the more central location of new retail facilities, close to the majority of the population and transit services. However, various aspects of post-socialist urban real estate and planning procedures rendered the siting of large modern retail facilities in town centres or sub-centres nearly impossible. Much of the hypermarket development was steered into off-centre or out-of-town locations in a fairly unregulated manner.

The difficulties in siting modern retail facilities in post-Communist cities included the constraints imposed by the lack of clarity with respect to the owner-ship status of re-privatized properties, the blockage for various reasons of large vacant or underused land (Jackson & Garb, 2002; Garb & Jackson, 2006), and the lengthy and uncertain procedures to change zoning status to allow retail activities. In contrast, large retail facilities were welcomed on greenfield sites in many small communities surrounding large cities. These had independent planning powers and competed with one another for the jobs anticipated from large retailers. Changing zoning involved far less bureaucracy in villages than in Prague and local mayors and councillors were lured by the prospect of land sales. The massive capitaliza-tion of international retailers relative to the incomes of civil servants also led to bribery to override residual attempts at land-use regulation. On the regulation side, there was a vacuum. The socialist system had engendered a widespread aversion to central planning in any form, including the regulation of retail location. The reform of territorial government and administration that came into force on 1 January 1991 removed the regional level of governance between the municipal and the national levels, which might have been the natural locus of such retail planning. Rising motorization rates (see Figure 9.1) also facilitated more car-dependent locations. The hypermarkets described below came from this first generation of hypermarkets in Prague, some in out-of-town locations, and others in off-centre infill locations within the Prague municipal boundaries.

9.3
The Prague hypermarkets travel survey

9.3.1
The hypermarkets

Four prominent Prague malls opened in the late 1990s were chosen for this study (Figure 9.2 and Table 9.1, below). These are spread across the city, and range from a classic exurban hypermarket (the cluster of retail development at Pruhonice,

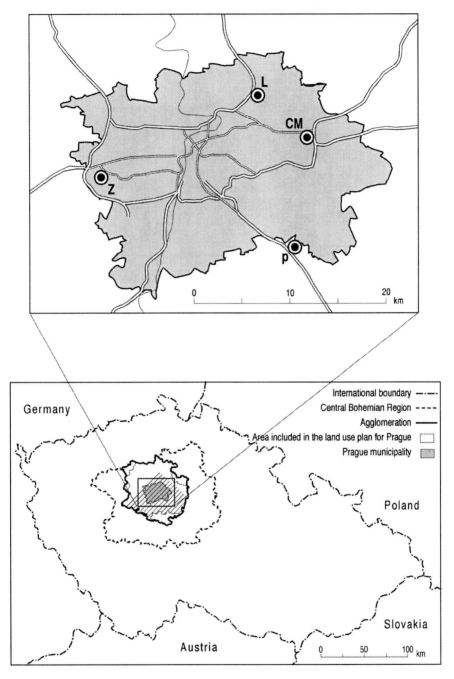

Fig. 9.2 The four Prague malls surveyed, located within the Prague municipal boundaries, the Prague Agglomeration, the Central Bohemia Region, and the Czech Republic. Z=Zlicin; P=Pruhonice; CM=Cerny Most, L=Letnany

Table 9.1 Shopping centre and survey information[6]

Mall information									Survey information (date and number of questionnaires)	
Location	Centre name	Date opened	Centre style	Gross leasable Area – GLA (m²)	Hypermarket percentage of GLA	Transit access	On highway or ring road	Relation to residential areas	Thursday	Saturday
Letnany	Letnany	Nov 1999	Mall	15,000	80%	Shuttle	No	Outside	25 Oct 2001 217	27 Oct 2001 251
	Hypernova	April 1998	Box	16,200	60%				8 Nov 2001 38	10 Nov 2001 45
Pruhonice	Makro	na	Box	Na	95%	Shuttle & bus	Yes	Outside	8 Nov 2001 106	10 Nov 2001 122
	Spektrum	April 1998	Mall	6,500	0%				8 Nov 2001 24	10 Nov 2001 22
Cerny Most	Centrum Cerny Most	Nov 1997	Mall	25,000	38%	Metro, shuttle	Yes	At edge	4 Oct 2001 208	6 Oct 2001 193
Zlicin	Shopping Park Praha	Nov 1998	Plaza	47,400	33%	Shuttle, metro	Yes	Outside	18 Oct 2001 189	20 Oct 2001 234

a ribbon sprawl development just outside the Prague municipal boundaries) to a more accessible mall, closer to the city centre and a residential neighbourhood. Two of the hypermarkets (Zlicin and Cerny Most) are located on opposite termini of a central subway line. Zlicin and Pruhonice are out-of-town malls: the former on the interchange of Prague's southwest radial highway with Prague's ring road, and the latter located on the southeast radial highway toward Brno, immediately outside the city boundaries.

9.3.2
The survey

The survey was conducted in October and November of 2001 via a questionnaire with 1649 respondents at 6 shopping centres located at the four different mall locations identified above (see Table 9.1 for the dates and number of questionnaires for each mall). Roughly 400 questionnaires were administered at each of the 4 sites on one weekday and one weekend day for each shopping centre. The distributors were instructed to circulate throughout the public areas in the shopping centres and approach individuals or groups to request their participation. In the case of a group, the person who responded completed the questionnaire. Our survey probably represents slightly less than one percent of the total daily visitation to these 4 malls, capturing 30,000 km of travel from places within the Prague agglomeration boundaries and an additional 45,000 of travel from further away.[7]

The questionnaires were designed to yield the following information:

1. Demographic information about the respondent (including age, gender, income ranking, household car ownership, household size).
2. Information about the trip that brought them to this shopping centre (the locations of the origin from which they came and their post-mall destination, what kinds of activity preceded and would follow the mall visit, how much time their incoming and outgoing trip would take, how long they anticipated staying or had stayed at the mall, how much they expected to spend there, their primary and secondary purposes for the trip, and how many times a month they came to this mall).
3. Information about the characteristics (mode, duration of visit, frequency) of the trip they used to make for the same purpose as their present trip prior to the existence of the new shopping centre.

This survey relies on several assumptions, which can be refined in follow-up studies. Thus, respondents' memory of prior shopping activity was assumed to be reliable (a reasonable assumption, since the malls had only been open for 2 to 4 years at the time of the survey), and that shopping was sufficiently habitual for the current trip to be representative of the visitors' usual shopping habits. In addition, in future work, possible overrepresentation in the survey of the weekend days and the smaller malls could be examined and compensated for, if necessary, by an appropriate frequency weighting.

The remainder of this chapter reports our analyses of the results of the survey, with special attention paid to three key characteristics of hypermarket use and travel: travel mode, trip distance, and shopping trip frequency. These indicators are crude, but important measures of the environmental and quality-of-life impacts of the shopping patterns captured in the surveys, and of the transition to these from shopping patterns reported to have prevailed prior to the use of the current mall.

Table 9.2 summarizes the key bivariate relationships of the key trip parameters in 26 comparisons of the difference in means of each parameter between subgroups for each of the independent variables. The findings are summarized in this way because they largely confirm the responses we expected of trip distance, mode, and frequency to various independent variables. The surprises here lie in the extent rather than the direction of these differences, and in the relationships that do not appear in the table: the relative unimportance of gender, for example.

Each of these three key trip characteristics is discussed further in a separate section, where a formal multivariate regression analysis is presented that explains between 34 percent and 44 percent of the variance of each trip characteristic[8]. In subsequent sections we discuss how these parameters changed in the transition to hypermarket shopping, and the striking absence of trip chaining.

Table 9.2 Bivariate relationships of key trip parameters

Trip parameter	Influencing factors and indicative examples (all significant at the 0.0001 level)
Distance (average round trip: **21.4 km**)	• **Travel mode** (car trips on average **20** km longer than pedestrian trips) • **Current shopping frequency** (trips undertaken biweekly or less average **12** km more than trips undertaken weekly or more) • **Duration** of mall visit (stays of over 2 hours average **10** km longer than stays of under one hour) • **Mall Location** (Zlicin trips on average **9** km longer than Letnany trips) • **Prior frequency** of shopping (trips undertaken biweekly or less on average **7** km more frequent than trips undertaken weekly or more often) • **Grocery** vs other trip purpose (non-grocery trips on average **6** km longer than grocery trips) • **Purchase amount** (visits with expenditure over 1000 crowns on average **5** km longer than those of under 1000 crowns) • **Day of week** (weekend or weekday) (Weekend trips on average **4** km longer than weekday trips)
Travel Mode (overall percent coming by car: **68%**)	• **Availability of car** (**17%** of those in car-less households come by car versus **75%** of those having one car in the household) • **Mall expenditure** (**39%** of the group spending under 500 crown, come by car versus **88%** of the group spending over 1000 crowns)

- **Reported income** (89% of those reporting above average income come by car, versus **65%** of the rest)
- **Distance** of trip (**39%** of those traveling under 6.5 kilometers round trip come by car, versus **72%** of those traveling over 6.5 km)
- **Mall location** (**57%** of shoppers at Letnany come by car versus **90%** of those at Pruhonice)
- **Age** (**46%-49%** of those over 62 or under 21 come by car versus **83%** of those in the 29-42 age bracket)
- **Prior shopping mode** (**32%** of those who used to shop by public transport prior to the mall's existence now shop by car versus **92%** of those who used to shop by car)
- **Frequency** (**72%** of those who come biweekly or less shop by car, versus **53%** of those who shop weekly or more)
- **Gender** (**60%** of women versus **77%** of men come by car; note: 71% of the car drivers are men, and only 15% of car passengers)

Frequency per month (average monthly frequency: **3.6**)

- **Number of passengers** in the car (those without a passenger come **3.1** times more than those with one or more passengers)
- **Mode** (pedestrians come **2.6** times more on average than those who come by public transport, who, in turn, come 0.5 times more often than those who come by car).
- **Distance** (those traveling under 11 km come **2.0** times more than those traveling over 11 km)
- **Prior frequency** of shopping (those who used to shop weekly or more now average **1.8** times more than those who used to shop biweekly or less)
- **Travel time** to mall (those traveling 15 minutes or less come **1.6** times more than those traveling 30-45 minutes)
- **Mall location** (Shoppers at Cerny Most come **1.1** times more than those at Zlicin)
- **Is public transport available** (those who declare that public transport is available for their trip come an additional **1.0** time a month more than those who do not)
- **Duration** of mall stay (those who spend under an hour come an additional **0.8** times a month compared with those spending between one and two hours)
- **Used to shop locally** (those who used to shop locally now shop an additional **0.6** times more than non-local shoppers)

9.4
Trip distance[9]

In addition to describing the analysis of the factors influencing trip length, in this section we discuss two important findings that have emerged from the study of the distribution of hypermarket travel distances: the presence of long-distance shopping and the large overall amount of hypermarket shopping in absolute terms, which can be estimated by linking the survey results to comprehensive 24-hour traffic counts at one of the malls.

9.4.1
The long distance surprise: Non Prague-based trips

As might be expected, the overwhelming majority of trips to the malls are Prague-based (PB); that is, they originate within the city of Prague or the Prague agglomeration—a ring about 30 km wide surrounding Prague that is used for functional analyses of the city (Figure 9.2). However, 15 percent of all trips *to* the malls and 14 percent of all trips *from* them (especially to/from Zlicin and Cerny Most) are from locations outside the Prague agglomeration. Since almost all the trips that have one trip end outside the agglomeration also have their second end outside, the number of trips having at least one terminus outside the agglomeration comprises 16.4 percent of all trips.

These non-Prague-based (non-PB) trips are distinctive and have striking implications for overall hypermarket travel. Over 91 percent of them are made by car (compared with 63 percent for Prague-based trips), and they average ten times the distance of PB trips: 99 km one way compared with 10.5 km for PB trips. For this reason, although non-PB trips constitute only 16 percent of overall hypermarket trips, they account for 50 percent *more travel* than the 84 percent of trips that come from within the Prague agglomeration (45,000 km of round-trips versus 30,000 km)!

Figure 9.3 shows the distribution (including average, median, inter-quartile range, and outliers) of roundtrip distances (in metres) of all trips, including those from outside the Prague agglomeration (on the left), and of the PB trips only (on the right).

In the diagram on the left (Figure 9.3), the non-PB trips are represented by the outer hump, the location of which is misleadingly close to the central hump. This closeness occurs because the travel modelling software replaces the actual

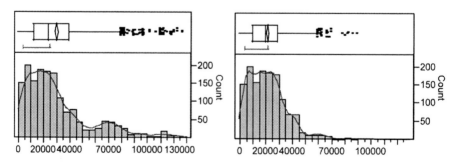

Fig. 9.3 Distribution of roundtrip distances (in m) for all trips (left) and Prague-based trips (right)

origin/destination of these trips with their point of entry to/exit from the Prague agglomeration. The distances representing non-PB trips in the data file distances are therefore drastically truncated. The true (and much longer) distances were derived separately from air-distances to the origin/destination points rather than the traffic model's network distances; they are shown in Figure 9.4.

This histogram provides a more accurate representation of the travel lengths, which appear with truncated values in the outer hump of the bimodal distribution in the previous figure. Whereas trips within the Prague agglomeration are clustered around a 21 km average (10.5 km each way), trips from outside the Prague agglomeration are distributed around an average distance ten times further away: a trip of just under 200 km on average (99 km each way). Half the non-PB trips are between 86 and 160 km one way. The distribution of non-PB trips is, obviously, truncated to the left, since shorter trips are registered within the Prague agglomeration and do not appear here. Beyond these two humps is a third distribution: a long thin tail of 28 trips (1.7 percent of the total sample) of over 350 km round trip (175 km each way) whose frequency does not decline until beyond 700 km round trip. The tail includes trips from Germany (353 km) and Slovakia (340 km).

In contrast with the PB trips, the non-PB trips are very sporadic (52 percent occur once a month or less compared with 16 percent for PB visitors); understandably, they are not standard grocery shopping trips. Only 35 percent of the non-PB

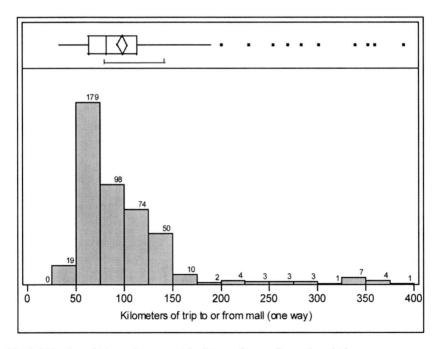

Fig. 9.4 Number of trips and one-way trip distance for non-Prague based trips

shoppers come for groceries (compared with 62 percent for the Prague-originating trips) and 7 percent are at the mall for work purposes (compared with 4 percent for PB visitors). Non-PB visitors stay for much longer; 38 percent stay for 2 hours or more (compared with 17 percent for PB visitors); and they spend more money than PB visitors. Not surprisingly, the overwhelming majority of these long-distance non-PB incoming trips originate at home (90 percent compared with the already high 85 percent of Prague-based trips). What is surprising is that 84 percent declare their post-shopping purpose also as 'home.' This is probably the case, but we must phrase trip-chaining questions very carefully to capture all stops, since it is difficult to imagine driving such distances to Prague and back without adding on a visit to other places in the city.

The long-distance trips discussed here probably represent an intermediate phase of retail deconcentration, with modern retail facilities located primarily in the capital city, so that people were willing to make a round trip from and to home of a hundred kilometres or more in order to shop at Prague malls.

Because of the methodological difficulties of merging the distance data of trips outside the scope of the traffic model with the rest of the dataset, and because these trips seem to be fundamentally different in kind, the non-PB trips have not been included in the further analyses of trip distances in reported here. The remainder of this chapter is a study of the travel behaviour of mall trip-making *within* the Prague agglomeration.

9.4.2
Regression model of trip length

A model accounting for 34 percent of the variance in roundtrip travel distance is given by the following nominal logistic regression (Table 9.3). Three factors alone account for 29 percent of the variance: (1) whether the trip origin is in/outside the municipal area; (2) trip mode; (3) shopping frequency.

Table 9.3 Regression coefficients for trip length model

Term	Std. beta	Prob> |t|
Intercept	0	0.0000
From Prague **municipal area** [No]	0.339	0.0000
Shopping **frequency** group {Two or less/month—3 or more}	0.223	0.0000
Primary purpose is groceries [No]	0.133	0.0000
Shopping **frequency** group {3 or 4/month —Four or more}	0.073	0.0015
Duration of mall stay {Up to one hour-One to two hours}	-0.077	0.0005
Mode {public transport-private vehicle}	-0.103	0.0000
Mode {Pedestrian—public transport & private}	-0.134	0.0000
Duration of mall stay {Up to two hours–over two hours}	-0.166	0.0000

Overall F ratio of 87.4, p>0.0001, R^2 adj. 0.34, n=1359.

There are some statistically significant influences on distance from some other bivariate variables, including the mall in question, age groups gender, and purchase amount (see Table 9.2). These relationships are, however, smaller or else test as insignificant in combination with other variables in a multivariate model. Car ownership does not influence trip distance directly, but through its influence on trip mode (trips made by car are somewhat longer).

9.4.3
Estimating overall generated travel

We can approximate the travel generation of the hypermarkets studied in absolute terms through linking the distances travelled in the population sampled in one of the malls, Shopping Centre Praha (Zlicin), with the total number of daily (24 hour) visitors to this mall.[10] The distance travelled in the Prague agglomeration trips sampled in this mall totalled 3,651 km on the weekday and 5,014 km on the weekend day. The total distance is slightly inflated by ignoring the fact that a small part of these shopping trips were added onto existing trips, but is greatly under-represented by excluding the far larger amount of travel that was not from the Prague agglomeration, most of which is reported to have been expressly for shopping.

Comparing the number of weekday and weekend day visitors in the questionnaires with the full daily count, we find that the sample in this survey represented 1.0 percent (weekday) and 0.7 percent (weekend day) of the total visits over the full day. Thus, the overall travel generated by this mall would be 354,250 km on a weekday and 716,448 km on a weekend day, yielding some 167 million km a year. This figure is reduced a little if we eliminate the days on which the malls are closed through holidays or travel is reduced through bad weather. These numbers accord with calculations derived in a different manner for a large mall in Warsaw (Garb & Dybicz, 2000). Assuming 0.2 kg of carbon produced per kilometre of car travel, even if we were only to include those 38 percent of total trips made by car drivers, this mall would produce over 12,000 cubic tons of carbon annually.

Given the 80 shopping centres in the Czech Republic when these surveys were made (Dragomir, 2001), hypermarket travel would have been responsible for 13 billion km of travel, and a million tons of carbon in the Czech Republic during the year of this study: 3.5 percent of total CO_2 from all fossil fuels in the Czech Republic. Even if we were to halve this number, because not all the 80 shopping centres nationwide are as large as Shopping Centre Praha and neither do they have this mall's average trip-distance (which is about 50 percent greater than an in-town mall), hypermarket shopping would still seem to be a significant source of travel and emissions.

9.5
Frequency

A model accounting for 30 percent of the variance in shopping trip frequency is given by the regression whose terms are shown in Table 9.4.

While the variable 'cars in household' is a statistically significant predictor, it contributes less than one percent to the explanation of variance. I have nonetheless included it in the model, because it remains significant even when travel mode and income are included in the model.

9.6
Travel mode

One can account for a good deal (44 percent) of the variance in mode choice with the six variables discussed below. In fact, 35 percent of the variance in mode can be explained by three variables: car ownership, pre-mall shopping mode, and shopping frequency.

The overall regression model for the choice between trip modes is given in Table 9.5. As expected, the following variables influence the choice of cars over public transport:

- a car in the household;
- larger purchases, of over 1000 crowns ($27 at the time of the survey): note that this effect can be shown to be separate from the effect of income, and does not seem to affect the choice of pedestrian over public transport;
- whether shopping before the existence of malls was done by car;
- whether the trip originated outside the Prague municipal area.

Table 9.4 Regression coefficients for trip frequency

Term	Std. Beta	Prob> |t|
Intercept	0	0.0000
Pre-mall frequency of shopping (monthly visits)	0.205	0.0000
Mall expenditure over 1000 [Under 1000 crowns]	0.160	0.0000
Day of week [Weekday]	0.123	0.0000
Persons in household	0.089	0.0014
Cars in household	0.070	0.0150
Primary purpose of mall visit [Entertainment/sport]	−0.064	0.0303
Income above average [not above average]	−0.095	0.0006
Primary purpose of mall visit [Groceries]	−0.103	0.0006
Primary purpose of mall visit [Other purchases]	−0.213	0.0000
Round trip length (m)	−0.267	0.0000

Overall F ratio of 43.8, p>0.0001, R2 adj. 0.29, n=1050.

Table 9.5 Regression coefficients for nominal logistic regression of trip mode

For Log Odds of	Term	Estimate	Standard error	Chi²	Prob>Chi²
Car /	Intercept	0.42	0.35	1.5	0.2230
Public	Mall expenditure [Under 1000 crowns]	−0.76	0.11	51.3	0.0000
transport	Round trip length	−0.0000032	0.000009	0.1	0.7065
	Pre-mall shopping mode [Private car]	1.56	0.16	91.1	0.0000
	Pre-mall shopping [Public transport]	−1.51	0.15	103.2	0.0000
	From Prague munic-ipal area [0]	0.45	0.16	7.7	0.0056
	A car in the house-hold? [No]	−1.50	0.15	94.2	0.0000
	Monthly mall visits	−0.05	0.04	1.5	0.2245
Pedestrian/	Intercept	−1.25	0.69	3.2	0.0719
Public	Mall expenditure [Under 1000 crowns]	0.005	0.28	0.0003	0.9867
transport	Round trip length	−0.0002554	0.000046	30.2	0.0000
	Pre-mall shopping mode [Private car]	0.49	0.36	1.8	0.1793
	Pre-mall shopping) [Public transport]	−0.63	0.30	4.5	0.0340
	From Prague munic-ipal area [0]	−0.04	0.44	0.008	0.9271
	A car in the house-hold? [No]	−0.53	0.20	7.1	0.0077
	Monthly mall visits	0.29	0.08	13.7	0.0002

Overall model R^2=0.44, Prob<0.0001, n=1041, full model Chi² 734.6.

Travel to malls on foot is chosen over public transport when there is no car in the household, for shorter distance trips, when shopping was done by public transport before the mall's existence, and in line with increasing shopping frequency.

The following results from this regression analysis are striking: distance *cannot* be shown to be capable of affecting the choice of car over public transport; whether an origin is inside or outside the municipal area, which strongly affects the choice of car, does *not* affect the choice of travel on foot over public transport; the absence of a car in the household *decreases* the likelihood of a trip being made on foot rather than by public transport (that is to say, once a trip is made other than by car, ownership of a car increases the likelihood of making the trip on foot). Also striking is the conservative nature of mode choice: that is, the pre-mall shopping travel mode influences the current choice of car over public transport more than current car ownership does.

Some other variables not included in the regression equation also show statistically significant relationships with mode choice. However, with the exception of *which* mall is visited, these variables do not explain more than a few additional percentage points of variance. For example, the day of the week affects the on foot/transit decision (with an increased likelihood of trips on foot on weekdays), but not the car/transit decision. Gender affects the car/transit decision (an increased likelihood of women using transit), but not the on foot/transit decision. A higher *frequency* of pre-mall shopping trips increases the likelihood of car trips (over and above the effect of pre-mall mode), but has no effect on the on foot/transit choice. However, while these effects are statistically significant and sometimes conceptually intriguing, they do not account for much of the variance.

9.7
Summary of regression findings

Figure 9.5 summarizes the multivariate regressions for each of the three key travel parameters (shopping trip distance, mode, frequency). This diagram should not be taken as a formal structural model, but as a convenient way of summarizing a large amount of information about what is and is not found in these regressions. It is important to note not only the factors that account for a good portion of the variance in each of the three (boxed) main trip parameters, but also the following: variables that are not capable of explaining any of the variance, and are thus not included in the diagram (gender or the reported availability of public transport for the trip, for example); whether variables explain the variance for only one parameter (visit duration only relates to distance, but not to mode or frequency, for example), or for two variables (trip purpose relates to both distance and frequency, but not mode). No variable occurs in the model of all three parameters. It is also

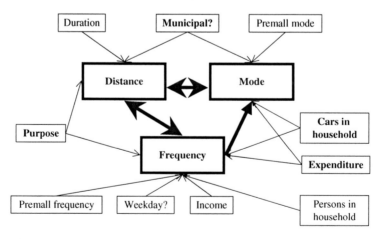

Fig. 9.5 Summary of multivariate regression findings

interesting to note the variables that remain influential despite the presence of what can be assumed to be mediating variables: for example, whether or not the trip is from within the municipal area of Prague (presumably well-served by public transport) affects trip mode even when travel distance is in the equation.

9.8
A striking lack of trip chaining in Prague shopping trips

The extent to which hypermarket visits feature in trips made for other purposes (trip chaining) rather than as the object of a dedicated trip must be an important part of the analysis of the impacts of hypermarket use and location. While the questionnaire was not designed to address trip chaining behaviour specifically, some surprising initial insights can be obtained.

Since weekday trips were only sampled in the afternoon, we could only examine chaining on the way home. We could not ascertain how many people stop at the hypermarket in the morning on their way to their day's activity. An examination of afternoon chaining, however, suggests that trip chaining plays a lesser part than we might anticipate. Thus, a stop-off on the way home from work occurs in only 11 percent of trips. These are divided almost equally between men and women; there is somewhat more chaining later in the afternoon. Thus, even during this time window of the return commute home, 79 percent of trips are reported to be made from and returning to home (57 percent of these by women). And, as Table 9.6 shows, the questionnaire responses reveal that shopping trips are overwhelmingly special-purpose trips from home and back. Only one of the malls (the Hypernova at the Pruhonice location) had 22 percent of the shoppers stopping there on their way home from work on the Thursday; however, this share was equal to just one half a percent of all the trips in the whole survey.

These findings are surprising in light of the fact that, in the literature on trip chaining in developed countries, work trips have come to be seen as an organizing element for household travel onto which other purposes, such as shopping, are added. While the results in this new and dynamic sub-area of travel analysis are still quite varied, they would lead one to expect a greater portion of linked trips. In the US, the National Personal Transportation Survey (NPTS) reports that 61

Table 9.6 Distribution of trips among various chaining types

Total % Row %	Home to home	Home to other	Work to home	Work to work	School to school	Other to home	Other to other	Total
Weekday	36.29	1.46	4.95	0.95	0.25	1.02	1.14	**46.07**
	78.79	3.17	10.74	2.07	0.55	2.20	2.48	100
Weekend day	46.76	2.54	0.19	1.02	1.14	0.57	1.71	**53.93**
	86.71	4.71	0.35	1.88	2.12	1.06	3.18	100
Total	**83.06**	**4.00**	**5.14**	**1.97**	**1.40**	**1.59**	**2.86**	100

percent of women and 46 percent of men make at least one stop on the way back from work (McGuckin & Murakami n.d.). Adiv reports that, on average, women make 2.1 stops on their work-to-home trips and men 1.8 (Adiv, 1983, as reported in McGuckin and Murakami n.d.). A major empirical review that aggregates 33 different household surveys comprising over 33,000 cases in the UK reports that 'only' 40 percent of main food shopping trips are linked.[11] Another surprising finding in the Prague survey in the light of the literature is that gender does not seem to have a significant effect on the kind of travel chain in which the shopping trip is embedded.

The implications of the foregoing are that shopping trips indeed *generate* travel rather than form part of or deflect existing travel. This finding underscores the environmental impact of retail travel and the associated choices of travel distance and mode. In Warsaw the significant portions of mall trips that are chained are closer to US and UK experience. The extremely low level of chaining that takes place in Prague remains a mystery.

9.9
The transition to current hypermarket shopping patterns

The sections above include details of the characteristics and factors influencing current mall shopping trips according to the responses of the shoppers in the survey. Some of the most interesting findings, however, are those regarding the reported characteristics of the equivalent shopping trips undertaken 'before this mall was available', particularly what can be derived from them regarding the *transition* from pre-mall to mall shopping. The malls covered in the survey had only been open for between 2 and 4 years before the survey date, so that pre-mall patterns would still have been relatively fresh in people's minds.

We must of course remember that differences between the period before a mall's existence and after its development are functions not only of the mall's presence, but of a lapse in time in a dynamic society. In the years between the opening of these malls (ranging between 1997 and 1999) and the 2001 survey date, incomes and motorization levels rose together with other changes affecting shopping patterns.

As set out below, the main change the survey reveals is that people replace frequent short duration trips, which were mostly not car-borne, with less frequent trips of longer duration made predominantly by car but also by transit. The total number of shopping trips, therefore, has dropped, though we may infer that the distance travelled in these less frequent trips is considerably longer. Trips made by car in the pre-mall period remain car trips; some of those formerly made by transit are lost to the car, while non-motorized trips are virtually eliminated. Mode choice becomes more strictly a function of income. In short, the shopping patterns of those who had cars was not altered much; but in the past, those lacking cars were likely to shop locally and on foot, and their shopping patterns have been altered radically.

Table 9.7 shows where people used to shop before they began shopping at this hypermarket, and how they used to get there. We can see that pedestrian and bicycle shoppers went predominantly (69 percent) to local retail outlets (local supermarkets or shops), while car-borne shoppers were free to go to predominantly (72 percent) more distant retail outlets (hypermarkets, supermarkets, company shopping clubs, or other centres).

The modified contingency diagram (Figure 9.6) shows the shift in shoppers' modes of travel as they moved from pre-hypermarket to hypermarket shopping. The horizontal axis shows the allocation among modes prior to the mall's existence, while the vertical axis shows the current allocation for each of these population segments. Almost all (92%) of the 47 percent of the people who used to shop by car before continued to shop by car. One third (32 percent) of those who used transit, and over half (56 percent) of those who used non-motorized transport, switched to the car. The switch to non-motorized transport among car and transit users was negligible, while only 8 percent of non-motorized shoppers remained non-motorized. In other words, car users were barely affected by the switch to hypermarkets; the number of transit users fell by one third; while non-motorized shopping trips declined by over 90%.

We can examine this transition from an environmental perspective. About 25 percent of all shopping trips surveyed switched to cars from modes considered more environmentally friendly. The 4 percent regained when car users report moving to more environmentally friendly modes in the switch to malls should be deducted from this. We can, therefore, estimate the additional amount of car travel engendered in the surveyed malls in the transition to mall-based shopping (Table 9.8).

If we project these proportions onto 6.5 billion km of annual hypermarket travel in the Czech Republic as a whole, as previously estimated (roughly, but extremely conservatively), we find that hypermarkets generate 4.6 billion kilome-

Table 9.7 Travel mode and type of former shopping (n=1542)

Col % Row %	Another centre	Company shop-ping club	Another hyper-market	Another super-market	Local super-market	Local shops	Other
Private car	70	50	78	57	24	24	41
	8	5	23	35	9	9	11
Public transport	22	19	14	26	5	11	41
	6	5	10	39	4	10	26
Walk or bicycle	9	31	8	18	71	65	18
	1	5	3	15	35	34	7

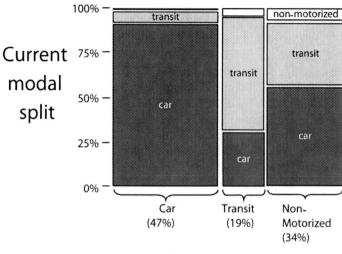

Fig. 9.6 Shifts in travel modes with move to current hypermarket (from Garb & Dybicz, 2005)

tres of car travel annually, 1.3 billion kilometres of which is by shoppers who did not previously use a car to shop.

At the same time, there are now far fewer shopping trips made by these more environmentally-demanding modes. The total **number of trips** made by the shoppers polled in these surveys was 60 percent greater in prior (pre-hypermarket) shopping patterns than currently (that is, the total reported frequencies times the number of people who reported that frequency was 7,614 for the prior shopping pattern, and is 4,663 in the current one).

Income significantly affects the *travel mode* of prior and current shopping, especially for people who shop non-locally. Thus, among pre-mall shopping undertaken *locally*, people whose (current) income is above-average report a somewhat greater amount done by car: 36 percent versus 23 percent (ChiSquare: 6.0, Prob>ChiSq: 0.049). Current income is more clearly reflected in the portion of car trips for shopping that used to be done *non-locally*: The shares are 79 percent for people with above average income and 56 percent for the rest. The respective public

Table 9.8 Breakdown of travel distances captured in survey

Total travel	$29,423\,km$	
Car travel (passenger or driver)	$20,766\,km$	71%
Car travel by people who did not previously shop by car	$5,760\,km$	20%

transport mode shares are 10 percent and 27 percent. For current shoppers, an above-average income all but eliminates non-car travel regardless of whether these shoppers used to shop locally or not; the car travel share jumps from 65 percent to 89 percent (ChiSquare: 50.6; Prob>ChiSq: <.0001). In other words, although these comparisons are based on current income reports, shopping travel mode prior to hypermarkets, especially for shopping that was done locally, may have been significantly less dependent on income than currently is the case, where travel mode is quite sensitive to income.

Shopping **frequency** drops from an average of 5 times a month to 3.6 times a month. The more frequent prior shopping used to be, the greater the amount by which the frequency drops. The extent of the drop is significantly larger for several categories: those who used to shop locally (a drop of 2.4 versus 1.0 for non-local shoppers; prob.< 0.0001); those who used to arrive on foot (a drop of 2.7 versus 0.7); those surveyed at the weekend (a drop in shopping frequency of 1.9 versus 1.2; Prob < 0.0001); those with an above-average income (1.6 versus 1; prob < 0.01); and those spending more than 1000 crowns (1.8 versus 1.2; prob< 0.0007).

There are interesting patterns in the extent of frequency change. While there is very little difference between the shoppers sampled on a weekend and a weekday regarding their prior frequency of shopping (averages of 5.0 and 5.3), there is a larger weekday/weekend difference in the frequency of *current* shopping (3.2 for weekend shoppers versus 4.2 for weekday shoppers), the sharpest average drop was for those who used to shop in local shops (2.9); the drop for those who used to shop in a local supermarket was moderate (1.9); there was almost no change in the shopping frequency of those who shopped in another hypermarket, however (0.3). The matrix of histograms (Figure 9.7) shows that the largest change in shopping frequency is of those who used to shop locally, with far less change in the frequency profile of non-local shoppers. The current shopping patterns of former local shoppers now approximate very closely the former infrequent shopping patterns of those who used to shop non-locally. Those who shopped non-locally in the past now shop even less frequently, with a monthly shop being the most common.

A series of logistic regressions (Figure 9.8) shows the response of trip mode to trip frequency in current trips (top), in prior trips (middle), and in prior local trips (bottom): those trips that used to be to local shops and local supermarkets. The choice to use public transport is relatively insensitive to trip frequency in all cases, while non-motorized and car trips are very responsive to the frequency of prior trips, especially that of prior *local* trips. We also see in these graphs the much larger mode share of non-motorized trips in pre-hypermarket shopping (R square of > 0.1 and Prob>ChiSq: <.0001 in all cases).

As shown in Figure 9.9, **shopping duration** (reported time spent at the hypermarket) stays the same or becomes longer for almost all the trips. (That is, most trips lie to the left of the white-barred diagonal.) Sixty five percent of trips were less than an hour in duration in prior (pre-hypermarket) shopping, whereas only 40 percent are now.

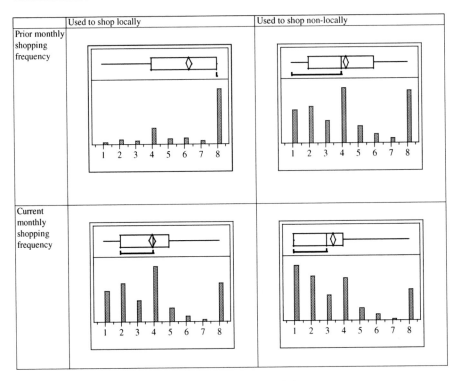

Fig. 9.7 Shifts in shopping frequency in local and non-local shoppers

9.10
Summary, conclusions and discussion

In this chapter, we have presented the key findings of a large-scale survey of shoppers in certain new hypermarkets in Prague. These findings relate not only to shoppers' current visitation patterns in these malls, but also to the patterns reported from a period prior to the mall in question becoming available. This concluding section summarizes these (and several additional findings) in a brief narrative, reflects on their implications for retail location policy, and briefly suggests further work that might usefully be undertaken with this dataset.

The transition to hypermarkets. The move to hypermarket shopping has resulted in people making longer duration shopping trips less often, so that the reported overall number of shopping trips made by the population sampled has dropped by almost 40 percent with the advent of hypermarket shopping. Most of this drop in frequency is a result of the substitution by hypermarket shopping of the one third of shopping that used to be done locally. These former local shoppers used to shop at least once a week, and very often several times a week, overwhelmingly on foot or by bicycle (68 percent) or by public transport (8 percent), and their mode

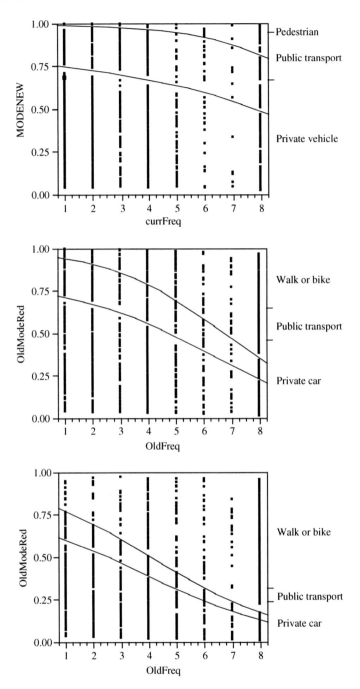

Fig. 9.8 The relation of mode to frequency in current (top), prior (middle), and prior local (bottom) trips

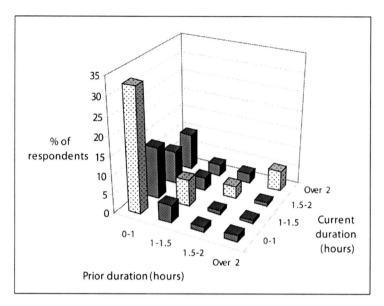

Fig. 9.9 Change in duration of prior-to-hypermarket and current shopping trips (white bars denote identical prior and current durations). N=1554

choice seems to have been far less influenced by income than it now is. In the transition to hypermarket shopping, transit trips were significantly reduced, while non-motorized trips were almost eliminated. For this reason, while the overall number of shopping trips has decreased with the advent of the hypermarkets, the overall amount of motorized trips has increased sharply. Indeed, 20 percent of the car trips made to the malls surveyed are trips that used to be by transit or non-motorized travel: this figure translates into roughly 1.3 billion kilometres car travel annually for the hypermarkets in the Czech Republic as a whole.

Travel distance in current hypermarket visits. A study of the distribution of trip distances indicates three different kinds of trips: those from *within* the Prague agglomeration (84 percent) with an average round trip of just over **20 km**; those 16 percent of trips that either originate in or end *outside* the Prague agglomeration (almost always both), with an average round trip of just under **200 km**, and a very thin (1 percent) but persistent long tail of long distance trips the frequency of which does not decline until about **700 km**. These non-Prague-based trips constitute a real surprise in terms of overall traffic generation, contributing much more travel (50 percent more) than the 86 percent of hypermarket visits considered to be normal Prague-based trips. The absolute amount of hypermarket travel is impressive, in the order of 150 million km a year for the Zlicin mall alone. This figure translates into a conservative estimate of at least 6.5 billion km of annual hypermarket travel in the Czech Republic, 4.6 billion kilometres of which is car travel, which generates something of the order of a million tons of carbon emissions.

Overall regression models of key trip parameters. About a third of the variance in three key trip parameters (distance, frequency, mode) can be explained through selected variables ascertained in the survey (together with two other parameters in each case). The multivariate regressions reveal no great surprise in terms of whatever may affect these parameters, but many small surprises regarding what does *not* affect them substantially, or what remains influential even in the presence of what would seem to be a mediating variable. As is often the case with a cluster of significantly collinear variables, effects that appear strongly in simple bivariate analyses of a variable can disappear when that variable is considered as part of a multivariate model. For example, the choice of mall surveyed (Pruhonice versus Cerny Most, for example) affects trip distance decisively when considered alone, but this effect disappears when the mall investigated is considered in tandem with other variables.

The regressions reveal a strongly conservative component in trip-making: shopping mode, frequency, and presumably distance are as strongly (and independently) related to the values of these variables in prior (pre-hypermarket) shopping patterns as they are to current variables. Further work drawing on theories of travel and shopping choice-making is needed to tease out the interrelationships in this dataset and the directions of causation (when does mode of shopping determine trip distance, and when does the converse apply?).

Trip chaining. With over 80 percent of hypermarket trips starting from and returning home, it seems that the overwhelming portion of travel is specifically for the purpose of visiting the mall: that is to say, hypermarket travel can be seen as predominantly generated travel rather than included in or diverting existing trips.

Further work. Since mall locations, trip origins, and destinations were all located to the closest traffic analysis zone (TAZ), future work could use GIS techniques to add a spatial dimension to the predominantly statistical analysis reported here. GIS techniques could, for example, help narrow down *where* the greatest conversion of pedestrian shopping to car-based shopping occurred, or help segment trips according to the population density and transport accessibility of their origin TAZ.[12] In other words, spatial attributes may help explain more of the variance in trip parameters, especially travel mode.

A GIS-assisted distinction drawn between **long-distance** out-of-agglomeration origins, **suburban** origins (within the agglomeration, but from locations outside the densely built-up area and public transport services), **urban** origins (in dense areas well served by public transport), and **walking-distance** origins, might well be crucial in explaining trip characteristics, and also in guiding retail location policy. Retail must address the needs of consumers in each of these groups and mediate the conflicts that arise in seeking to serve them all. For example, the two malls at the termini of Prague's subway system (Cerny Most and Zlicin) may serve shoppers travelling outward by subway to shop as well as those who travel inward by car from surrounding villages and more remote locations. Shoppers at these malls can avoid travelling in the congested urban areas. If malls were better linked to the surrounding residential areas, they could also be visited by pedestrians and cyclists for trips involving small loads. Shuttles could also be useful. As discussed elsewhere (Garb & Dybicz, 2006), the location of malls with respect to workplaces is also important: Warsaw has malls characterized by a sizeable portion of 'stop-on-the-way-home-from-work' trips; such characteristics are lacking in the Prague malls we examined.

Thus, the empirical findings presented here show not only the importance, but also the complexity of regulating the nature, location, and accessibility of retail. Although the current toolbox of retail regulation is fairly extensive, it may still need to be upgraded to accommodate this complexity.

During its first decade of expansion, Central European retail followed, by default, the North American model of relatively unfettered market-driven expansion.[13] In USA, there are no national policies governing retail location and very few state-level initiatives as a result of the country's geographical size, lack of land-use powers at the federal level, and strong emphasis on local policy determination. The general trend in USA is one of local ordinances intended to temper the encroachment of new 'big box' stores. The circumstances and consequent actions vary from community to community; they tend to be reactive in the face of new proposed development rather than an overall strategy for retail policy as seen at a national level elsewhere.[14]

In Western Europe, on the other hand, a diverse and sophisticated toolkit of measures for regulating retail has evolved. Zoning has been used to restrict retail development to town centres or to urban areas with good access by all transport forms. In other cases, countries have set thresholds for the maximum size of new retail projects, the kinds of goods sold, and even the opening hours to reduce competition with small retailers. In the Dutch case, impacts on existing retail in smaller formats is avoided through specifying a small number of national 'large-scale concentrated retail establishments,' which have a *minimum* size threshold. Other tools regulate retail through the manipulation of incentive structures and stakeholder relations rather than zoning. Examples include redistributing to small businesses in traditional locations a portion of the business taxes paid by large retailers to retailers in out-of-town locations, or allowing a regional planning authority to veto the retail development proposals of another adjacent authority if these plans can be claimed to have an adverse regional effect. At various points in time, some countries have mandated obligatory retail research that maps out the needs for proposed retail development and its impact.

The empirical findings reported in this paper indicate the subtlety and contextual specificity with which these and other tools must be formulated and applied and the complex linkages with policies on motorization and other forms of deconcentration (of jobs and housing). In some respects, the environmental characteristics of malls can be improved by locating them on public transport routes in central locations: about a quarter of the trips can then come by transit and average travel distances could be almost halved (Garb & Dybicz, 2006). While offering no silver bullet, this step would support the rationale of policies intended to steer new retail development to accessible locations and would lead to significant improvement.

Nonetheless, the situation is complex. Hypermarkets significantly *reduce* the number of trips made, although they convert those remaining into motorized and longer-distance trips. We must also remember that such 'improved' urban accessibility would be irrelevant for the majority of trips, since more than 60 percent of the total distance travelled to the Prague hypermarkets came from or went to *outside* the Prague agglomeration. Whether the spread of large retail facilities to smaller cities, presumably closer to the homes of these non-Prague shoppers, lessens these long-distance trips to Prague hypermarkets remains to be seen.

As residential sprawl begins to develop around post-Communist cities, a trip to an out-of-town mall may replace a trip into the urban area as the environmentally-preferable mode of shopping for suburban residents.[15] For them, a trip to central retail involves a longer travel distance on more congested urban roads. Even in a country like England, which has fairly ubiquitous modern retail provision, modelling shows that the provision of in-town location increases the *distance* travelled by shoppers coming from out of town. Moreover, they have to drive on congested urban roads rather than inter-urban highways (Hay, 2005).

The complexity of retail travel impacts and the need for a segmented approach to retail policy is apparent. We need to encourage commuters to chain their shopping trips; we must allow urban dwellers access to modern retail without having them travel out by car; we must allow suburban dwellers access to retail without driving into the city especially for this purpose. The location of hypermarkets at the extremities of transit lines (as is the case with Zlicin and Cerny Most, in the Prague survey) may be a good compromise between the sustainable support of city shoppers travelling out and suburban shoppers travelling in.

While the shaping of where, how, and how often people shop has a significant effect on their quality of life, we should consider whether the more substantial quality-of-life impacts of hypermarkets, especially out-of-town hypermarkets, might not lie in the travel and traffic generated. More significant, perhaps, might be the isolation of the retail function from other urban functions. Every euro spent in a hypermarket is a euro drawn from local neighbourhoods or downtown areas. Local and downtown shopping trips can be chained through walking to other town centre destinations. This chaining encourages a flow of revenue and people and generates opportunities for the activities, land-use functions, and social interactions that are vital for urban and neighbourhood spaces. The profit on a euro spent in a hypermarket typically returns to the West European corporation that owns the shops and the West European institutional investors who own and lease the mall. There is also the question of the consolidation of substantial segments of the market into larger companies, as enabled by mega-stores. The effects of such consolidation are felt all the way up the supply chain to the farmers, whose bargaining power diminishes in the face of the purchasing power of a Tesco, Walmart or a Carrefour.

Thus, in addition to the effect studied in this chapter (added car travel), there are deeper quality-of-life issues at stake when a family shifts from shopping twice a week at the local grocery to a monthly car-borne trip to a hypermarket.

Notes

[1] The author conducted this research in his capacity as Director of European Programs with the Institute for Transport and Development Policy (ITDP; see www.itdp.org). This project was sponsored by a Rockfeller Brothers Fund grant to ITDP. I am grateful to Jirina Jackson, Tomek Dybicz and Gregory Newmark for their role in preparing and administering the questionnaire, to the UDI (Prague) for data entry and use of their excellent services in providing TAZ-to-TAZ network distance matrices, to Tomasz Dybicz whose prior work in Warsaw provided a useful reference point, and for his assistance in calculating trip distances for Prague; to Shaul Zionit who introduced me to the joys of using JMP(SAS) for data analysis; and to the editors of this volume for their useful comments and for urging a formal multivariate model in preference to a more piecemeal bivariate approach.

[2] For a far more detailed account of the three stages of the Central European retail revolution, see Dries, Reardon, & Swinnen (2004).

[3] For an overview of the impact of socialism on urban spatial structures, see Bertaud (2006).

[4] I know of no single good overview of the spatial organization of retail in Central Europe during the Socialist period, but Elmar Kulke provides an excellent review of the East German situation (Kulke, 1997).

[5] Number of hypermarkets drawn from INCOMA consultancy Shopping Center statistics. Motorization rates are drawn from UDI (Prague) *Yearbook of Transportation*–2004, Prague: UDI, 2004. Motorization rates for Prague, also given in this handbook, would be about 100 cars per thousand higher than the national average.

[6] This table is derived from information in Newmark, Plaut & Garb (2004), and from a table of Prague hypermarket descriptions prepared by UDI (Prague).

[7] Careful visitation counts by car and shuttle were carried out for one of the malls: Shopping Park Praha,. The survey was conducted by M. M. Agentura (Prague) in December of 2000. The total number of visits for the 24 hours on a weekday was 18,336 and 33,433 for the weekend. Our surveys thus represent 1.0% and 0.7% of these numbers respectively.

[8] Each of these three trip parameters (distance, mode, frequency) is statistically related to the other two as well as to a variety of other variables, in themselves related; with these obvious colinearities the direction of causation is sometimes open to different interpretations.

[9] All calculations for distance exclude trips from outside the agglomeration, since these are assigned by the traffic model to entry points at the edge of the agglomeration. The distribution of distance is mildly non-normal, and a slight improvement in the regressions (significances, R^2, normality of residuals) can be obtained through the use of the square root of distance rather than distance itself. These gains, however, do not invalidate any of the interpretations made and so do not seem sufficient to merit the use of a less intuitive measure and unit (square root of distance).

[10] These were collected by M. M. Agentura (Prague) in Dec. 2000.

[11] Bennison, D., J. Byrom, et al.. (2000). *Linked Shopping Trips: a Report for Tesco Stores Ltd.*, Department of Retailing and Marketing, Manchester Metropolitan University as cited in Oxford Institute of Retail Management (2004). NRPF Scoping Paper: *Linked Trips and the Viability and Vitality of Centers of Retail Activity*, Templeton College, University of Oxford. These reports stem from the fact that the issue of how shopping figures into linked trips (or 'complex trips,' combined trips, or 'joint purpose trips' as they are also called) has assumed importance in the UK, as part of the debate on how out-of-town and town-edge stores effect the vitality of town stores. There is concern to use make sure that new large stores will remain accessible enough to city centres so that trips to them will link to the adjacent city centre.

[12] The beginning of such work was presented as part of: Yaakov Garb and David Epstein, *Rapid Retail Deconcentration in Post-Communist Prague: Causes and Travel Consequences*, a presentation to the conference Spatial Deconcentration of Economic Land Use and Quality of Life in European Metropolitan Areas, Jerusalem Nov 20-22, 2005, and subsequent work on this dataset at the University of Michigan by David Epstein.

[13] See, for example, Walter (2003) for a detailed study of retail regulation in the Polish context, which shows that while existing legal tools were adequate, their lack of enforcement led to a more-or-less free

market development context. The drive toward retail modernization overrode any concerns of spatial consequences. Impact analysis of new retail facilities was required, but these were prepared by the developer and there were no guidelines as to what to measure, or what the goals or benchmarks were. As might be expected, such reports focused on (unsubstantiated) claims about increased employment opportunities and highly local (parking-lot level!) assessment of impacts on air quality.

[14] This summary and the following summary of West European retail is derived from a comprehensive survey of the topic by Y. Garb and S. Lichfield, forthcoming from ITDP.

[15] See the discussion of the Centrum Janki mall outside Warsaw in Garb & Dybicz (2005) and Garb & Dybicz (2006).

References

Adiv A (1983) The structure of the work trip based on analysis of trip diaries in the San Francisco Bay Area. In: Carpenter S, Jones P (eds) Recent advances in travel demand analysis. Gower, Aldershot, England, pp 117–136

Bertaud A (2006) The spatial structures of central and eastern European cities: more European than socialist? In: Tsenkova S, Nedovic-Budic Z (eds) The urban mosaic of post-socialist eastern Europe. Springer, New York, p. 91

Dragomir M (2001) Consumers' hypermarket mania driving 3-year retail expansion. Prague Business Journal, August 6–12

Dries L, Reardon T, Swinnen J (2004) The rapid rise of supermarkets in central and eastern Europe: implications for the agrifood sector and rural development. Development Policy Review 22(5):525–556

Garb Y, Dybicz T (2000) A preliminary estimate of traffic generation in Warsaw malls and the CO_2 reduction potential of improved retail siting. Unpublished memo prepared for the Institute for Transportation and Development Policy

Garb Y, Dybicz T (2005) Global lessons from the travel impacts of retail decentralization in Central Europe. Paper presented at the Annual Meetings of the American Planning Association, March 2005

Garb Y, Dybicz T (2006) The retail revolution in post-socialist Central Europe and Its lessons. In: Tsenkova S, Nedovic-Budic Z (eds) The urban mosaic of post-socialist eastern Europe. Springer, New York, p. 231

Garb Y, Jackson J (2006) Central Europe's brownfields: catalyzing a planning response in the Czech Republic. In: Altrock U, Güntner S, Huning S, Peters D (eds) Spatial planning and urban development in the new EU member states. Ashgate, Aldershot

Hay A (2005) The transport implications of planning policy guidance on the location of super-stores in England and Wales: simulations and case study. Journal of Transport Geography 13:13–22

Jackson J, Garb Y (2002) The search for brownfield beadership in central European cities: overview and case study of the Czech Republic. Policy report. Institute for Transportation and Development Policy, New York/Prague

Kulke E (1997) Effects of the economic transformation process on the structure and locations of retailing in East Germany. Journal of Retailing and Consumer Services 4:49–55

McGuckin N, Murakami E (n.d.) Examining trip-chaining behavior: a comparison of travel by men and women. Manuscript

Michalak WZ (2001) Retail in Poland: an assessment of changing market and foreign investment conditions. Canadian Journal of Regional Science 243:485–504

Newmark GL, Plaut PO, Garb YJ (2004) Shopping travel behaviors in an era of rapid economic transition: evidence from newly built malls in Prague, Czech Republic. Transportation Research Record 1898:165–174

Oxford Institute of Retail Management (2004) NRPF scoping paper: linked trips and the viability and vitality of centers of retail activity. University of Oxford, Templeton College

PMR Publications (2004) News item in the Central Europe Retail Headlines Newsletter accessed at http://www.pmrpublications.com/ but no longer available without charge

Walter M (2003) Einzelhandelsentwicklung in Polen: Probleme der planerischen Steuerung des Einzelhandels in Warschau. Masters thesis. Institute for Town and Regional Planning. Berlin Technical University

10 Employment deconcentration in European metropolitan areas: A comprehensive comparison and policy implications

Martin Dijst[1] and Carmen Vázquez[2]

[1] *Faculty of Geosciences, Utrecht University; P.O. Box 80115, 3508 TC, Utrecht, The Netherlands*
[2] *Department of Geography and Planning, Faculty of Humanities, University of Castilla-La Mancha, Avd. los Alfares 44, 16002 Cuenca, Spain*

Abstract: This chapter features a cross-national comparison of economic deconcentration in 12 European metropolitan areas analysing two attributes of employment deconcentration: the magnitude, which refers to the scale of deconcentration; and the physical form. The discussion is positioned in the framework of two dimensions of governance systems: welfare-state regime and central-local government relations. Our expectation that deconcentration would take place on a smaller scale and in a more concentrated form in comprehensive welfare state systems than in liberal regimes is confirmed for one decentralized comprehensive welfare state case and three decentralized liberal state metropolitan areas, but not for the other seven cases. Arguments accounting for this mismatch are put forward. In addition, the effects of deconcentration on the quality of life and the impact of policies are discussed

Key words: Employment deconcentration, European metropolitan areas, sprawl, governance systems, quality of life

10.1
Introduction

All Western countries are developing towards an economic, social, and political network society (Castells, 1996; Graham & Marvin, 2001). Investments in high-quality transport systems together with the implementation of new Information and Communication Technologies (ICT) offer opportunities for changes in the spatial organization of economic activities world wide. Management, research and development, production, services and other economic activities make new trade-offs between the accessibility of information, people and goods, and costs of locations. The same is true for the locational decisions of households, which reflect changes in preferences for dwellings and environments stimulated by new economic and mobility opportunities. As a consequence, new spatial configurations of land uses have been developed (Ingram, 1998), ranging from concentration to deconcentration with various impacts on the quality of life.

The reorganization of economic activities in the form of their deconcentration is a process that has taken place on a large scale in American metropolitan areas (Garreau, 1991; Lang & Le Furgy, 2003). Various economic activities have also

E. Razin et al. (eds.), Employment Deconcentration in European Metropolitan Areas, 265–291.
© 2007 *Springer.*

found new locations in European metropolitan areas at the edge of central cities and on suburban locations (Parr, 1999, 2003; Kloosterman & Musterd, 2001; Phelps & Parsons, 2003; Halbert, 2004; Bontje & Burdack, 2005). Considering the large differences between North America and Europe in history, political and cultural contexts, and urbanization patterns (Schwanen *et al.*, 2004), we could expect large differences between these Western continents in the scale and form of economic deconcentration. This is one of the main issues we address. In the earlier chapters, we discuss deconcentration in three selected economic sectors and 13 metropolitan areas and their main determinants for the 1990s patterns and processes of employment. What is lacking is a broad cross-national comparison of the case studies that is positioned in the framework of governance types developed in the first chapter. Such a comparison is the main purpose of this chapter.

The comparison of economic deconcentration processes in metropolitan areas is led by two related hypotheses: the *multi-dimensional centrality hypothesis* and the *governance system hypothesis*. The first hypothesis is related to the position of cities within economic cycles. The three North European countries, Denmark, the UK, and the Netherlands, represent economically prosperous countries, which underwent globalization and transformation of the economy a long time ago. New windows of opportunities have been created through innovations in transportation and ICT. As shown by Pred (1977), Friedmann (1986), Sassen (1991) and Castells (1996), for example, multinationals in particular are responsible for changes in the locations of production, administration, research and development, and control functions, which lead to the centralization of various activities in particular places and to the specialization of other places in some activities at the expense of others. As a consequence, many production activities have been moved to developing countries, while control, innovation, financial and business activities increasingly dominate the economies of the North European countries. In contrast, Italy and Spain are lagging behind economically. They are experiencing the early stages of economic transformation. The same can be said for the Czech Republic, which experienced a change from a socialist to a capitalist economy in the 1990s. Finally, Israel is a highly-developed country in the Middle East, surrounded by developing countries and under the utmost demographic and political pressures, but which, like the three north European countries, has been experiencing economic transformations for several decades.

We expect that the position of countries and cities in economic cycles will have an impact on the deconcentration processes in the selected metropolitan areas. Using the metaphor of 'centre and periphery' (Wallerstein, 1979) and the idea of different levels of (spatial) aggregation, economic deconcentration can be hypothesised as a phenomenon of multi-dimensional centrality. This statement means that we expect economic deconcentration to occur first and most intensively in leading economic (central) countries, like Denmark, the UK, the Netherlands, and Israel. Within these countries, the largest cities in which the strategic control and organization activities are located experience the greatest pressures on available land, which will cause large-scale deconcentration. Because of their high rents and transportation costs, these cities push out certain economic activities to the edge of the central cities or even further away where the trade-off between accessibility and locational costs are more acceptable (Janelle, 1969; Clark, 2000). As a consequence, these processes result in an expanded area of centralization and specialization or the development of a metropolitan area.

This hypothesis is mainly based on the spatial decisions taken by multinationals. However, the opportunities local, regional, national, and international public authorities have for intervention in market processes could also have large impacts on spatial configurations. The impact of governance systems is the subject of the second hypothesis. Based on the work of Esping-Anderson (1990), in chapter 1 we distinguished between two dimensions of governance systems: welfare-state regime and central-local government relations. These two dimensions define four extreme governance systems.

First, the *centralized comprehensive welfare-state model*, represented by the Dutch cases, is characterized by a strong hierarchy of government levels and centralized detailed planning regulations, and a broad societal consensus over sustainable development.

The second governance type, the *decentralized comprehensive welfare state*, differs from the centralized version in the sense that local government is more powerful and autonomous functionally and fiscally and that land-use planning is more decentralized and left to regional and local authorities. Although in Denmark land-use planning is centralized (Larsen, 2005), this type of governance system is exemplified by Copenhagen.

The third type of governance system is the *centralized liberal system*, best exemplified by Britain since Thatcher. The British cases are confronted with centralized compact development policies, but liberal *laissez-faire* mechanisms provide incentives for public authorities to deviate from the national plans.

Finally, in a fully *decentralized liberal system*, which can be found in the United States, markets predominate and local authorities have relatively strong political and financial autonomy.

Although the governance systems of south European countries, post-communist countries, and Israel are all very far from the United States prototype of a decentralized liberal state (Larsen, 2005; see also Razin in this book), compared with northern Europe these countries lean towards a decentralized liberal system model. However, the case studies do show variations in governance system. Madrid and Valladolid in Spain can both be characterized by the concentration of decision power at the regional level with strong influences from commercial interests. The governance systems of the cases in the Czech Republic, Italy, and Israel could all be characterized by local autonomous planning highly influenced by market-based actors. It is assumed that the type of governance system has a large impact on economic deconcentration processes. It is expected that, in welfare-state systems, deconcentration is taking place on a smaller scale and is much more concentrated than in liberal regimes.

In this concluding chapter, we address both hypotheses. Furthermore, based on the comparative analysis, we discuss the main quality-of-life and policy impacts and implications for policy in metropolitan areas in various settings. The next section provides a comparison of employment deconcentration patterns in the selected metropolitan areas that stand to the fore in this book. This comparison is based on the magnitude and spatial form of deconcentration and the leading economic sectors (manufacturing/construction, consumer, and producer services). Although the data, definitions, and methods applied in the countries vary, we have sought to provide more solid foundations for generalizations than the discussions on observations and impressions presented in the former chapters. In the third section, we set these patterns of deconcentration against the governance types to which the cases belong. In section 10.4, we discuss the quality-of-life impacts of employment deconcentration and related planning policies. Finally, the chapter concludes with a discussion of the main findings and policy implications.

10.2
Employment deconcentration patterns

10.2.1
Methodological approach

In this section, we analyse data on employment deconcentration processes that took place in the 1990s in 12 metropolitan areas. Two attributes of employment deconcentration are discussed: the *magnitude*, which refers to the scale of deconcentration, and the *physical form*. Employment data have been classified into three economic sectors:

- Consumer services: supermarkets, department stores, travel agencies, hairdressers, public transport companies, and post offices
- Manufacturing and construction: producers of cars, textiles, beverages, metal, furniture, and so forth, and construction companies
- Producer services: companies working in finance, accountancy, and advertising.

Besides development in employment in these three economic sectors, the sum of employment in these three sectors ('total') has been analysed separately.

The analysis of the form of deconcentration is based on a subdivision of the metropolitan areas into concentric zones starting from the centre of the central city. This subdivision resulted in four functional zones:

- CBD or centre of the central city
- The rest of central city
- Inner suburban ring
- Outer suburban ring.

This quantitative approach is supplemented by qualitative observations on the sprawl and clusters of deconcentrated land uses taken from the national chapters in this book.

A comparison of the countries is a useful task, but not one that is easy to accomplish. The countries show wide variations in the availability of data (substantial variations in the level of economic and spatial disaggregation, for example), the definitions of variables, and the methodology applied. For example, the data from the Czech Republic only allowed a distinction to be drawn between two zones: the outer suburban zone and the central city/inner suburban zone. For Chieti-Pescara (Italy), Valladolid (Spain), Copenhagen (Denmark) and Tel Aviv (Israel) the central city could not be divided into a centre and the rest of the central city. As a consequence, not all cases are included in some tables and figures, which means that the results of this comparative analysis should be interpreted as indicative for employment deconcentration processes.

10.2.2
Developments in growth

The scale of economic growth experienced in the 1990s in each metropolitan area is the subject of Table 10.1. As this Table illustrates, by far the largest growth in employment took place in the Dutch case studies, the Northwing of the Randstad and Breda. In this period, the growth of the Dutch economy was well above that in other European countries and the US (Bogaerts *et al.* in this book). In terms of employment growth, the Italian cases and Brno have lagged behind the other countries. In all the cities the most important driver for the spatial reconfiguration of economic land use was the producer services. This growth was again especially high in the Dutch cases, but Madrid also shows a very large increase in the number of jobs in this economic sector. In comparison with producer services employment in consumer services has grown less. The exceptions are the Czech Republic, Israel, and the UK. The earlier chapters show that expansion in retailing in these countries is caused by various factors. In the Czech Republic, the transition of the former socialist system into a market economy attracted new (foreign) investments in big-box hypermarkets. The rapid demographic growth caused by the migration of Jews and weakened central controls can be seen as the main drivers for job growth in retailing in Israel. The planning efforts in developing shopping centres could explain the growth in retail employment in the UK cases.

Table 10.1 informs us also about the *magnitude* of *economic deconcentration*. This is operationalized by the growth of employment in the suburban zone (the sum of the inner and outer suburban rings) as a percentage of total metropolitan employment in approximately 1990. The figures clearly show that the scale of deconcentration was relatively large in the northern countries Denmark, the UK, and the Netherlands and also in Israel, which seems to be in accordance with the multi-dimensional centrality hypothesis. The large scale of deconcentration in Madrid was not expected. In the past two decades, Madrid has undergone a process

Table 10.1 Growth in employment in 12 metropolitan areas by economic sector for the period appr. 1990–2000 (1990 = 100) and for suburban zone (%)

Metropolitan area	Total abs. metrop. employment appr. 1990*	Growth total*	Growth consumer services	Growth manufacturing/construction	Growth producer services	Growth suburban zones 1990–2000 abs.	Growth suburban as % of 1990
Copenhagen	898027	111	109	97	129	65226	7.3
Bristol	406200	121	126	96	131	59900	14.7
Southampton	379800	122	126	99	133	71500	18.8
Northwing	756573	154	103	104	202	294794	39.0
Breda	136185	133	96	113	196	18563	13.6
Prague	432419	117	132	78	139	7365**	1.7**
Brno	190092	94	118	76	93	−1365**	−0.7**
Madrid	1413728	119	93	128	187	246799	17.5
Valladolid	132566	113	114	104	122	5611	4.2
Rome	1230107	104	91	102	106	29068	2.4
Chieti-Pescara	128337	97	98	103	126	5352	4.2
Tel Aviv	482200	117	122	88	149	96400	20.0

* Sum of consumer and producer services and manufacturing/construction.

** Includes only outer suburban zone.

of economic internationalization and high economic growth; the spatial pattern is led by market forces and regional planning policies favouring municipalities located mostly in the southwest of Madrid (Valenzuela *et al.* in this book). The extent of deconcentration in the Dutch Northwing might be surprising for a country perceived as a prototype of central planning and compact urbanism. However, as can be seen from Table 10.1, the total growth of employment in the Northwing is by far the largest, which is difficult to accommodate in the central city alone. Dutch planning has not always been focused on the strengthening of central cities, but has also sought to concentrate urban growth outside the central cities in designated centres (Bogaerts *et al.* in this book). In the UK, deconcentration has been influenced by labour-market and real-estate conditions, especially in Bristol (Smith in this book). Finally, in Tel Aviv, locations were sought for economic activities along major highways and highway junctions with competitive land prices and high accessibility (Razin & Shachar in this book).

In Figure 10.1, the growth in employment in each ring is shown for all the metropolitan areas. From this figure we notice large variations in the spatial config-uration of employment growth. For total employment growth in all metropolitan areas, the differences between the functional zones is largest in Spain and the Netherlands and the least in the cases of the Czech Republic, Denmark and Italy. Although, less strongly than in the suburban zones, in general employment is expanding in the central cities. Also, most centres of the central cities show a stable number of jobs or even a (small) growth (in Bristol and Southampton for example). In Madrid, Valladolid, Tel Aviv and Breda, the growth in the outer suburban ring is substantial.

What differences do we observe in the spatial distribution of growth between the economic sectors? The change in employment in *consumer services* in the functional zones is mainly a reflection of the decline in population in the central cities and growth of the suburban population. In the Netherlands, Italy, and Denmark few differences between the rings can be observed. On the other hand, suburban employment growth in this sector is substantial in Madrid, Prague, Bristol, Southampton, and Tel Aviv. This growth is explained not only by resi-dential suburbanization, but also by changes in retailing policies with less control over or even the stimulation of the expansion of retailing outside the central cities. For example, Israel is characterized by intense competition in terms of land, rent, and legality between local authorities and developers over retail establishments (Razin & Shachar in this book). In the Czech Republic, the foreign investments in hypermarkets in combination with an aversion to central planning stimulated the suburban growth in retail employment (Sýkora & Ouředníček in this book).

In general, owing to the nuisances associated with some facilities, the downtown areas of the central cities are not kindly disposed to *manufacturing/construction*. Although in general the centres lost employment in the 1990s, in the centres of Madrid and Bristol this sector showed an increase in the number of jobs. In Madrid's case it was construction, not the manufacturing sector that led the deconcentration process; in fact, employment in the construction sector shows the

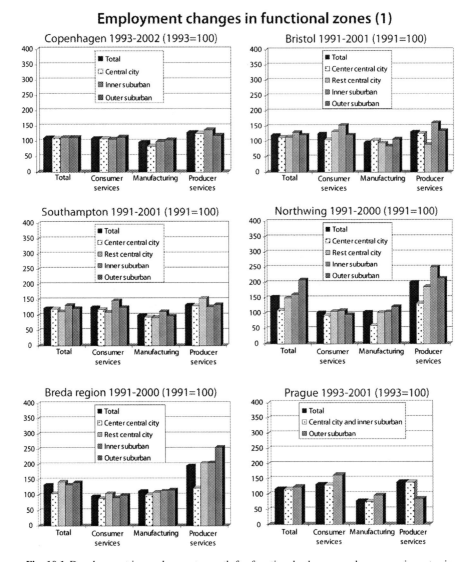

Fig. 10.1 Development in employment growth for functional urban zones by economic sector in 12 metropolitan areas

highest rate of increase during the whole period and its evolution is a reliable image of the dynamism and expansion of the districts/municipalities within the Madrid metropolitan area. In Bristol, the evidence suggests that manufacturing experienced a relative deconcentration within the 30 km zone, even though employment also continued to grow within the city-centre area. This pattern has been complicated by the contraction of employment in aircraft manufacture in Bristol's north fringe as a

Employment changes in functional zones (2)

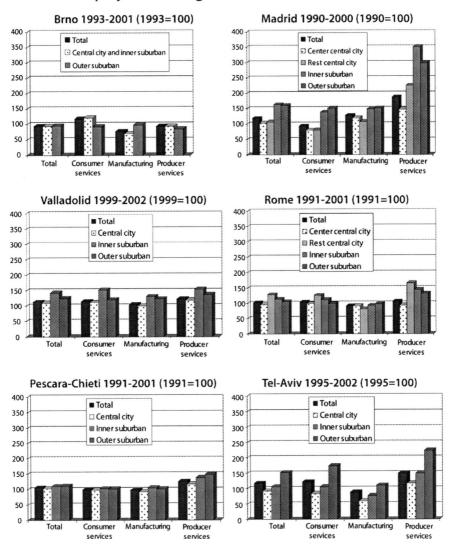

Fig. 10.1 continued

result of the end of the cold war in the early 1990s and the changing structure of the air transport industry in the late 1990s. With the exception of Italy, the locations that have shown an increase in popularity for employment in manufacturing are the outer and, to a lesser extent, the inner suburban rings. This spatial pattern also reflects the changes in the locational preferences of manufacturers for suitable and sufficient land at accessible locations and the greater emphasis that has been put on the quality of life by the public and planning authorities. In Italy, the employment growth was larger in the rest of the central city. In Rome, historically the small and medium-sized companies were located along a few axes in the metropolitan area (Montanari *et al.* in this book).

Although, compared with consumer services and manufacturing, the growth in the number of jobs in the *producer services* in the downtown areas of the central cities can be said to have been substantial, these urban areas are surpassed by the suburban rings. Producer services have found their preferred place of location in the inner suburban ring, as in the Northwing, Madrid, Valladolid, Copenhagen, and Bristol, and the urban ring of the central cities in Rome and Southampton. The outer suburban rings attracted a lot of jobs in Breda, Chieti-Pescara, and Tel Aviv.

We can conclude that, in general, growth in employment is largest in the ring that encircles the urban centres (Rome) and in the inner suburban ring (Madrid, Valladolid, Bristol, Southampton, and Northwing Randstad). Employment growth in the outer suburban rings is relatively large in Madrid, Tel Aviv, and Breda. Differentiated by economic sector, we found that the growth in employment in the manufacturing/construction sector showed the greatest deconcentration. The least deconcentrated sector in terms of growth was the producer services, while the consumer services took an intermediate position.

10.2.3
Development in positions of functional zones

So far, we have discussed the job growth and the magnitude of economic deconcentration in the entire metropolitan area and various rings of this area for total employment and by economic sector. In order to characterize the *form of deconcentration processes* in these metropolitan areas, this picture is complemented by an analysis of the change in position of each functional zone within the metropolitan area to which it belongs. This analysis is the subject of this section. To that end, we have calculated the ratios of employment in pairs of functional zones. In Table 10.2, the ratios are presented of successively central city-suburban zones, centre-rest central city, and finally, inner-outer suburban zones. Our data do not allow us to assess whether deconcentration has taken the shape of a concentrated or a scattered form. Qualitative descriptions taken from the national chapters can give some insight into these specific form characteristics.

In the early 1990s, the central cities of the Italian and Spanish cases had the strongest positions in their metropolitan areas. These areas could be characterized as strong monocentric urban systems. This is particularly the case for consumer services and manufacturing/construction. In approximately 1990, in most cases producer services had a strong position in the central cities. In contrast with the Italian and Spanish cases, Copenhagen, the two British cities, and Tel Aviv suburban zones seemed much more important as employment locations than the central city. The Dutch cities took an intermediate position. Table 10.2 shows that,

Table 10.2 Ratios of total number of employees in central city and suburban zones in appr. 1990 and 2000*

Functional zone	Central city/suburban		Centre/rest central city		Inner/outer suburban	
Metropolitan area	1990	2000	1990	2000	1990	2000
Copenhagen	0.62	0.61	–	–	1.47	1.47
Bristol	0.67	0.62	2.65	2.64	0.75	0.81
Southampton	0.35	0.33	1.28	1.38	0.26	0.29
Northwing	0.88	0.67	0.79	0.59	3.22	2.49
Breda	0.84	0.80	0.54	0.40	1.59	1.51
Madrid	3.39	1.99	1.67	1.62	4.88	4.96
Valladolid	8.42	6.59	–	–	4.30	5.03
Rome	3.72	3.32	7.83	5.86	3.03	3.27
Chieti-Pescara	1.52	1.41	–	–	0.50	0.50
Tel Aviv	0.61	0.42	–	–	0.73	0.51

* Ratios for Prague and Brno could not be calculated (see section 10.2.1)
– No division could be made between the centre and the rest of the central city (see section 10.2.1)

within the central city of Rome, the centre of the town had a dominant employment position, followed at a considerable distance by the centres of Madrid, Bristol, and Southampton. In Madrid and Rome in 1990, employment in the suburban zones was largely concentrated within the inner suburban ring. Copenhagen and the two Dutch cases are also characterized by the relatively limited employment shares of the outer suburban zone, which reflect the effectiveness of their deconcentration policies.

Since 1990, the central city has seen its dominant position in employment diminish in all the selected metropolitan areas. This positional change was most striking for Madrid and Valladolid in Spain, although in both the central cities remain important in terms of employment. In all the countries, the deconcentration trend is most striking for producer services, which have found new locations at the edge of central cities. In general, the deconcentration of manufacturing/construction is rather limited, which indicates that deconcentration took place before the 1990s, as in northern Europe. However, in Italy and Spain this economic sector still seems to find reasonable locations in central cities. In the 1990s, the three northern European countries, Denmark, the UK, and the Netherlands, experienced the least change in position. In these countries the deconcentration processes that had originated some decades before the 1990s continued. The same applies to Tel Aviv. Within the central cities, the position of the centres hardly changed for the two British cases and Madrid. These results for the British cities seem to reflect the impact of the Sequence Approach in planning, which favoured new developments in town centres over other centres (Hills *et al.*, 2005). Large-scale urban renewal in Madrid could keep employment in Madrid (Valenzuela *et al.* in this book). Downtown Rome lost employment in favour of the rest of the central city in absolute and in particular in relative terms. Nevertheless, this central area of the city still dominates, as in the two British cases and Madrid. These four central cities also experienced a strengthening of the position of their inner suburban zones. Together with Copenhagen and the two Dutch cases, in 2000 the supply of jobs in the inner suburban zones of Rome and the Spanish was much higher than in the outer suburban zones. The converse is true for the suburban zones of Chieti-Pescara, Bristol, Southampton, and Tel Aviv.

Based on our observations reported in the last two subsections, we can conclude that, in the 1990s, in the selected metropolitan areas the central cities and, in most cases, also the centres of these cities, lost ground as the main source of jobs in favour of the suburban areas. Nevertheless, in absolute terms job growth in most of these areas continued through the 1990s. The change in the position of the central cities started much earlier in the northern European countries and Israel than in southern and eastern Europe. Furthermore, the scale of deconcentration in the large metropolitan areas of these countries seems more substantial than in the smaller areas. These findings seem to confirm the multi-dimensional centrality hypothesis, which states that deconcentration occurs first and most intensively in the economically leading countries and the largest cities. However, the findings also show that Spain in particular seems to be catching up quickly.

The results also show that the deconcentration processes have taken a rather compact form in The Northwing of the Randstad, Breda, Copenhagen, Rome, Madrid, and Valladolid. However, the growth figures per zone show that the number of jobs in the outer suburban zone of the Spanish cases is increasing rapidly. Employment is deconcentrated at a larger distance from the central city in the small metropolitan area of Chieti-Pescara in Italy, in the UK, and in Tel Aviv. In spite of these changes, the central cities of the Italian and Spanish cases still dominate the metropolitan area and as a consequence can be characterized as monocentric. Although Prague and Brno in the Czech Republic are not mentioned in Table 10.2, our impression is that the same conclusions can be drawn for them. The other metropolitan areas show more polycentric developments. Besides the position within economic cycles, we expect that the type of governance systems also has an impact on the scale of deconcentration and particularly on the form of these spatial reconfigurations. This issue is addressed in the next section.

10.3
Deconcentration patterns and governance types

In this section, we consider the hypothesis that deconcentration is taking place on a smaller scale and is much more concentrated in welfare-state systems than in liberal regimes. Our selected metropolitan areas belong to four different types of governance systems: centralized comprehensive welfare state; decentralized comprehensive welfare state; centralized liberal; decentralized liberal. In Table 1.2 of chapter 1, the expected association of these types of governance system and economic deconcentration patterns is shown. In Table 10.3, we set this expectation against the findings from our analysis. The assessment of the *magnitude* of *economic deconcentration* is calculated as the employment growth in the suburban zone expressed as a percentage of total employment in the early 1990s (see Table 10.1). The data we have used in this chapter only allow us to define *form of deconcentration* in terms of the distance of employment from the central city or centre of the central city (see Table 10.2).

As Table 10.3 shows, the confrontation of patterns of employment deconcentration with the governance types to which the countries belong both corroborate and confuse the previous assumptions. Only four cases match our expectations: Copenhagen, Chieti-Pescara, Madrid, and Tel Aviv. The other metropolitan areas deviate from our expectations in magnitude and form of economic deconcentration. Based on the results of earlier chapters, in this section we put forward an interpretation of these results.

Although the Dutch cases fall under the centralized comprehensive welfare-state governance model as expected, the patterns of the Northwing of the Randstad and Breda are much larger than we expected. As explained in section 10.2.2, this size is the result of the enormous growth of employment in the 1990s and the fact that Dutch planning also stimulated growth in designated areas outside the central cities. This growth in the Dutch cases was largely brought about by the expansion of producer services. As a consequence of this growth, the

Table 10.3 The expected relationships between governance system and pattern of economic deconcentration (*italics*), the confirmed (**bold italics**) and deviated relations (**bold regular**)

Pattern of economic deconcentration	Governance system			
	Centralized comprehensive welfare state	Decentralized comprehensive welfare state	Centralized liberal	Decentralized liberal
Magnitude and form	*The Netherlands*	*Denmark*	*United Kingdom*	*Czech Republic Israel Italy Spain*
Small scale Concentrated	*Northwing Randstad Breda*	**Copenhagen**		**Rome Prague Brno Valladolid**
Small-scale Less concentrated	*Northwing Randstad Breda*	*Copenhagen*	*Bristol Southampton*	**Chieti-Pescara**
Large-scale Concentrated	**Northwing Randstad Breda**	*Copenhagen*	*Bristol Southampton*	*Madrid*
Large-scale Less concentrated			**Bristol Southampton**	*Tel Aviv*

competition for scarce space in the central cities of these cases increased, with rising rents as the result. Companies with a high requirement for floor space, such as distribution firms or business administration, have moved to suburban locations (Bogaerts *et al.* in this book).

The deconcentration pattern of Copenhagen fits the hypothesis reasonably well. The form of deconcentration is concentrated, which is probably a consequence of the centralized land-use planning that we find in the Netherlands. The Danish and Dutch cases have been highly successful in containing urban sprawl. This success is not one which originates from the 1990s it started much earlier in both countries. For decades, the principles of Dutch planning most successful in limiting sprawl are *concentration of urbanization* and *spatial diversity*. Various Planning Memorandums have stimulated the channelling of residential growth into suburban or urban centres since the 1960s, and similarly for economic functions in the 1990s. Deconcentrated developments took place in a rather concentrated manner along highways at infrastructure nodes and on designated sites. A new policy of *compact urban growth* formulated in the Fourth Physical Planning Memorandum stimulated urban growth in existing central cities and on new greenfield sites directly adjacent to the built-up areas of the larger cities (MVROM, 1988). As an important instrument to stimulate compact developments, the Fourth Physical Planning Memorandum (MVROM, 1991) introduced the ABC location policy for firms. This policy was aimed to encourage the location of firms at public transport locations. The intention was to reduce the use of private cars. The extent of the success of this policy is, however, questionable. Many new employment- and visitor-intensive economic developments were located on sites along highways that were not accessible by public transport. High rents and poor accessibility by car at public transport locations, limited support of this policy by private and public actors, and the enormous demand for space were responsible for the disappointing results. A highly successful policy in force since 1973 is Dutch retail policy. This prevented the establishment of out-of-town shopping malls. As a consequence, most shops are still located within the built-up areas of cities and towns and within walking or cycling distance of home for local residents (Evers, 2002). It is, however, expected that in future more extensive and less concentrated forms of economic deconcentration will occur (Bogaerts *et al.* in this book) as a consequence of the liberalization of policies and the deconcentration of planning power from national authorities to lower administrative levels.

As in the Netherlands, in Denmark the policy options to curb sprawl and employment deconcentration also favour direct land-use planning constraints and equalization mechanisms. In fact, on a regional scale, in Greater Copenhagen urban development has been controlled through a successful comprehensive planning for nearly sixty years. The main principle – the Finger Plan – has been implemented and the development in radial urban fingers along railway lines and with green wedges between the fingers is easy to recognize on a map. In the decades 1960–1980, not all secondary centres outside the city of Copenhagen were developed as planned. The successful centres have mainly become shopping centres.

However, employment was deconcentrated from Copenhagen to business parks in the periphery, small enclaves in urban areas or in traditional industrial areas, along motorways and relatively isolated sites. The Regional Plan for Greater Copenhagen of 1989 reintroduced and reinterpreted the finger structure. At that time, only half the office floor space constructed in the 1990s in Greater Copenhagen was located within walking distance of a station. The desired balance of power among the three administrative levels, conflicts between planning and sectoral considerations, the interests of individual property owners and the difficulties of brownfield developments have hindered the location policy. However, the strongly-decentralized public sector is ready to undergo some administrative changes; the county units and Greater Copenhagen Authority will be abolished from January 2007 and Denmark's 271 municipalities will be reduced to 98; in such a context, land-use planning will be a matter between the state and the municipalities.

Intermediate levels of policies and patterns of deconcentration, that is to say small-scale less concentrated or large-scale concentrated deconcentration types, could characterize a centralized liberal governance model. However, as Table 10.3 shows, the deconcentration pattern of both Bristol and Southampton can be characterized as large scale and is taking place at a relatively large distance. This pattern does not mean that no employment growth is taking place in the city centres. Compact policies, including those to keep out-of-town retail developments within fixed limits, and the regeneration of centrally-located declining concentrations of economic activities contributed to the growth of employment in the city centres of Bristol and Southampton. However, deconcentration dominated the metropolitan scene. The integration of public policy interventions within metropolitan areas is made problematic in the UK because of the fragmentation of jurisdictions across the city-regions. Local government reorganization in 1996–97 made matters more difficult at the metropolitan level with further fragmentation of local policy responses in relation to land-use planning, transport, and education. In this context, economic deconcentration is assumed to be part of the urban economic restructuring that has made these city-regions more economically successful, but seems also to have stimulated economic deconcentration in outer suburban zones. This process of deconcentration to the fringes of Bristol and Southampton was also supported by residential deconcentration, followed by employment in consumer services, and the availability of new office space (Smith in this book).

Although the Czech Republic, Israel, Italy, and Spain are certainly very far from the United States prototype of a *decentralized liberal state*, our impression is that these countries lean towards this model in a comparative European perspective. Based on experiences from the US, it was expected that case studies from these European countries would show more large-scale, less concentrated deconcentration patterns than the countries in northern Europe. Metropolitan areas located in Spain or Italy could have been expected to display a less planned pattern of deconcentration, resulting from loose management practices and low levels of enforcement of laws and regulations. However, less explicit policies towards deconcentration and lower levels of enforcement did produce mixed results concerning the magnitude and form of deconcentration. The two largest metropolitan areas, Rome and Madrid, differ in scale of deconcentration, but are both characterized by highly-concentrated forms. These metropolitan areas seem to have retained a strong monocentric employment distribution, mainly reflecting market mechanisms. Only the small metropolitan area of Chieti-Pescara in Italy shows some less concentrated forms of deconcentration.

Formally, the governance system of Italy is characterized by a clear, hierarchical planning system. However, coordination across the various levels is difficult to establish (Larsen, 2005; Montanari *et al.*, in this book). So, other factors seem to be responsible for the concentrated form of deconcentration we find in the capital of Italy. First, the relatively small growth in employment in Rome and even a decline in Chieti-Pescara (Table 10.1) did not put excessive pressure on land use in these metropolitan areas. Second, in Rome the locational decisions of firms are highly influenced by the urban scenery. This city has a historic and environmental heritage of inestimable value, which constitutes the exogenous variable or the main market attribute. As a consequence, there is a centripetal force of attraction. In general, it can be stated that, in Italy, when centres continue to be attractive, they are valued, whereas the peripheries are second best to locate in. In Rome, historically the small and medium-sized companies were located along a few axes in the metropolitan area, but, compared with other European cities, the percentages of employment located in the central city are still high. Deconcentration in the metropolitan area of Rome occurs between the centre and the borders of the central city. The lack of high value in the two centres of Chieti-Pescara has contributed to the deconcentration processes within this metropolitan area. During the last few years in Rome there has been a tendency to recover peripheral buildings and existing spaces through renovation. These policies were intensified and supported by community programmes. Currently, the City Master Plan identifies 18 new urban and metropolitan centres. The underlying goal is the revitalization of the peripheries through "a distribution of central city values throughout the suburbs" (Marcelloni, 2003: 132). The strategy is that of finding peripheral locations within the municipality, not outside it.

Spain only recently became a democracy (1978) and a member of the European Union (1986). Madrid in particular is rapidly developing as an internationalized economy with interests in Europe and Latin-America, thereby undergoing large-scale economic deconcentration. The arrival of democracy in Spain in the second half of the 1970s[1] and the shaping of the new Autonomous Community structure[2] had a negative effect on the survival of the metropolitan development authorities and planning coordination both across and within sectors, and across different government levels. The municipalities together with market forces have left their mark on the spatial configurations of employment. Since the early 1980s, like many other Spanish cities, Madrid has enjoyed an enormous improvement in urban quality. The city's transformation has affected every single sector. The improvements include the configuration of a modern arterial network and one of the best public transport systems in Europe; the protection and refurbishing of buildings;

the eradication of shanty-towns and areas of sub-standard housing; the creation of over 12 km² of new residential areas; the restructuring of a substantial part of the municipal periphery; and the improvement of public amenities of all kinds (López de Lucio, 2000). These transformations slowed down the deconcentration of urban functions outside Madrid. Until recently, deconcentration processes in Spanish cities have mainly been residential. However, during the 1990s, a combination of purposeful deconcentration policies and market forces encouraged employment deconcentration in Madrid. Large growth in employment (Table 10.1) and increased prices for real estate and costs for the rehabilitation of obsolete premises in central areas triggered firms to find new locations outside the central city. This deconcentration was further stimulated by public subsidies and tax incentives to spread economic activities, like offices (technological and business parks), consumer (shopping and leisure centres), and public services. The development of new transport infrastructures, which improved accessibility in the metropolitan area, contributed to a gradual erosion of the existing monocentric spatial pattern. Nevertheless, the central city of Madrid still dominates employment opportunities in the metropolitan area. The same is true for Valladolid, where economic deconcentration processes are still at an early stage.

In contrast with Italy and Spain, economic deconcentration in the other Mediterranean country, Israel, is far less concentrated. The rapid demographic growth caused by the migration of Jews and weakened central controls can be seen as the main drivers for this deconcentration pattern. Since the 1990s, an avalanche of more than a million immigrants over a total population of 6.5 millions inhabitants set the authorities the problem of finding sizeable new areas for housing, consumer services, and employment in a country that lacks the abundance of land that characterizes North America. On the other hand, Israel does have a tradition of centralized planning within a democratic framework, even though decision-making powers are less centralized than the formal legal and bureaucratic structures would suggest. In fact, since the mid-1980s local government authorities have become increasingly dependent on self-generated revenues, thus strongly competing to attract commercial and industrial land uses (Razin, 1998; 2004). This context of high demand for land and eroding central control, competition between municipalities, and market forces explain the dynamic economic deconcentration identified in Tel Aviv, which largely represents that occurring on a smaller scale in Israel. The rapid deconcentration tends to favour the outer rings with proximity to major highways and highway junctions.

The Czech Republic can now be characterized, like the Mediterranean countries, as a decentralized liberal governance system. During the period of communism and central planning, there was a strong preference for the concentration of development in major urban centres. Investment and growth went into large housing and industrial complexes at the urban edge of medium and large cities. Since the beginning of the post-communist transition, the most important features of urban change in Prague and Brno can be characterized by the commercialization of the historic cores and adjacent areas of the inner cities, commercial and residential suburban-

ization into the outer city and urban hinterland, and selective revitalization in inner
city areas (Sýkora *et al.*, 2000). The transition of the former socialist system into a
decentralized decision-making system within a market economy with an aversion
to central planning attracted new (foreign) investments in big-box hypermarkets
and warehousing in particular. These firms consume a relatively large amount of
land; they were situated outside the central cities, particularly around Prague. As
the country's major command and control centre, deconcentration processes in
Prague did not involve producer services or offices unless they were an integral
part of retail or warehousing. Brno's economic development depends strongly on
the reindustrialization that took place in the new industrial zones and the individual
production plants in suburban areas. While non-residential suburbanization was
driven by the demand of international firms expanding on Czech markets in the
second half of the 1990s, residential suburbanization was driven by the (limited)
investments of Czech households in a context of overall population stagnation.
Despite the recent forceful dynamics in economic deconcentration, compared with
the other European case studies the deconcentration patterns of both Prague and
Brno can best be characterized as 'small' and 'concentrated'.

To end this section, we can conclude that offsetting the economic deconcentration patterns against the relevant types of governance system does not clearly
confirm the assumptions about the impact of governance systems on deconcentration patterns. Large deviations can be found for the Dutch, British, and Czech
cases, and Rome and Valladolid. Explanations of the variations in deconcentration
patterns have to be sought in the various contextual factors, such as the *scarcity of
urban land, urban scenery, administrative fragmentation,* and *level of coherence.*
For the Netherlands, the relatively large-scale deconcentration was caused by the
relatively large economic and employment growth, which led to heavy demands for
land. However, the strong interventionist approach accommodated this growth in
land-use concentrations. This approach is in contrast with that in Israel, where the
huge demand for land for urban functions in a rather weak policy context resulted
in the deconcentration of employment to the outer suburban zones. The (small) loss
of jobs in central Rome in combination with the attractive urban scenery did not
push economic functions out of the central city in the 1990s. One can wonder what
will happen in this city when employment growth reaches the levels of Madrid and
Tel Aviv. Although deconcentration is substantial, the relatively large investments
in the built environment of Madrid have tempered the deconcentration processes in
this metropolitan area. Just like Rome, the Czech Republic could also face serious
deconcentration processes the moment the economy becomes more integrated into
the international economy and economic prosperity rises.

In addition, the demand for urban land and urban scenery, administrative
fragmentation, and a lack of coherence seem to be explanatory factors for the
deviations. In the UK, the fragmentation of administration and the absence of integrative (sub) regional plans contributed to the relatively heavy domination of outer
suburban zones in Bristol and Southampton. The desire to stimulate economic
growth, which overruled the negative impact on environment and accessibility

(Hills *et al.*, 2005), also contributed to the growth of the outer suburban zones in these British cases.

10.4
Quality of life and policy impacts

The quality of life in metropolitan areas can be seriously affected by economic deconcentration. This has three dimensions: economic, social, and environmental. The economic dimension consists of the supply of new jobs, infrastructural costs, transport and travel costs (Cervero, 1989, 1996; Cervero & Kang-Li Wu, 1998), and tax incomes. The social dimension refers to access to jobs and amenities (Van Ham *et al.*, 2001), choice of services, and so forth. Environmental quality-of-life indicators include the loss of open land, traffic pollution (Naes and Sandberg, 1996), and nuisance and hazards associated with the proximity of certain economic activities to residential areas (Garb *et al.*, 2004). As mentioned in chapter 1, in contrast with residential deconcentration, relatively little is known about the impact of the economic variant of deconcentration on the quality of life. The aim of this section is to generate some insights into these effects and to link them to the governance-system typology mentioned in Table 10.3. We hypothesised that the extent and types of policy put in place to influence the quality of life depends on the type of governance system. In general terms, we expected that the *comprehensive welfare states* (Denmark and the Netherlands) would have policies in place to manage the economic, social, and environmental outcomes of economic deconcentration. These countries will influence the effects through land-use controls/regulatory growth controls and by applying policy instruments capable of avoiding unequal outcomes. These policy initiatives could also be found, although marginally, in *central liberal states* (United Kingdom). In contrast, the *decentralized liberal systems* (Czech Republic, Israel, Italy and Spain) will be characterized by much fewer efforts to influence the quality of life and the policies they apply will be much more 'market-based', such as setting up financial penalties and incentives to stimulate the regeneration of the older urban centres.

A thorough test of the quality-of-life impacts of various economic deconcentration patterns has shown that the most sensitive quality-of-life issue is accessibility; this refers to congestion and proximity to work and shopping centres. A change in deconcentration configuration is likely to elicit a change in these social indicators, a change which would be much greater than for economic indicators, such as income, local taxes or local employment, for example. There are significant policy implications in the areas of commuting and households' residential and employment choices (Felsenstein, 2005).

As expected, only in Denmark, the Netherlands, and the United Kingdom is the management of economic deconcentration an explicit policy goal. These countries do not mention the quality-of-life impacts explicitly, but they do refer to the sustainability outcomes of economic deconcentration in the form of diminishing accessibility, increasing congestion, and the declining viability and vitality of town centres (Hills *et al.*, 2005). In the Netherlands, spatial planning policies have been fairly successful in managing economic growth. In the previous section, we mentioned the important role of the 'concentration' principle in this respect. Two other principles have contributed in particular to the quality of life of metropolitan areas: spatial coherence and spatial differentiation (Bogaerts *et al.* in this book). 'Spatial coherence' was aimed at stimulating the development of a mixture of coherent urban activities in urban and suburban areas; 'spatial differentiation' focused on the preservation of open areas, the differentiation of residential environments, and the protection of residential functions against the nuisance and hazards of certain economic functions. Various land-use controls and regulation policies were applied to reach these aims (*op. cit.*). Nevertheless, monofunctional areas have been developed in the Northwing and Breda metropolitan areas. Furthermore, changing people's travel patterns through physical policies would seem to be difficult, if not impossible (Schwanen *et al.*, 2004).

In the Danish case, the improved balance between workplaces and the pattern of human settlements did not prevent increasing commuting problems. Both the proportion of long-distance commuters and the average commuting distance increased. The lack of success in managing the location of workplaces based on the strategies used in regional planning is blamed for the increasing total transport and the share travelling by car. Nevertheless, the quality of life in Copenhagen seems to be high. Thanks to the Finger Plan, the metropolitan area has a relatively well-developed urban and green structure. The urban areas situated in the fingers have relatively good access to public transport. Retail regulations fostered the development of mixed functions in urban areas. Brownfield developments upgraded older urban structures (Hills *et al.*, 2005). The wedges between the fingers give high access to green and natural scenery. In addition, there are plentiful stretches of coastal areas and beaches near at hand. As in the Netherlands, the credit for the current environmental quality must be attributed to the fact that Denmark has a long tradition of environmental concern, well-developed legislation, a well-established environmental movement, and active political interest in sustainable development on all administrative levels. This environmental consciousness is also underlined by Denmark's contribution to 'Local Agenda 21' activities (Matthiessen *et al.*, 2002).

In the United Kingdom, the management of economic deconcentration is an explicit policy aim. However, compared with Denmark and the Netherlands, this tradition is relatively young. From the mid-1990s onwards, policies aimed at reducing deconcentration processes in order to promote sustainable development have increased in popularity (Hills *et al.*, 2005). Relevant policy instruments are the Green Belt, which preserves open space, and the Sequential Approach, which favours retail development in town centres. Nevertheless, large-scale deconcentration to suburban zones is dominant in the British metropolitan areas. Economic deconcentration in Bristol and Southampton has improved the accessibility of employment, especially for the residents of the urban fringe (Smith in this book). However, the other side of the deconcentration coin shows that, between 1981 and 2001, there was a massive increase in the number of commuting kilometres travelled and in the average distance travelled for work, despite the converging spatial distribution of housing and employment. Serious environmental damage has ensued in the form of noise, congestion, and carbon emissions. So while there has been a broadly positive economic impact of economic deconcentration (the successful economic restructuring of the metropolitan areas of Bristol and Southampton), both the social and environmental consequences of economic deconcentration have been less well managed (*op. cit.*). In neither of these metropolitan areas is the fragmented governance system capable of facilitating the management of the negative consequences of economic deconcentration. For that purpose, the resurgence interest in sub-regional planning could be an important step forwards (*op. cit.*).

In the countries that belong to the decentralized liberal governance systems group, the management of economic deconcentration is not an explicit planning goal (Hills *et al.*, 2005). In Israel, the spatial plans are based on the principle of limiting sprawl and concentrating urban developments (not explicitly economic developments) in relatively large and dense suburbs. From an economic point of view, the accelerated suburbanization of economic activities has not so far eroded the fiscal soundness of the Tel Aviv municipality. On the contrary, the relatively small population and accelerated suburbanization of the population have helped maintain a very high ratio of business to residential land uses. Moreover, out-migration from the central city has not been associated with an increasing concentration of poor people in the city. Tel Aviv remained attractive for the prosperous population categories (Razin & Shachar in this book).

In Spain, economic deconcentration has to a certain extent been stimulated by the local government authorities in order to boost their economies (Hills *et al.*, 2005). In both Spanish cases, but mainly in Madrid, this deconcentration process generated a high increase in the demand for inter-municipal mobility. In addition to their mononuclear form, the centripetal traffic network and increasing car ownership contributed to an increase in congestion and pollution in both central cities. In general, planning at the metropolitan or regional scale lacks efficiency in achieving a better adjustment in the territorial assignation of employment and housing by subordinating local planning to supra-municipal objectives. Local planning has mainly pursued housing-related aims, while the location of companies appears to conform to different criteria (Angelet, 2000). There are few explicit policies to influence the quality of life impacts in Spain.

The mismatch between residential deconcentration during the 1980s and the limited employment deconcentration in the Italian cases resulted in thick traffic flows and congestion on the road networks. During the rush hour in Rome, private transport represents 67 percent of total trips and the motorization rate is one of the highest in the world, generating problems of air pollution and noise (Montanari *et al.* in this book). The poor quality of the metropolitan public transport system and the absence of integrated planning for economic and residential deconcentration, which is reinforced by the lack of a powerful metropolitan authority, have contributed to these quality-of-life problems. Nevertheless, the relatively small scale of economic deconcentration in Rome and Chieti-Pescara explains why these metropolitan areas so far face relatively limited environmental and social problems. Rome's City Master Plan aimed at developing a polycentric city could help limit the detrimental effects of future employment growth on the quality of life.

In the formerly centrally-planned economies, the ownership of assets was concentrated in the state, earnings inequality in the dominant state sector was low, and public policies were designed to limit income differences (Aghion & Commander, 1999). Given the initial conditions at the start of the transition, it is hardly surprising that the liberalization of the economy and the introduction of market processes led to greater income inequality (Nee & Peng, 1996). The spatial mismatch between jobs and residences is emerging in Prague and Brno (Sýkora & Ouředníček in this book), contributing to increased travel in metropolitan areas and negative effects on the quality of life. The compact character of the former socialist cities is changing through the rapid commercial and residential suburbanization that now threatens sustainable metropolitan development in the Czech Republic.

The case studies discussed in this book show that the issue of the management of the quality-of-life effects of economic deconcentration has only been contended with in the comprehensive welfare- and centralized-liberal states. These countries applied various land-use controls and regulation policies to stimulate the positive and diminish the negative quality-of-life aspects. Strategic plans such as the Finger Plan in Copenhagen and regulation policies such as the development of mixed land uses, preserving open landscapes, and retail regulations seem to have been highly successful from a quality-of-life perspective.

10.5
Conclusions and policy implications

Compared with North America, European employment deconcentration is a relatively young and small-scale process. Nevertheless, it is an issue, especially in regard to its quality-of-life effects. These are put high on the agenda of European politicians and policymakers. Economic deconcentration processes of consumer and producer services and manufacturing/construction within European large and medium-sized metropolitan areas have been analysed and discussed in the preceding national chapters and in this comparative chapter. Two hypotheses structured our discussion. The *multi-dimensional centrality hypothesis* is based on the idea that economic deconcentration is related to the position of a city in its economic cycle: deconcentration occurs first and most intensively in leading economic countries and in the largest cities. In the *governance system hypothesis,* it is assumed that the positioning on the deconcentration spectrum, varying from the archetypical American *sprawl type* to the European *compact model,* depends on the type of governance system. Besides these two hypotheses, the quality-of-life impacts of economic deconcentration and the effect of planning policies have been discussed. In this concluding section, we highlight our main findings and discuss some policy implications.

The European experience with economic deconcentration as discussed in this book shows that economic deconcentration is a complex phenomenon and that the variations in deconcentration patterns in Europe are wide, probably wider than in North America. The complexity is apparent in various dimensions of economic deconcentration: stage, scale, and form. In accordance with the first hypothesis, the various case studies are to be found in various *stages of economic deconcentration*. The deconcentration processes in the North European metropolitan areas and Tel Aviv started much earlier than the 1990s when the processes started in the metropolitan areas of southern and eastern Europe. This deconcentration is shown by the dominance of suburban locations with respect to employment. As a consequence, the urban structure of the metropolitan areas of the economically leading countries has a much more polycentric character. The economies in southern and eastern Europe are lagging behind or catching up and they have a rather monocentric structure. In a world of intensifying globalization and integration, these economic deconcentration processes in metropolitan areas are expected to continue. Although this development means that the relevance of central cities in metropolitan areas will decline, in absolute terms employment in the central city is still increasing. In the 1990s, except for Chieti-Pescara and Tel Aviv, all central cities and even most centres in these central cities experienced an expansion of the number of jobs.

The fact that economic deconcentration processes started earlier in the metropolitan areas in northern Europe and Israel does not mean that, compared with other regions, the *scale of deconcentration* in these areas is much smaller. On the contrary; our analysis has shown that the scale, measured by the growth of employment in suburban zones as a percentage of total employment in 1990, was on the average higher. The growth of the national economies and, for Israel, the massive immigration of Jews stimulated the deconcentration of economic land uses. In southern Europe in the 1990s, only Spain was catching up quickly with the leading economies. This achievement can largely be explained by the improvement of the Spanish position within the economic cycle.

The driver for spatial reorganization that has received the largest share of attention in this book has been the governance and land-use planning regime. Based on the various characteristics of governance systems, we expected that deconcentration would have taken place on a smaller scale and in a much more concentrated form in comprehensive welfare state systems than in liberal regimes. This hypothesis is confirmed for the decentralized comprehensive welfare state case (Copenhagen), and three decentralized liberal state metropolitan areas (Chieti-Pescara, Tel-Aviv, and Madrid). However, large deviations can be found for the other 8 metropolitan areas. The deconcentration in the Northwing of the Randstad and Breda is much more substantial than expected, but concentrated. In contrast, the large-scale deconcentration in Bristol and Southampton is less concentrated. Finally, Rome, Prague, Brno, and Valladolid all experienced unexpected small-scale but concentrated developments.

The European experience shows that a comprehensive explanation can be found through *combining* both hypotheses and by taking into account the *specific contexts* in which the economic activities and interventions of public authorities develop. This is illustrated in the penetration of hypermarkets in eastern European countries. This penetration is largely led by German (Metro/Makro), British (Tesco) and French (Auchan and Carrefour) multinationals. These post-communist countries offer many opportunities for economic growth because of the transition of the former socialist system into a market economy. However, these investments in hypermarkets are also favoured by the strong aversion to central planning in these countries (see Garb and Sýkora & Ouředníček in this book). These developments in retailing are further supported by the residential and car-ownership decisions of households. The Netherlands is another example. The unexpected large-scale deconcentration in this country is caused by the relatively large economic and employment growth, which stimulated high demands for land. However, the scarcity of land in combination with a strong interventionist approach stimulated the development of relatively heavy clusters of land-use concentrations in central cities and suburban locations. In contrast, limited economic growth in Rome caused a (small) loss of employment in the central city. Economic functions could be kept in the central city of Rome by the attractive urban scenery. The same is true for the large investments in the built environment of Madrid, which limited economic deconcentration. In addition to the scarcity of land and the urban scenery, the level of administrative fragmentation and coherence is a relevant contextual factor. This is exemplified by the UK, where administrative fragmentation and the absence of integrative (sub) regional plans contributed to the relatively large domination of outer suburban zones in Bristol and Southampton. The national consensus to restrict urban deconcentration to further a sustainable development melted away under the pressure to stimulate economic growth (Hills *et al.*, 2005).

Although the relationship between type of governance system and pattern of economic deconcentration deviated from our assumptions, the extent and the types of policy in place to influence the quality of life are largely in accordance with our expectations. The case studies show that the issue of the management of the quality-of-life effects of economic deconcentration is only dealt with in the comprehensive welfare and centralized liberal states. Various land-use controls and regulation policies were applied in order to influence the quality of life. Strategic plans such as the Finger Plan in Copenhagen and the development of mixed land uses, preserving open landscapes, and retail regulations were highly successful in this respect.

On the basis of our findings, we now address the issue of the future outlook for the economic deconcentration of the metropolitan areas discussed in this book. We have concluded that changes in the role of metropolitan areas can have a major impact on the demand for land for economic functions. From a quality-of-life perspective, the accommodation of this demand for land seems to be relatively unproblematic for countries that are familiar with comprehensive welfare planning. Countries like Denmark and the Netherlands have for a long time had a suitable planning organization and set of policies to improve the quality of life in their metropolitan areas. However, driven by the constant need to enhance competitiveness to reach higher levels of economic development, in both countries liberal-conservative and liberal-Christian governments stress the responsibility for planning of lower-level of administrative authorities and a liberalization of planning regulations. This delegation could limit the effectiveness of public authorities to achieve sound spatial configurations of economic functions from a quality-of-life perspective. The substitution in the Netherlands of the compact-city planning concept by the network-city concept, which offers the opportunity to develop new locations along infrastructural networks between major central cities, could lead to such a situation.

In contrast, the Mediterranean and East European countries are less well-equipped with appropriate planning organizations and policies to manage economic deconcentration and its quality-of-life impacts. In these contexts, market mechanisms, which bring together demand and supply for land, largely conduct the spatial configurations of land use and quality of life. This pressure on land is relatively unproblematic in a situation where there is an abundance of land or where demand for land is not very big, as in the Italian and Czech cases. However, the moment these metropolitan areas face large growth in employment, the pressure on land markets will increase. In a liberal state, the responsible public authorities have neither the ability nor the desire to protect or improve the quality-of-life in their jurisdictions. In such a situation, outer suburban developments or even American sprawl and the associated economic, social, and environmental costs could develop. This situation is exemplified by Madrid, where in spite of large investments in the central city, employment in the outer suburban zone has grown substantially. This vulnerability could be diminished when these countries become more inspired by the North European countries to curb economic deconcentration processes and its negative quality-of-life impacts.

Notes

[1] After the death of the dictator Francisco Franco in 1975, the current democratic Constitution was approved in a referendum in 1978 and the first democratic municipal governments were in power following the April 1979 elections.

[2] Under the Spanish Constitution of December 27th 1978, Spain became a parliamentary monarchy based on social values, democracy, and the rule of law. The previous centralized regional structure was replaced by a new model of Autonomous Regions, provinces (50 in all), and municipalities. The Autonomous Regions (17 plus the autonomous cities of Ceuta and Melilla) have their own legal identity. The regions considered distinctive for linguistic, cultural or historical reason have received a greater transfer of powers from central government. Since the 1980s Spain has become one of the most politically decentralized countries in Europe; because of that seventeen regional governments were fully competent to deal with town and country planning regulations.

References

Aghion P, Commander S (1999) On the dynamics of inequality in the Transition. Econ Tran 7(2):275–298

Angelet Cladellas J (2000) La descentralización del empleo y de la residencia en las áreas metropolitanas de Barcelona y Madrid. Urban 4:124–144

Bontje M (2004) Sustainable new economic centres in European metropolitan regions: a stakeholders' perspective. Eur Plann Stud 12(5):703–722

Castells M (1996) The rise of the network society. Blackwell Publishers, Oxford

Cervero R (1989) Jobs-housing balancing and regional mobility. J Am Plann Assoc 55:136–150

Cervero R (1996) Jobs-housing balancing revisited: trends and impacts in the San Francisco Bay Area. J Am Plann Assoc 62(4):492–511

Cervero R, Kang-Li Wu (1998) Subcentring and commuting: evidence from the San Francisco Bay Area, 1980–1990. Urban Studies 35(7):1059–1076

Clark WAV (2000) Monocentric to polycentric: new urban forms and old paradigms. In: Bridge G, Watson S (eds) A companion to the city. Blackwell Publishers, Oxford, pp 141–154

Esping-Anderson G (1990) The three worlds of welfare capitalism. Princeton University Press, Princeton, NJ

Evers D (2002) The rise (and fall?) of national retail planning. Tijdschrift voor economische en social geografie 93(1):107–113

Felsenstein D (2005) Translating economic land use deconcentration into quality of life impacts, Deliverable 05 (Final Report), SELMA project, Hebrew University, Jerusalem

Friedmann J (1986) The world city hypothesis. Dev Change 17:69–83

Garb Y, Van Kamp I, Kuijpers M, Ouředníček M, Sýkora L (2004) Quality of life indicators, Deliverable 02, SELMA project

Garreau J (1991) Edge city: life on the new frontier. Anchor Books, Doubleday, New York

Graham S, Marvin S (2001) Splintering urbanism. Networked infrastructures, technological mobilities and the urban condition. Routledge, London

Halbert L (2004) The decentralization of intrametropolitan business services in the paris region: patterns, interpretation, consequences. Econ Geo 8(4):381–404

Hills S, Atkinson R, Smith I (2005) WP8 Policy analysis and prescriptions: policy analysis report. University of the West of England, Bristol

Ingram GK (1998) Patterns of metropolitan development: what have we learned? Urban Studies 35(7):1019–1035

Janelle DG (1969) Spatial reorganization: a model and concept. Ann Assoc Am Geogr 59:348–364

Kloosterman RC, Musterd S (2001) The polycentric urban region: towards a research agenda. Urban Studies 38(4):623–633

Lang RE, LeFurgy J (2003) Edgeless cities: examining the noncentered metropolis. Housing Policy Debate 14(3):427–460

Larsen JN (2005) Governance, policy and determinants of economic land use deconcentration (WP6-report). Danish Building Research Institute, Copenhagen

López de Lucio R (2000) Madrid 1979–1999. Perfiles de una transformación urbana desconocida. Urban 4:106–123

Marcelloni M (2003) Pensare la città contemporanea. Il nuevo piano regolatore di Roma. Roma-Bari, Laterza, Roma

Matthiesen CW, Søgaard H, Anderberg S (2002) Environmental performance and European cities: a new key parameter in the competition between metropolitan centres. In: Davies WKD, Townshend IJ (eds) Monitoring cities: international perspectives. International Geographical Union, Urban Commision, University of Calgary and University of Lethbridge, Calgary pp 119–142

MVROM (1988) Fourth spatial planning memorandum. Ministry of Housing, Physical Planning and the Environment, The Hague

MVROM (1991) Fourth spatial planning memorandum extra. Ministry of Housing, Physical Planning and the Environment, The Hague

Naes P, Sandberg SL (1996) Workplace location, modal split and energy use for commuting trips. Urban Studies 33(3):557–580

Nee V, Peng L (1996) Market transition and societal transformation in reforming state socialism. Annu Rev of Sociol 22:401–435

Parr JB (1999) The Metropolitan area in its wider setting. In: Summers AA, Cheshire PC, Senn L (eds) Urban change in the United States and Western Europe, comparative analysis and policy (Second edition). The Urban Institute Press, Washington, pp 215–242

Parr JB (2003) The polycentric urban region: a closer inspection. Regional Studies 38(3):231–240

Phelps NA, Parsons N (2003) Edge urban geography: notes from the margins of Europe's capital cities. Urban Studies 40(9):1725–1749

Pred A (1977) City-systems in advanced economies. Hutchinson, London

Razin E (1998) Policies to control urban sprawl: planning regulations or changes in the "rules of the game". Urban Studies 35:321–340

Razin E (2004) Needs and impediments for local government reform: lessons from Israel. Journal of Urban Affairs 26:623–640

Sassen S (1991) The global city. Princeton University Press, Princeton, NJ

Schwanen T, Dijst M, Dieleman FM (2004) Policies for urban form and travel: The Netherlands experience. Urban Studies 41(3):579–603

Sýkora L, Kamenický J, Hauptman P (2000) Changes in the spatial structure of Prague and Brno in the 1990s. Acta Universitatis Carolinae Geographica 35(1):61–76

Van Ham M, Hooimeijer P, Mulder CH (2001) Urban form and job access: disparate realities in the Randstad. Tijdschrift voor Economische en Sociale Geografie 92(2):231–246

Wallerstein I (1979) The capitalist world economy. Cambridge University Press, Cambridge

Index

The GeoJournal Library

1. B. Currey and G. Hugo (eds.): *Famine as Geographical Phenomenon.* 1984
   ISBN 90-277-1762-1
2. S.H.U. Bowie, F.R.S. and I. Thornton (eds.): *Environmental Geochemistry and Health.* Report of the Royal Society's British National Committee for Problems of the Environment. 1985
   ISBN 90-277-1879-2
3. L.A. Kosiński and K.M. Elahi (eds.): *Population Redistribution and Development in South Asia.* 1985
   ISBN 90-277-1938-1
4. Y. Gradus (ed.): *Desert Development.* Man and Technology in Sparselands. 1985
   ISBN 90-277-2043-6
5. F.J. Calzonetti and B.D. Solomon (eds.): *Geographical Dimensions of Energy.* 1985
   ISBN 90-277-2061-4
6. J. Lundqvist, U. Lohm and M. Falkenmark (eds.): *Strategies for River Basin Management.* Environmental Integration of Land and Water in River Basin. 1985
   ISBN 90-277-2111-4
7. A. Rogers and F.J. Willekens (eds.): *Migration and Settlement.* A Multiregional Comparative Study. 1986
   ISBN 90-277-2119-X
8. R. Laulajainen: *Spatial Strategies in Retailing.* 1987
   ISBN 90-277-2595-0
9. T.H. Lee, H.R. Linden, D.A. Dreyfus and T. Vasko (eds.): *The Methane Age.* 1988
   ISBN 90-277-2745-7
10. H.J. Walker (ed.): *Artificial Structures and Shorelines.* 1988   ISBN 90-277-2746-5
11. A. Kellerman: *Time, Space, and Society.* Geographical Societal Perspectives. 1989
    ISBN 0-7923-0123-4
12. P. Fabbri (ed.): *Recreational Uses of Coastal Areas.* A Research Project of the Commission on the Coastal Environment, International Geographical Union. 1990
    ISBN 0-7923-0279-6
13. L.M. Brush, M.G. Wolman and Huang Bing-Wei (eds.): *Taming the Yellow River: Silt and Floods.* Proceedings of a Bilateral Seminar on Problems in the Lower Reaches of the Yellow River, China. 1989
    ISBN 0-7923-0416-0
14. J. Stillwell and H.J. Scholten (eds.): *Contemporary Research in Population Geography.* A Comparison of the United Kingdom and the Netherlands. 1990
    ISBN 0-7923-0431-4
15. M.S. Kenzer (ed.): *Applied Geography.* Issues, Questions, and Concerns. 1989
    ISBN 0-7923-0438-1
16. D. Nir: *Region as a Socio-environmental System.* An Introduction to a Systemic Regional Geography. 1990
    ISBN 0-7923-0516-7
17. H.J. Scholten and J.C.H. Stillwell (eds.): *Geographical Information Systems for Urban and Regional Planning.* 1990
    ISBN 0-7923-0793-3
18. F.M. Brouwer, A.J. Thomas and M.J. Chadwick (eds.): *Land Use Changes in Europe.* Processes of Change, Environmental Transformations and Future Patterns. 1991
    ISBN 0-7923-1099-3
19. C.J. Campbell: *The Golden Century of Oil 1950–2050.* The Depletion of a Resource. 1991
    ISBN 0-7923-1442-5
20. F.M. Dieleman and S. Musterd (eds.): *The Randstad: A Research and Policy Laboratory.* 1992
    ISBN 0-7923-1649-5
21. V.I. Ilyichev and V.V. Anikiev (eds.): *Oceanic and Anthropogenic Controls of Life in the Pacific Ocean.* 1992
    ISBN 0-7923-1854-4

The GeoJournal Library

22. A.K. Dutt and F.J. Costa (eds.): *Perspectives on Planning and Urban Development in Belgium.* 1992   ISBN 0-7923-1885-4
23. J. Portugali: *Implicate Relations.* Society and Space in the Israeli-Palestinian Conflict. 1993   ISBN 0-7923-1886-2
24. M.J.C. de Lepper, H.J. Scholten and R.M. Stern (eds.): *The Added Value of Geographical Information Systems in Public and Environmental Health.* 1995   ISBN 0-7923-1887-0
25. J.P. Dorian, P.A. Minakir and V.T. Borisovich (eds.): *CIS Energy and Minerals Development.* Prospects, Problems and Opportunities for International Cooperation. 1993   ISBN 0-7923-2323-8
26. P.P. Wong (ed.): *Tourism vs Environment: The Case for Coastal Areas.* 1993   ISBN 0-7923-2404-8
27. G.B. Benko and U. Strohmayer (eds.): *Geography, History and Social Sciences.* 1995   ISBN 0-7923-2543-5
28. A. Faludi and A. der Valk: *Rule and Order. Dutch Planning Doctrine in the Twentieth Century.* 1994   ISBN 0-7923-2619-9
29. B.C. Hewitson and R.G. Crane (eds.): *Neural Nets: Applications in Geography.* 1994   ISBN 0-7923-2746-2
30. A.K. Dutt, F.J. Costa, S. Aggarwal and A.G. Noble (eds.): *The Asian City: Processes of Development, Characteristics and Planning.* 1994   ISBN 0-7923-3135-4
31. R. Laulajainen and H.A. Stafford: *Corporate Geography. Business Location Principles and Cases.* 1995   ISBN 0-7923-3326-8
32. J. Portugali (ed.): *The Construction of Cognitive Maps.* 1996   ISBN 0-7923-3949-5
33. E. Biagini: *Northern Ireland and Beyond.* Social and Geographical Issues. 1996   ISBN 0-7923-4046-9
34. A.K. Dutt (ed.): *Southeast Asia: A Ten Nation Region.* 1996   ISBN 0-7923-4171-6
35. J. Settele, C. Margules, P. Poschlod and K. Henle (eds.): *Species Survival in Fragmented Landscapes.* 1996   ISBN 0-7923-4239-9
36. M. Yoshino, M. Domrös, A. Douguédroit, J. Paszynski and L.D. Nkemdirim (eds.): *Climates and Societies – A Climatological Perspective.* A Contribution on Global Change and Related Problems Prepared by the Commission on Climatology of the International Geographical Union. 1997   ISBN 0-7923-4324-7
37. D. Borri, A. Khakee and C. Lacirignola (eds.): *Evaluating Theory-Practice and Urban-Rural Interplay in Planning.* 1997   ISBN 0-7923-4326-3
38. J.A.A. Jones, C. Liu, M-K.Woo and H-T. Kung (eds.): *Regional Hydrological Response to Climate Change.* 1996   ISBN 0-7923-4329-8
39. R. Lloyd: *Spatial Cognition.* Geographic Environments. 1997   ISBN 0-7923-4375-1
40. I. Lyons Murphy: *The Danube: A River Basin in Transition.* 1997   ISBN 0-7923-4558-4
41. H.J. Bruins and H. Lithwick (eds.): *The Arid Frontier.* Interactive Management of Environment and Development. 1998   ISBN 0-7923-4227-5
42. G. Lipshitz: *Country on the Move: Migration to and within Israel, 1948–1995.* 1998   ISBN 0-7923-4850-8
43. S. Musterd, W. Ostendorf and M. Breebaart: *Multi-Ethnic Metropolis: Patterns and Policies.* 1998   ISBN 0-7923-4854-0
44. B.K. Maloney (ed.): *Human Activities and the Tropical Rainforest.* Past, Present and Possible Future. 1998   ISBN 0-7923-4858-3

The GeoJournal Library

45. H. van der Wusten (ed.): *The Urban University and its Identity.* Roots, Location, Roles. 1998   ISBN 0-7923-4870-2
46. J. Kalvoda and C.L. Rosenfeld (eds.): *Geomorphological Hazards in High Mountain Areas.* 1998   ISBN 0-7923-4961-X
47. N. Lichfield, A. Barbanente, D. Borri, A. Khakee and A. Prat (eds.): *Evaluation in Planning.* Facing the Challenge of Complexity. 1998   ISBN 0-7923-4870-2
48. A. Buttimer and L. Wallin (eds.): *Nature and Identity in Cross-Cultural Perspective.* 1999   ISBN 0-7923-5651-9
49. A. Vallega: *Fundamentals of Integrated Coastal Management.* 1999
ISBN 0-7923-5875-9
50. D. Rumley: *The Geopolitics of Australia's Regional Relations.* 1999
ISBN 0-7923-5916-X
51. H. Stevens: *The Institutional Position of Seaports.* An International Comparison. 1999
ISBN 0-7923-5979-8
52. H. Lithwick and Y. Gradus (eds.): *Developing Frontier Cities.* Global Perspectives –Regional Contexts. 2000   ISBN 0-7923-6061-3
53. H. Knippenberg and J. Markusse (eds.): *Nationalising and Denationalising European Border Regions, 1800–2000.* Views from Geography and History. 2000
ISBN 0-7923-6066-4
54. R. Gerber and G.K. Chuan (eds.): *Fieldwork in Geography: Reflections, Perspectives and Actions.* 2000   ISBN 0-7923-6329-9
55. M. Dobry (ed.): *Democratic and Capitalist Transitions in Eastern Europe.* Lessons for the Social Sciences. 2000   ISBN 0-7923-6331-0
56. Y. Murayama: *Japanese Urban System.* 2000   ISBN 0-7923-6600-X
57. D. Zheng, Q. Zhang and S. Wu (eds.): *Mountain Geoecology and Sustainable Development of the Tibetan Plateau.* 2000   ISBN 0-7923-6688-3
58. A.J. Conacher (ed.):*Land Degradation.* Papers selected from Contributions to the Sixth Meeting of the International Geographical Union's Commission on Land Degradation and Desertification, Perth, Western Australia, 20–28 September 1999. 2001
ISBN 0-7923-6770-7
59. S. Conti and P. Giaccaria: *Local Development and Competitiveness.* 2001
ISBN 0-7923-6829-0
60. P. Miao (ed.): *Public Places in Asia Pacific Cities.* Current Issues and Strategies. 2001   ISBN 0-7923-7083-X
61. N. Maiellaro (ed.): *Towards Sustainable Buiding.* 2001   ISBN 1-4020-0012-X
62. G.S. Dunbar (ed.): *Geography: Discipline, Profession and Subject since 1870.* An International Survey. 2001   ISBN 1-4020-0019-7
63. J. Stillwell and H.J. Scholten (eds.): *Land Use Simulation for Europe.* 2001
ISBN 1-4020-0213-0
64. P. Doyle and M.R. Bennett (eds.): *Fields of Battle.* Terrain in Military History. 2002
ISBN 1-4020-0433-8
65. C.M. Hall and A.M. Williams (eds.): *Tourism and Migration.* NewRelationships between Production and Consumption. 2002   ISBN 1-4020-0454-0
66. I.R. Bowler, C.R. Bryant and C. Cocklin (eds.): *The Sustainability of Rural Systems.* Geographical Interpretations. 2002   ISBN 1-4020-0513-X
67. O. Yiftachel, J. Little, D. Hedgcock and I. Alexander (eds.): *The Power of Planning.* Spaces of Control and Transformation. 2001   ISBN Hb; 1-4020-0533-4
ISBN Pb; 1-4020-0534-2

The GeoJournal Library

68. K. Hewitt, M.-L. Byrne, M. English and G. Young (eds.): *Landscapes of Transition.* Landform Assemblages and Transformations in Cold Regions. 2002
ISBN 1-4020-0663-2
69. M. Romanos and C. Auffrey (eds.): *Managing Intermediate Size Cities.* Sustainable Development in a Growth Region of Thailand. 2002   ISBN 1-4020-0818-X
70. B. Boots, A. Okabe and R. Thomas (eds.): *Modelling Geographical Systems.* Statistical and Computational Applications. 2003   ISBN 1-4020-0821-X
71. R. Gerber and M. Williams (eds.): *Geography, Culture and Education.* 2002
ISBN 1-4020-0878-3
72. D. Felsenstein, E.W. Schamp and A. Shachar (eds.): *Emerging Nodes in the Global Economy: Frankfurt and Tel Aviv Compared.* 2002   ISBN 1-4020-0924-0
73. R. Gerber (ed.): *International Handbook on Geographical Education.* 2003
ISBN 1-4020-1019-2
74. M. de Jong, K. Lalenis and V. Mamadouh (eds.): *The Theory and Practice of Institutional Transplantation.* Experiences with the Transfer of Policy Institutions. 2002
ISBN 1-4020-1049-4
75. A.K. Dutt, A.G. Noble, G. Venugopal and S. Subbiah (eds.): *Challenges to Asian Urbanization in the 21st Century.* 2003   ISBN 1-4020-1576-3
76. I. Baud, J. Post and C. Furedy (eds.): *Solid Waste Management and Recycling.* Actors, Partnerships and Policies in Hyderabad, India and Nairobi, Kenya. 2004
ISBN 1-4020-1975-0
77. A. Bailly and L.J. Gibson (eds.): *Applied Geography.* A World Perspective. 2004
ISBN 1-4020-2441-X
78. H.D. Smith (ed.): *The Oceans: Key Issues in Marine Affairs.* 2004
ISBN 1-4020-2746-X
79. M. Ramutsindela: *Parks and People in Postcolonial Societies.* Experiences in Southern Africa. 2004   ISBN 1-4020-2542-4
80. R.A. Boschma and R.C. Kloosterman (eds.): *Learning from Clusters.* A Critical Assessment from an Economic-Geographical Perspective. 2005
ISBN 1-4020-3671-X
81. G. Humphrys and M. Williams (eds.): *Presenting and Representing Environments.* 2005   ISBN 1-4020-3813-5
82. D. Rumley, V.L. Forbes and C. Griffin (eds.): *Australia's Arc of Instability.* The Political and Cultural Dynamics of Regional Security. 2006   ISBN 1-4020-3825-9
83. R. Schneider-Sliwa (ed.): *Cities in Transition.* Globalization, Political Change and Urban Development. 2006   ISBN 1-4020-3866-6
84. B.G.V. Robert (ed.): *Dynamic Trip Modelling.* From Shopping Centres to the Internet Series. 2006   ISBN: 1-4020-4345-7
85. L. John and W. Michael (eds.): *Geographical Education in a Changing World.* Past Experience, Current Trends and Future Challenges Series. 2006
ISBN: 1-4020-4806-8
86. G.D. Jay and R. Neil (eds.): *Enterprising Worlds.* A Geographic Perspective on Economics, Environments & Ethics Series. 2007   ISBN: 1-4020-5225-1
87. Y.K.W. Albert and H.G. Brent (eds): *Spatial Database Systems.* Design, Implementation and Project Management Series. 2006.   ISBN: 1-4020-5391-6
88. H.J. Miller (ed.): *Societies and Cities in the Age of Instant Access.* 2007.
ISBN: 1-4020-5426-2